The Monks of War

The Monks of War

THE MILITARY RELIGIOUS ORDERS

Desmond Seward

'The strange association of a monastic and military life which
fanaticism might suggest, but which policy must approve.' GIBBON

'Know ye that Paradise lieth under the shadow of swords.' MUHAMMAD

ARCHON BOOKS
1972

Library of Congress Cataloging in Publication Data

Seward, Desmond, 1935–
   The monks of War

   Bibliography: p. 316–328
   1. Military religious orders—History. I. Title.
CR4701.S48 1972   271'.05   73–39239
ISBN 0–208–01266–4

First published 1972 by Eyre Methuen Ltd, London.
Simultaneously published in the United States of
America as an Archon Book by The Shoe String Press, Inc.,
Hamden, Connecticut. Printed in Great Britain

Contents

Illustrations

Acknowledgements and thanks for permission to reproduce the plates are due to Aerofilms for plate 1; *Deutschordenszentralarchiv* for plate 2b; the British Museum for plate 3; Photoverlages Franz Stodtner, Berlin, for plate 4b; *Foto Mas* for plates 6 and 11b; *Foto PAN* for plate 7; *Foto Oronoz* for plate 9; *Foto Alvao* for plate 10; Friedrich Rahlves, Hanover, for plate 11a; and the Royal Library, Valetta, for plate 14b.

All the maps were drawn by Neil Hyslop.

Acknowledgements

I must acknowledge my deep gratitude to Dr Jonathan Riley-Smith of St Andrew's University and to Dom Alberic Stacpoole of Ampleforth Abbey. Both supplied me with valuable references besides reading parts of the typescript. In addition, Dr Riley-Smith let me see the typescript of his own monumental work, *The Knights of St John in Jerusalem and Cyprus 1050–1310*, before its publication in 1967, while as a former soldier and present monk Dom Stacpoole's comments have been particularly useful. Without their advice and encouragement this book would never have been completed.

Nor can I forget the kindness of the late Sir Harry Luke, Knight Grand Cross of the Venerable Order of St John, Bailiff of Egle and a former Lieutenant Governor of Malta, who died in 1969. He too gave me advice and encouragement.

Finally, I would like to thank, once again, Mr Richard Bancroft, Superintendent of the British Museum Reading Room, and the members of his staff for their usual courteous and patient assistance.

Abbreviations

C.A.R.H.P.	*Collecçam de documentos e memorias da Academia Real da Historia Portuguesa* (Lisbon 1720)
Dugdale	*Monasticon Anglicanum*, ed. W. Dugdale, 8 vols (London 1817–30)
H.R.S.E.	*Historiae Ruthenicae Scriptores Exteria*, 2 vols (Berlin 1841)
M.L.A.	*Monumenta Livoniae Antiquae* (Riga & Leipzig 1835–47)
M.P.L.	*Patrologiae cursus completus. Series Latina*, ed. J. P. Migne, 221 vols. (Paris 1844–55)
R.H.C.	*Recueil des historiens des croisades* (Paris 1841–1906):
R.H.C. oc.	*Historiens occidentaux*, 5 vols (1844–95)
R.H.C. or.	*Historiens orientaux*, 5 vols (1872–1906)
R.H.C. arm.	*Documents arméniens*, 2 vols (1869–1906)
R.H.C. Lois	*Lois. Les Assises de Jérusalem*, 2 vols (1841–3)
S.R.L.	*Scriptores Rerum Livonicarum*, 2 vols (Riga & Leipzig 1848–53)
S.R.P.	*Scriptores Rerum Prussicarum*, 6 vols (Leipzig 1861–74)

Author's Note

To emphasise the brethren's monasticism, the title *Fra.* is used throughout (except for *Frey* when speaking of Spanish brethren). This is an abbreviation of the official Latin *Frater* for which *Br.* is hardly satisfactory – *Fr.* was the normal usage amongst all military orders but nowadays is too easily confused with the priest's *Father*. I have therefore employed *Fra.* which is still the suffix for professed brethren of the only military order to survive in anything like its original form, the Knights of Malta. It is worth emphasising that Middle English could refer to Hospitallers and Templars as 'freres' or 'friars' – the Templars were sometimes called 'Red Friars'.

For the sake of clarity, in the chapters on the Iberian orders I have used Castilian, Portuguese and Catalan names rather than English – Juan, João and Joan, Alfonso, Afonso and Alfons, are an aid to identification amid a multitude of Johns and Alfonsos. Similarly, *comanador* and *comendador* help to establish whether a commander came from Aragon or Castile, while the Portuguese branch of the Order of Santiago is referred to throughout as '*Saõ Thiago*'.

FOR

JONATHAN RILEY-SMITH

AND

ALBERIC STACPOOLE

I

INTRODUCTION

Rejoice, brave warrior, if you live and conquer in the Lord, but rejoice still more and give thanks if you die and go to join the Lord. This life can be fruitful and victory is glorious yet a holy death for righteousness is worth more. Certainly 'blessed are they who die *in* the Lord' but how much more so are those who die *for* Him.

Bernard of Clairvaux

Verily, of the faithful hath God bought their persons and their substance, on condition of Paradise for them *in return*: on the path of God shall they fight, and slay, and be slain: a promise for this is pledged in the Law, and in the Evangel, and in the Koran – and who more faithful to his engagement than God? Rejoice, therefore, in the contract that ye have contracted: for this shall be the great bliss.

The Koran

CHAPTER I

The Christian ideal of death in battle

This book is intended as a general introduction to military religious Orders up to the Counter-Reformation. By then their brethren had ceased to lead a monastic life, while Jesuits had taken their place as the Church's Janissaries, and despite an Indian summer at Malta the knights' later days as lay confraternities are of minor importance. Only by concentrating on their heroic period when the brethren really were monks with swords can one hope to understand their grim calling.

The thought of Christians devoting their lives to warfare in the service of God seems a paradox. Professional soldiers have a name for uproarious gaiety: 'I know not how but martial men are given to love,' wrote Bacon, 'I think it is but as they are given to wine, for perils commonly ask to be paid in pleasures.'[1] Nevertheless there have been men consecrated to battle, the brother knights of the military orders, noblemen vowed to poverty, chastity and obedience, who lived a monastic life in convents which were at the same time barracks, waging merciless war on enemies of the Cross; to enter their chapels was to see monks in hooded habits chanting the office, but on active service the horsemen in black or white uniforms were no different from other troops save for an iron discipline. The spirit of the cloister and the glebe had been transferred to the parade ground and battlefield. Such men tried, literally, to *fight* their way into heaven.

The three greatest orders were the Templars, the Knights of St John and the Teutonic Knights, but there were many others less well known, including one which was exclusively English, the Hospitallers of St Thomas. These brotherhoods were created in the twelfth century to tame a brutal warrior nobility

[1] Essay X – 'Of Love'.

and to provide the Roman Church with stormtroopers, for
chivalry had not yet eradicated pagan savagery, while legions
were needed to defend the Holy Land. St Bernard of Clairvaux
took over the new Templar concept of soldiers under religious
vows and synthesised knight with monk, producing a strange
vocation which unconsciously substituted Christ for Woden,
Paradise for Valhalla. Again the syncretic genius of Catholicism
harnessed a pagan hero cult – just as once it had metamor-
phosised gods into saints and converted temples into churches –
transforming the ideal into a spiritual calling whose followers
sacrificed their lives for Christ not only in the monastery but
on the battlefield with a startling mixture of humility and
ferocity. While retaining much of the Germanic war-band,
by adapting the monastic organisation they became the
first properly staffed and officered armies since the Roman
legions.

They fought and prayed in many lands and on many seas.
Even Gibbon admitted that in Palestine 'the firmest bulwark
of Jerusalem was founded on the Knights of the Hospital of St
John, and of the Temple of Solomon; on the strange association
of a monastic and military life which fanaticism might suggest,
but which policy must approve'.[1] Outremer, land of the
crusades – and the West's first colony – was doomed from the
start, but because of the brethren's sacrifices it endured for
nearly two centuries. And after the kingdom of Jerusalem had
been finally destroyed the Hospitallers, first from Rhodes and
then from Malta, devoted themselves to guarding Christian
merchantmen in the Levant against Barbary corsairs and
Turkish pirates.

In Spain the brethren of Calatrava, Alcántara and Santiago
were the spearhead of the Reconquista, consolidating the
Christian advance, destroying the exotic Moslem civilisation of
Córdoba and Granada. On the vast and lonely *meseta* where
no peasant dared settle for fear of Moorish raiders, the monkish
frontiersmen ranched herds of cattle and sheep, a practice
which reached North America by way of the Mexican *haciendas*.
In the later Middle Ages politicians used them to capture the
whole machinery of Castilian government. From Portugal they

[1] *The History of the Decline and Fall of the Roman Empire*, vol. VI, p. 65.

initiated the expansion of Europe with expeditions half-missionary, half-commercial. Henry the Navigator was Master of the Order of Christ (successor to the Portuguese Templars), and directed a research centre which employed the foremost scientific geographers of the day while his ships sailed under the Order's flag.

The strange soldier monks were equally active in Northern Europe, in Latvia, Lithuania and Estonia, and had a part in shaping the destinies of Poland and Germany. All these countries were permanently influenced by them, racially, economically and politically. The heritage of the Drang nach Osten, today's Oder-Neisse line, was largely bequeathed by the Teutonic Knights, whose lands, the *Ordensstaat*, reached almost to Leningrad. It was they who created Prussia by exterminating the pagan Baltic race once known as Prussians and by the most thorough colonisation seen in the Middle Ages. Their terrible forest campaigns against the Lithuanians have been called the most ferocious of all medieval wars. The Polish Corridor was not a complication invented by the Treaty of Versailles, but began when the knights seized Danzig from Władislaw the Dwarf in 1331. The first Hohenzollern ruler of Prussia was also the last Hochmeister of the Teutonic Knights to reign in Prussia. Hindenburg's victory over the Russians among the Masurian Lakes in 1914 was deliberately named Tannenberg after the defeat of 1410 when the Hochmeister had been killed and his knights almost wiped out by the Slavs. Their grim hierarchy foreshadowed the Potsdam parade ground while the brethren's black and silver cross is still the emblem of the German army, and indeed was the model for the Iron Cross itself.

Few historical romances have been written about the military brethren, which is surprising, for no story is more dramatic. The *Götterdämmerung*-like fight to the death of the knights at the storm of Acre, Hochmeister von Juningen's refusal to leave the doomed field of Tannenberg, and the Commanders of St John, too badly wounded to stand, waiting in chairs at the breach at St Elmo for the Turks' final assault, these are only the best known of many deeds of epic heroism. The suppression of the Templars, whose last Grand Master, Jacques de Molay, was burnt alive over a slow fire for heresy, has inspired occasional novels, but it needs a grand opera to do justice to this sinister tragedy; of the other twenty-one Masters of the Temple five died in battle, five of wounds, one of starvation in a Saracen prison. Popular histories of the great siege of Malta appear from time to time, while Eisenstein took for the plot of his film, *Alexander Nevsky*, the story of the bloody defeat of the Teutonic Order on the ice at Lake Peipus in 1242, and Sienkiewicz wrote a novel, *The Teutonic Knights*, of which a Polish film has recently been made, though the real inspiration in the latter cases was Slavonic glory. There is also Henri de Montherlant's play, *The Master of Santiago*, but his Master rules a crumbling survival, not a vital conquering force. Otherwise there is little else.

Whatever their order or century all belonged to similar communities whose inspiration and organisation were the same on the banks of the Jordan as on those of the Tagus, on the Baltic Sea or the Mediterranean. Military brethren were just as much a part of western monasticism as Benedictines or Franciscans. This book is not concerned with chivalry, only with men in monasteries who went out to battle. Just as mendicant friars lived a conventual life preaching the Gospel, brother knights lived a conventual life defending it. But the Counter-Reformation's failure to renew the vocation and the orders' consequent decline into mere confraternities has obscured their original role. Only by accepting this monasticism, only by admitting mystical love of Christ, asceticism and even humility, can one realise the appalling ferocity of their ideal. During all the wars of extermination and berserk Thermoplyaes they themselves never doubted that theirs was a religious calling; 'who fights us fights Jesus Christ' claimed the Teutonic Knights.

'Filled with holy frenzy' crusaders seldom offered Moslems a choice between true religion and death before attacking. In contrast it is written in the Holy Koran 'Ye shall do battle with them *unless* they profess Islam'. Jihad was never 'the total expression' of Islam even if certain sectaries exploited it for reasons of personal ambition. The reverse was true in Europe; Holy War was an ideal admired by all Christians, the crusade an inspiration which endured for centuries. Only after the

Christian onslaught in Syria and Spain did Moslems feel the need for permanent if undeclared Jihad against the 'polytheists', and to stress the more savage suras. This clash between the Catholic and Islamic faiths induced a rabid intensity of fanaticism which has never been surpassed, whose most zealous exponents were the military brethren.

In theory they were a protection against the infidel, in practice merciless aggressors. The Teutonic Order's deliberate liquidation of the Prussian race is sufficient testimony; as a chaplain chronicler proudly recorded 'they drove them forth so that not one remained who would not bow his neck to the Yoke of Faith – this with the help of the Lord Jesus Christ who is blessed for ever and ever'.[1] Simple men, the brethren easily became unbalanced, prayer and mortification intensifying rather than eradicating those violent instincts which still lurked in a Woden-haunted unconscious. 'Take this sword; its brightness stands for faith, its point for hope, its guard for charity. Use it well . . .' ran the Hospitaller rite for profession.

> Let us all show joy of heart
> For, lo, the Heathen feel the smart

sang the pious Germans. Monasticism had made a sacrament of battle.

It would be unjust to brand the knights as medieval Red Guards or S.S., yet the defenders of Malta and the Marienburg had more than a little in common with the Nazi and Marxist zealots. The Convent of Rhodes and the Prussian *Ordensstaat* were the first modern states – in the sense of the 1930s and 1940s – totalitarian dictatorships organised for war in the service of an ideal. It is irrelevant that this ideal was religious rather than social or racial. Military Christianity foreshadowed the baneful philosophy of Treitschke, an admiring historian of the Teutonic Order, that war is the enemy of materialism. But though one may find it hard to understand how they could reconcile violent and destructive lives with the message of the New Testament one cannot deny their bravery. Such men, remote and fearsome even to their contemporaries, possessed extraordinary courage, dying in battle at worst with a twisted

[1] Petrus von Dusburg, 'Cronica Terre Prussie'. *S.R.P.*, vol. I.

love of God, at best with real sanctity. If fanaticism was there so also was sacrifice, fortitude and the watchman's spirit, a determination to guard the defenceless, 'to defend widows and orphans from the enemies of Christ'.[1] Certainly they became ruthless professionals but then so often did the most altruistic of Hitler's opponents. War is evil yet inescapable and the brethren's real mission was to humanise an inhuman trade. Military Christianity was a compromise which at least diverted feudal brigandage, saving countless European peasants from famine and murder. Ultimately the expedient worked, exorcising Woden's ghost.

'Those who live by the sword shall perish by the sword.' Yet the brothers sought not only to live by the sword, but to conquer heaven with it as well. Many Christians of the past, including great saints, considered this ambition both healthy and admirable. To comprehend such a paradox we must try and see the knights as they saw themselves, spotless warriors of Christ rather than bloodstained fanatics. Whatever their faults they took their vows in hope of self-sanctification, and thought of themselves as men of God. The intention is not to list short-comings obvious enough but to understand an ideal, for the brethren do indeed deserve the title, 'monks of war'.

[1] From the Hospitaller rite of profession.

II

LATIN SYRIA
1099–1291

The Crusades and the international Orders:
Templars – Hospitallers – St Lazarus – Montjoie – St Thomas

... such are they whom God chooses for himself and gathers
from the furthest ends of the earth, servants from among the
bravest in Israel to guard watchfully and faithfully his
Sepulchre and the Temple of Solomon, sword in hand, ready
for battle.

Bernard of Clairvaux

And who fights for the cause of God their works he will not
suffer to miscarry: He will vouchsafe their guidance and dis-
pose their hearts aright. And he will bring them into the
Paradise of which he hath told them.

The Koran

CHAPTER 2

The birth of a new vocation

The three greatest military orders, the Templars, the Hospitallers, and the Teutonic Knights, were founded in the twelfth century, an earlier renaissance which saw the birth of Gothic architecture, the zenith of papal monarchy, and an intellectual revolution that would culminate with Aquinas. Perhaps its most outstanding figure was the Cistercian monk Bernard of Clairvaux, last of the Fathers of the Western Church. The Templars had been in existence for a decade when he met their founder, Hugues de Payens, in 1127 but this meeting was the real moment of the military brethren's genesis for St Bernard at once understood how Hugues's inspiration matched the conflicting vocations of chivalry and the cloister.

The Abbot of Clairvaux, the greatest moral force of his day, proclaimed the superiority of love to knowledge and presided over the change in religious emotion when the humanity of Christ was at last fully appreciated: a crucifix of the tenth century has a figure of Christ the King in majesty, *Christos Pantocrator* the terrible judge, while one of the twelfth has a compassionate representation of the tortured man. Later Francis of Assisi brought this message to the masses with explosive results, but in the first half of the century popular enthusiasm found an outlet in new monastic orders, especially the Cistercians. Bernard joined them in 1113, when they were confined to one monastery, Citeaux, and at his death in 1153 there were 343 such houses.

However, the ethics of the ruling class remained those of the *Nibelungenlied* and the Icelandic sagas. As late as the tenth century a heathen religious order called the Joms-Vikings appeared in Scandinavia, restricted to warriors of proven bravery who submitted to a harsh discipline, sleeping in barracks without women. Death in battle was their dearest ambition – to join Woden in Valhalla. The House-Carles who gave so grim an account of themselves at Hastings had been founded by King Sweyn Forkbeard, a former commander of these Jomsburg brethren, and many European noblemen had Scandinavian blood. The traditions of the northern war-band were very much alive in the twelfth century and the *chansons de geste* expressed the same pagan ideals: physical prowess, the joy of plunder and the duty of revenge.

The Church tried desperately to stop the unending bloodshed. An early expedient was the 'Truce of God', specified days on which noblemen swore not to fight. The long-term policy was chivalry, an attempt to tame murderous instincts by providing a Christian ideal of the warrior; ultimately knighthood, originally a reputation for skill in battle, became almost a religious calling, hallowed by quasi-sacramental rites – vigils, weapon blessings, even vows of chastity. The code of the Germanic comitatus gave way to one of prayerful self-sacrifice, which exalted the protection of the defenceless. Sagas were replaced by romances of King Arthur and Amadis of Gaul, the berserk transformed into Don Quixote. It was an example of the Catholic Church at her syncretic best, civilising the barbarian invaders of the Roman Empire. But this process took centuries so there was urgent need of another, quicker solution.

The ascetic impulse produced a papal revolution. Gregory VII (1073–85) set the papacy firmly on a course towards the position of leader and judge of Western Christendom, demanding that temporal power be subordinated to spiritual just as the body depends on the soul, envisaging a papal army, the *militia Sancti Petri*. Europe listened to the priest-kings with new respect. When in 1095 Pope Urban II called upon the faithful to recover Jerusalem – occupied by the Moslems since 638 – his appeal inspired extraordinary enthusiasm. Palestine's importance was heightened by the new appreciation of Christ's humanity; the scenes of the Passion were still pointed out at Jerusalem. That His City should belong to infidels was contrary to the law of God. And Holy War would provide a magnificent outlet for the destructive energy of barbarous nobles.

These saw the crusade as a summons by God to render military service and also as an opportunity to win new manors in the way they had been won in England and southern Italy. Shouts of '*Deus li volt*' resounded throughout Europe and a great host of warlike pilgrims from all classes converged on the Holy Land singing the ancient, triumphant hymn 'Vexilla regis prodeunt':

> Behold the royal ensigns fly,
> The Cross's shining mystery;
> Where Life itself gave up its breath
> And Christ by dying conquered death . . .

Its tune was an old marching song of the Roman legions.

If he had thundered 'When ye encounter infidels strike off their heads', Muhammad had also said 'deal calmly with the infidels, leave them awhile in peace', referring to Christians as 'nearest in affection to believers'. However, unprovoked onslaughts by the aggressive Western Church caused a violent reaction. The battles between Islam and Catholicism were to be the most fanatical the world has ever seen, fought for victory or Paradise. Fortunately the Moslem world was in chaos from India to Portugal, and Syria was more vulnerable than it had been for a century, broken up into principalities ruled by Turkish atabegs, while the Fatimid Caliphate at Cairo was in decline.

Jerusalem was stormed in July 1099. The rabid ferocity of its sack showed just how little the Church had succeeded in Christianising atavistic instincts. The entire population of the Holy City was put to the sword, Jews as well as Moslems, 70,000 men, women and children perishing in a holocaust which raged for three days. In places men waded in blood up to their ankles and horsemen were splashed by it as they rode through the streets. Weeping, these devout conquerors went barefoot to pray at the Holy Sepulchre before rushing eagerly back to the slaughter. The kingdom of Jerusalem had been founded in blood and was to end in blood.

Those who stayed in Palestine were adventurers, mainly French, with nothing to go back to, and the state they created reflected the feudalism of their own land. It came to include four great baronies, the principality of Galilee, the county of Jaffa and Ascalon, the lordship of Kerak and Montreal, and the

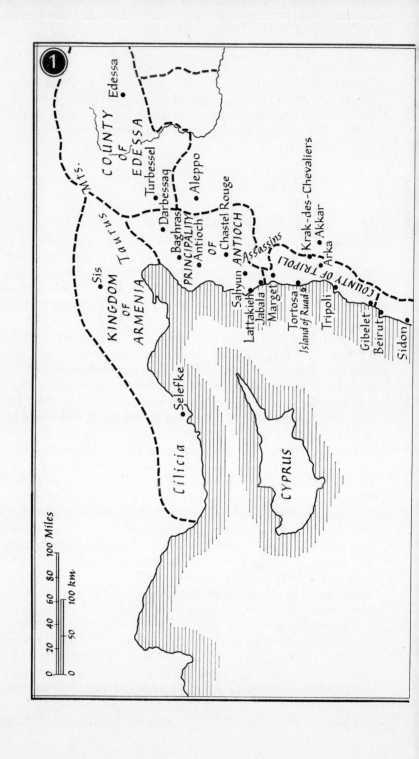

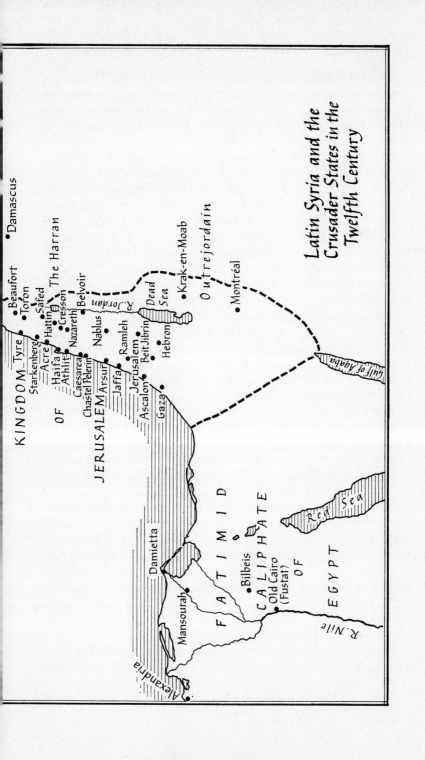

Latin Syria and the
Crusader States in the
Twelfth Century

Damascus

Beaufort
Toron
Safed
The Harran
Hattin • Cresson
Acre Nazareth
Starkenberg
Tyre
Haifa
Athlit
Caesarea
Chastel Pelerim
Arsuf
Jaffa
Jerusalem
Ascalon
Gaza

KINGDOM

OF

JERUSALEM

Belvoir
R. Jordan
Dead Sea
Krak-en-Moab
Montréal
Outrejordain
Gulf of Aqaba

Nablus
Ramleh
Beit Jibrin
Hebron

FATIMID

CALIPHATE

OF

EGYPT

Red Sea

Damietta

Mansourah

Bilbeis
Old Cairo (Fustat)

R. Nile

Alexandria

lordship of Sidon, together with twelve smaller fiefs. There were also three lesser states, the principality of Antioch and the counties of Tripoli and Edessa. Without the assent of the Haute Cour, or great council of the realm, in theory no political action was valid, though the king was extremely powerful. Outremer was shaped like an hour-glass, extending for nearly five hundred miles from the Gulf of Aqaba on the Red Sea to Edessa, which lay east of the Euphrates. At the centre, Tripoli, it was only twenty-five miles broad and never more than seventy miles across in the south. There was a chronic shortage of manpower, while the desert frontier was far from impenetrable, holding water and fodder. The 'Franks' put their trust in sea power and fortresses. Genoese, Pisan and Venetian fleets soon controlled the sea, eager for commerce as the lure of spices, rice and sugar cane, of ostrich plumes from Africa and furs from Russia, of carpets from Persia, of inlaid metal work from Damascus, of silks and of muslin from Mosul and of countless other luxuries, attracted merchants who settled in the coastal towns. But the new land was no more than a beach-head sustained by the belief that God wished His children to occupy His personal fief.

There was a large native Christian population, Maronite, Melkhite, Syrian and Armenian. About 1120 Fulcher de Chartres wrote of how 'Some of us have married Syrians, Armenians or even baptised Saracens . . .', and how his people were no longer Frenchmen but Palestinians who were accepted by the natives as fellow countrymen.[1] Morfia, the queen of Baldwin II himself, was the daughter of an Armenian prince. Many officials and merchants were Christianised Arabs, while great barons employed Moslem secretaries. But if European visitors talked of *poulains*, Syrian-born Franks, it is too much to say that a new Franco-Syrian race had been born. The local Christian churches were treated with contemptuous tolerance, Latin rite patriarchs being installed at Jerusalem and Antioch. French was the language of administration and the ruling classes remained French.

Nevertheless, to the Franks Jerusalem was home. The king

[1] Fulcherius Carnotensis, 'Historia Iherosolymitana', *R.H.C. oc.*, vol. III, p. 468.

dressed in a golden burnous and keffiyeh and gave audiences cross-legged on a carpet. Nobles wore shoes with up-turned points, turbans, and the silks, damasks, muslins and cottons that were so different from the wool and furs of France. In the towns they lived in villas with courtyards, fountains and mosaic floors, reclining on divans, listening to Arab lutes and watching dancing girls. They ate sugar, rice, lemons and melons and washed with soap in tubs or sunken baths, while their women used cosmetics and glass mirrors, unknown in Europe. Merchants, grown accustomed to bazaars, veiled their wives, and professional wailers were seen at Christian funerals. Coins had Arabic inscriptions. Yet this success in sinking roots vitiated the brutal missionary urge necessary for a detested minority to survive on the edge of a vast and hostile world empire. What shocked the European visitor to Outremer was its frivolity amid all the luxury. It was not only a higher civilisation which softened the Franks. The climate, with its short but stormy winters and long sweltering summers, and the new diseases, caused heavy mortality despite Arab medicine. The majority of the population was Moslem. Life, perpetually overshadowed by the sinister spectres of death, torture or slavery, could only be endured by men of strong self-discipline.

The sophistication of the neighbouring Eastern Empire has often been contrasted with the crusaders' barbarism, even if no western ruler died the horrible death of many Byzantine emperors, publicly torn to pieces by their own people. Its continuity from the Rome of Augustus was unbroken while learning and the material techniques of civilisation had never disappeared. Now for the last time it was reviving, under the Comnenoi emperors. The Franks were overawed by Constantinople with its million inhabitants, although they thought them soft and corrupt. Schism with Rome was not yet an accomplished fact, but the West had little understanding of Eastern Christendom. The Byzantine army was still extremely formidable, consisting almost entirely of mercenaries, English and Danish infantry and Patzinak and Cuman cavalry.

At this date the Armenians were still fierce mountain warriors, though their old kingdoms in Greater Armenia, the

land of Mount Ararat where Noah's Ark rested, had been
absorbed and their princes murdered by the Byzantines so that
they were unable to resist the Seldjuk onslaught. The 'Haiots'[1]
did not despair and throughout the eleventh and twelfth
centuries many trekked down to Cilicia, the southern shore of
Asia Minor. Led by Ruben, a cousin of their last king, they
carved out a new country among the glens and crags of the
Taurus Mountains, half wrested from the crumbling imperial
administration, half conquered from the Turks. They welcomed
Outremer and their nobility married Frankish ladies and
acquired a feudal character.[2] But if an ally against Islam,
Armenia was nevertheless a rival of the Latin states.

Frankish success in battle depended on skilful use of specially
equipped cavalry over carefully chosen ground.[3] Infantry with
spears, long Danish axes and crossbows provided cover until
the moment for a single decisive charge.[4] There were two sorts
of cavalry, knights and sergeants, the former's armour consisting of a conical steel helmet, a chain mail tunic with sleeves
and hood worn over a quilted undershirt, padded breeches and
a kite-shaped shield. Later the shield became smaller, the
conical helmet was superseded by the helm covering the whole
face, and mail stockings were adopted, with a burnous and
keffiyeh to ward off the sun. They carried a lance held under the
arm, a long two-edged cutting sword and occasionally a mace.
On the march the knight rode a hack or mule, mounting his
carefully trained war-horse when action was imminent. These
'destriers' were enormous animals, often seventeen hands high,
more akin to a dray-horse than a cavalry charger, and taught to
bite, butt and kick. Sergeants were similarly armed, but did not
wear the chain hauberk. They charged with the knights,
riding in the rear ranks.[5] To time the charge correctly, res-

---

[1] The Franks called them 'Hermins' and their country of Cilicia 'Erminie'.
[2] See F. Macler, 'Armenia', *C.M.H.*, vol. IV.
[3] See R. C. Smail, *Crusading Warfare (1097–1193)* (C.U.P., 1967).
[4] 'The foot, on both the line of march and the battle-field, were usually
placed between the enemy and the knights . . . a living barrier armed
with spears and bows.' p. 130.
[5] Dr Smail believes that sergeants fought as foot soldiers. Ibid., p. 91.

training troops beneath blistering sun and the enemy's arrows, demanded real leadership.

Their Turkish opponents used classic Turanian tactics, highly manœuvrable mounted bowmen shooting from the saddle, who never attacked frontally, but tried to divide and surround the enemy before closing in with short sabres or yataghans. Their arrow fire was extremely rapid and they liked to attack the Franks on the march, aiming at the horses, leaving their opponents no time to prepare defensive formations. There were some armoured cavalrymen but even these rode Arab ponies chosen for speed.[1]

The Franks had a certain admiration for Turks, but little for Egyptians.[2] The caliph at Cairo – whom the Franks called King of Babylon – was the pope-emperor of the Shias, who did not bear allegiance to the Caliph of Baghdad, head of the other great Moslem sect, the Sunni. Fatimid armies were made up of Arab horsemen, who charged home with the lance or waited to receive the Frankish charge, and Sudanese archers on foot. Their discipline was wretched. However, just before their conquest by Saladin's family the Egyptians began to employ cavalry of Turkish type, recruited from Caucasian slaves known as Mamelukes.

Battles between Frank and Turk were like the combats of bull and matador, but when the bull got home the effect was shattering, victories being won in the face of incredible odds.[3] Not only were the Franks and their horses bigger and heavier, but they were better at in-fighting and could deal out terrible punishment. The perennial problem of Outremer was to muster enough of these tank-like noblemen.

When the first king of Jerusalem, Baldwin I, died in 1118 the land was still in wretched disorder, infested with criminals;

---

[1] Ibid., p. 75, 'Turkish tactics'.
[2] Smail (op. cit., p. 87 n. 6) quotes William of Tyre on the Egyptians in one disastrous campaign. 'The vile and effeminate Egyptians ['Egyptiis vilibus et effeminatis'] who were more of a hindrance and a burden than a help . . .' See 'Historia rerum in partibus transmarini gestarum', *R.H.C. oc.*
[3] For the Frankish charge see Smail, pp. 112–15, 200–1 'on many occasions the divisions of the army charged in succession' (i.e. attack in echelon).

with some justice Latin Syria has been compared to a medieval Botany Bay.[1] Many Franks had been sent on the crusade as penance for atrocious offences such as rape and murder and reverted to their unpleasant habits. Pilgrims were a natural prey, though one of the principal objects of the crusade had been to make the Holy Places safe for them. Baldwin's successor, Baldwin II, had no means of policing the kingdom. The English merchant Saewulf wrote of the miseries of pilgrims in 1103 and about the same time the German abbot Ekkehard recorded robberies and martyrdoms as daily occurrences. William of Tyre observed that in the early days of the kingdom the Moslem peasants of Galilee kidnapped solitary pilgrims and sold them into slavery.

Hugues de Payens was no mere adventurer, but Lord of the castle of Martigny in Burgundy, a cousin of the counts of Champagne, and may have been a relative of St Bernard whose family home was near Martigny. He arrived in Syria in 1115 and by 1118 had become a self-appointed protector of pilgrims on the dangerous road from Jaffa to Jerusalem, harried ceaselessly from Ascalon. This ragged eccentric persuaded seven knights, also from Northern France, to help him, all taking a solemn oath before the patriarch to protect pilgrims and observe poverty, chastity and obedience. They looked very odd, dressing only in what old clothes were given to them, but King Baldwin was impressed and gave the 'Poor Knights' a wing of the royal palace, the mosque of al-Aqsa, thought to be the Temple of Solomon. He also joined the patriarch in subsidising them. The Templars had begun their career, as a police force.[2]

Even before the crusade there was a hospital of St John the Almoner for pilgrims at Jerusalem, near the Church of the Holy Sepulchre, which was both an infirmary and a guest

---

[1] Sir Ernest Barker, *The Crusades* (O.U.P., 1949), p. 48.
[2] For the earliest account of the Templars' origin see William of Tyre, op. cit., bk. 12, ch. VII, p. 520–1, 'Ordo militiae templi instituitur'. Jacques de Vitry, *Historia orientalis seu Hierosolymitana*, adds details, such as those about the gift of the Temple, which he must have had from the brethren themselves.

house.[1] It had been founded about 1070 by some merchants of Amalfi. In 1100 a certain Fra. Gerard, about whom little is known, was elected master. Probably he arrived before the crusaders. After the kingdom's establishment the increased number of pilgrims necessitated a reorganisation and Gerard abandoned the Benedictine rule for St Augustine's while another more important St John was adopted as patron, the Baptist himself. The new order became deeply respected, acquiring estates in many European countries,[2] and in 1113 Pope Paschal II took them under his special protection.[3] Possibly Gerard employed Poor Knights to protect his hospitals which spread throughout Outremer.

King Baldwin must have lost many men in the bloody victory of Tel-Shaqab in 1126. The solution appeared to be another crusade. Not only did Hugues de Payens have some link with St Bernard but Hugues, Count of Champagne, founder of the abbey of Clairvaux, had joined the Poor Knights, while another recruit may have been St Bernard's maternal uncle. In 1126 two brethren were sent to France with letters for St Bernard from the king and the next year Hugues de Payens himself came to ask Bernard for a new crusade.

Other founders of religious orders had asked the abbot's advice, St Norbert of the Premonstratensian canons and the English Gilbert of Sempringham. Indeed there was a spate of new vocations during this period : Carthusians, Grandmontines, Tironians, besides those of Savignac and Fontevrault. Cistercians and Templars were produced by the same wave of asceticism. However, Hugues and his companions did not see themselves as a religious order until they met the great abbot. A

---

[1] For the Hospitallers' origins see William of Tyre, op. cit., bk. 18, ch. 4, pp. 822–3, 'Describitur, unde habuit ortum et initium domus Hospitalis' (in the 'Estoire d'Eracles', a thirteenth-century French translation, this is charmingly rendered 'Comment li Hospitalier orent petit commencement'). Also Riley-Smith, The Knights of St John in Jerusalem and Cyprus, p. 32 et seq where all traditions and sources concerning the order's origins are fully examined.
[2] Delaville le Roulx, Cartulaire Général des Hospitaliers de Saint Jean de Jérusalem 1100–1310, vol. I, cart. no. 30.
[3] 'The Papal bull of 1113, Pie postulatio voluntatis, was the foundation charter for the new order.' Riley-Smith, op. cit., p. 43.

document of 1123 refers to Hugues as 'Master of the Knights of the Temple'[1] but his little band was merely a voluntary brotherhood and recent research seems to indicate that they were having difficulty in finding recruits and were on the verge of dissolution.[2] Hugues had come about another crusade, not to ask for a rule.

St Bernard, who took a strong liking to Hugues, recognised a means of channelling the feudal nobility's surplus energy which would convert 'criminals and godless, robbers, murderers and adulterers'. He promised Hugues that he would compile a rule and find recruits. 'They can fight the battle of the Lord and indeed be soldiers of Christ.' Military Christianity had found its real creator.

In 1128 a council was convened at Troyes and on Bernard's advice Hugues attended it. Though the abbot was not present he sent a rule which was debated and endorsed by the council. Copies of the Templar constitutions survive from the thirteenth century and these state that the first part of the rule was 'par le commandement dou concile et dou venerable père Bernart abbés de Clerevaus'.[3]

He thought of Hugues's new brethren as military Cistercians. Significantly, brother-knights wore a white hooded habit in the cloister, like Cistercian choir monks, while lesser brethren wore brown, as did Cistercian lay brothers. On active service this habit was replaced by a cloak. An emphasis on silence, even to the extent of using signs in the refectory, came from the same source, while the simplicity of Cistercian altar furnishings was paralleled by the plainest weapons and saddlery possible, with no trace of gold or silver. Brethren slept in dormitories in shirt

---

[1] '*Magister Militum Templi*' – it is perhaps significant that 'Magister Militum' had been the title of the Commander-in-chief of the later Roman Empire.
[2] 'Un document sur les débuts des Templiers', ed. J. Leclercq in *Revue d'histoire ecclésiastique*, LII (1957).
[3] See H. de Curzon, *La Règle du Temple* (Paris, 1887). For a résumé of its principal statues see Melville, *La Vie des Templiers*, pp. 42–7. (Marion Melville does not consider the rule to be St Bernard's despite its Cistercian form – p. 20.) For the Templar translation of the *Book of Judges* see Melville, pp. 81–3, who comments that it transforms scripture into 'une sorte de roman de Chevalerie'.

Fig. 1. A Templar in his habit—white with a plain red cross on his shoulder. From P. Helyot, *Histoire des Ordres Religieux, Monastiques et Militaires* (Paris 1714–21).

and breeches, as Cistercians still do today. Unless on night duty, attendance at matins was strictly enforced, for they said Office together in choir, not the full Roman Office, but the Little Office – psalms and prayers easily memorised by men who could not read; on campaign thirteen 'Pater Nosters' were said in lieu of matins, seven for each canonical hour and nine for vespers. Religious services alternated with military exercises. There were two main meals, both eaten in silence with sacred reading from a French translation of the Bible, special emphasis being placed on the Books of Joshua and the Maccabees. All found inspiration in the ferocious exploits of Judas, his brothers and their war-bands, in reconquering the Holy Land from cruel infidels. Brethren ate in pairs to see that the other did not weaken himself by fasting. Wine was served with every meal and meat three times a week; their mortification was the rigours of war. Each knight was allowed three horses but with the symbolic exception of the lion, hawking and hunting were forbidden. He had to crop his hair and grow a beard, being forbidden to kiss even mother or sister, and no nuns were to be affiliated to the Order. His Master was not merely a commanding officer, but an abbot. For the first time in Christian history soldiers would live as monks.[1]

St Bernard's rule was the basis of those of all military orders, even if only indirectly, whether the framework was Cistercian or Augustinian, for he had defined a new vocation. Its ideals were set out in a pamphlet, *In Praise of the New Knighthood*,[2] written to attract recruits. The Templars found themselves heroes almost overnight and donations poured in from the kings of Aragon and Castile, from the Count of Flanders and many other princes. Hugues was especially well received in England and Scotland[3] while in France the Archbishop of Rheims instituted an annual collection. Europe was thrilled by these holy warriors who guarded the throne of David.

When Hugues returned to Palestine in 1130 he began to erect

[1] The best easily available description of the brethren's daily life is in Melville, op. cit., ch. XVII.

[2] 'De Laude Novae Militiae' in *S. Bernardi Opera*, vol. III (*Editiones Cistercienses*) ed. Dom J. Leclerq and Dom H. M. Rochais (Rome, 1963).

[3] See Lees, *Records of the Templars in England in the Twelfth Century*.

a system of preceptories or commanderies. This evolved slowly, ultimately depending on temples in the front line territories, Jerusalem, Antioch, Tripoli, Castile-Leon, Aragon and Portugal, each ruled by a master who owed allegiance to the Master at Jerusalem. However, centralisation was not complete until the next century. Temples, with preceptories, were also set up in France, England (including Scotland and Ireland), Sicily (including Appulia and Greece) and Germany. These were used to administer estates, as training or recruiting depots, and as homes for elderly brethren. It was very different from the days when the Templars' only resources had been a scanty portion of the bishop's dime.

By the mid thirteenth century the hierarchy would comprise a Master; his deputy the Seneschal; the Marshal, supreme military official; the Commander of the Land and Realm of Jerusalem, who was both treasurer and in charge of the navy and estate management; the Commander of the City of Jerusalem, who was hospitaller; and finally the Draper or keeper of the wardrobe – a sort of quartermaster general. The Master was chosen by an elaborate combination of vote and lot designed to ensure impartiality, a procedure which recalled the election of the Venetian Doge. Powerful though he was, important decisions were taken by the General Chapter. Provincial Masters had all the Grand Master's rights in their own lands save when he was present in person. The Marshal was the Order's third most important officer and provincial Marshals were responsible to him. This organisation took many years to evolve, but became increasingly necessary, for there were many recruits. Their number was swollen by confrère knights who served for only a short period, donating half their property, and who could marry. Cistercian *confratres* were the model for these auxiliary brethren.[1]

The Order's ecclesiastical privileges were very great since, though it soon acquired its own clergy, priest brothers, it was exempt from episcopal visitations, being responsible to the Pope

[1] Other great officers were the Gonfanonier (Standard Bearer), the Vice-Marshal, and the Turcopolier. For a more detailed account of the Templar hierarchy see Melville, op. cit., pp. 84–101.

alone; the bull *Omne datum optimum*[1] allowed these chaplains to celebrate Mass and dispense the sacraments during an interdict. As clerics, brethren could only be tried in ecclesiastical courts; it has been said that they were both a Church within a Church and a State within a State.

Brother knights saw themselves as solemnly professed religious. These were fighting men who joined the Order not just to fight but for prayer, making holy the only work they knew, as they could not hope to acquire the literacy necessary to become choir monks, while a lay brother's life was not suited to them on physical grounds. As members of a fighting class they had cultivated an entirely different set of muscles, the sensitive hands and bow legs of the horseman and the swordman's wrist and shoulder – an agricultural labourer's strength was in his bowed back. A Cistercian thinks of cutting down a tree as prayer, given the right conditions, and the Templar had a similar attitude towards a Moslem. In St Bernard's words 'killing for Christ' was '*malecide* not *homicide*', the extermination of injustice rather than the unjust, and therefore desirable; indeed 'to kill a pagan is to win glory for it gives glory to Christ'. Any cavalry soldier will speak of the characteristic noises in a squadron, the squeak of leather and jangle of metal harness, but above all troopers cursing beneath their breath at restive mounts. It was prayerful ejaculations rather than swearing in the ideal Templar squadron. The first object of a monk is self-sanctification, and long before the crusades Popes Leo IV and John VIII had declared that warriors pure in heart who died fighting for the Church would immediately inherit the kingdom of God. Death in battle meant consecration as a martyr, a road travelled by 20,000 Templars, knights and sergeants in two hundred years of war.

Yet basically their ideals were those of contemplative monasticism. A monk abandons his will and his desires to search for God; the monastic life is often described as a martyr-dom in which the monk must die to be reborn. Many of the

[1] Until recently this bull was ascribed to 1139 but Dr Riley-Smith has shown that it cannot be earlier than 1152 – and also that in that year the Templars were still not yet exempt from the patriarch's jurisdiction. See *English Historical Review* (April 1969).

early brethren ended in contemplative houses and it is no exaggeration to call the first Templars military Cistercians. Active service – usually of a fire brigade nature, galloping off at a moment's notice to deal with Turkish razzias – was the only interruption in an essentially ascetic existence. The worst hardship of monastic life is not self-denial or celibacy, but obedience to a superior's least command; a Templar was not even allowed to adjust his stirrup without permission. In battle they neither gave nor asked for quarter and were not allowed to ask for ransom. 'They neglected to live, but they were prepared to die in the service of Christ', full of that holy delirium which according to Ekkehard, filled the first crusaders.[1] These soldiers with cropped hair and hooded white mantles were unmistakable. They faced death if captured; after the Field of Blood in 1119 the atabeg Togtekin gave Frankish prisoners to his soldiers for archery practice or hacked off their legs and arms, leaving them in the streets of Aleppo for the townsmen to finish, though this was before the days of the brethren, who suffered much worse. For a brother to lose the black and silver gonfalon 'Beau Séant' meant expulsion from the Order. This was the ultimate penalty, also inflicted for desertion to the Saracens, heresy, or murdering a fellow Christian. Their lives were spent in the strange land of Christ and his mother, Palestine, with its brooding landscape, stony hills and lowering mountains, brief springs and burning summers. Celibates, they shared to the full in the new, lyrical devotion to Our Lady, preached so exquisitely by St Bernard and enshrined in simple popular songs. The brethren loved Outremer, the Holy Land, nearest to the kingdom of God.

Did they love it too well? Frequently they were reminded by popes and theologians that the Holy War was not an end in itself and that bloodshed was intrinsically evil. Such arguments were too subtle for men who did the actual fighting. A Templar's attitude towards his enemies became one of unadulterated fanaticism. Bernard had revived the old Northern war-band, substituting Christ for Woden. From the very beginning there were Western Christians who mistrusted the ideal. An English mystic, the Cistercian abbot Isaac of Étoile, wrote in St Bernard's

---

[1] Ekkehard of Aura in 'Hierosolymitana', *R.H.C. oc.,* vol. V.

2*

lifetime '. . . this dreadful new military order that someone
has rather pleasantly called the order of the fifth gospel was
founded for the purpose of forcing infidels to accept the faith at
the point of the sword. Its members consider that they have
every right to attack anyone not confessing Christ's name,
leaving him destitute, whereas if they themselves are killed while
thus unjustly attacking the pagans, they are called martyrs for
the faith. . . . We do not maintain that all they do is wrong, but
we do insist that what they are doing can be an occasion of
many future evils.'[1]

However, most contemporaries admired this new vocation
and when Hugues de Payens died in 1136 – in his bed – the
Temple had a rival, the Order of the Hospital of St John the
Baptist. Gerard had been succeeded as Master in 1120 by Fra.
Raymond du Puy, an organiser of genius. The Order's nursing
work had already made it rich and popular, more than a
thousand pilgrims a year being accommodated in Jerusalem,
while its hospitals and guest houses spread throughout the
kingdom. It received grants of land from Godefroi de Bouillon
and also acquired property in France, Italy, Spain and England.
Raymond was expert in providing an administration for these
European possessions, setting up houses whose revenues were
spent in forwarding food, wine, clothes and blankets for
hospital use; some were specifically charged with providing
luxuries, such as white bread, for the sick. The papacy gave St
John many privileges: Innocent II forbade bishops to interdict
Hospitaller chapels; Anastasius IV gave them their own priests;
and the English Adrian IV gave them their own churches. In
1126 a constable of the Order is mentioned, suggesting some
sort of military organisation, but the first firm date for armed
activity is 1136, when King Fulk gave them land at the key
position of Beit·Jibrin on the road from Gaza to Hebron. This
was the first of their huge fortresses, the castle of 'Gibelin'. The
Hospitallers owed an enormous debt to St Bernard, who had
made it possible for them to take up arms. Christian war had not
only become spiritually respectable, but a means of self-sanctification. Without the great Cistercian the brethren of St John

[1] Trans. G. Webb and A. Walker, quoted in L. Bouyer, *The Cistercian
Heritage* (Mowbray, 1958).

T. III. p. 82.

Fig. 2. An early Hospitaller in the original habit, worn until the fourteenth century (the white cross on the shoulder would have been smaller and had not yet developed into the familiar eight-pointed Maltese version). From Helyot.

would never have evolved into a military order. By 1187 they controlled more than twenty great strongholds in Outremer.[1]

The rule developed very slowly. A Christian must love Christ in other Christians and this command was the basis of the Hospital's nursing vocation. In the rule of the Temple it was laid down that a brother must be expelled from the order for killing a Christian but only reprimanded for killing a Saracen slave; Christ did not live within Saracens. Nursing made the Hospitallers more humane while the presence of women within the Order must also have had a softening influence. Fra. Raymond seems to have taken the Augustinian rule as a framework and then experimented with various ideas from the Poor Knights' constitutions.[2] The brethren took vows of poverty, chastity and obedience and were to expect only bread and water for sustenance, and obey the orders of the sick whom they visited every day. There was provision for surgeons who messed with the knightly brethren, while much attention was given to the maintenance of the hospital. As with the Templars there were four classes: knights, sergeants, serving brethren and chaplains. Similarly, there was provision for confrère knights. A bull of Alexander III of 1178 states that 'according to the custom of Raymond' the brothers could only carry arms when the standard of the cross was displayed – to defend the kingdom or attack a pagan city. The habit was a black mantle with a white cross on the chest, shaped like a bell tent and very clumsy in battle, and a black skull cap (though outside the house brethren sometimes wore a white turban).[3] There were also nursing sisters attached to each hospital. In the twelfth century fighting was only a secondary activity for Hospitallers (not even being mentioned in the Order's statutes until 1182), and militarisation was a long and slow process.

Eventually the structure came to resemble the Templars, and

[1] Dr Riley-Smith considers that fighting was very much an auxiliary activity – 'an extension of its charitable duties' (op. cit., p. 55) – which did not become so important as the latter until the thirteenth century.

[2] See King, *The Rule, Statutes and Customs of the Hospitallers, 1099–1310*.

[3] See Riley-Smith, op. cit., p. 257. Vainer brethren seem to have spent their regulation pocket money on clothes of better cloth, embroidered with gold thread, or on silk turbans etc.

knights ruled the brotherhood. The bailiffs, as the great officers were known, included the Master, elected by the same process as the Master of the Temple, and the only bailiff to hold office for life; the Grand Preceptor (sometimes called Grand Commander) of Jerusalem, the Master's lieutenant; the Treasurer; the Marshal; the Draper or quartermaster general; the Hospitaller; and finally the Turcopolier who commanded the 'Turcopoles', light native horse.[1] Commanderies were small units of knights and sergeants administering adjoining groups of properties. In Syria the commanders were directly responsible to the Master, but elsewhere the system was more complex, European commanderies being grouped into priories, and the priories into provinces corresponding to countries. Like the Templars, supreme power lay with the General Chapter. A smaller assembly, the conventual chapter, reminiscent of a cabinet, assisted the Master, acting as a secret privy council for affairs of state and a full public council to hear appeals. A quorum constituted 'the venerable chamber of the treasury'. Each province, priory and commandery had its own chapter.[2]

Day-to-day routine was no less monastic than that of the Templars, the Little Office being said while, like non-military religious, brethren received the sacraments more frequently than layfolk – it was said that when they had received the Body of the Lord they fought like devils. Yet the Hospitallers' spiritual life was deepened by their devotion to the sick, for wherever they had estates they also had hospitals and guest-houses. Then, as now, accommodation was hard to find and pilgrims had cause to be grateful. Caravans were regularly escorted from the coast up to Jerusalem. Here there was a hospital with beds for 1,000 patients, for Syrian-born Franks as well as visitors were weakened by frequent ptomaine poisoning and plagues of insects, afflicted by sand-fly fever, opthalmia, desert sores or endemic septicaemia. It has been suggested that the brethren's great hospitals were founded on Byzantine models, but their latest historian believes that the

[1] See Ibid., pt. II.
[2] Grand Commander in the West was an office occasionally bestowed on a great bailiff like the Prior of St Gilles (southern France). Ibid., p. 366.

brethren owed more to Arab medicine.[1] Certainly they took
the place of a field medical corps for after a battle, besides
wounded, there were always casualties suffering from terrible
bruises beneath their chain mail, from shock or from heatstroke.
This twofold vocation, to nurse and to fight, gave them an
important role in the life of Latin Syria, and like the Templars
they too were exempt from episcopal control.

The rule of the Temple specifies that a knight who catches
leprosy must leave the Order and join the brethren of 'St
Ladre'.[2] Leprosy, which included all forms of skin disease, was
very prevalent in Syria. The Hospitallers of St Lazarus were
the first military order to emerge after the Temple and the
Hospital. Probably there had been a leper house of St Lazarus
at Jerusalem before the conquest, run by Greek or Armenian
religious who observed the Basilian rule, the Eastern equivalent
of St Benedict's. Early in the twelfth century it was taken over
by Frankish Hospitallers following the Augustinian rule.[3] A
tradition that St Lazarus' first Master was that Gerard who was
also first Master of St John could mean that he supplied
brethren to found a specialised nursing order; the Hospitaller
customs state that those who contract leprosy must lose the
habit – like Templar lepers these may well have joined 'St
Ladre'. There is also a strange legend that the early Masters
were always lepers. They administered a network of 'lazar
houses' in both Syria and Europe organised on a commandery
framework similar to that of St John. After the Second Crusade
Louis VII established a house at Boigny near Orléans, while
Roger de Mowbray founded another at Burton Lazars in
Leicestershire;[4] many leper hospitals in France and England

[1] Ibid., pp 334–5.

[2] H. de Curzon, op. cit.

[3] Dr Riley-Smith believes that the tradition of a Basilian rule may stem
from the fact that a considerable number of the Order's first brethren were
Greek-rite Italians – many names from southern Italy are found witnessing
the earliest known charters of St Lazarus.

[4] See J. Nichols, *History of the County and Antiquities of Leicestershire*, vol. II,
pt. I (London, 1759); also 'The Hospital of Burton Lazars', *V.C.H.
Leicestershire*, vol. 2, pp. 36–9; the founder's charter is in Dugdale, *Monasticon
Anglicanum*, vol. VI (2), p. 632.

depended on these commanderies, who in turn depended on the great house of the Order at Jerusalem. This had itself been richly endowed, and Raymond III of Tripoli was a confrater of the brotherhood. Probably the habit was black and resembled St John's; its green cross was not adopted until the sixteenth century. The Lazar Knights were never numerous and had only a handful of non-leper brethren for protection, though no doubt in times of crisis unclean knights also took up arms. This always remained a primarily hospitaller order even if it took part in several battles.

The only other fighting brotherhood in twelfth-century Outremer was the Knights of Our Lady of Montjoie.[1] A bull of Alexander III of 1180 recognised them as an order who followed the Cistercian rule and, besides ransoming captives, took an oath to fight Saracens, a fourth of their revenues being set aside for this purpose. Montjoie was a hill castle outside Jerusalem which took its name from the pilgrims' cries of joy when they saw the Heavenly City from its summit. The actual founder was a Spaniard, Count Rodrigo, a former knight of Santiago, who gave the new brethren lands in Castille and Aragon, while King Baldwin IV entrusted them with several towers at Ascalon. Their habit was white with a red and white cross. Rodrigo himself, a thoroughly unstable character, was the first Master, and the order did not prosper. It had difficulty in attracting recruits, as most Spaniards preferred to join their great national orders. After 1187 the remnants retired to Aragon where they became known as the Order of Trufac, their Castilian commanderies being appropriated by the Templars. The little brotherhood's interest lies in its combination of two separate vocations.

Ostensibly the fighting brethren's ideal was the defence of Christians. Yet this was in complete contrast to the early Church's condemnation of all violence; 'Blood will have blood' and even a defensive war cannot avoid becoming aggressive. 'To lay down one's life for others' now became a precept of fanaticism, as the finest death for a knight brother was to die in battle. Yet it was surely better to harness a destructive element

[1] See Delaville le Roulx, 'L'Ordre de Montjoie', *Révue de l'Orient Latin*, vol. I (Paris, 1893); this article is still the definitive study.

in society than to leave it to ravage the homelands. The new brethren were the first organised armies of Western Europe since the legions and cataphracts had gone down before the barbarians and were another stage in the Church's restoration of the Roman Empire. Bernard's genius had transformed a Germanic warrior cult into a religious vocation just as pagan gods had been metamorphosed into saints and fertility rites into Christian festivals. Christ had ousted Woden.

CHAPTER 3

The bulwark of Jerusalem

The county of Edessa was the most exposed of the Frankish
territories, lying on both sides of the Euphrates, a Mesopotamian
march rather than a Syrian state. Despite its rich cornland it
had few castles, being scantily furnished with the indispensable
Frankish knights. Everything depended on the count. Joscelin I
was a brilliant captain of heroic character whose very presence
warded off raiders. However, his half-Armenian son, who
succeeded him in 1129, was cowardly and irresolute. Swarthy,
hook-nosed and shifty-eyed, Joscelin II typified those Franks
who had ceased to be crusaders and become *colons*. Perhaps he
did not smoke opium like some of his fellow *poulains*, but no
doubt he made frequent use of Turkish baths and wore silk
trousers. His cultivated Arab or Turkish neighbour was far
more congenial to him than some aggressive brute newly
arrived from northern Europe. The grim paladin had been
followed by a Levantine intriguer. Joscelin preferred to live in
the pleasant castle of Turbessel on the west bank of the
Euphrates rather than in his perilous capital, whose protection
he left to a sort of town guard, recruited from the Armenian and
Syrian merchants. Suddenly, in November 1144, the 'blue eyed
devil' of Aleppo, the terrible atabeg Zengi, laid siege to
Edessa and stormed it the day before Christmas Eve.

Western Christendom was appalled. Bernard of Clairvaux
used his last energies to preach the Second Crusade and by the
autumn of 1147 two armies reached Anatolia, one led by the
Emperor Conrad III, the other by Louis VII of France. In
October the Germans were cut to pieces in a Turkish ambush at
Dorylaeum and fled to Nicaea, where the French joined them.
Conrad fell ill and returned to Constantinople, but Louis
continued through Anatolia, relentlessly harried by the Turkish
bowmen. By January, lashed by winter storms, short of food,
his men's morale had collapsed. After a particularly murderous

attack in which Queen Eleanor was almost captured and
Louis nearly killed, the king lost all confidence in his powers of
generalship and handed over the command to the Templar
Master.

Everard des Barres was an ideal Poor Knight, half fervent
religious, half skilled soldier. He had joined Louis in France with
a detachment of 300 Spanish Templars, many of whom had
probably joined the Order only for the duration of the crusade,
which they were allowed to do on payment of a premium. For
the first time Templars wore the red cross on their mantles. The
king was impressed by Everard's diplomatic skill in dealing with
the Byzantines, and by his brethren, who alone retained their
discipline. The Master restored order, bringing the battered
army through to the coast, where Louis took ship with his
cavalry, leaving the infantry to struggle on.

Though thousands had perished, Conrad rejoined his men,
and the joint army – French, German and Syrian – assembled
at Acre in June 1148. Raymond du Puy was summoned to the
council of war, an acknowledgement of his brethren's military
importance. A disastrous decision was taken, to attack the emir
Unur of Damascus, the one Saracen prince anxious for a
Frankish alliance, an error which eventually led to the
unification of Moslem Syria. The attempt failed amid mutual
recriminations; crusaders considered the barons of Outremer,
the *poulains*, to be half-Turk, while Latin Syrians regarded
their northern cousins as dangerous, unwashed fanatics. By 1149
the Second Crusade had petered out, having done irreparable
harm to Frankish prestige.

The survival of Jerusalem was largely due to the ability of
Baldwin III (1143–62) and his choleric brother Amalric I
(1162–74). Syrian-born with Armenian blood and married to
Byzantine princesses, they were fully alive to their native land's
growing danger. Energetic warriors, they hoped to extend
their territory. Already Frankish castles had been built on the
Gulf of Aqaba across the caravan route from Baghdad to
Cairo. King Baldwin's capture of Ascalon in 1153 was the
occasion of a peculiarly unedifying display by the Templar
Master, Bernard de Tremelay. The detachment of 'the avenger
who is in the service of Christ, the liberator of Christian people'

had breached the city wall, whereupon Fra. Bernard, posting guards to prevent other Franks entering, went in with forty hand-picked brethren. They were killed to a man, but the Master's rashness was attributed to greed rather than gallantry.[1] On the other hand the king's decision to persevere with the siege was due to Raymond du Puy's persuasion. The Hospitallers were becoming soldiers too.

Together the brethren could now put nearly 600 knights into the field, half the total muster of the kingdom, while their possessions accumulated steadily. Count Raymond II (1137–1152) of Tripoli was a Hospitaller confrater and in 1142 entrusted his brothers-in-religion with the key position of his county, the enormous fortress of Qalat al-Hosen, which they rebuilt as Krak-des-Chevaliers. Raymond III (1152–87) was also a confrater of the Hospitallers and during his long captivity they acquired the strongholds of Arka, Akkar, and many others. With these they were the greatest landowners in the county, though rivalled by the Templars who had large possessions in the north. In Antioch there was a similar division of territory, while many castles in the kingdom itself were handed over to them. Their constitutional role grew accordingly, both Masters sitting as members of the Haute Cour, the commanders of Antioch and Tripoli doing likewise in their local courts. The three keys of the royal treasury, in which was deposited the crown, were entrusted to the patriarch and to the Masters of the Temple and the Hospital, an apt symbol of their power. The princes continued to endow them with fiefs. Many lords preferred to retire to some luxurious villa on the coast, while the brethren had the money and men to run the vast Syrian fortresses and also solve such irksome problems as finding husbands for heiresses or furnishing wards with guardians. Donations and recruits poured in from Europe in a steady flow.

Their chief critics were the local clergy. These military orders were almost a Church within a Church, whose priests were not only exempt from diocesan visitations but also from any financial obligation. Brethren wrangled with bishops over dues, tithes and jurisdictions and were accused of admitting

[1] For the death of Bernard de Tremelai see the 'Estoire d'Eracles', R.C.H. oc., vol. I, bk. 17, ch. XXVII, p. 805.

excommunicated men to their services. When in 1154 the Patriarch of Jerusalem ordered them to desist, the Hospitallers burst into his sermons, shouting him down and shooting arrows at his congregation. Templars contented themselves with merely shooting at his church door. In 1155 the patriarch travelled to Rome to ask the pope to place the military brethren under his authority, but Fra. Raymond followed him, obtaining a confirmation of all Hospitaller privileges. Reluctantly the clergy of Outremer accepted the brethren's independence, but their chroniclers always gave them a bad press.

The brethren were remarkably adaptable, turning their hands to many skills. Some learnt Arabic (great officers kept Saracen secretaries) and the brothers' spy service was un-paralleled. They had to fill such institutional vacuums as banking, for only they possessed the necessary vaults, organisa-tion and integrity. The Templars became professional finan-ciers; all monies collected for the Holy Land were conveyed by them from their European preceptories to the temple at Jerusalem while pilgrims and even Moslem merchants deposited their cash at the local temple. Brethren needed money for arms and equipment, to build fortresses, to hire mercenaries and to buy off enemies, so the funds in their strongrooms could not be allowed to lie idle; the church's embargo on usury was circum-vented by adding the interest to the sum due for repayment and Arab specialists were employed for dealings in the money markets of Baghdad and Cairo while an excellent service of bills of exchange was provided. In many ways the military brethren foreshadowed the great Italian banking houses.

Both Templars and Hospitallers found it cheaper to transport troops in their own ships, and passages were available to pilgrims; at one time the Templars conveyed 6,000 pilgrims each year.[1] Their boats were popular, for they maintained a flotilla

[1] 'Marseilles, indeed, as the centre of transport from France to the Holy Land, had in 1253 and 1255 to pass statutes to regulate the traffic. Not more than fifteen hundred pilgrims were to be taken in any one ship. First-class passengers, with deck cabins, were to pay 60 sous; second-class, between decks, 40; third-class, on the lowest deck, 35; and fourth-class, in the hold, 25. Each pilgrim received a numbered ticket . . .' Joan Evans, *Life in Mediaeval France* (Phaidon, 1969), p. 98.

of escort ships and could be trusted not to sell their passengers into slavery at Moslem ports, as did certain Italian merchants. It was natural to use empty space for merchandise so they exported spices, silk dyes, porcelain and glass, taking full advantage of their exemption from customs dues, and soon rivalled the Levantine traders who banked with them.

Such activities hardly harmonise with the name of Poor Knights. As Jacques de Vitry pointed out, the Templars owned no individual property, but in common seemed anxious to possess everything. Nevertheless their life was as ascetic as ever. Certainly by this time purely contemplative orders were no strangers to high finance; Cistercian techniques of agriculture brought great wealth to the white monks – the entire wool crop of many English abbeys was often sold for years ahead. Certainly rivalry over revenues made for little love between Poor Knights and Knights of St John, yet nonetheless both would unite in times of real danger.

In 1154 the young Fatimid caliph was murdered by his homosexual favourite, Nasr, who fled to Syria and was captured by the Templars. To save his skin he asked for instruction in the Christian faith. He did not deceive the unsympathetic brethren. They accepted Cairo's offer of 60,000 dinars for him, and Nasr was taken home by the Egyptians in an iron cage to be first horribly mutilated by the caliph's four widows and then, still living, crucified at the Zawila Gate, where his rotting corpse hung for two years. At least one contemporary chronicler appears to have been disturbed by the brothers' business acumen.

Certainly one Armenian joined the brethren as a knight and probably many more were admitted to the sergeant class (which also numbered Christian Arabs). The Templars had an unfortunate experience with Fra. Mleh, a member of the Cicilian ruling family, 'hom pleins de grant malice et trop desleaus'. After taking vows as a Poor Knight he attempted to murder his brother, Prince Thoros, and fled to Damascus where he turned Moslem. In 1170 he came back with Turkish troops to conquer Cilicia, after attacking the Templar stronghold at Baghras. 'Ce desloial Hermin' cherished a venomous hatred for his former co-religionists and treated Templar prisoners with particular cruelty. At last, outraged by their prince's apostasy, his own people killed him.[1]

Fra. Raymond died in 1158. He was succeeded as Master of the Hospital by Fra. Gilbert d'Assailly. Until 1168 King Amalric's Egyptian policy had been a realistic one of alliance with the viziers of the Shia caliph against the Sunni Nur ed-Din who now ruled Aleppo and Damascus. However, it was clear that the Fatimid regime was near its end and Amalric negotiated an alliance with the Emperor Manuel; the Byzantines would attack by sea while the whole muster of Jerusalem struck overland. Success depended on the cooperation of the emperor, who was busy campaigning in Serbia. Amalric was prepared to wait but Fra. Gilbert intervened with an offer of 500 knights and 500 Turcopoles, in return for the town of Bilbeis.[2] At this the barons refused to wait any longer before enjoying the fabulous riches of Cairo. Fra. Bertrand de Blanquefort, the Templar Master, refused to support the expedition; there was not sufficient manpower to wage a campaign and at the same time cope with the counter-attack which was certain to come from the north-east.

The Franks captured Bilbeis, but the troops got out of hand and a massacre, including the local Christians, took place. The Egyptians were panic-stricken and the caliph himself wrote to Nur ed-Din for help, whereupon the atabeg sent his Kurdish general Shirkuh with 8,000 horsemen who by-passed Amalric and entered Cairo. Shirkuh was proclaimed vizier but soon afterwards ate himself to death and was succeeded by his nephew, Salah ad-Din Yusuf ibn Ayub, better known as Saladin. Within two years the last Fatimid caliph was dead and Shia Egypt had returned to the Sunni fold; the Frankish protectorate was replaced by a Cairo-Aleppo axis, the most formidable coalition yet to threaten Outremer.

The Hospital was nearly bankrupt as it had staked all available funds on a successful outcome. Fra. Gilbert was not noted for stability and the failure of his gamble unbalanced him. He

[1] See William of Tyre, op. cit., bk. 20, ch. XXVI, p. 990 – 'Milo Armenus, frater domini Toros' – 'De la grant desloiauté Meslier le frere Toros'.
[2] See Delaville le Roulx, *Les Hospitaliers*, pp. 65–76 and *Cart. Gen.* no. 402 – the charter which confirmed this great gamble.

appears to have had a nervous breakdown in the rummer of
1170, when he retired to a cave in the Hauran to become a
hermit. Eventually he was coaxed out, but, despite the General
Chapter's pleas, abdicated; later he was drowned crossing the
English Channel. The Knights of St John had suffered a
grievous setback and it took them years to recover their losses
in money and manpower.

It is hardly surprising that there were many cases of mental
and moral breakdown among the brethren. Whether one thinks
like Freud that religion is spiritualised sex or agrees with Jung
that it is necessary for a man's sanity, most people admit that
monks and nuns seem to achieve a happy, balanced life based
on prayer and humane activities. But military brethren mixed
blood with prayer, their conventual life continually interrupted
by the call to arms. These vigorous men, products of a violent
age and class, had to find an outlet in war or administration.
Many unsuitable recruits joined the brethren to seek a vocation
as rare as that of a Carthusian hermit.

In 1173 'the new Maccabees', as the English pope Adrian IV
called the Templars, had a fierce quarrel with the king over the
Assassins. These *Hashishiyun*, eaters of hashish, were an extremist
sect of the Shias, whose founder had pushed the doctrine of
Jihad – paradise the reward for death in combat with unbelievers – to its extreme, his followers being persuaded that
their master could give them a foretaste of heaven. This was
done under the influence of hashish when they were brought
into a green garden of delight. As the Koran specifies, it was
furnished with wine, couches, flowing fountains and 'the
Houris, with large dark eyes, like pearls hidden in their
shells . . . damsels with retiring glances, whom no man or
djinn hath touched before'.[1] To return there devotees would
die. Their weapon was the poisoned knife, flat cakes their trade
mark, and they terrorised Moslems and Christians alike. The
sect's organisation had a superficial resemblance to the
brethren's. They had several 'eagle's nests' in the Nosairi
mountains of the Lebanon, whose governor was called the
Sheikh al-Gebel, the Old Man of the Mountains. In 1173
this was Rashid ed-Din Sinan, who was much alarmed by the
[1] From Sura LVI – 'The Inevitable' and Sura LV – 'The Merciful'.

recent extinction of the Fatimid caliphate. Suddenly he sent an embassy to King Amalric announcing his imminent conversion to Christianity and asking to be relieved of the tribute imposed by the Templars. The king knew just how much belief to place in Sinan's conversion, but peace in the Nosairi and the use of the Assassin intelligence network were worth having. He remitted the tribute announcing that his own ambassadors would visit the Sheikh. As the Assassin envoys were returning home they were ambushed by some Templars, under the one-eyed Fra. Gautier de Mesnil, and decapitated. Amalric was so furious that to his courtiers he appeared out of his senses.[1] He had had trouble from Templars before, hanging ten for surrendering a castle without permission. He ordered the Master, Eudes de St Amand, to hand over the culprit. Fra. Eudes refused but offered to send the erring brother to Rome – the pope alone could try the case. However, Amalric burst into the Master's quarters, and seized Gautier whom he flung into prison.

Next year Nur ed-Din died. Saladin now ruled Damascus as well as Cairo and was proclaimed King of Egypt and Syria in 1176, with the Caliph of Baghdad's official blessing. A Kurdish adventurer who hacked the way to the throne, once there he became a Moslem St Louis, something of a mystic, an ascetic who fasted, slept on a rough mat and gave alms unceasingly – in Gibbon's amusing phrase, 'while he emulated the temperance he surpassed the chastity of his Arabian prophet'.[2] His ambition was to restore the unity of Sunni Islam which included a Jihad against the Franks. Nevertheless with his sensitive, inquiring mind he saw that there was much good in Christianity, even if it lacked the Third Revelation, and was intrigued by the Frankish code of chivalry. The Franks had a deep respect for his bravery and magnanimity; there was even a legend that in his youth he had been knighted by the constable of Jerusalem.

Amalric died the same year, succeeded by perhaps the most gallant figure of the whole Frankish venture, the leper king,

[1] On Gautier de Mesnil, Eudes de St Amand and King Amalric see Melville, op. cit., pp. 103–4 and William of Tyre, op. cit., bk. 20, ch. XXX, pp. 997–9.
[2] See *The Decline and Fall*, ch. LIX.

Baldwin IV (1174–85), who inherited the throne at thirteen, a year after his leprosy had been discovered. He literally dropped to pieces during his reign, a via dolorosa on which he showed, with moving courage, political realism and remarkable powers of leadership.

Outremer's strategic position was deteriorating rapidly. In 1176 the Seldjuk Sultan of Iconium wiped out the army of Emperor Manuel at Myriocephalum; Byzantium, finished as a military power, would never again intervene in Syria. Lesser Armenia was growing at the expense of Antioch, unedifyingly ready to ally with Moslem neighbours. Worse, however, was the kingdom's encirclement. Saladin would take Aleppo in 1183 and was steadily consolidating his empire.

In November 1177 Saladin led the whole of his army, 26,000 Turks, Kurds, Arabs, Sudanese and Mamelukes, in a raid on the plain between Ramleh and Ascalon. Blockading the leper king in Ascalon with a small garrison he marched on Jerusalem. Baldwin broke out with 300 Knights and, joined by Eudes de St Amand with eighty Templars, circled Saladin by hard riding. The little force caught him off his guard in the ravine of Montgisard and, with the leprous youth and the Bishop of Acre carrying the True Cross at their head, the heavy Frankish horsemen smashed into the Egyptian army. It was a bloodbath and Saladin and his troops fled into the Sinai desert, where they all but perished of thirst.

Next time Baldwin was not so lucky. On the morning of 10 June 1179 the king ambushed a raiding party, commanded by Saladin's nephew, at Marj Ayun. Resting, he himself was surprised some hours later by Saladin's entire army and routed with heavy loss. The Templars charged too soon and Fra. Eudes was taken prisoner, but in accordance with his Order's rule refused to be ransomed. William of Tyre abuses the fire-breathing Master, 'homo nequam superbus et arrogans, fel et orgueilleus',[1] but Eudes was a man of principle and died in prison the year after, probably from starvation.

The sinister Gerard de Ridefort became Master of the Temple in 1185. A penniless gentleman from Flanders he had

[1] William says that the Master literally breathed fury – 'spiritum furoris habens in naribus' – op. cit., bk. 21, ch. XXIX, p. 1057.

taken service with Raymond III on condition that he be given
the hand of the heiress of Botrun. Raymond did not keep his
promise and the embittered Gerard joined the Templars. His
driving ambition and aggressive self-confidence soon took him
to the top, but he embodied all his Order's worst faults. A
Master had to live with princes, and an impressive household
pandered to Gerard's pathological pride; his personal staff
included bodyguards and Arab secretaries, with two great
officers always in attendance.[1] It is interesting to compare Fra.
Gerard with one of the companions of St Francis, Fra. Elias,
Master General of the Franciscans, whose head was so turned
by power that he would only appear in public on horseback. One may condemn Gerard without condemning his
brethren.

One of the two co-heiresses of Baldwin who died in 1185 was
his sister, Sibylla, married to Guy de Lusignan, a brainless
adventurer gifted with good looks. When the child king
Baldwin V died in 1185 many in Outremer hoped to enthrone
Sibylla's younger sister Isabella, who would leave affairs of
state to the one man capable of saving the kingdom, the
Regent Raymond III of Tripoli. However, an unscrupulous
faction including the patriarch and the vindictive Master of
the Temple rallied to Guy. Fra. Gerard extorted the third
key of the royal treasury from the Hospitaller Master, Roger
des Moulins, who flung it from his window and would have
nothing to do with the coronation. Guy was crowned king,
guarded by a phalanx of Poor Knights, whose Master com-
mented 'ceste corone vaut bien le mariage dou Botron'.

Early in 1187 the Lord of Outrejourdain, Reynald de
Chatillon, rode out from his desert stronghold, Krak-en-Moab,
to slaughter a Damascene caravan with which the sultan's
sister was travelling, and which thought itself protected by the
truce. Reynald was an archetypal robber baron, a murderous
throwback to the northern progenitors of the French aristocracy and a perfect specimen of the brutal noblemen whom

[1] A famous description of the splendid establishment at the Temple of
Jerusalem was written by an enthralled Franciscan priest, Johann von
Wurzburg, who visited it in the 1170s. See 'Johannis Wirburgensis Pres-
byterii Descriptio Terrae Sanctae', *M.P.L.*, ch. CLV.

St Bernard hoped to civilise. His most lunatic exploit was in
1182 when he transported ships, piece by piece, over the
desert to the Red Sea and raided the pilgrims on their way to
Mecca, earning the Franks the hatred of the whole Moslem
world. Insanely brave and totally unscrupulous, he had much
in common with Fra. Gerard. Outremer's affairs were exposed to the meddling of two irresponsible berserks at a time
when the kingdom desperately needed wise and cautious
leadership.

In May a raiding party of 7,000 Moslem cavalry was tackled
at the Springs of Cresson near Nazareth by 150 Knights,
comprising Fra. Gerard, 90 Templars, 40 secular knights, and
the Master of the Hospital, Roger des Moulins, with his
Marshal Jacques de Mailly and their escort. Ridefort taunted
Fra. Jacques 'Vos amez trop cele teste blonde'.[1] A Moslem
eye-witness records how even the blackest head of hair went
white with fright as the Frankish horsemen hurtled towards
them. But the odds were too great. Fra. Roger went down
riddled with arrows, and only Fra. Gerard escaped with two
brethren, all three badly wounded. It had been his decision to
charge. He was a typical medieval man who believed in trial
by battle – God always gave the victory to Christians unless
they displeased him, just as he had done with the people of
Israel. Perhaps in his Order's great refectories the Master had
heard priest brethren read the words of Judas Machabeus to
faint-hearted warriors: 'There is no difference in the sight of
the God of heaven to deliver with a great multitude or with a
small company: for the success of war is not in the multitude
of the army, but strength cometh from heaven.'[2]

On 1 July 1187 Saladin crossed the Jordan with an army of
60,000 men. The whole muster of Outremer assembled, 1,200
Knights and perhaps 20,000 sergeants, turcopoles and foot
soldiers. Of the knights about 300 belonged to the Temple,
250 to the Hospital. There was also a small detachment of the
brethren of Montjoie, and possibly another from St Lazarus.

[1] See 'L'Estoire de Eracles Empereur et la conqueste de la terre d'outremer'.
R.H.C. oc., bk. 28, ch. XXVI, p. 40.
[2] I Maccabees, III – 18, 19 (Douai version).

Prince Bohemond III of Antioch sent his son with 50 knights. No more than 600 could have been provided by the kingdom, this being the total 'knight-service'. They were better equipped than men of the First Crusade. Chain stockings and a mail shirt were worn in place of the long hauberk. The shield was smaller, and sometimes the helmet was flat-topped like a saucepan, with a grille to guard the face, though not yet the great barrel helm of the next century. Lay knights wore a keffiyeh and a surcoat, while the brethren had their white, brown and black cloaks. This was not an alien expeditionary force, but an army of *poulains* marching out to defend their homeland. Many brethren and most secular knights and sergeants had been born there; some were of mixed blood, Syrian and Armenian, or even pure Arabs. *Colons* and natives were united by their Christian faith and common peril.

Instead of trusting Count Raymond's experienced judgement, Guy relied on those two berserks Reynald de Chatillon and Fra. Gerard. Saladin had captured Tiberias and was besieging Raymond's wife in the castle, but the count advised Guy to wait at Saffaria where there was water. Gerard persuaded the king to change his mind, coming to the royal tent 'quant ce vint la nuit'[1] and telling Guy that Raymond was a traitor, that he would be disgraced before God and his subjects if he did not recapture Tiberias. Guy succumbed to the fanatic, and gave the order to march. Friday, 3 July, was the hottest day of an unnaturally hot summer. After a grim trek through waterless desert the Frankish army pitched camp on a hill called the Horns of Hattin. Its well was dry. Saladin could hardly believe his eyes, but gave thanks to God, while his troops encircled the hill. The Christians spent a terrible night without water, awaiting death.

At dawn the Moslems set fire to the scrub. Flames and smoke swept up the slopes maddening men and horses tortured by thirst. The infantry soon broke and were slaughtered by the thousand, but the horsemen fought on in the appalling heat. After many charges over impossible ground and having beaten back attack after attack under a hail of arrows, King Guy's force was reduced to 150 dismounted knights, and surrendered.

[1] *R.H.C. oc.*, II, bk. 23, ch. XXXV, p. 52.

The Moslems captured the True Cross in its gold reliquary.[1] Saladin was merciful, treating the king with kindness. Most prisoners were spared, but there were two exceptions. Reynald de Chatillon, the harrier of pilgrims, was struck down by Saladin himself and the Hospitallers and Templars, save for Fra. Gerard, were handed over to dervishes who hacked them to pieces. To a man they had refused to save their lives by accepting Islam.

While the male population of Frankish Syria was driven off to the slave markets of Damascus, Saladin proceeded to occupy their towns. Jerusalem had one man for every fifty women and children, but by putting up a gallant defence was allowed to ransom a large proportion of its citizens, in humane contrast with the Christian sack of 1099. The Hospitaller and Templar financial officials were scandalously parsimonious, as there was not a single knight to take responsibility. However, Saladin let the penniless go free. Acre surrendered on the same conditions and within a month, apart from a few castles, only Antioch, Tripoli and Tyre resisted. A contemporary chronicler attributed the disaster of Hattin to the filth, luxury and adultery of Jerusalem, but whatever the cause Christendom had lost the 'City of the King of Kings' and with it the Temple and the Hospital.

Reduced to Tripoli, Tortosa, Antioch and Tyre, the kingdom at first seemed doomed. The conviction that God had deserted him could produce a sudden, staggering demoralisation in medieval man and Count Raymond died of a broken heart. However, Saladin concentrated on the few remaining strongholds inland which cut his supply lines. The brethren realised that resistance would help the coastal towns. In January 1188 the Hospitallers of Belvoir in Galilee cut to pieces a besieging army. For a whole year the Moslems invested Belvoir as well as the Templars at Safed, battering the two castles with rock-throwing mangonels and trebuchets, ceaselessly mining,

[1] *R.H.C. oc.*, II, bk. 23, ch. XLIII, p. 65 – 'En cele bataille fu la Sainte Crois perdue'. Marion Melville makes much of a story that a Templar escaped with the True Cross which he buried in the sand; later he returned but could not find it. Yet Arabic sources definitely state that the Cross was captured.

mounting assault after assault The winter's drenching rain and mud nearly defeated the besiegers but at last, in December 1188, Safed surrendered, followed by Belvoir in January 1189. The sultan spent June 1188 before Krak-des-Chevaliers, but the Hospitallers were not easily frightened. He then invested Tortosa where he was beaten off by the Templar garrison. Marqab, the Hospitallers' coastal stronghold, he left in peace. His caution was due to the arrival of 200 knights from Sicily, who relieved Krak at the end of July. In September, at Darbessaq, the Templars astonished the Moslems by their bravery, standing motionless and silent in the breach. The castle resisted for a fortnight and then with Prince Bohemond's permission capitulated, as did Baghras, another Templar stronghold. Their garrisons retired to Antioch. These campaigns deflected Saladin from the reduction of Tyre, the centre of Christian resistance.

In July 1188 the sultan released King Guy, who swore he would never again bear arms against Islam, and shortly after Fra. Gerard was allowed to ransom himself, a flagrant breach of the Templar rule. The Master found many brethren at Tyre, as well as Hospitallers who had come in haste from Europe. Then in April 1189 a fleet arrived from Pisa with further reinforcements. The following August Guy suddenly laid siege to Acre, whose garrison outnumbered his troops by three to one. Perhaps one may detect Gerard's baneful counsel in breaking the oath sworn to Saladin; sworn to an infidel under duress it had no validity. The long siege of Acre has been compared to the siege of Troy but was the beginning of the Frankish recovery.

Saladin invested Guy's camp and besiegers found themselves besieged. Yet all the time reinforcements were arriving by sea – small parties of French, German and Danish crusaders. On 4 October Guy attacked Saladin for the first time since Hattin. It was a savage battle, though honours were even. Fra. Gerard, who commanded the advance guard, refused to leave the field and was taken prisoner. He was executed immediately on Saladin's express orders. Crusaders continued to arrive, including a contingent of Londoners, while since May 1189 Frederick Barbarossa had been marching to the Holy Land with 100,000 men. In 1190, however, while fording a river in Seleucia the fine old Emperor was drowned and the German army disintegrated – not more than 1,000 reached Acre. The siege dragged on; the Franks could not take Acre, neither could the Moslems dislodge them. Famine and plague broke out. By the spring of 1191 the crusaders were desperate.

On 20 April 1191 the fleet of Philip Augustus of France anchored off Acre, bringing food, men and siege engines. The Third Crusade had finally materialised. King Philip postponed an assault until the arrival of Richard I of England on 7 June and contented himself with concentrating a heavy bombardment on the Tour Maudite, Acre's principal bastion; both Templars and Hospitallers had their own mangonel. After recklessly overtaxing his subjects Richard had made countless enemies during a leisurely journey, in the course of which he paused to conquer Cyprus, then a Byzantine island ruled by a rebel emperor. Yet in the Holy Land he became 'Richard Cœur de Lion', the hero that he is in Grétry's opera and Scott's novel. The 'Accursed Tower' crumbled. A series of ferocious assaults culminated with a particularly savage attack by the English on 11 July which broke the garrison's spirit; next day Acre surrendered after negotiations conducted by the Hospitallers.

The French king installed himself in the Temple, upon which the brethren broke into vociferous complaints led by their new Master, Fra. Robert de Sablé from Maine, who had been elected with Richard's support. The king soon moved out, a humiliating concession which shows the power of the brethren. At the end of July, Philip sailed for France leaving Richard in undisputed command.

Saladin, who loathed the Templars but recognised their integrity, asked them for their word that the prisoners would not be harmed, but knowing Richard's cruel and unstable temperament they refused it; on 20 August, Richard ordered his English troops to butcher nearly 3,000 men, women and children. Two days later he marched on Ascalon down the coast road with the sea covering one flank, the Hospitallers for his advance guard and the Templars covering his rear. Later they changed places. Because of dense papyrus swamps the column was forced to turn inland, on to the plain before Arsuf.

Saturday, 7 September 1191, was a day of sweltering heat.
The Moslems began a terrifying din, drums rolling, cymbals
clashing, trumpets braying and dervishes howling. Horses
began to fall beneath the arrow storm, but Richard was determined to wait until he could charge on as broad a front as
possible. The Hospitaller Master, Fra. Garnier de Nablus, a
former prior of England, whose knights were on the left, told
him that they could not be kept back much longer, but Richard
ordered them to hold and they held. As the rear guard, the Hospitallers, had suffered most of all – the Order's Marshal could
not restrain himself. The whole Frankish cavalry galloped with
him. The Turkish squadrons disintegrated while the Moslem
infantry ran for its life. For the Christians it was a victory of
some significance; the sins which brought about the judgement
of Hattin were forgiven and once more God was on their side.

The sultan started to evacuate coastal towns. Unfortunately,
instead of marching on Jerusalem, Richard delayed to refortify
Jaffa. In November he set out for the Holy City. By January
he was only twelve miles away, but the winter rains were unusually hard and Saladin's army was behind him, so Richard
withdrew to Ascalon on the advice of the brethren and the
poulains, a wise if melancholy decision. At the Templars' suggestion he set about re-fortifying Ascalon. The first months of
1192 were spent in deciding the future of the crown of Jerusalem.
Queen Sibylla had died childless in October 1190 and the
Syrian baronage was anxious to be rid of her lamentable
husband. Her younger sister, Isabella, had her marriage to the
weak Humphrey de Toron forcibly annulled and, protesting,
was married to Conrad of Montferrat in November. In July
1191 Guy, supported by Richard as a Poitevin, had won the
right to keep the crown. Now the English king knew him better
and in April 1192 summoned the Syrian magnates to a council.
Unanimously they chose Conrad for their king. However, a
week later Conrad was struck down by the Assassins. Within
another week Isabella was married to Richard's nephew, Henry,
Count of Champagne, young, able and popular, who was
crowned in place of Conrad.

There remained the problem of the ex-king. On his way to
Palestine, Richard had sold Cyprus to the Templars. They soon

1a. The castle of Krak-des-Chevaliers in Palestine. A stronghold of the
Hospitallers from 1144 to 1271.

1b. The Marienburg in West Prussia, headquarters of the Teutonic Order
and residence of the Hochmeister from 1309 to 1466. Now called Malbork,
and in Poland, it was severely damaged during the Russian advance in 1945
but has since been restored. A photograph taken before 1939.

2a. The commandery of the Teutonic Knights at Rheden in West Prussia as it must have appeared at the end of the thirteenth century. The four wings form chapel, dormitory, refectory and chapter house, fortified on the outside, while the cloisters are on an upper floor in case enemies should penetrate to the courtyard.

2b. The commandery of the Teutonic Knights at Blumenthal-über-Aichach in Bavaria, founded in 1296. The medieval castle-monastery is on the left. From a seventeenth-century print.

upset the islanders by their arrogant administration. In April 1192 there was a fierce rising and the Templar commander, Fra. Armand Bouchart, fourteen brethren and a hundred troops only survived by taking refuge in the citadel of Nicosia. A few days later Fra. Armand launched a lethal counter-attack which was successful, but the Templars returned the island to Richard. He sold it to Guy, who borrowed the necessary down-payment from the merchants of Tripoli and then left the Holy Land for ever.

In September Richard made a treaty with Saladin; peace for five years and the Franks to keep the coastal towns from Tyre to Jaffa. The Third Crusade had failed to attach Jerusalem to the narrow strip of land ninety miles long, never more than ten miles wide, which was the new Outremer, a string of coastal towns. In October 1192 Richard left Palestine. The next year Saladin died the death of a saint at Damascus and his sword was buried with him, for the prophet had said that 'Paradise lies under the shadow of swords'. The Moslem counter-crusade slackened. His heirs, the Ayubite dynasty, were busy disputing his inheritance and Outremer settled down under King Henry's capable government. The Temple of Solomon and the Hospital were lost with Jerusalem, and so the brethren moved their chief houses to Acre.

In September 1197 Henry fell from a window and the wretched Isabella was married for a fourth time, to Amalric de Lusignan, Guy's youngest brother. He had inherited Cyprus in 1194 on Guy's death and had recently been given a crown by the Emperor Henry VI. Amalric took up residence at Acre, a good friend of the Orders; they had intervened on his behalf when he quarrelled with King Henry. In Cyprus, Amalric built a kingdom which endured for three centuries.

Lusignan Cyprus resembled Outremer in that it was ruled by a French-speaking king and had an aristocracy with an Italian merchant class. Castles and churches were built in the French style and the new Cypriot culture was Latin and feudal, Roman clergy being installed and Orthodoxy persecuted. Both Hospitallers and Templars founded commanderies, the most notable being at Kolossi whence the sweet St John wine still comes. However, brethren never obtained the power they had in Syria, for the king was stronger and his thirteen barons weaker than in Jerusalem. Cyprus was a beautiful country and free from border warfare, yet ultimately it ruined Outremer. Settlers preferred its fertile soil, lemon and orange groves, and gentler climate, to the stones, heat and danger of Palestine, while the possession of Cypriot manors by the Syrian baronage lessened their stake in Jerusalem's survival.

The one important event in Amalric's reign was the abortive German crusade of 1197. Its sole achievement was to found the third great military order, the Teutonic Knights, in 1198, who were installed in the St Nicholas Gate at Acre. As the new brotherhood developed in the Baltic rather than in Palestine, its rise is dealt with in another chapter.[1] About this time another order was emerging, the Hospitallers of St Thomas of Canterbury at Acre, usually called Knights of St Thomas Acon. During the siege of Acre, William, chaplain to the Dean of St Paul's, moved by the English crusaders' misery, began nursing the sick and wounded. After the city's capture, aided by King Richard, he built a small chapel and purchased a cemetery, founding a hospital and a nursing brotherhood restricted to Englishmen.[2] Probably they did not turn military until the Fifth Crusade. Like the Teutonic Knights their constitutions seem to have been copied from the Templar rule, despite hospitaller activities. The habit was a white mantle and red cross, which had a white scallop shell on it. The new Order acquired lands in Cyprus, Sicily, Naples and later Greece, while in England its headquarters was the Hospital of St Thomas Acon in London, on the site of what is now the Mercers' Hall. The original house was the actual birthplace of Thomas Becket and had been presented to the brethren by his sister and brother-in-law. The brethren of St Thomas were always a small brotherhood, most Englishmen preferring to join the Hospitallers of St John.

The principality of the tough Cilician highlanders was expanding and their ruler, Lavon II, had nearly succeeded in

---

[1] See ch. 5, 'The Crusade on the Baltic'.

[2] The main source for these details is Ralph de Diceto's *Ymagines Historiarum*. See 'The Historical Works of Master Ralph de Diceto, Dean of London', ed. Stubbs, *Rolls Series*, vol. II (London, 1876), p. 80.

capturing Antioch with its half-Armenian baronage. Lavon had occupied the Templar castle of Baghras, commanding the road from Antioch into Cilicia, after Saladin had evicted the brethren; the Poor Knights seem to have taken a very un-oecumenical attitude towards Eastern Christians in general and had unpleasant memories of Prince Mleh, their renegade brother. Lavon then tried peaceful means, marrying his niece to Bohemond III's son, Raymond, to procure an eventual merger of the two principalities. He appreciated the advantages of both papal and imperial support. Something of a shotgun marriage was arranged and the Monophysite Armenian Church recognised the nominal supremacy of the pope's juris-diction with little enthusiasm. The union was never very effective, though the Armenian bishops took to Western mitres and croziers. Their strange Gregorian liturgy disturbed the Latins, but in January 1198 at Sis, in the presence of a papal legate, the Jacobite patriarch and an Orthodox archbishop, Lavon was crowned King of Armenia by the Catholics from Etchmiadzin. The Western coronation rite was used. Frankish influence grew stronger and the 'sparapet' became a 'cunstabl', the 'nakharar' a 'baron'. There was more intermarriage and in old age Lavon himself married Amalric's daughter, Sibylla de Lusignan.

On the death of Bohemond III in 1201 the Templars and their new Master, Philippe du Plaissiez, opposed the succession of his baby grandson, Raymond-Ruben, whilst supporting his younger son, Bohemond of Tripoli. They would not tolerate an Armenian regency. In the ensuing war against Lavon the brethren were joined not only by the Antiochenes but also by Malik az-Zahir of Aleppo. However, the latter soon made peace after being badly mauled by the fierce Haiots. Then it was the turn of the Templars, a war of night raids followed by dawn pursuits in the hills along stony mountain paths, and of am-bushes in the steep valleys of the Taurus. The struggle lasted for nearly twenty years, the Hospitallers supporting Raymond-Ruben, the Templars Bohemond. They were also fighting each other, and Innocent III reprimanded the Templar Master, saying that his Order's job was to fight Moslems, not Hospitallers.

The Armenians trusted the brethren of St John and gave them Selefke, the key fortress of Eastern Cilicia, from where they launched frequent razzias into Moslem territory, probably assisted by Teutonic Knights; it was no doubt on one of these that the Hochmeister Hermann Bart was killed in 1210. The Germans' presence exacerbated their feud with the Templars, who disputed their right to wear the white habit, chasing them out of Acre. The same year the Poor Knights allied with Malik of Aleppo and Kaikawas of Konya. Brethren and Turks rode together into Cilicia where they captured the mountain stronghold of Partounk and even threatened Sis, the capital. Lavon was horrified and made peace, returning Baghras to the Templars, a triumph for their ruthless diplomacy. In 1213 Prince Bohemond's son, Raymond, was stabbed to death by assassins at Tortosa and the next year the patriarch of Jerusalem met the same fate. As he had been a loud critic of the Hospitallers, and the assassins paid them tribute, some contemporaries suspected their connivance. At last, in 1216, Raymond-Ruben captured Antioch and its citadel from the Templars, installing a Hospitaller garrison under Ferrand de Barras, the castellan of Selefke, and handed over Jabala to Fra. Joubert, castellan of Marqab. But in 1219 the Antiochenes rose and brought back Bohemond, who confiscated all Hospitaller possessions. The Order appealed to Rome in vain, though the pope did succeed in reconciling Hospitallers and Templars in 1221. The latter were no longer active in Armenian politics since their old enemy, King Lavon, had died and Raymond-Ruben had been murdered. Not until 1231 did Bohemond make peace with the Hospitallers.

King Lavon had left a daughter, Zabel, by Sibylla de Lusignan, and in 1222 the *cunstabl*, Constantine of Lampron, married her to Bohemond IV's younger son, Philip, who joined the Armenian Church, then out of communion with Rome. Nevertheless, the Hospitallers continued to support him. The new king behaved with such arrogance that he was murdered in 1226, Zabel being forcibly married to Constantine's son, Hethoum. When the sixteen-year-old queen fled by night from Sis to the Hospitallers at Selefke pursued by the regent, the castellan Fra. Bertrand sold both fortress and fugitive to

Constantine, a cynical if practical decision. Later his Order supplied Armenia with an annual tribute of 400 horsemen while both Constantine and Hethoum became Hospitaller *confratres*. Happily Hethoum proved a kind husband and a great king, who reconciled his Church with Rome and followed a policy of alliance with Antioch. Firm government put an end to the brethren's intrigues.

The long struggle had shown them at their worst. Nonetheless one must see them as monks with a genuine sense of spiritual brotherhood, albeit monks living in barrack-room cloisters. They obeyed their Masters just as monks do an abbot and the good of their Order came before everything. Their 'caravan priests' must have had considerable influence as spiritual directors – ideologists who decided difficult points of Christian dialectic, campaigning with the brethren rather like the commissars who rode with the Red cavalry in the Russian Civil War. Only they could hear the brother-knights' confessions.

They were not without writers – the fact that they were not intellectuals and could not read Latin did not mean that brother-knights were illiterate. The Templars produced several poets, *troubadors* and *trouveurs*, including one Grand Master, Fra. Robert de Sablé. Towards 1180 'the Templar of Temple Bruer' (a preceptory near Sleaford in Lincolnshire) was writing Norman French verse translations of 'Thais', and of Latin poems on Anti-Christ and on St Paul's descent into Hell; one is dedicated to his superior, 'Henri d'Arci, frère del Temple Salemun'. This unknown English poet of the Order also produced a prose translation of the 'Vitae Patrum'.[1] Such austere and didactic literature was obviously considered suitable for brother-knights. Undoubtedly their best mind was a Hospitaller, Guglielmo di San Stefano, who wrote a scholarly but brief history of his Order besides legal treatises which show considerable knowledge of the Nichomachean Ethics and of Roman law. In 1286 he commissioned a clerk at Acre to translate Cicero into French. It is significant that Fra. Guglielmo was not a chaplain but a brother-knight.[2] However, such men were probably exceptions rather than the rule; some clerical

[1] See Legge, *Anglo Norman Literature and its Background*, p. 191.
[2] See Riley-Smith, op. cit., pp. 272–3.

contemporaries sneered at the military brethren's lack of erudition.

Innocent III launched the Fourth Crusade in 1204, as usual a mainly French affair. However, *en route* the Venetians' blind but exceedingly cunning Doge, Enrico Dandolo, persuaded the crusaders to help the pretender Alexius Angelus to secure the Byzantine throne. When the new emperor failed to make good extravagant promises of payment, the crusaders stormed Constantinople on 12 April. For three days they plundered and murdered their fellow Christians; even priests joined in the sack, which culminated with the desecration of Hagia Sophia, the Orthodox St Peter's, where a drunken prostitute was sat on the patriarchal throne. Then the conquerors elected a French emperor and a Venetian patriarch, carving out baronies and duchies. The second Rome had fallen at last. A horrified pope cried out that Greeks could not be blamed for hating Latins whom they knew only as treacherous dogs, but instead of reinstating the rightful patriarch he confirmed the Latin usurper and the pseudo-emperor. Everywhere Orthodoxy was persecuted, its monks evicted from their monasteries to make way for Cistercians or military brethren. Left in peace the Eastern Empire might have revived, as so often in the past, to provide a strong bulwark against Islam; the ephemeral Latin Empire would soon fall before despised 'Griffons', to be overrun in turn by the Turks. But few Frankish colonists would set foot in Palestine while land could be had in Greece or on some Aegean island. For the barons 'Romania' was a paradise and the court of the princes of Achaia has been compared to Camelot.

On Amalric's death Cyprus went to his son Hugh, while Jerusalem passed to his young step-daughter, Maria, who in 1210 married John de Brienne, a soldier of fortune who at the age of sixty was surprisingly vigorous. Since 1201 the ruler of Saladin's empire had been the Sultan Saif ad-Din al-Adil, known to the Franks as Saphadin. Once an ardent champion of the counter-crusade and belonging to a Moslem military brotherhood distinguished by special trousers, he was now ageing. Exhausted by family quarrels, Saphadin adopted a peaceful policy towards the Christians.

For six years Outremer enjoyed peace largely because of the Albigensian crusade. Ostensibly a holy war against the melancholy and repellent sect of the *Catharii*, Manichaeans who abominated the flesh, it was a campaign by the nobles of northern France against those of Languedoc whose lands they coveted. The French commanderies of the Hospital and Temple took a small part in the cruel and unjust struggle. At this time heresy menaced Catholic Europe and Innocent III encouraged the foundation of fresh orders to cope with it. Either extremist tendencies were contained within the Franciscans or else combated by the Domicans who staffed the new Inquisition. The mendicant friars' organisation reflected that of military brethren, with provinces and Master Generals.

The Fifth Crusade materialised in 1217 to the secret dismay of Syrian Franks. In September King Andrew II of Hungary and Duke Leopold of Austria landed at Acre, joined in November by King Hugh of Cyprus. King John summoned his barons, including the Masters – the Templar Guillaume de Chartres, the Hospitaller Garin de Montaigu and the German Hermann von Salza. However, the next few months were frittered away in fruitless campaigns. Eventually King John decided that a hard blow at Egypt was more likely to regain Jerusalem than any direct assault. Accordingly, a Christian armada from Acre sailed up the Nile to invest Damietta in May 1218. The Egyptians attempted to cut the Franks off from the sea by a great iron chain across the Nile, but in August the Crusaders stormed the 'Tower of the Chain', opening the approach to the city walls. Old Saphadin died, his end hastened by mortification. More reinforcements arrived from Europe with an arrogant legate, Cardinal Pelagius. Damietta was bombarded, each order having artillery. On the night of 9 October 1218 the Egyptians made a surprise attack on the Latin camp but were beaten back by King John and the Hospital Marshal, Fra. Aymar de Layron, with only thirty knights, until sufficient help arrived to drive the Mamelukes into the Nile. On the 29 August 1219 the Franks attempted to storm the town, but were repulsed with very heavy losses, the Templars losing fifty brethren, the Hospitallers thirty-two, including their gallant Marshal.

Finally Saphadin's son and successor al-Kamil, offered the Franks all Moslem Palestine including Jerusalem if they would abandon the siege. King John and the Teutonic Order wished to accept, but Pelagius and the other brethren refused. On 5 November Damietta fell and the Franks held the town for two years. Kamil, alarmed by the news that Genghis Khan's hordes were making a bloody entrance into the Islamic world, again offered peace: Damietta for Palestine. This time all three Masters agreed with the king, but the greedy, overbearing cardinal refused. He wanted Cairo. John retired to Acre in disgust, but in 1221 Pelagius summoned him back. Once more Kamil offered generous terms, but in July the crusaders marched on Cairo.

Incredibly, they became bogged down in the network of canals before the great city and were surrounded by the Turks; starving, without hope of rescue, King John was lucky enough to save himself and his army in return for Damietta. Kamil, who lacked none of his uncle's charm, invited the crusader magnates to a banquet and sent provisions to their troops. When news came to Damietta that it must be surrendered, Italian merchants who hoped to use the town as a trading base rioted, a Templar being killed and a Teutonic Knight wounded during the uproar. Four years of crusade had been wasted through the arrogant folly of a prince of the Church.

St Francis of Assisi came to Outremer at this time and even obtained an interview with Sultan Kamil, who was intrigued by the Christian dervish. Francis was a testimony to the dynamism of Western Christianity. The triumph of the Church, however arrogant, took its force from this vitality, as did the fighting brethren themselves who indeed had their own saints. The Hospitaller, St Hugh of Genoa, was a mystic noted for asceticism, who always slept in the hospital near the sick, performing the humblest duties such as washing patients or laying out corpses; yet to have attained the rank of commander of Genoa, Fra. Hugh must have seen plenty of fighting. Nor were the brothers' good qualities confined to nursing. The diplomat St Gerland de Pologne, commander of Calatagirona, who had the unenviable task of representing the Master of St John at Emperor Frederick's court, was a legendary father

Fig. 3. A canonness of St John in the Rhodian period. From Helyot.

to the Sicilian poor, and was famed for his gift of mending
broken friendships. There was another saint among the Hospitallers: a serving brother called Fra. Gerard Mercati, later a
Franciscan, who died a hermit in 1241 still wearing the white
cross on his grey habit. Even nursing sisters produced a saint
the much loved Ubaldesca. One must not underestimate the
spiritual force of the brethren's vocation, to be as the Hospitaller
rite of profession put it: 'A servant of the gentlemen that are
poor and sick and a person devoted to the defence of the
Catholic faith.' Bloodstained the brethren may have been, but
nonetheless they were emulators of the Good Samaritan, including the Poor Knights.[1] The minnesinger Wolfram von Esenbach
visited Outremer during this period and was so overcome by
admiration that in 'Parsifal' he compared the Templars to
Knights of the Holy Grail.[2]

In Europe nursing sisters were at first attached to the
Hospitaller commanderies, but were later grouped together in
separate houses where they led a contemplative life, praying
for their brethren who fought the infidel. Their habit was red
with a white-crossed black cloak. The first convent was at
Sigena in Aragon, which was occupied in 1188. The famous
English convent of Buckland in Somerset, a former house of
Augustinian canonnesses, was founded by assembling all
nursing sisters in England and served by chaplain brethren.
Such houses sent revenues to the Master like any commandery.

The papal monarchy had attained its zenith with Innocent
III, but was now over-reaching itself. Ultimately the struggle
between empire and papacy destroyed both and was reflected
in the next crusade, that of the Emperor Frederick II. He had
inherited Sicily from his Hauteville mother and was more of a
Norman than a Hohenstauffen, a 'baptised sultan' with Arab
soldiers and a harem at Palermo. The papacy was to call him
'Anti-Christ', yet he was loyally supported by the German
Hochmeister, Hermann von Salza. For many years he was

[1] For contemporary writers who admired the Templars see Melville, ch.
XVI, 'Un archeveque et deux trouvères' (Jacques de Vitry, Guiot de
Provins, and Christien de Troyes).
[2] For Wolfram von Esenbach's admiration for the Templars see Melville,
p. 182.

Frederick's most trusted agent, playing a key role in his master's policies, but never forgetting to exact privileges for his brethren. Against bitter Templar opposition, it was Frederick who secured from the pope the Order's right to wear a white mantle, and the Golden Bull of Rimini gave heathen Prussia to the German Knights. Probably it was Salza who persuaded the emperor to acquire the crown of Jerusalem by marrying its heiress Yolande, John de Brienne's daughter. As soon as the marriage took placé she was relegated to the harem while, after a surprisingly ineffective campaign in Italy against his unnatural son-in-law, John became Emperor of Constantinople, a splendid climax to his career as professional monarch.

The Sixth Crusade was launched under inauspicious circumstances. The Holy Roman emperor had just been excommunicated, while during a brief stay in Cyprus his arrogance and treachery alienated the Syrian baronage before his arrival in Palestine in 1228. There the clergy were ranged against him, with the exception of the Teutonic Order. Even so, he brought off a diplomatic *tour de force*. The emperor, who had Saracen subjects in Sicily and spoke Arabic fluently, understood and liked Moslems, admiring Islamic culture. His adversary, Kamil, was a civilised tolerant ruler who disliked war. The sultan was intrigued by news of this strange emperor who dressed like an emir, with the Koran embroidered on his silk robes. As a result Frederick obtained a treaty which gave him Nazareth, the castles of Montfort and Toron, and Jerusalem, with a corridor to Jaffa, though the Moslems retained the Dome of the Rock and the 'Temple of Solomon'. No doubt Salza had advised the emperor to save the sultan's face by yielding a little. Fra. Hermann had once written to a cardinal at Rome: 'Do not forget that before the loss of the Holy Land, in nearly all cities which belonged to the Christians the Saracens were free to practise their religion just as today the Christians in Damascus and in other Moslem lands still freely practise their religion.'[1]

Both the Masters of the Temple and Hospital, Pierre de Montaigu and Bertrand de Thessy, were infuriated by the treaty, ratified without their seals. Hospitallers and Poor Knights marched beside the emperor-king to take possession

[1] See Masson, *The Emperor Frederick II of Hohenstauffen*, p. 147.

of the Holy City, not under his command but under orders given in the name of Christ, a typical piece of medieval chicanery. Frederick installed himself in the Hospital at Jerusalem and gave the old royal palace, Manoir-le-Roi, to the Teutonic Order. When 'Anti-Christ' wore the imperial crown at the Church of the Holy Sepulchre, he was alone save for the indispensable Salza and his German brethren.[1]

Master Pierre de Montaigu of the Temple then wrote to the sultan suggesting that he assassinate Frederick on his way back to Acre. Kamil immediately forwarded this interesting letter to the emperor, who surrounded the Temple at Acre, but Fra. Pierre was safe inside and very wisely refused to emerge.[2] Frederick returned soon after to Italy where he confiscated all Templar preceptories. Their Syrian brethren retaliated by chasing the Teutonic Knights out of Acre. Frederick always believed that Pope Gregory was behind Pierre's plot, but, thanks to Salza's inspired diplomacy, he made his peace with the papacy, which in 1231 recognised both the emperor and his son Conrad as kings of Jerusalem. The next decade in Syria was a struggle between their supporters and the barons, a condition best described as legalised anarchy. Yet it was also a period of territorial expansion, for the Franks recovered strongholds which they had not occupied since 1187. Al-Kamil, frightened by news of Moslem disasters in Persia and the terrible Mongols, was too preoccupied to care about infidels in Jerusalem.

The brethren's headquarters were in Acre, but their strongholds were outside the capital. The Germans had Montfort, which they called Starkenberg, near Acre; the Hospitallers, Marqab in Tripoli by the sea; and the Templars, Chastel Pelerin. The latter, at Athlit, a fortified peninsula rather than a castle, was protected by sea on three sides with an immense wall of dressed stone on the landward end, and had freshwater

---

[1] Until very recently it was supposed that Frederick crowned himself king but it has now been shown that this was not the case – he merely wore the imperial crown. See H. E. Mayer, 'Das Pontifikale von Tyrus und die Krönung der Lateinischer Koenige von Jerusalem', *Dumbarton Oaks Papers*, no. 21 (1967).

[2] Only Matthew Paris mentions this plot. See Riley-Smith, op. cit., p. 168.

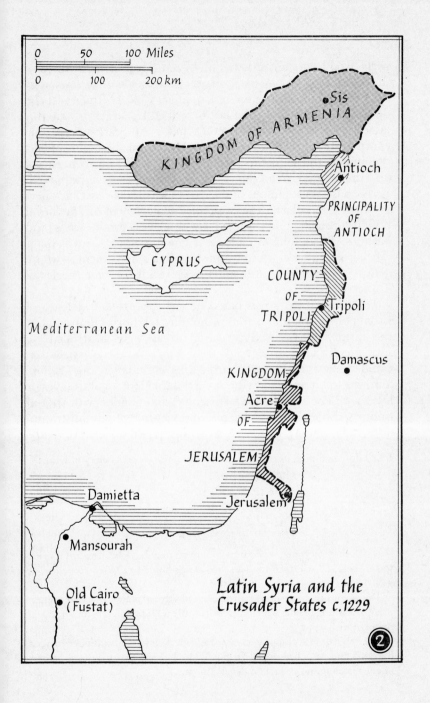

Latin Syria and the
Crusader States c.1229

Scale: 0, 50, 100 Miles; 0, 100, 200 km

KINGDOM OF ARMENIA

Sis

Antioch

PRINCIPALITY OF ANTIOCH

CYPRUS

COUNTY OF TRIPOLI

Tripoli

Damascus

Mediterranean Sea

KINGDOM

Acre

OF

JERUSALEM

Jerusalem

Damietta

Mansourah

Old Cairo (Fustat)

②

wells, woods, orchards, herds and even salt mines. All three of the chief Orders possessed many fortresses with names that still evoke Outremer's romantic quality; Chastel Rouge, Roche de Roissel and Belvoir, the last described by an Arab writer as 'among the stars like a falcon's nest'. At Starkenberg, one enormously tall watch-tower, separated from the main *enceinte*, dominated the landscape from its hill, while the conventual apartments were in a keep surrounded by a single curtain wall. Perhaps the most famous of the castles was Krak-des-Chevaliers of the Hospitallers, 'the supreme achievement of medieval military architecture', ringed by massive curtain walls and bastions. It contains a cloister, a chapter house, and a magnificent chamber – possibly the castellan's apartment – whose delicate rib vaulting and stone roses recall the monasteries of France.[1]

Medieval strategy was based on the capture and defence of strongpoints, the sole means of holding territory.[2] Throughout the history of Latin Syria large areas were controlled by strategically sited strongholds from which razzias or *chevauchées* could be launched; swift, hard-riding commando raids whose aim was to hit and run with any available loot – gold, slaves or livestock. The castellan was a senior commander with special military duties. Such fortresses were centres of administration and trade, halting places for caravans where taxes were paid.[3]

[1] An oddly haunting inscription was found in the Great Gallery of Krak:

> *SIT TIBI COPIA*
> *SIT SAPIE(N)CIA*
> *FORMAQ(UE) DET(UR)*
> *INQ(UI)NAT O(MN)IA SOLA*
> *SUP(ER)BIA SI COMI(TETUR)*

– wealth may be yours, wisdom too, and you may have beauty, but if pride touch them, all will turn to dross. See Deschamps, *Le Crac des Chevaliers*, p. 218.

[2] 'The acquisition or successful defence of strong places was the highest prize of warfare, besides which success in battle was of secondary importance.' Smail, op. cit., p. 139.

[3] Ibid., pp. 60, 61 – castles 'served as residences, as administrative centres, as barracks and as police posts'. Dr Smail also believes that they were centres of colonisation and economic development.

The brethren spent much time garrisoning them; at Marqab
the walls were always patrolled by four knights and twenty-
eight sergeant-brethren. Sometimes they were magnificent,
with mosaic floors and wall paintings, especially the refectory
and the castellan's apartments where visiting lords were entertained. As in non-military monasteries guests sat at meals in
silence listening to devotional reading, but the food and table
equipage before them were as splendid as any in Outremer.[1] The
chapels were superb, and the Little Office was said
punctiliously. Life in these frontier strongholds really was a
military and monastic existence.

Whenever a serious crisis loomed, garrisons were reduced to a
bare minimum, the brethren riding forth to join their Order's
main army. If they failed to return, the isolated fortresses,
though seldom more than ten miles from the coast, had little
chance of discovering whether another 'Hattin' had taken place.
Technically their defences were impregnable, but although
there was food, water and provisions for a thousand men there
were never enough troops to man the walls. The besieging army
would give no quarter unless the garrison surrendered, while
there was little likelihood of relief as the kingdom's forces were
too small. Day by day the atmosphere in the great silent castles
grew tenser. Assaults were constantly launched, accompanied
by the cacophony of a Mameluke military band, the howling of
enraged fanatics and the crash of missiles from the siege artillery.
These 'bombs' included blazing barrels of Greek fire, a brew
of sulphur and naphtha, the medieval version of napalm. Great
tunnels were burrowed under the foundations, shored up with
pit props and then set alight to bring the walls tumbling down.
Sometimes engineers were attacked from underground by
counter-mines, picks and knives or were smoked out with
stinkpots or even flooded out with water. Native troops,
Armenians and Christian Arabs, were unreliable and prone to
panic. Sieges quickly turned into wars of nerves so that fortresses
rarely fell by storm but usually surrendered under terms; in
1187 Sahyun, reputedly the most impregnable of all the

[1] Behaviour in the refectory was not always decorous – brethren would
sometimes beat or throw bread and wine at the paid servants who waited
on them. See Riley-Smith, op. cit., p. 254.

Frankish strongholds, yielded to Saladin after only three days.

None of the lesser orders possessed fortresses, with the possible exception of the Tower of St Ladre, next to the Lazar House between Athlit and Caesarea. Even so the little brotherhood of St Thomas was making steady if modest progress. In 1231 the Bishop of Winchester, Peter des Roches, gave English brethren a new church at Acre, urging them to follow the Templar rule – though they did not forget their hospital work – and bequeathing them a large sum of money.[1]

In 1239 King Tibald of Navarre landed in Outremer with many French lords and over 1,000 knights, but that November some were surrounded and killed on a raid near Ascalon. Fortunately Tibald and the three great Orders had not accompanied them. Jerusalem was sacked by Moslem troops who then withdrew. However, Tibald recovered Beaufort, Safed and Ascalon. He was followed by Richard, Earl of Cornwall, who through skilful negotiation recovered much land in the south-west. During this period of Moslem weakness when a real advance was possible, Templars and Hospitallers squabbled ceaselessly, intriguing with imperial agents and fighting each other in the narrow streets of Acre. When the Templars and the Syrian barons seized Tyre, the last imperial stronghold, Frederick was still supported by Hospitaller and German brethren. As long ago as the 1170s there had been bad blood between Temple and Hospital. It flared up with particular violence in 1197 over a trifling dispute for a small estate in Tripoli; for years afterwards younger brethren drew their swords when they met members of the rival order in the streets, despite papal rebukes. Harmony was briefly secured when Pierre de Montaigu, elected Master of the Templars in 1218, cooperated with his brother, Fra. Garin de Montaigu, Master of St John from 1208–28, though relations deteriorated once more after their deaths.

The Poor Knights captured Nablus in 1242, massacring its inhabitants, including Christian Arabs, and in 1243 reoccupied the Temple of Jerusalem. They began to refortify the Holy City. However, Sultan Ayub had new allies in the Kwarismian

[1] 'Quingentas marcas' (50 marks), a very large sum for the period. See Matthew Pans, *Chronica Majora*, ed. Luard, vol. III, p. 490.

Turks who were fleeing from the Mongols. In July of that year 10,000 savage tribesmen stormed Jerusalem, which was lost to the Franks for ever. In the meantime Outremer and the Moslem princes of northern Syria were mustering. The barons brought 600 knights and the Templar Master, Armand de Périgord, 300, as did the Hospitaller Master, Guillaume de Châteauneuf. There was a detachment of Teutonic Knights, even a few brethren of St Lazarus, together with knights from Antioch and Tripoli and several thousand Turcopoles and foot-soldiers. The Saracen princes brought a large force of Mameluke and Bedouin cavalry.

On 17 October 1244 at La Forbie near Gaza the allied army left a strong position to attack the Egyptian forces. Instantly they were charged by the ferocious Kwarismians, carrying lances with red streamers. On the right the Franks held out but on the left and in the centre the wild onslaught proved too much for the Saracen troops who turned and fled. Together Kwarismian and Egyptian Turks surrounded the Franks and cut them to pieces. No less than 5,000 Christians fell, including Fra. Armand, his Marshal Hugues de Montaigu and 312 brethren. 325 Hospitallers perished, while their Master was taken prisoner and all the St Lazarus brethren were killed.[1] Only 26 Hospitallers, 33 Templars and 3 Teutonic Knights escaped.[2] Even if the Egyptian Sultan was too busy to complete Outremer's destruction the little kingdom could never replace the loss of manpower. The Hospitaller Master spent the next six years in captivity at Cairo. Fortunately his Order had evolved machinery to deal with such cases and elected his Lieutenant, the Grand Preceptor of Jerusalem, Fra. Jean de Ronay, Vice-Master.

There was little central authority in the kingdom itself, though the regent, Henry of Cyprus, appointed various members of the Ibelin family as *baillis*. However, the Holy Land received a new God-sent leader who landed at Damietta in June 1249, Louis IX of France, the hero-king of the Christian West who once said that the only way to argue with

---

[1] A Templar, Fra. Roger l'Aleman, taken prisoner, apostatised but then escaped; he was expelled from the Order. Melville, p. 206.

[2] See Matthew Paris, op. cit., vol. IV, p. 342.

an infidel was to thrust one's sword into his belly. His foreign
policy, almost totally dependent on divine guidance, was
noticeably inept. This forbidding character was relieved by
magnanimity, kindness and a sense of humour, which explains
some of his magnetic attraction for his contemporaries, Moslems
included. He was never known to break his pledged word, not
even to Saracens.

Louis occupied Damietta with over 2,000 knights, including
400 from Frankish Roumania, and a full complement of
Templars, Hospitallers and Teutonic Knights. The king waited
till the Nile floods had receded before advancing on Cairo. His
progress was hampered by the network of canals, so in December he halted before the largest of the Nile's branches, the
Bahr as-Saghir, near the town of Mansourah. On the 8 February
1250, Shrove Tuesday, the army, led by the king's brother,
Robert d'Artois, forded the river at dawn under strict instructions not to attack. Count Robert, arrogant and impetuous,
charged as soon as he had crossed. The Egyptian army was
taken by surprise and the Mamelukes fled in terror while their
commander, the aged Vizier Fakr ad-Din, caught dyeing his
beard, was cut down. Robert ordered a pursuit and the Templar
Master Guillaume de Sonnac, 'bon chevalier preux et hardi',
trying to restrain him was called *poulain* and coward for his
pains. The grim old man replied that neither he nor his
brethren were frightened, that they would ride with him but
none of them would come back alive. The Turks rallied under a
brilliant Kipchak captain, Baibars Rukd ad-Din '*Bundukdari*'
(the Crossbowman), ambushing the Franks in the streets of
Mansourah. Robert was unhorsed and killed while Fra. Guillaume, who lost an eye, brought back 5 out of his 200 brethren.

Baibars then attacked Louis and a terrible battle lasted until
sunset, charge following charge. Eventually the Mamelukes
were driven from the field, but the crusaders were exhausted,
with little stomach left for an equally ghastly struggle three days
later. Every time Turkish horsemen galloped forward the air
was black with arrows and barrels of Greek Fire from Mameluke
catapults. Old Fra. Guillaume was caught defending a barricade
set ablaze by naphtha, but fought on amidst the flames till he
lost his remaining eye and fell mortally wounded. However,

inspired by Louis's almost supernatural heroism, the Franks held their ground and eventually beat off the dreadful Baibars.

In the next eight weeks the Christian army was stricken with dysentery and typhoid while its ships were captured by the Egyptian navy. Louis decided to retreat in April, but his enfeebled troops were easily surrounded. After a hopeless resistance the king, who was dangerously ill with typhus, surrendered. The poorer crusaders were slaughtered or herded off to the slave market, but after every sort of indignity Louis and his knights were allowed in May to ransom themselves in exchange for Damietta and on payment of the huge sum of one million bezants. The king asked the Templars to lend him 60,000 bezants but the Commander Etienne d'Otricourt and the Marshal Renaud de Vichiers refused. For once Louis lost his temper and sent the faithful Joinville to collect the money from a Templar galley. As the Templar Treasurer refused to deliver the keys, Joinville smashed the chests with a hatchet.

King Louis spent the next four years at Acre administering the kingdom, and subjected the Templars' great officers to a humiliating punishment. Their Marshal, Hugues de Jouy, had negotiated a treaty at Damascus without the king's permission. Renaud de Vichiers, now Master, had to come before him, barefoot, and retract the treaty, kneeling in full view of the whole army. As a result Fra. Hugues was banished for life from the Holy Land.

The king obtained the release of many important prisoners, including the Hospitaller Master, Guillaume de Châteauneuf, with thirty of his brethren, fifteen Templars and ten Teutonic Knights, though negotiations nearly broke down when the Poor Knights made their abortive alliance with Damascus. An attack on Jaffa by the Damascene army caused the Franks to launch a punitive expedition, during which the little detachment of Lazarus Knights came to grief.[1] Joinville describes the incident as follows: 'While the king was before Jaffa, the Master

---

[1] Writing in 1250 of the last fifty years' main events, Matthew Paris noted 'The houses of the Temple, of the Hospital, of St Mary of the Germans, and of St Lazarus have twice been taken prisoner, killed and scattered.' He was referring to La Forbie and the disasters of St Louis. Op. cit., vol. V, p. 192.

of Saint Lazarus (Fra. Raynaud de Flory) had spied out near Ramleh, a town some three good leagues away, a number of cattle and various other things from which he thought to collect some valuable booty. So being a man of no standing in the army, and who therefore did exactly as he pleased, he went off to that place without saying a word to the king. But after he had collected his spoils the Saracens attacked him, and so thoroughly defeated him that of all the men he had in his company no more than four escaped.'[1]

Louis's hopes of a Franco-Egyptian alliance came to nothing and his one lasting treaty was with the Assassins through the mediation of the Hospitaller and Templar Masters. Louis's mother, Queen Blanche, the Regent of France, died in 1254 and the king returned home. He left behind a seneschal, Geoffroi de Sargines, with a French 'regiment' but Latin Syria could not replace the losses in manpower it had suffered during his Egyptian campaign and the kingdom would never again know firm government. Not even a saint could save Outremer.

[1] See Joinville, *Histoire de Saint Louis*, p. 300.

CHAPTER 4

Armageddon

Latin Syria was now a mere string of coastal *entrepôts* in which commercial, municipal and clerical factions squabbled viciously, heedless of the Cypriot kings' futile efforts to assert their authority. Most barons had left for Cyprus, so military orders, holding what little territory remained inland, were the dying kingdom's last support, and even they quarrelled and fought with each other. Yet this self-destroying anarchy was menaced by a ferocious Mameluke state, the chimera of a Mongol alliance offering a sole, illusory hope of salvation. In 1256 the rivalry between the Genoese and Venetians developed into civil war over the control of the monastery of St Sabas in Acre. The Venetians were supported by the Pisan and Provençal merchants, the Templars, the Teutonic Knights, and the brethren of St Lazarus and St Thomas. The Genoese were backed by the Catalan merchants, the Hospitallers and Philippe de Montfort, Lord of Tyre. There was a battle in the streets of Acre ending in a temporary victory for the Hospitallers and Genoese. An even bloodier battle followed, after which the Genoese withdrew to their own quarter of the town.[1] Syrian Franks recognised no authority.

Yet this period was one of important development for the Hospitallers under Fra. Hugues Revel, 'maistre prodome et sage'.[2] Their militarisation was complete, chaplains having been finally subordinated to knight-brethren, while their hierarchy was crystallising. First came conventual *baillis* (great officers), then bailiffs of Syria followed by ones from overseas. All priories and commanderies had to contribute one third of

[1] See Matthew Paris, *Chronica Majora*, vol. V, p. 745.
[2] 'In the magistracy of Bertrand de Comps between 1236 and 1239, brother knights were given precedence over the priests and it was later said that Bertrand had done more for them than any other Master.' Riley-Smith, op. cit., p. 238. See *Cronica Magistrum Defunctorum*, XVII.

their revenues for the use of the Order to offset losses in income from lands captured by the Mamelukes. The increasingly aristocratic and military emphasis found expression in the Hospitaller's new uniform. By 1248 the cumbersome monastic cloak had been superseded by a black surcoat with a white cross, soon replaced by a red surcoat with a white cross. The original habit was retained for convent life. As early as 1250 the Templar rule stipulated that a postulant must prove himself a knight's son or the descendant of knights, and priest-brethren were restricted to fewer offices. Similar modifications appeared in the Hospitaller constitutions.[1]

The word 'knight' has a certain fairy-tale flavour which obscures the fact that such a man was a specialised, fighting machine. Remembering his impact in battle as the 'armour' of the age, the nearest modern equivalent is 'tank-commander' – perhaps an even better analogy is the 'scout' pilot of the Royal Flying Corps in the 1914–18 War. 'Chivalry' was his personal code of honour based on highly formalised standards evolved by a professional military class, just as *'Bushido'* was that of the Japanese officer in the Second World War. They were often employed by a baronial household in administrative as well as military posts, or they plied for hire as mercenaries. The more fortunate acquired manors but most were poor, their armour constituting the greater part of their wealth. The suit of armour was undergoing change however. Plate knee-caps, gauntlets and leg-plates began to be worn, and shields were smaller, while the helmet was the great barrel-helm, though some preferred a light steel-cap under a mail hood. The most curious innovations were ailerons, square pieces of *cuir bouilli*, on which the owner's coat of arms were painted, standing up vertically from his shoulders. Naturally the brethren were provided with excellent equipment.

The Franks could afford to indulge in such petty squabbles as the 'War of St Sabas' only because their Moslem enemies were

---

[1] It was laid down by the Hospitallers' Chapter-General of 1262 'that no Prior nor bailiff nor other brother knight receive a brother unless he who is to be knighted should be the son of a knight or of knightly family'. Delaville le Roulx, *Cartulaire Générale*, vol. 3, p. 42 (trans. from 'The Thirteenth-Century Statutes of the Knights Hospitallers', ed. King).

distracted by the threat of Mongol invasion. At the end of the twelfth century the nomadic tribes of the Gobi desert had united under Genghis Khan, and the standard of the Nine Yak Tails had swept like a roaring whirlwind through Asia – 'the scourge of Heaven's fury in the hands of the merciless Tartars'. By the middle of the thirteenth century they had conquered Baghdad, throwing the last caliph, tied in a bag, into the river. Some of them were Nestorian Christians. The legend of Prester John, the great Christian potentate of the East, probably arising from rumours of the Coptic kings of Ethiopia, was well known in Latin Syria and resulted in much wishful thinking about the Great Khan Mongka. King Louis had sent ambassadors to the '*kuriltai*' at Karakorum, while King Hethoum of Armenia went in person, acknowledging Mongka as overlord in return for military assistance. In 1259 the great Khan's brother Hulagu, Ilkhan of Persia, whose wife, Dokuz Khatun, and whose best general, Kitbuqa, were Nestorians, led the horde into Syria accompanied by a strong detachment of Armenian and Georgian Knights. Aleppo soon fell, followed by the other Moslem towns of the north. On 1 March 1260 three Christian princes, Kitbuqa, Hethoum of Armenia and Bohemond VI of Antioch, rode triumphantly into Damascus. At Baghdad, Hulagu had shown special favour to the Nestorian Catholics and Kitbuqa was equally kind to the Christians in his new city. By now no great Moslem power existed east of Egypt.

Unfortunately Mongka's sudden death and the subsequent struggle for the throne forced Hulagu to withdraw most of his troops. Kitbuqa was left at Damascus with a small force, whereupon Sultan Qutuz of Egypt advanced into Syria with a large army. He asked the Christian lords for help and the Haute Cour discussed his appeal with some sympathy. The Tartars were uncomfortable neighbours who only tolerated vassals, not independent allies, and the *poulains* preferred civilised infidels to barbarous Christians. However, Hochmeister Anno von Sangerhausen warned them that the Saracens would turn on the Franks if they were victorious. Outremer remained neutral. On 30 September 1260 Mongols and Mamelukes joined battle at Ain Jalud – 'the Pools of Goliath'. Kitbuqa was surrounded, his troops wiped out and he himself captured and beheaded –

Turkish captains playing polo with his head. Next month Qutuz was murdered by the sinister Baibars, who became sultan in his place and ruler of Damascus as well as Cairo.

'His Sublime Highness, the Sultan an-Nasr Rukn-ad-Din', the same 'crossbowman' who had defeated St Louis, was a soldier of genius even if, in the words of a French historian he was also a treacherous and ferocious beast of prey.[1] This former slave soon controlled all Saladin's former empire, building countless roads which gave the armies of the Mameluke sultans a mobility unknown to their predecessors. Determined to annihilate both Franks and Armenians, Baibars launched his first sledge-hammer blow in 1265. After taking Caesarea, he laid siege to Arsur, which the Hospitallers had recently bought from the Ibelin family. There were 270 knights in the town, who fought bravely for forty days. Eventually the Mameluke heavy artillery and mangonels on moveable towers breached the walls of the lower town. By now ninety Hospitallers had fallen. The citadel was crowded with refugees and unreliable native troops, and the castellan surrendered within three days. It was understood that he and his remaining knights would be allowed to withdraw to Acre, but Baibars dragged them off to Cairo in chains.

The following summer '*Bendocdar*' invested the Templar fortress of Safed in Galilee. The bleak stone stronghold controlled 160 villages. Again it was a story of local auxiliaries panicking. After three assaults had failed Baibars offered a free pardon to all Turcopoles, who started to desert. The Templars began to lose their own nerve and sent a Syrian sergeant, Fra. Leo, to negotiate terms with Baibars. He returned with a guarantee of safe conduct to the coast. The knights accepted and opened the castle gates, whereupon the sultan offered them a choice of Islam or death. Next morning, when they were paraded outside the walls to give their answer, the castellan stepped forward, begging his brethren not to apostatise. Baibars had him skinned alive and the brethren decapitated, after which he decorated his new possession with their rotting heads.

Meanwhile, the emir Qalawun raided Cilicia. King

[1] '. . . ces Césars mamelûks, bêtes de proie traîtresses et féroces, mais soldats de génie, connaisseurs et manieurs d'hommes . . . ' Grousset, vol. III, p. 615.

Hethoum's two sons and the Templars from Baghras met them near Darbessaq. But they were too few and after killing Prince Thoros and capturing Prince Lavon the Mamelukes swept on to Sis, the Armenian capital, which they burnt to the ground. The little mountain kingdom was utterly laid waste and never completely recovered.

Three years later, after capturing Jaffa and the Templar fortress of Beaufort, Baibars attacked and stormed Antioch. Amid the usual atrocities one incident shocked even the Turks. The canonnesses of St John had cut off their own noses with scissors and gashed their cheeks to avoid rape. The appalled Moslems slaughtered them on the spot. Save for the isolated coastal town of Lattakieh the principality had vanished. The Templars saw that northern Syria was lost and wisely withdrew their outposts at Baghras and La Roche de Roissel. As his subjects said, the sultan 'never destroyed the hiding place of error without giving it to the flames and drenching it in blood'. Baibars wrote a sardonic letter to Bohemond at Tripoli congratulating him on being absent. Gloatingly, the 'crossbowman' went on to describe the desolation he had created, the butchery of Antiochene priests and citizens, the desecration of churches and how cheaply ladies had been sold in the slave market.

The kingdom was tottering, though in 1269 Hugh III was crowned at Tyre, the first Levantine-born king since 1186. Baibars' relentless campaigns were sapping even the Hospital's resources; in 1268 Master Hugues Revel had written that his Order could muster only 300 knights in Syria. The Sultan humiliated them further in 1271. He had already taken Chastel Blanc from the Templars when on 3 March he laid siege to Krak-des-Chevaliers. The finest castle of the Christian world, which had defied Saladin, was garrisoned by the Marshal of St John with 200 knights and sergeants of his order. A Saracen writer called this vast and lonely stronghold 'a bone stuck in the throat of the Moslems'. On 15 March mangonels breached the gate-tower of the first curtain wall and on 26 March battered a way through the inner wall. Most brethren escaped to one of the great towers, but Baibars set up mangonels in the courtyard and their last refuge shuddered beneath a crashing barrage. On 8 April they surrendered and were conducted to Tripoli. An exultant Baibars wrote triumphantly to Hugues Revel: 'You fortified this place, entrusting its defence to the best of your men. All was in vain and you only sent them to their deaths.' In June the 'crossbowman' surrounded Starkenberg. The castellan, Johann von Sachsen, had few knights and his Turcopoles went mad with fear. After a week he yielded and was lucky enough to obtain a safe conduct to Acre for himself and his garrison.

There was no help to be had from Sicily or Rumania. The Latin Empire had fallen to the Greeks in 1261 and the Frankish lords of Achaia were fighting for survival. Even Cyprus was attacked by Egyptian galleys in 1271, though Mamelukes were poor seamen and their raid was easily beaten off. The Frankish paradise was at its zenith with a way of life epitomised in the tournaments outside St Hilarion, the castle named *Dieu d'Amour* by the barons. Indeed it is remarkable that Cypriot kings tried to save their other, beleaguered kingdom so often, when it meant leaving this gay and beautiful land.

Providentially 'the Lord Edward' had arrived from England in May, but with less than 1,000 men. Had he had more, this cold, methodical giant would have proved himself a really effective crusader. King Hugh's Cypriots refused to help him, but the Ilkhan Abaga, who honoured Kitbuqa's memory, was more generous and 10,000 Mongol horsemen galloped into Syria where they taught the Mamelukes a bloody lesson. Unfortunately they were not strong enough to face the full might of Baibars, who was marching up from Damascus, and withdrew. Edward did little more than lead a series of small and ineffectual raids but impressed the sultan sufficiently to conclude a ten years' peace with Acre. Baibars even paid Edward the compliment of trying to assassinate him – the legendary occasion when the prince's young wife was supposed to have sucked the poison from the stab wound. Another less romantic story says that the English Master of the Temple, Thomas Berard, provided an antidote. Edward seems to have made much of the English Order, helping the brethren of St Thomas build their new church at Acre and endowing them generously. It seems, from the letters they afterwards wrote him, that their advice was always welcome. But in September 1272 he sailed from Acre. For the rest of Baibars' reign the Franks were left in comparative peace.

Edward profited from his experience, which taught him how to conquer Wales. Previous English kings had been unable to cope with impassable terrain and fast-moving enemies but he now employed Syrian methods: sea-to-land assaults, sea lines of communication, and advances consolidated by castle administration points, whose small garrisons could be quickly switched from place to place along the coast.[1] This strategy proved remarkably effective. While it is impossible to say if his great fortresses like Conway or Beaumaris were copied from Palestinian models, the king had learnt how to use them in Outremer.

King Hugh III finally abandoned his ungrateful kingdom in 1276. The new Master of the Temple, Guillaume de Beaujeu,[2] a relative of the French royal family and an incurable intriguer, had systematically hindered the king's policies, and next year Charles proclaimed himself king with the enthusiastic support of Fra. Guillaume. Hugh tried to return in 1279, but, though the Hospitallers were sympathetic, his attempt was frustrated by armed opposition from the Poor Knights. Returning to Cyprus, the angry monarch burnt out the Templar preceptories at Limassol and Paphos. However, Charles's government collapsed when he lost Sicily in 1282. King Hugh then returned, opposed by both Templars and Hospitallers, to die at Tyre in 1284. By now the kingdom was really a feudal republic in which merchants, brethren and barons quarrelled noisily. In 1279 the Knights of St Thomas had written to King Edward describing the alarming condition of the Holy Land and their own gloomy forebodings. The Templars and their Master became involved in the deplorable squabble at Tripoli between Bohemond VII and Gui Embriaco, Lord of Gibelet. The Poor Knights, who

[1] I must thank Dom Alberic Stacpoole for this analysis of strategy and tactics.
[2] Fra. Guillaume de Beaujeu was '. . . a great nobleman "mout gentil-home", a cousin of the King of France, so generous, openhanded and charitable that he was famous for it'. This, at any rate, was the opinion of his secretary, the Templar of Tyre. *R.H.C. arm.*, II, p. 779.

were always baronial in their attitude to authority, consistently
supported the rebel against his over-lord, razing Botron to the
ground (the castle once coveted by Gerard de Ridefort), and
Templar galleys attacked those of the prince-count. This
struggle lasted from 1277 to 1282, from the moment when Gui
abducted an heiress until the day when he and his brothers were
buried in a ditch up to their necks and left to starve.

Strategically the Frankish position never ceased to deteriorate
despite some slight success. In October 1280 a Mongol army
occupied Aleppo, while in the same month a raiding party of
Hospitallers from Marqab chased by 5,000 Turcomans suddenly
turned on its pursuers and cut them to ribbons. When the
Mongols had withdrawn, 7,000 vengeful Saracens led by the
Emir of Krak surrounded the great castle, but the garrison of
no more than 600, led by brethren in red surcoats, galloped out
to rout the astonished infidels. Another Tartar expedition
entered Syria in the autumn of 1281 accompanied by King
Lavon III of Armenia and a Georgian force. A detachment
from Marqab joined them, including the English prior of St
John, Joseph de Chauncy from Clerkenwell. However, the allied
army was defeated outside Homs. Two years later the Mamelukes overran Lattakieh, the last remnant of the principality of
Antioch. Outremer was crumbling piece by piece, its manpower
dwindling with every battle.[1]

Without warning Sultan Qalawun and a vast army appeared
before the mountain stronghold at Marqab on 17 April 1285.
The Hospitallers had their own mangonels mounted on the wall
towers and succeeded in putting the Mameluke machines out of
action. However, on 23 May a mine brought an important
tower crashing down. The horrified castellan then discovered
that other tunnels had been dug under the moat, reaching below
the inner towers. Realising that the castle was lost he managed
to obtain excellent terms from Qalawun. The garrison were
allowed to withdraw to Tortosa, while the twenty-five Knights

[1] For the last twenty years of Outremer we are largely dependent on the
Chronicle of the Templar of Tyre (in the 'Gestes des Chyprois'). Its author
was probably Gérard de Montréal who belonged to the Palestinian gentry
and was not a Templar but merely 'ecrivain sarrasinois' or Arabic secretary
to Master Guillaume de Beaujeu.

of St John in the keep were permitted to retain their arms and take away all personal property. Never again would the Office be said in the beautiful chapel.

Coastal Syria was still a western land, even if sadly shrunken. Most fiefs had been overrun, and the wealthiest class comprised the merchants and many nobles then living in the towns, like the mayor of Tripoli, Bartholomé Embriaco, who belonged to the Gibelet family, while younger sons often joined the military orders. At Beirut the Ibelins stayed on in their magnificent villa, with a rich income from local iron mines. Syrian Franks enjoyed comforts almost unknown in Europe. There were still farmers who not only cultivated the fields round the towns but also tilled those near the inland castles. These *colons*, often half-castes, had only one country, Latin Syria. The capital of Outremer had an evil reputation for the pirates, smugglers and white slavers of the Mediterranean swarming in its noisy streets. Nonetheless the *poulains* were proud of Acre, aware that it stood for two centuries of crusade. Its architecture was splendid in the French style – the royal palace, the luxurious houses of the barons and merchants, the beautiful new Gothic Church of St Andrew, and the vast headquarters of the Orders. So imposing was the Hospitaller church that the city was called St Jean d'Acre. With double walls and many towers manned by hand-picked troops, a fortified promontory, it was inconceivable that infidels should take this strong seaport.

Perhaps thirty brother-knights were resident in its Hospital, the Temple holding as many Poor Knights. Most brethren were on garrison duty in the great castles or scattered throughout their wide properties, busy with estate management, collecting taxes and inspecting supply depots. It was not only diminished resources which sapped the strength of the military brotherhoods for, as with other religious orders, there was evidence of growing laxity. Knight-brethren no longer slept in dormitories but in their own cells and senior officers enjoyed considerable comfort. Their founders' stern ideals were out of fashion.

Acre was especially gay in 1286 when, after the coronation of Henri II, the epileptic boy who was also King of Cyprus, his court spent a fortnight celebrating. Nothing so lively or so decorative had been seen in Palestine since the old court at

Jerusalem. There were tournaments and sumptuous banquets, while in the 'Herberge del Ospitau de Saint-Johan'[1] pageants of King Arthur and the Round Table were enacted, Syrian and Cypriot nobles playing the parts of 'Lanselot, et Tristan, et Pilamèdes', and other games 'biaus et délitables et plaissans'.[2] The king then returned to his other kingdom, leaving two Ibelin *baillis*. Yet the city was as turbulent as always and in 1287 Pisan and Genoese galleys fought in the harbour; the latter even attempted to sell their Pisan captives in the Moslem slave market, but were dissuaded by the outraged brethren.

In February 1289 Qalawun marched into Syria. The Templars' spies learnt from an emir in their pay that the sultan's objective was Tripoli. But the prosperous merchants did not want to believe this alarming news. Fra. Guillaume's weakness for political intrigue was too well known. To their incredulous horror Qalawun arrived in front of the city at the end of March with 40,000 cavalry, 100,000 foot soldiers and a menacing train of mangonels. Tripoli, with its famous schools, silk factories and fertile gardens, seemed strong enough, defended by Venetian, Genoese and Cypriot contingents. The Italians' galleys guarded it against any attack from the sea. There was also a large detachment of Templars commanded by the Marshal Geoffroi de Vendac and a smaller force of Hospitallers led by the Marshal of St John, the redoubtable Matthieu de Clermont. Nonetheless many citizens prudently embarked for Cyprus. An incessant battering by nineteen mangonels eventually demolished two key towers whereupon the Venetians decided that the city was lost and sailed away. Soon after, on 26 May, the Mamelukes assaulted the undermanned walls with fanatic bravery and the defence collapsed. Most brethren died fighting in the storm, but the two Marshals escaped by boat. For the citizens it was a blood bath in the style of Baibars. Nearly all were butchered and their families herded off to the slave markets. Outremer was foundering, yet even now the Franks did not see their doom.

Not even a spectacular disaster could revive the crusader spirit. However, a band of out-of-work labourers from northern

[1] See 'Les Gestes des Chyprois', *R.H.C. arm.*, II, p. 793.
[2] Loc. cit.

Italy volunteered and sailed for Acre, where they arrived in August 1290, a drunken rabble. There had been a fine harvest, caravans were coming down from Damascus and the capital, gayer than ever, was crowded with Moslem visitors. The 'crusaders' had not been in the city very long before they rioted and cut the throat of every Saracen in sight, though the *poulains* and the brethren did their utmost to save them. Qalawun was infuriated and prepared to invade Syria. Once again Templar spies got wind of his plans and once again the Franks refused to listen to Fra. Guillaume's warning. He was so alarmed that on his own initiative he tried to negotiate with Cairo. Qalawun's terms were a gold piece per head of Acre's population. The Master was howled down by the citizens, and accused of cowardice.

The sultan died in November but made his son, al-Ashraf, swear to destroy the Christian capital, and in March 1291 an enormous Mameluke army marched on Acre – 160,000 infantry and 60,000 cavalry. Their artillery was awe-inspiring, including not less than 100 mangonels. The two greatest were known respectively as *al-Mansour* (the Victorious)[1] and *Ghadaban*, (the Furious) while the smaller, but almost equally lethal, catapults were called 'Black Bulls'. *Al-Mansour* threw stones weighing one hundredweight. On 5 April al-Ashraf invested the city.

By this time the Franks were not altogether unprepared. The Orders had thrown in every brother available so that out of a population of fifty thousand, 14,000 were foot soldiers and 800 were mounted men-at-arms. There was no shortage of experienced leaders. All Masters were present, the Templar Guillaume de Beaujeu, the Hospitaller Jean de Villiers and the Hochmeister Konrad von Feuchtwangen. Unfortunately the latter had only been able to bring a few German brethren. St Lazarus provided twenty-five knights while there were nine from St Thomas under their Master. Other troops included a Cypriot contingent, the Pisan and Venetian garrisons, the French regiment led by Jean de Grailly, a few Englishmen commanded by the Swiss Otto de Grandson, armed citizens of Acre, and the Italian rabble who had caused the war. King

[1] Ibid., p. 808, '. . . le Mensour ce est a dire le Victorious'.

Henri's young brother, Prince Amalric, was nominal commander-in-chief. The troops were divided into four divisions,
each entrusted with a sector of the double walls. These and the
twelve great towers were in excellent condition, while much of
the city was protected by water, and, as the Franks retained
control of the sea, ships could arrive at any time with food and
reinforcements.

On the night of 15 April Master de Beaujeu led 300 brethren
and the English troops on a sortie to burn the Mameluke siege
engines, but their horses became entangled in the enemy's
tent-ropes and they were ignominiously chased back to Acre,
losing eighteen knights. Later the Hospitallers launched
another night-raid, this time in pitch darkness, but it was
equally disastrous. Spirits sank, only to be restored on 4 May
by the arrival of King Henri from Cyprus with 500 infantry
and 200 knights.

But the young king and his advisers soon realised that the
situation was hopeless. Turkish engineers were steadily undermining the towers, which began to crumble beneath a ceaseless
bombardment from the sultan's mangonels, a hail of enormous
rocks and timber baulks. Lighter machines hurled pots of
Greek fire or burning pitch which burst when they hit their
targets and the sky was ablaze with naphtha arrows. Henri
tried to negotiate, but the implacable al-Ashraf would accept
nothing but complete surrender. By 15 May the first wall and
all its towers had been breached. Filling the moat with the
bodies of men and horses as well as sandbags the Saracens
swept through the main gate, encouraged by 300 drummers on
camels. Charging on horseback down the narrow streets the
Templar and Hospitaller brethren drove them out, but by
evening the desperate Franks were forced to withdraw behind
the inner wall. Next day many citizens put their wives and
children on board ship for Cyprus, but unfortunately the
weather was too bad to put out to sea.

In European legend a 'last stand' has always been an
admired death. Icelandic sagas show a man's lonely fight to
the end against hopeless odds as something of beauty, a genuine
aesthetic achievement, like Roland's refusal to blow his horn
at Roncesvalles or the Nibelungs' grim finish. For the brethren

S·ADALBERTUS PRUSSORUM APOSTOLUS

MAGISTER ORDI·TEUTON·

SACERDOS ORD·TEUTONIC·

PETRI de DÜSBURG
Ordinis Teutonici Sacerdotis.
CHRONICON PRUSSIÆ,
cum
Anonymi cujusdam
CONTINUATIONE,
alysq
ANTIQUITATIBUS
PRUSSICIS.

CHRISTOPH HARTKNOCH
è Mss·Codicibus recensuit
Notisq illustravit.

Francofurti & Lipsiæ
Sumptibus Martini
Hallervordi Bibliop.
Königsb. A°1679.

CHRISTIANUS PRIMUS EPISCOPUS PRUSSIÆ

H·C·Sartorius sculp·Norimb·1670

3. The Hochmeister Fra. Werner von Orselen (1324–30) with the priest-
brother Fra. Petrus von Dusburg. From the frontispiece to the 1679 edition of
Fra. Petrus's chronicle of Prussia..

4a. The minnesinger Tannhäuser—the original of Wagner's hero—in the habit of a Teutonic Knight *c.* 1300. From the Manessa Codex at Heidelberg University.

4b. Monumental effigy *c.* 1340 of Hochmeister Fra. Luther of Brunswick (1331–4).

the beauty was spiritual as well as heroic and they knew that the reward of such a death could be heaven itself. They were fortunate to possess such a belief.

Just before dawn on Friday, 18 May 1291, the sultan ordered a general assault, announced by first one great kettle drum, then by massed drums and a battery of trumpets and cymbals, 'which had a very horrible voice'.[1] Mangonels and archers sent an endless shower of fire bombs into the doomed city, the arrows 'falling like rain', while Mameluke suicide-squads led by white-turbaned officers attacked through the dense smoke all along the wall in deep columns. At the St Anthony gate they were hurled back by Marshal Matthieu de Clermont, the Hospital's chief battle commander, who then counter-charged at the head of a band of Templars and Hospitallers to recapture the 'Accursed Tower'.

He was unsuccessful, and after a short breathing space at the Temple, where he saw the Master's lifeless body brought in, Fra. 'Mahé' deliberately went out to find his own death. The Templar chronicler wrote that the Marshal returned to the battle taking all his brethren with him for not one would desert him, and they came to 'la rue de Jenevés' and there he fought fiercely 'and killed, he and his companions, many Saracens and in the end he died, he and the others, like brave gallant Knights, good Christians, and may God have mercy on their souls.'[2]

The elderly Guillaume de Beaujeu had also attempted to recover the 'Accursed Tower', with only a dozen men. On the way there he met the Master of St John, who joined him, and the two stumbled grimly towards the Mamelukes, forcing a path through fleeing soldiers and over piles of dead and wounded, many horribly burnt by Greek fire, amid screams, groans, triumphant yells from the Turks and a few defiant

---

[1] Ibid., p. 812, '. . . une grant nacare . . . quy avoit mout oryble vois'.
[2] Ibid., p. 816, '. . . frere Mahé de Clermont . . . come chevaliers preus et hardis, bon crestiens. Et Dieus ait l'arme de yaus!' It is worth remembering that this account of the Marshal's last stand was written by the Templar of Tyre who spoke to eye witnesses. The Hospitaller Master wrote later of the Marshal '. . . estoit nobles et preus et sage as armes. Diex li soit deboinaires!' See Delaville le Roulx, vol. III, cart. no. 4157.

4

shouts of 'S. Jean' or 'Beau Sire, Beau Séant'. But the little band in red and white surcoats could do nothing against the victorious horde and were so blinded by smoke, naphtha flames, and dust from falling rubble that they could not see one another. Still the heroic old men and their bodyguards fought on, while a small group of Italians rallied to them. Finally a crossbow quarrel hit Fra. Guillaume beneath the left armpit, and he reeled back. The Italians pleaded with him to stay but the Master cried: 'Gentlemen, I can't go on because I'm a dead man – look at this wound.'[1] He collapsed and his aides took him into the Temple where he soon died. Fra. Jean also was badly wounded and his brethren carried him weeping and protesting down to a ship.[2] Death would have been welcome, for on a day like this the gates of Paradise were open.

Acre was now lost irretrievably. The terrified population, women, children, babies and old men, ran to the harbour in frantic despair, though many able-bodied citizens died fighting. King Henri had already sailed for home and there were too few ships. Horrible struggles took place on the crowded jetties and overloaded boats sank. A deserting Templar, Fra. Rutger von Blum, seized a galley and made his fortune by extorting ruinous passage money from the hysterical ladies of Acre fleeing from rape, mutilation and death, or at best slavery. To add to the horror a great storm blew up. The Saracens soon reached the jammed quays to butcher the screaming fugitives. Every one of the Teutonic Knights except their Hochmeister died in the sack, as did all the brethren of St Thomas and St Lazarus. Among the few male prisoners taken by the Mamelukes were several Templars who apostatised; years afterwards visitors to Cairo saw some slaves who had once been Poor Knights. However, most of their brethren who had not yet been killed held out in the Temple, by the sea.

[1] Ibid., p. 813, 'Et il lor respondy hautement que chascun l'oy: Seignors, je ne peu plus, car je suy mort – vées le cop'.

[2] In the letter quoted above which the Master of the Hospital afterwards wrote to the Prior of St Gilles, '. . . en larmians souspirs et en très grande tristrece, vous anonchons le maleuret trebucement d'Acre, le boine cité, hec! con grande doleur . . .', he says that 'nous meymes fume en cel jour feru àmort d'une lance entre les garites . . . '

The Order's Marshal, Pierre de Sevrey, was there to direct its defence. A large number of women and children had fled to them for protection and the Templars showed that they could be generous, putting as many refugees as possible aboard the Order's galleys, and sending them off to join the king's fleet. There was not enough room for everyone, and all the brethren, even the wounded, stayed behind. An eyewitness who saw the ships leave wrote afterwards that 'when they set sail everyone of the Temple who remained raised a great cheer, and thus they departed'. After several days al-Ashraf offered good terms, which Fra. Pierre accepted, and some Mamelukes were admitted. They hoisted the crescent flag of Islam but then began to rape the women and boys, whereupon the infuriated Templars killed them. The infidel flag was torn down and 'Beau Séant' hauled up again. That night the Marshal sent away the Commander, Tibald Gaudin, by boat with the Temple treasury, the holy relics, and some non-combatants. Next day the sultan once more proposed excellent terms, admitting that his men had got what they deserved, so Fra. Pierre went out to discuss surrender. He was immediately seized and beheaded. Some of the brethren were old men, most of them wounded and all exhausted, yet they decided to fight to the finish. They beat off assault after assault. 'They can fight the battle of the Lord and indeed be soldiers of Christ. Let them kill the enemy or die, they need not be afraid.' But the brethren had no reply to mangonel fire and the tunnels which riddled the foundations. On 28 May, the mines were fired. Part of the massive wall collapsed and 2,000 Turkish troops poured in to meet a bloody reception. The weight was too much for the tottering building, which came crashing down and Saracens and brethren perished together in a flaming hecatomb.[1]

Outremer died with its capital. Tortosa, Beirut, Sidon, Tyre, Haifa and Chastel Pelerin remained to the Franks, but they had made their supreme effort at Acre and were exhausted. All these places were quickly abandoned, though the Templars at Sidon made some show of resistance. By the end of August only the waterless island of Ruad was left, two miles from the

[1] Grousset tells the story particularly well, vol. III, pp. 760 et seq.

coast opposite Tortosa, with a small garrison of Poor Knights.
The local Christians, including the Latin peasants, fled into
the hills while 'la Douce Syrie' was methodically laid waste by
the sultan's army, who dug up irrigation channels, felled and
uprooted orchards, poisoned wells and devastated even the
richest farm lands to make sure the accursed Franks would
never return. Acre became a city of ghosts.[1] Those *poulains*
and brethren who survived took refuge in Cyprus.

Historians differ in their judgements on the brethren in
Latin Syria. Older and more traditional writers like the Abbé
Vertot or, in our own century, Sir Edwin King, see them as
spotless knight errants who were in truth Gibbon's 'bulwark' of
the crusader kingdom. Others regard them as a chief cause of
that 'Frankish anarchy' which eventually hamstrung any
attempt at constructive policy. Thus Sir Ernest Barker wrote:
'It was the two great orders of the Templars and the Hospitallers which were, in reality, most dangerous to the kingdom
... They built up great estates, especially in the principality
of Tripoli; they quarrelled with one another, until their
dissensions prevented any rigorous action; they struggled
against the claims of the clergy to tithes and to rights of jurisdiction; they negotiated with the Mahommedans as separate
powers; they conducted themselves towards the kings as
independent sovereigns.' René Grousset, writing of the decline
of Outremer, condemned them still more strongly: 'They took
no heed of this contemptible state save for the odd occasion
when they would embroil it in their personal battles for their
own special ends.'

Yet the most hostile historian cannot deny their good intent.
For the Holy Land meant everything to them. Certainly
Templars were avaricious, Hospitallers scarcely less so, but
both were prodigal of their treasure and their lives in defending a land which they loved passionately; they would hardly
have been human had they refrained from politics, while to be

---

[1] Israeli archaeologists have only recently disproved an impression, based
on contemporary chronicles, that Acre was completely destroyed; almost a
third of the crusader city remains, including the Hospitaller refectory and
several streets in the Genoese quarter. I owe this information to Dr Riley-
Smith.

combative and aggressive are necessary qualities in front-line troops. If their asceticism wilted during the thirteenth century, so did that of almost every monastic order. The latest historian of St John gives the truest picture: 'In Syria it possessed great palatinates in the north, in which it could behave as an independent prince and from which it directed a highly aggressive war against small Muslim neighbours. But in the Holy Land itself, the kingdom of Jerusalem, its estates were never independent of the crown and, faced by two great Saracen powers, it supported a policy of integration into Oriental politics by means of alliances, being suspicious of Crusades that could upset a delicate *status quo*. Its political influence in the twelfth century has been exaggerated. It achieved power slowly and haphazardly, its rise accompanied by humiliating reverses. Its emergence as one of the few institutions governing the settlement came about by default as others grew weaker in the collapse that followed the Battle of Hattin; that is, while the monarchy passed to an absentee dynasty in the West.'[1] This verdict applies no less to the Templars.

What has not been attempted – until now – is to contrast the Templars and Hospitallers in Syria with the Spanish military orders in their own land or the Teutonic Knights on the Baltic; as will be seen, in Spain the Reconquista would have been impossible without such brethren, who alone could provide professional armies to consolidate the Christian advance, while in Prussia the *Deutschritter* built an entire new state. In this wider context it must surely be recognised that during that long, losing battle which was Latin Syria the contribution of the brethren of the Temple and the Hospital, who possessed all the gifts of their Spanish and German cousins, was beyond price. The odds were against them, yet they were indeed Joshuas in the promised land even though at the end they must go up to Armageddon.

[1] Riley-Smith, op. cit., p. 475.

III

THE CRUSADE ON THE BALTIC
1200–1560

German orders in Prussia and Livonia:
Teutonic Knights – Brethren of the Sword

... they rush at their opponents as though such enemies were
sheep. However few their numbers they are not in the least
afraid of being in a cruel and alien land, ringed by foes, for
as the Machabees believed 'NOTHING FORBIDS GREAT
NUMBERS SHOULD BE AT THE MERCY OF SMALL;
WHAT MATTER MAKES IT TO THE GOD OF
HEAVEN, FEW BE HIS SOLDIERS OR MANY WHEN
HE GRANTS DELIVERANCE? ARMED MIGHT AVAILS
NOT TO WIN THE DAY; VICTORY IS FROM ABOVE.'
And so it often happens – many times will one brother harry a
thousand infidels two thousand of whom flee at the sight of two
brethren.

Bernard of Clairvaux
'De Laude Novae Militiae'

Seven brethren from a Teutonic house together with a few
noblemen built a fort in the Kulmerland beside a sacred oak
tree. It is said that at first they had to fight a vast horde of
natives, beyond number, but as time passed – perhaps fifty-
three years – they drove them out [*exterminaverunt*] so that
no one remained who would not bow his neck to the yoke of
faith; this with the help of the Lord Jesus Christ who is
blessed for ever and ever. Amen.

Fra. Petrus von Dusburg
'Cronica Terre Prussie'
III, 3 (in *S. R. P.* vol. 1)

CHAPTER 5

The Crusade on the Baltic

Throughout the history of the *Deutschritter* the German genius is very evident, romantic idealism implemented with utter ruthlessness. Tradition claims that a Hospital of St Mary of the Germans had been founded at Jerusalem in 1127. After the debacle of 1187 members of this establishment were included in a new foundation, a field hospital set up in 1190 by merchants from Bremen and Lubeck during the siege of Acre. Their first headquarters was a tent, made from a ship's mainsail, on the sea shore.[1] In 1198 some noblemen who had come with the abortive German crusade joined these brethren to form a military order, 'the Teutonic Knights of St Mary's Hospital of Jerusalem'. Heinrich Walpot von Bassenheim, a Rhinelander, was appointed Master, recruits were enrolled and the new Order was given statutes similar to the Templars' but with provision for hospitaller work. There were three classes of brother: knight, priest, and sergeant. Brother-knights, who had to be of noble birth and German blood, wore a white cloak with a black cross over a white tunic; priests wore a longer skirted version, while the sergeants' cloak was grey, its cross truncated with only three arms. In certain hospitals a fourth class existed – nursing women known as half-sisters.

The new brotherhood's hierarchy resembled that of the Poor Knights. Under the *Hochmeister* were his great bailiffs: the *Grosskomtur*, the *Ordensmarschall* (sometimes called *Grossmarschall*), the *Spittler* (Hospitaller),[2] the *Tressler* (Treasurer), and the *Trapier* (Quartermaster). The General Chapter of the knights, which elected the Hochmeister, met every September on the feast of the Holy Cross. A *komturei* contained not less than twelve knight-brethren under a *pfleger* or *hauskomtur*. The houses

[1] Dusburg, 'Cronica Terre Prussie', I, 1.
[2] The Spittler's headquarters would later be at Elbing at the mouth of the Vistulka – the modern Elblag – in western Prussia.

4*

of a province formed a *landkomturei* or *ballei*. In charge of
German *balleien* was the *Landmeister* whose headquarters were
at Mergentheim in Swabia.

The empire endowed the new brethren generously with lands
in Germany, Sicily and southern Italy, while they were also
given Greek estates by the Frankish lords of Achaia. Teutonic
Knights could not hope to compete in Syria with Templars or
Hospitallers so they devoted their energies to Armenia, where
their chief strongholds appear to have been Amouda – a plain
keep of Rhineland pattern – and Haruniye. King Lavon the
Great became a *halbbruder* or confrère. In 1210 most brethren
perished with their third Hochmeister, Hermann Bart, on an
obscure Cilician campaign.

Fra. Hermann von Salza, his successor, was the real founder
of the Order's greatness.[1] Born about 1170, in his youth he
attended the court of the dukes of Thuringia, where he was
supposed to have acquired distinguished manners, and certainly
he knew how to win the favour of princes. In 1219 King Jean de
Brienne awarded the Hochmeister the privilege of bearing the
Gold Cross of Jerusalem under the Order's black cross in his
achievement of arms to commemorate the knights' bravery at
the siege of Damietta. In 1226 the Emperor Frederick II made
Fra. Hermann and his successors Princes of the Empire, while
the Pope presented him with a magnificent ring afterwards used
at the inauguration of every Hochmeister. It is a testimony to
Salza's statesmanship that he succeeded in remaining on good
terms with both papacy and emperor; at the 'coronation' of the
excommunicated Frederick as King of Jerusalem in 1229
Teutonic Knights mounted guard in the Holy Sepulchre and
Fra. Hermann read the emperor's proclamation in French and
German. The sceptical, ruthless Frederick appears to have had
a genuine regard for the dedicated religious, and encouraged
his order's progress. In 1229 a second headquarters was built –
the castle of Starkenberg, north-east of Acre. However there is
not sufficient space to deal fully with their activities in
Palestine where they were always overshadowed by Templars

---

[1] 'This man was eloquent, affable, wise, careful and far seeing, and glorious
in all his actions.' Dusburg, op. cit., I, 5.

and Hospitallers. The German brothers were to find their true destiny in Europe.

King Andrew II of Hungary was worried about eastern Transylvania, savagely raided by heathen Kumans. In 1211 he gave its mountainous Barcasag district to the Teutonic Order. The brethren adapted methods of warfare learnt in Syria and Armenia, building a network of wooden fortresses, and the Turkish Kumans proved neither so numerous nor so skilful as their Anatolian cousins. By 1225 the 'Burzenland' had not only been pacified but settled with German colonists. King Andrew grew alarmed; in any case the Kumans were now being integrated with the Magyars. Suddenly he descended on the Burzenland with a large army and evicted the knights. After loud protests Fra. Hermann began to look elsewhere.

Livonia, the modern Estonia and Latvia, was peopled by pagan Baltic and Finnish tribes. To the east it was bounded by Russian princes, whilst to the north it was scantily settled at Reval by Danes. The idea of a Holy War in northern Europe was not new. In 1147 the ubiquitous St Bernard had summoned all Germans to a crusade against the heathen Wends who lived across the Elbe. Livonia was a fair enough prospect for land-hungry Teutons. In 1201 Albrecht von Buxhövden sailed from Lubeck with a great fleet of colonists to found Riga at the south of the river Dvina, in the land of the Baltic Livs. The town prospered and many Livonians were converted. Nevertheless the little colony could not afford to depend on stray crusaders for protection, and in 1204 Albrecht, now Bishop of Riga, founded the Sword Brethren, who took the Templars' rule. The habit was white, marked with a red sword and cross. Their purpose was the defence of 'Mary's Land', commemorated in the lines spoken by the Master in the ceremony of profession:

> Dis Schwert entfange von meiner Hand
> Zu schützen Gotts und Marien Landt.

They are supposed to have admitted postulants of ignoble birth, but recent research seems to disprove this legend.[1] Master Wenno von Rhorbach was murdered by one of his own

---

[1] See Herder, *Der Orden Schwertbrüder* (Cologne, 1965), who identifies the origins of a surprisingly large number of Sword Brethren.

brethren in 1208[1], yet they were fine soldiers. For Albrecht colonisation was as much part of the crusade as conversion. First his *Schwertbrüder* built the castle of Wenden as a headquarters, then they invaded Estonia with an army half-German, half-Livonian, penetrating the deep pine forests to rout the natives and their Russian allies; in 1227 they conquered the island of Oesel (Saaremaa), shrine of the god Tarapilla. German burghers settled in the new towns and the colony rested on sound foundations when its bishop died in 1229.

The bishop, later Archbishop of Riga, was the true governor of Marienland, and at first a system of dividing conquered territory between bishop and brethren worked very well. Large estates were given to German nobles, in return for military service. Shortly after Albrecht's death the Sword Brethren proclaimed a Holy War against 'the Northern Saracens' and made steady progress. They had many preceptories, administered by *vogts*, their chief strongholds being Wenden and Fellin, though the Master's headquarters were now at the Jurgenhof in Riga. Eventually they sought to wrest sovereignty from the bishop. However in 1237 their second Master, Fra. Wolquin Schenk, was defeated and killed with most of his brethren at Siauliai by the Kurs in alliance with the Lithuanian prince, Mindaugas.[2]

In the meantime Hochmeister Hermann von Salza had seen other opportunities. The seaboard from the Vistula to the Niemen and its hinterland of lakes, marshes, sandy heaths and pinewood were inhabited by the heathen *Prusiskai*, a Baltic

---

[1] 'Among the Knighthood's brethren at that time there was a certain Wigbert whose heart was far more inclined to love the world rather than religious discipline and who had caused much discord among his brothers ... he was a real Judas ... like a wolf among sheep ... in the upper room where he had gone on the pretext of communicating some secret, suddenly, with the axe ['bipenne'] which he always carried, he struck off the Master's head ...' Heinrich von Lettland, p. 132, 'Chronicon Livonicum vetus' in *S.R.L.*, vol. I. (Balthasar Rüssow, 'Chronica der Provintz Lyfflandt', *S.R.L.*, vol. 2, p. 13, mistakenly dates the murder to 1223.)

[2] '... there arrived unexpectedly from Livonia Fra. Gerlac the Red announcing that Master Wolquin with many brethren, pilgrims and people of God had been killed – slain in battle.' Dusburg, op. cit., III, 28,

people who spoke a language closely related to Lithuanian.[1] The latter, in the primeval forest north and east of Poland, resembled the Prussian tribes in everything except disunity and were now coming together under the able Mindaugas. Balts worshipped idols in sacred groves and fields, and attributed divine powers to the entire creature-world, including their own animals.[2] They practised human sacrifice, by burning or beheading, and buried animals alive at funerals; dead warriors were cremated astride their horses while widows were often made to hang themselves. Stockades of towns and temples were adorned with animal skulls to ward off the evil eye, their grim shrines served by weird priests and soothsayers. The Prussians' domestic habits were as unpleasant as their religion. The old, the sick, the blind and the lame were invariably slaughtered. Drunkenness from mead and fermented mares' milk was a major pastime while tribesmen often drank the living blood from their horses' veins. Inter-tribal warfare was endemic.

Konrad, Duke of Mazovia, was so cowed by their raids that he abandoned the whole province of Chelmno. In 1228 the bishops of Kujawia and Plock organised a Polish military order, the Brotherhood of Dobrzyn, as protection. Already Konrad had offered Chelmno to Fra. Hermann together with any other territory his brethren might conquer. Next year the Hochmeister obtained a document from his friend the emperor, known as the Golden Bull of Rimini, later confirmed by the pope, which gave him full sovereignty over these lands with nominal papal suzerainty. Two knights arrived in 1229 and built the castle of Vogelsang ('Birdsong') on the Vistula but were soon killed by the Prussians.[3]

The year after, one of the Teutonic Order's great heroes came with twenty knights and 200 sergeants to take possession of

[1] '. . . terram horroris et vaste solitudinis.' Dusburg, op. cit., II, 10.
[2] They mistook every created thing for God, says Fra. Petrus, '. . . the sun, the moon and the stars, thunder and lightning, and even four legged beasts, down to the toad'. Ibid., III, 5. The Order never forgot this gruesome paganism: An eighteenth-century knight historian wrote 'La Prusse, vaste pays encore plongélors dans les tenèbres de l'idolatrie' – Wal, vol. I, p. 194.
[3] '. . . castrum dictum Vogelsanck quod dicitur latine cantus avium . . .' seems to be a ponderous joke on Fra. Petrus's part. Dusburg, op. cit., II, 10.

Vogelsang. It was Fra. Hermann Balke, styled *Landpfleger*
(Preceptor), whose skill in war was equalled by his modesty and
generosity. It is no exaggeration to call Balke the Pizarro of the
Baltic lands. Most of his troops were volunteers who regarded
themselves as Crusaders, the brethren acting both as command
structure and panzers. Help also came from Bohemia and
Silesia. Transport was supplied by the sea-faring merchants of
Lübeck. In 1231 Hermann crossed the Vistula and stormed a
fortress-temple, hanging the Prussian chief from his own sacred
oak tree. This *Landpfleger* used his enemies' tactics of forest
ambush. At first the Prussians were scornful of his tiny force, but
soon they came to dread it. White-robed horsemen attacked
them even in the snow, and riding over frozen rivers or
charging out of blizzards like winter ghosts their great cloaks
served for camouflage. 'Often under the weird glitter of the
Northern Lights combat was joined upon the ice that covered
the rivers and marshes, until the solid crust broke beneath the
weight of the warriors and the men of both sides were engulfed
to their chilly doom.'[1] Tribesmen who fought on horseback with
sword and battleaxe or on foot with bows found the uncanny
strangers' terrible charge irresistible, very different from un-
disciplined Polish levies. The '*Pruzzes*', as the Germans called
them, retreated to simple forts which were easily overrun by the
brethren. Like Pizarro, Balke allied with one tribe to defeat
another; natives who submitted and accepted Christianity were
left in possession of their lands, and enlisted as Baltic Turcopoles. Systematically he reduced the territory between the
Vistula and the Niemen, penetrating up the rivers, consolidating
ground gained by wooden castles. In 1232 Kulm (Chelmno)
was founded on the left bank of the Vistula; in 1233 Marienwerder. The same year a crusade was launched, brethren
joining forces with Duke Konrad and Duke Swientopelk of
Pomerellen, and a great victory was won on the Sirgune where
1,500 Prussians fell. In 1234 the Hochmeister himself came to
inspect Kulm and Thorn (Thorun). The year after, the Order of
Dobrzyn was united with the Teutonic Order. Elbing was

[1] Treitschke, op. cit., p. 40. At least one great victory was won over the
Prussians 'tempore hyemali, cum omnia essent gelu intensissimo indurate'.
Dusburg, op. cit., III, 11.

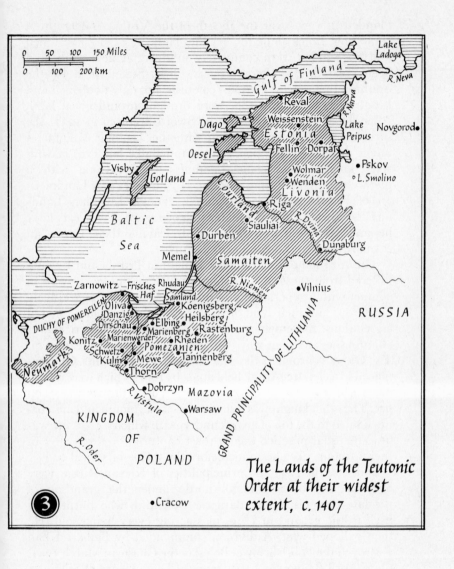

The Lands of the Teutonic Order at their widest extent, c. 1407

founded in 1237 near the mouth of the Vistula and brethren could now attack along the Frisches Haff. By 1238 Pomezanien and Pogezanien were completely subdued. A new polity had been created, the *Ordensstaat*, or Order-State, ruled by the brethren themselves; German colonists, not only noblemen and burghers but peasants too, were brought in and given land. After the disastrous defeat of the Sword Brethren in 1237[1] the survivors applied for affiliation with the Teutonic Knights, a union ratified by the pope. Hermann Balke left Prussia with sixty knights to become Landmeister of Livonia with a hierarchy of officers similar to the Hochmeister's. A Landmeister of Prussia was also appointed, though Livonian Landmeisters always enjoyed greater independence. Two years later he and Hermann von Salza died, leaving their Order an extraordinary and magnificent destiny.

The vocation of the Teutonic Knight in Prussia and Livonia differed from those of his comrades in Palestine, who were in contact with a superior civilisation. Prussians were aggressively barbarous and their land of swamps and forests held no sacred associations. Extremely treacherous, the tribesmen were expert at ambushes and their ways with prisoners did not endear them. The Order's chronicles describe the fate of two knights. One was placed in a cleft tree-trunk held apart by ropes which were released, crushing the wretched brother, whereupon the tree was set on fire. The other knight was lashed to his horse, mount and man being hauled to the top of an oak underneath which a great fire was lit. The usual practice was to roast captured brethren alive in their armour, like chestnuts, before the shrine of a local god.

Suddenly in 1237 the principalities of Kievan Russia were overwhelmed by a Mongol horde under the grandson of the late Genghis Khan, Batu the Splendid, who burnt Kiev itself to the ground in 1240, massacring every living soul. He then galloped west. A division commanded by Baibars Khan destroyed the Polish army of Boleslav the Chaste in March 1241. On 9 April Baibars met the troops of Duke Henry of Silesia at Liegnitz: 30,000 Poles and Bavarians with a force of Templars

[1] In fact Master Wolquin had been negotiating for the incorporation of his brotherhood into the Teutonic Order for the last six years. See Dusburg, op. cit., III, 28.

and Hospitallers and a strong detachment of Teutonic Knights under the Prussian Landmeister, Poppo von Osterna. The Christians were misled by the dense formations of the Mongols and underestimated their strength. The Mongols seem to have taken Duke Henry by surprise. The Christians broke before the whirlwind onslaught of the Nine Yak Tails, and were annihilated, the brethren dying almost to a man, though Fra. Poppo managed to escape. The duke's head was impaled on a lance while nine sacks of severed ears were taken to Batu. The fugitives believed that they had been defeated by witchcraft; the Yak banner was a demon 'with a devil face and a long grey beard'. Fortunately Batu returned to Mongolia on hearing of the death of Khan Ogodai.

Encouraged by the disasters of the Slavs, undeterred by Liegnitz and with papal encouragement the Livonian Landmeister sought to enlarge his territory at the expense of the Russian schismatics. In 1240 brethren crossed the river Narva to take Pskov; their objective was Novgorod, of whose wealth alluring reports had been brought by German merchants. There was little love between the Orthodox Christians of Russ and Catholic Teutons. Novgorod was ruled by Prince Alexander Yaroslavovitch, surnamed Nevsky after his victory on the river Neva in 1240 when he had defeated the Swedes. Alexander chose his ground with care. The knights were successfully manœuvred on to the ice of Lake Peipus, which could support lightly armed Slavs, but not heavy German cavalry, who died by the hundred with their Landmeister. Eisenstein's film *Alexander Nevsky* caricatures the scene, but does at least provide some idea of the dread which the brethren inspired among Balts and Slavs; their huge horses, faceless helmets, black-crossed shields and billowing white cloaks gave them a truly nightmarish appearance. The 'Ice Slaughter' put an end to Teutonic hopes of expansion into Russia beyond the Narva.

Although a Christian, the Duke of Pomerellen, Swientopelk, at first the brethren's enthusiastic ally, had become increasingly restive. Like Andrew of Hungary he now realised that a dangerous power was emerging as his neighbour. Too many Germans had settled in Pomerellen. The building of Elbing on the lower Vistula and the Order's claim to the Vistula delta alarmed him as much as the Germanisation of his erstwhile Prussian enemies. Liegnitz and Lake Peipus gave him his opportunity. In late 1242 he attacked the brethren without warning. At the same time, assisted by their untamed kinsmen in the east, the apparently submissive Prussian tribesmen revolted, returning to the old religion. 40,000 Germans perished in the Kulmerland (Chelmno) alone. One tribe, the Pomezanians, stayed loyal, but only Thorn and a few castles held out. Livonia was laid waste by Mindaugas and his savage Lithuanians. It took a full-scale crusade to rescue the brethren from their unwilling subjects, and in 1254 an army of 60,000 Germans and Bohemians arrived, led by King Otakar II and Rudolf of Habsburg. The region most thickly populated by Prussians, the peninsula of Samland north of the Pregel estuary, was overrun, and the Sambians, the foremost Prussian tribe, were conquered. The town of Königsberg was founded and named after King Otakar. Fra. Poppo von Osterna, now Hochmeister, restored order and by 1260 had overcome all the western tribes.[1]

In Livonia the Lithuanians were beaten off and under two capable Landmeisters, Gruningen and Struckland, the Kurs were tamed, Memel being built to prevent arms reaching them. The wily Mindaugas gave up the struggle and was seemingly converted to Christianity. With the pope's blessing he was crowned King of Lithuania and even endowed the Order with lands. The brethren's aim was now to unite Livonia to Prussia by overrunning Samaiten, the Lithuanian seaboard. However, in 1260 Livonia was raided by tribesmen whom Mindaugas could not, or would not, control. Through the treachery of the Kurs the Landmeister was defeated at Durben, perishing with 150 knights, including the Marshal of Prussia. Immediately Mindaugas, throwing off Christianity, attacked, joined by the Russians, while everywhere Kurs and Estonians rose in revolt. Providentially both Alexander Nevsky and Mindaugas died in 1263 and by 1267 the rebellious Kurs had been finally brought to heel.

[1] However, in Pomerellen the brethren left the native Slav nobility, who were firmly Christian, in possession of their lands.

Durben had also caused a Prussian rebellion which lasted thirteen years – the great apostasy, as the brethren termed it. The tribes at last united under the able and determined leaders, Herkus Monte and Glappon, who had lived in Germany and understood the brethren's tactics, the value of a Lithuanian alliance, a wooded terrain's military possibilities, and how to besiege castles. To survive, brethren acted on the axiom 'who fights the Order fights Jesus Christ'. Double apostates who worshipped consecrated snakes with sacred amber fires did not deserve mercy.[1] The Order began a systematic policy of bloody extermination, slaughtering the population wholesale, destroying villages and burning crops. Tribes disappeared without trace, Prussian leaders being hunted down like animals. Brethren copied Prussian tactics, sending raiding parties guided by loyal tribesmen deep into the forests.[2] No quarter was given. By 1273 the Prussian Landmeister Konrad von Thierberg, having broken his rebellious subjects for good, went on to conquer the so far independent tribes. Their last leader, Skurdo, laid waste his own lands and took his people to Lithuania. By the end of 1283 only 170,000 Prussians remained. The promised land was cleansed of Moabites.[3]

No doubt brethren found ample justification in the Old Testament: 'So Joshua smote all the country of the hills and of the south, and of the vale, and of the springs, and all their kings: he left none remaining, but utterly destroyed all that breathed as the Lord God of Israel commanded. And Joshua smote them from Kadesh-barnea even unto Gaza and all the country of Goshon even into Gibeon. And all these kings and their land did Joshua take at one time, because the Lord God of Israel fought for Israel.' Many Landmeisters must have seen themselves as

[1] '. . . in errores pristinos sunt relapsi . . .'. Dusburg, op. cit., III, 89.
[2] On one occasion Martin von Gollin – probably a *halbbruder* – seized a Lithuanian ship and sailed back, down the rivers, to Thorn, 250 miles away. Fra. Petrus further records that this Gothic Chindit always attacked Prussian villages at dusk – to catch the warriors taking their sauna. Ibid., III, 199.
[3] '. . . and all the tribes in the said land had been conquered or driven out ['expugnate essent et exterminate'], so that not one was left who would not humbly bow his neck to the Most Holy Roman Church.' Ibid, III, 221.

Joshuas, and Livonian battle flags were emblazoned with an image of the Blessed Virgin.[1] The Gospel had indeed become a flaming Sword.

The reduction of Prussia and Livonia demanded remarkable qualities and the rule produced extraordinary men.[2] There is some analogy with Plato's Guardians, who could neither marry nor own property. Self-renunciation was absolute, and the brethren, who slept clothed with a sword at hand, rose four times at night for the office, taking the discipline – that is, self-flagellation – every Friday. Punishment included flogging, while property was in common, the sole personal possessions being a sword, the habit and a right to bread and water, while no brother was allowed to use his family coat-of-arms. As with the Templars the beard was always worn, and the Bible was read at meals.[3]

Triumph on the Baltic was balanced by collapse in the Levant. In 1271 Starkenberg was lost; in 1291 the German Hospital vanished with Acre. Armenia was falling to Mamelukes, Romania to renascent Byzantines. The Hochmeister's head-quarters were at Venice, where he waited in vain for the crusade to recover the Holy Land. Then in 1308 the Arch-bishop of Riga, hoping to regain the lost sovereignty of Albrecht von Buxhövden, begged Pope Clement V to suppress the Teutonic Order because of its luxury, sensuality, cruelty and injustice; soon there were accusations of sodomy and witch-craft. The following year Hochmeister Siegfried von Feuchtwangen hastily transferred the Order's headquarters to Marienburg, which henceforth became the *Grosskomturei*, the Prussian Landmeister's office being merged with the Hochmeister's. Now their crusade was concerned solely with Balts and Slavs.

---

[1] The Livonian Master's banner depicted the Blessed Virgin in Glory. See 'Banderia Prutenorum', *S.R.P.*, vol. IV.

[2] The Engelsberg *komturei* was known as 'Angels' Hill' because those living in it led lives of angelic piety (angelicum ducunt vitam) boasts Fra. Petrus; one may suspect that the natives had a different name for them. Dusburg, op. cit., III, 22.

[3] See Perlbach for the rite of profession; the rite contains a sword blessing – Benediccio ensis ad faciendum militum'. *Statuten des Deutschen Ordens*, p. 129.

CHAPTER 6

The Ordensland: an Army with a Country

Marienburg (known as 'Malbork' since 1945) was the symbol of the Order, a combination of fortress, palace, barracks and monastery. Like all military religious the celibate brethren had a deep and tender devotion to the Virgin Mary of whom an enormous yet gracious statue dominated the castle. Nonetheless the splendour of their court was greater than that of many of the visiting European kings. It was presided over by the reigning Hochmeister, whose white habit was embroidered with a great black and gold cross charged with the Hohenstauffen eagle and the lilies of St Louis. He was always escorted by four carefully chosen knights-in-waiting, the *Hochmeister companiones* who stood at his side to prevent a repetition of the tragedy of 1330. (That year Werner von Orselen, a demanding superior noted for piety, had severely punished a certain Fra. Johann von Biendorf for gross immorality; one dark November evening as the Hochmeister was attending Vespers in his private chapel the revengeful knight stabbed him to death.)[1] Hochmeisters more than rated such semi-regal state; their Prussian and Livonian lands were outside the empire so they were real sovereigns. Under Hochmeister Luther, Duke of Brunswick, a talented musician, the great castle became another Wartburg, the setting of scenes worthy of *Tannhäuser*. There were frequent song contests and on one occasion a pathetic figure appeared from the past, a Prussian harpist who sang in his own almost forgotten tongue. Jeering, the knights awarded this ridiculous ghost a prize, a

---

[1] A horrified Petrus von Dusburg added a sad postscript describing the murder to the chronicle which he had finished only three years before and which had probably been commissioned by the unfortunate Hochmeister.

sack of rotten walnuts, before sending him back to the forest
and his sacred oak trees. Marienburg was a truly Wagnerian
capital and indeed the minnesinger Tannhäuser seems to
have been a *Deutschritter* for a short period.

A young knight might serve some years in a frontier blockhouse, but the greater part of his career was passed in the
commanderies. He could be posted to the Levant – Greece or
Armenia – while there were commanderies in Italy and even
France, though after the thirteenth century few brethren lived
outside Germany or the Baltic lands. It has been suggested
that Hermann von Salza himself gave the Order a bureaucratic
tradition derived from Norman Sicily, and certainly the
administration followed a uniform pattern from the Mediterranean to the Baltic.[1] Officials developed the art of scientific
book-keeping; financial and legal experts were employed and
archives meticulously kept, including a personal dossier on
each brother. Each Landkomtur was responsible for his district's colonisation, later tax collection and the maintenance
of roads and schools, as well as defence, while he was also
president of the provincial Landthing. The chief relaxation of
all brethren was hunting; not for pleasure but the necessary
extermination of primeval fauna – wolf, bear, lynx, elk, aurochs
and bison – which terrorised the settlers or ruined their crops.
If elderly or infirm, brothers retired to a kind of Chelsea
Hospital at Marienburg. Most came from the Rhineland or
Westphalia – Westphalians predominating in Livonia. The
latter, more dour and reserved, disliked the Rhinelanders'
noisy volatility and tended to think them frivolous. Celibacy
did not seem so ghastly a privation to the medieval mind
as it does to the modern and the Order offered an adven-
turous career to landless younger sons; a fair number of
ne'er-do-wells took the habit to avoid criminal proceedings.
For fear of nepotism the brotherhood would not admit Prussian
junkers.

The settlement of Prussia was the outstanding colonial
enterprise of the Middle Ages. Cultivation spread slowly
inland from the Baltic and up the lower Vistula until the
southern and south-eastern borderlands came under the

[2] This point is made by Carsten in *The Origins of Prussia*, p. 7.

plough. German and Dutch peasants, led by a *locator*,[1] who combined the functions of immigration agent and village mayor, were given freeholdings in return for rent in kind. Market places were set up. There were no labour dues and peasants were not tied to the soil. Noblemen came too, and were granted estates, forming the new gentry.[2] Most Prussians were reduced to serfdom though steadily Germanised. Marshes were drained, sea walls built, forests cleared and the sandy soil conquered by the heavy German plough. Customs duty was levied, but there were no inland tolls on the well-kept roads or the rivers, which were patrolled by the brethren. Understandably, there was little brigandage. By the fourteenth century, Prussia had the most contented peasant freeholders in Europe. The brethren had learnt the value of commerce in the Levant, maintaining a Baltic fleet of merchantmen and warships. To some extent they had copied the Templars' banking methods, and bills of exchange were accepted at the larger commanderies. They also enforced a uniform system of weights and measures. In 1263, at the height of the Prussian rebellion, they obtained papal permission to trade and exported grain in vast quantities from the Order's estates. The Hochmeister minted his own coinage at Thorn and kept a monopoly of the yellow Prussian amber, much prized for rosaries. As a member of the Hansa merchant league he was well able to sympathise with his burghers' ambitions. Furs, salt, timber, cloth, falcons, horses, silver and wax were exported, and Ordensland burghers grew rich, with every reason to be grateful to their Hochmeister. They belonged to arms clubs, riding fully armed with the brethren in emergencies.

The Hochmeister was a limited monarch whose bailiffs comprised a council very like a modern cabinet of ministers and whose household revenues were kept separate from those of the *Ordensstaat*. One law governed Prussia, that of the Hochmeister and his council, applying to laymen and clerics alike. The Church was very much the servant of the ecclesiastical state. There was no archbishop and all four bishops were priest-

[1] Ibid., pp. 30 and 52.
[2] Only about 100 knightly families received estates from the Order during its first 50 years in Prussia. Ibid., p. 54.

brethren of the Order. It is this uniformity of law and administration, coordinating foreign policy, internal government, church affairs, trade and industry, which gives substance to the claim that Prussia was the first modern state.

The Ordensland could boast a literature, although like most contemporary princes many of its rulers could neither read nor write.[1] Several brethren wrote biblical commentaries, among them Fra. Heinrich von Hesler (fl. c. 1300) and the Ermeland canon Tilo von Kulm (fl. c. 1340). Fra. Heinrich's commentaries, *Evangelium Nicodemi* and *Apocalypsis* are interesting for their criticism of the landowners' harsh treatment of the peasants. Hagiography was not neglected and Fra. Hugo von Langenstein (fl. c. 1290) wrote a life of St Martina which was much admired in its day. He also compiled the *Mainauer Naturlehre*, a strange work which deals with geography, astronomy and medicine. The Order's mystics did not emerge until the end of the fourteenth century, though its first great historians were at work much earlier. The tradition begun by the *Chronica Terre Prussie* of Fra. Petrus von Dusburg – translated into rhyming German by Fra. Nikolaus von Jeroschin – would reach its height in the fifteenth century with the 'Annals' of Johann von Pusilge.[2] The chronicle of Fra. Petrus (fl. c. 1330) has an introduction in which each weapon is sanctified by its scriptural precedents, giving holy war an almost sacramental quality. There were also various translations of the Old Testament, especially of Job and the Maccabees, which, like the chronicles, were read in the refectories.

Chroniclers also flourished in Livland. Conquest and settlement, the union of the *Schwertbrüder* with the Teutonic Knights and the early years of 'Marienland' were vigorously recorded as the *Chronicon Livonicum Vetus* by Heinrich von Lettland (d. 1259). In the next century the story was continued by Hermann von Wartberge. One should mention too a short chronicle in German, *Die Riterlichen Meister und Brüder zu Lieflant*,

---

[1] 'As late as the fifteenth century one of the Grand Masters was "neither doctor nor clerk," that is to say he could neither read nor write.' Treitschke, *Das deutsche Ordensland Preussen*, trans. Eden and Paul, p. 97.

[2] 'In this essentially political world, only one science was diligently fostered, that of historiography.' Ibid., p. 98.

by Dietleb von Alnpeke. These early Livonian chronicles strike a noticeably grim note, compounded of savagery and anxiety, even when compared with those of Prussia which are harsh enough. The German presence on the shores of the northern Baltic was far more precarious than in Prussia – at times the 'Crusaders', both brethren and colonists, saw themselves as a beleaguered garrison rather than as triumphant Conquistadores.

The Teutonic Knights' one real aesthetic achievement was their architecture. A typical *'domus conventualis'* was a combination of austerity and strategic necessity. By 1300 there were 23 of them in Prussia alone. At first these houses consisted of a strong watch tower on the Rhineland pattern, with curtain walls enclosing wooden conventual buildings, the whole surrounded by moats and earthworks. However, towards the end of the thirteenth century they began to build commanderies of a specific design. Chapel, dormitory, refectory and chapter house formed four bulky wings, fortified on the outside, often with a free-standing watch tower (see pl. 2a). There were cloisters, but these were on an upper floor in case enemies should enter the courtyard. The brethren's architects evolved a style which, although borrowing from Syrian, Italian, French and even English sources, remained their own.

Marienburg was the outstanding example. Here, the original fortified monastery grew into four great wings of several storeys enclosing a courtyard with arcaded galleries on two storeys against such rooms as chapel, chapter house, dormitory, kitchen and armoury. Square towers at the corners were linked by a crenellated rampart along the roof. In the days of the Prussian Landmeisters the *Hochschloss* followed the basic pattern: a quadrangle with cloisters enclosing a courtyard, strengthened by towers at each angle. The Marienburg one was built in stone, but the later outworks, the *Mittelschloss* and the west wing, were of brick. The *Mittelschloss* contained the great refectory with star-shaped vaulting resting on delicate, attenuated granite pillars. The Hochmeister's apartments were in the west wing and his personal dining-room, the charming 'summer refectory' centred round a single pillar whose stem supported a mass of decorative brick vaulting. This graceful mingling of brick and stone produced an ethereal, almost mystical effect. The

nineteenth-century Romantic poet Eichendorf was so moved
by its 'light diaphanous quality' that, standing in the summer
refectory he coined the phrase 'music turned to stone'. There
were other great castle-commanderies at Thorn, Rheden,
Mewe, Königsberg and Heilsberg. At Marienwerder the
bishop's palace was both castle and fortified cathedral in one
vast, yet undeniably elegant, red brick building. The Ordensburgen's sombre history was relieved by the gaiety of their
exquisite architecture.

The commanderies dominated the landscape of the *Ordensland*.
However, there were other buildings in the brethren's distinctive
style, walled towns, and churches such as the Marienkirche at
Danzig with its fantastic red gables. In Livonia, stone was plenti-
ful, and brick was seldom used, but otherwise its architecture
was very similar to that of Prussia. Towns were strengthened
with massive citadels. At Reval and Narva there were tall towers
named *Langer Hermann*, perhaps to commemorate the brave
Landpfleger. The independent-minded Livonian bishops built
castles in emulation of their Prussian colleagues, similar to the
domi conventuales of the brethren, as the requirements of a dean
and chapter were very like those of a *hauskomtur* and his twelve
brother-knights. It was no accident that the twentieth-century
S.S. named their own fortresses *Ordensburgen*.[1]

Livonia differed from Prussia in many ways. The Archbishop
of Riga together with the four bishops disputed power with the
Order, frequently appealing to the papacy or even to the
heathen Lithuanians. So independent was the Hochmeister's
viceroy, the Landmeister, that many historians do not realise
that he and his thirteen *vogts* were no longer Sword brethren
but Teutonic Knights. The settlers, both burghers and junkers,
came mainly from Lower Germany and spoke *Ostniederdeutsch*.
Riga, Dorpat (Tartu), and later Reval (Tallin), belonged to
the Hansa and operated a highly lucrative staple at Novgorod,
a virtual monopoly of Russian-Baltic trade. However, outside
these towns there was little commercial activity and Livonia
always remained more rural than Prussia. There were no
peasant colonists and the Lettish and Estonian natives, save

[1] Oddly enough Hitler's *wolfschanz*, from whence he directed his own *drang
nach Osten*, was near the site of the Teutonic Order's *Komturei* of Rastenburg.

for a few Germanised nobles, were brutally exploited by the Baltic barons.[1] Statutary labour service was strictly enforced. Dogs were said to howl and children fly screaming at the sight of a German. There were frequent and bloody *jacqueries*. On the night of 23 April 1343 the wretched Estonians rose and murdered 1,800 Germans before morning.[2] A tatterdemalion army marched on Reval to meet a terrible end, and Landt-meister Burckhardt von Dreileve exterminated the population of a whole province 'with ingenious tortures'. Yet Estonia was Danish until 1346, even if its colonists were mostly from the Reich. Brethren brought the serfs to heel, but the true oppressors were the junkers.[3]

The Order's policy towards its conquered subjects is inter-preted, by German, Slavonic and Baltic historians, notably Heinrich von Treitschke, as aggressive Teutonic nationalism, but this is an exaggeration. True, Latin or German had to be used for purposes of administration but the Baltic languages were not only difficult to learn, but unwritten. Intermarriage with natives was forbidden because they were suspected of paganism. Prussians were forbidden to inhabit German villages because they could not use the heavy plough and would lower the standard of agriculture. No Jew was permitted to settle in Marienland, nor indeed in any part of the *Ordensstaat*, though

[1] 'Not all these classes, however, were represented. Only knights and a few townsmen were found in the Eastern Baltic lands.' See Hermann Aubin, 'The lands east of the Elbe and German colonisation eastwards', *C.E.H.*, vol. I, pp. 367–8.

[2] 'In the year 1343 when the aforesaid Master [Fra. Burkhardt von Dreileve] had descended upon the schismatics [i.e. the Orthodox Russians] with an armed fleet, behold, on the eve of St George's Day [night of 22–3 May] the converts of the diocese of Reval fell back into their old religion; they killed their own lords and all Germans including little children, dashing babies against rocks or throwing them into the water or into fires, and doing to women that of which I am ashamed to speak, cutting them open with swords and impaling the infants hiding in their wombs with spears . . . ' Hermann von Wartberge, 'Chronicon Livoniae', *S.R.P.*, vol. II, p. 70.

[3] 'The result was the formation in these north-eastern marches of a populace without rights, for it consisted of underlings who were substantially slaves, whereas the Prussian peasants, learning to speak German, simultaneously acquired German freedom.' Treitschke, op. cit., p. 57.

this was for purely religious reasons. The brethren's prejudices were political and economic, never racial, even if class coincided with race. They were Christians first, Germans second, and the foundation of the *Ordensstaat* was the extirpation of paganism. Even so Livland has an unfortunate resemblance to the state which Nazi cranks hoped to set up in Eastern Europe by exterminating the natives or reducing them to helotry. It is significant that the leading racialist of the Third Reich, Alfred Rosenberg, was a Baltic German born at Reval.

An undeniably dubious aspect of the Order's activities was its Polish policy. In 1331 Władyslaw the Dwarf called in the knights to repress a rebellion at Danzig, and after an unusually spectacular massacre the brethren kept the rich town for themselves. Poland, now uniting under strong kings, became the brethren's deadly enemy and routed them at Plowce in 1332, yet by herself could not overcome the Order. Her kings often appealed to the papacy, but the brethren always contrived a skilful defence. In 1343 Casimir the Great ceded Pomerellen and Danzig by the Treaty of Kalisz, abandoning the struggle.

Pagan Lithuania was the Order's *raison d'être*. Its inhabitants resembled Prussians in their customs, but were united by the gifted Liutaras dynasty. Under Gediminas (1315–41), secure in his forests and marshes, the Lithuanian state absorbed the Ukraine as far as Kiev and the Black Sea. Their Ruthenian neighbours[1] civilised the wild gentry, a few of whom became Orthodox Christians. Polish merchants and artisans were encouraged to settle by the grand-duke, who nevertheless maintained the holy green snakes and the sacred fire of sweet-smelling amber in his palace at Vilnius (Wilno). His country-men waged endless war with the knights.

The terrain was primeval forest, whose only roads were the water-ways. The brethren attacked from the sea, sailing up the rivers, but as soon as they built castles the natives overran them. Alternatively the knights raided through pathless woods and fens, like Indian scouts in North America. Trained in woodcraft by Prussian trackers they carried their armour and provisions for many months by packhorse or porters through

[1] '. . . Rutenos . . . subditores et co-operatores paganorum . . .' Herman von Wartberge, 'Chronican Livoniae', *S.R.P.*, vol. 2, p. 115.

dense pine trees which hid the sun and stars. Their armour, heavier now with plates for legs, arms and shoulders, could only be donned when they reached the banks of the Niemen. They endured all the hazards of ambush and wild animals, of storms and starvation. Sometimes they lost their way and perished slowly; frequently the wounded were abandoned. Some brethren went mad from forest '*cafard*'. If captured they were sacrificed to the Lithuanian gods with fiendish tortures. Seventy expeditions were launched from Prussia into Samaiten between 1345 and 1377, another thirty by the Livonian Landmeister.[1] These forest razzias were the Teutonic version of the Hospitallers' sea caravans. The brethren were dreaded. In 1336 they besieged and overran a stockade on the Niemen. Rather than fall into their hands, the Lithuanians burnt all their possessions in a great funeral pyre, killed their wives and children and then beheaded each other. One old woman had decapitated more than 100 warriors with an axe and when the knights broke in she split her own head.

In 1346 the Danish king sold Reval and northern Estonia to the Order, but Samaiten, the Lithuanian seaboard inhabited by a peculiarly warlike and barbarous tribe, still prevented the junction of Prussia and Livonia. The brethren had a man equal to the task, Fra. Winrich von Kniprode, who ruled from 1351 to 1382, and raised the Ordensland to the status of a European power, himself personifying its magnificence. An attractive, indeed magnetic figure, noted for his Rhinelander's cheerfulness, he was a man of vision.[2] Elected after an already brilliant military career he introduced administrative reforms which revitalised the whole Order. Imposing as Marienburg was, Fra. Winrich built a new palace worthy of a prince's capital: the superb *Mittelschloss* with its beautiful gardens.

[1] A typical example is that described by Hermann von Wartberge which took place in 1378. 'In that same year, on the sixth day before St Valentine's, Fra. Wilhelm [von Freimersen] the Master of Livonia went briskly "strenue ivit" with his men against the Lithuanians at Opythen where for nine days he killed, burnt, laid waste and destroyed all things.' Op. cit., p. 115.

[2] 'Wynricus de Knyprode . . . vir decorus et personatus, magne relligiositatis [*sic*] et multe prudentie.' See 'Historia Brevis Magistrorum Ordinis Theutonici Generalium', *S.R.P.*, vol. IV.

Here he presided with true south German gaiety over a splendid court welcoming a never-ending stream of foreign visitors for whom he provided sumptuous banquets and entertainments, with music and jugglers. Among those who came were Knights of St John, from the German commanderies of the *Johanniterorden*.[1] Tournaments, in which as religious the brethren did not take part, were frequently arranged. However there was wisdom in the Hochmeister's extravagant hospitality, for the papacy had promised the full spiritual privileges of a crusader to those who assisted the Order, and throughout the fourteenth century the princes and noblemen of Europe flocked to fight the Lithuanians. The blind king, John of Bohemia, who died at Crecy, had lost his eye in Samaiten; he was accompanied in Prussia by his secretary, the composer Guillaume de Machaut. Marshal Boucicault, the French paladin, fought at the brethren's side,[2] while Henry of Derby, later Henry IV of England, paid two visits to the Hochmeister's court, though this was after Winrich's day.[3] No doubt he was enrolled as a *halbbruder*, a confrère knight. A young Yorkshireman, the twenty-year-old Sir Geoffrey Scrope – brother of a future Archbishop of York – fell fighting at Fra. Winrich's side in 1362 and was buried in Königsberg Cathedral, where for centuries a window commemorated him.[4] Many English and Scots took part in the wars of 'the High Master of the Dutch Knights', while

[1] For a brief but illuminating summary of Templar and Hospitaller possessions in Pomerania and Brandenburg, see Carsten, op. cit., p. 13.

[2] See 'Le Livre des faicts du Marechal Boucicaut: Comment messire Boucicaut alla la troisième fois en Prusse, et comment il voulut venger la mort de messire Guillaume de Duglas', *S.R.P.*, vol. II.

[3] 'A.D. 1390. In this yer Ser Herry, erl of Derby, sailed into Prus, where with help of the marschale of Prus and of a kyng that hite Witot, he ovyrcam the kyng of Lettow and made him for to fle. Thre of his dukes he took and foure dukes he killed with many lordes and knytis and swieris mo than thre hundred.' (King Henry's contribution has been somewhat exaggerated!) See John Capgrave, *Chronicle of England*, ed. Hingeston (London, 1858).

[4] See Metcalfe, *A Great Historic Peerage, the Earldom of Wiltes* and *Burke's Landed Gentry* – 'Scrope'. Sir Geoffrey's brother was the future Archbishop Scrope of Shakespeare's 'Henry IV' who was executed for High Treason.

Chaucer's reference to such an episode in the career of his knight is well known:

> Ful ofte time he hadde the bord bigonne
> aboven alle naciouns in Pruce
> In Lettow hadde he reysed and in Ruce
> No Cristen man so ofte of his degree.

The Ordensland's campaigns had the attraction of big-game hunting in the nineteenth century. The courtly, charming Hochmeister understood how to make the best use of such enthusiasm.

Fra. Winrich tried to raise the spiritual and educational level of the Order. There were to be two learned brethren in every *komturei*, a theologian and a lawyer. A law school was set up at Marienburg, and the Hochmeister at one time contemplated founding a University of Kulm. So many recruits joined the brethren that there were not enough posts for them; there were probably seven hundred knights in Prussia by the end of Winrich's reign. He solved the problem by setting up convent houses as well as commanderies. These consisted of twelve knights and six priest-brethren, emphasis being on the Office and spiritual life. There were four such houses in Marienburg alone.

More junkers were employed in official posts and their levies organised into a formidable militia. However, Winrich protected the peasantry against them, and indeed earned the title of the peasants' friend.[1] He was equally jealous of his burgher's privileges, defending them from foreign competition and issuing an excellent new coinage.

Fra. Winrich was determined to exterminate 'the skin-clad Samogitians' of Samaiten and their foul deities, to whom human sacrifice was far from unknown. Two extremely able grand-dukes, Algirdas and Kestutis, led the enemy during thirty years of unbroken warfare, but the crisis came in 1370 when a vast army marched on Königsberg and was beaten back by the Hochmeister himself at Rhudav (Rudawa). He lost his Marshal[2]

[1] So folk songs called him, according to Treitschke, op. cit., p. 85.
[2] '. . . the man whose heart was as hard as his name Henning Schindekopf.' Ibid., p. 75.

with 26 komturs and 200 other brethren, but the Lithuanians, who lost their Grand-Ducal standard, would never face him again. Throughout, Winrich showed himself a wily statesman, supporting one grand-duke against another. When he died in 1382 his brethren controlled Samaiten in all but name, though it was raided incessantly by the uncowed tribesmen, uniting Prussia with Livonia. It was the zenith of the Order's power. Fra. Winrich's military record of massacre and extermination may not seem over-Christian – expeditions against the Samogitians often degenerated into mere man hunts[1] – but there is no need to doubt the brethren's conviction that those who fought them fought Jesus Christ.

Suddenly the ground was cut from beneath their feet. In August 1386 Grand-Duke Jogaila became a Catholic, married the Polish Queen Jadwiga and was crowned King of Poland and Lithuania as Władyslaw II. The holy fire at Vilnius was extinguished for ever, and next year Jogaila set about converting his subjects. However, the Order claimed, with some justice, that many were still heathen or Orthodox schismatics. Only recently in, 1377, Grand-Duke Algirdas had been cremated with his horses in the forest. As late as 1413 a French visitor, Guillebert de Lanoy, noted that some tribesmen still burnt their dead, splendidly dressed, on oak pyres within the sacred groves.[2]

The *Ordensstaat* was strong enough to defy Jogaila's vast empire, as his viceroy in Lithuania, Grand-Duke Vitautas, took an independent line and even allied with the brethren, abandoning Samaiten, though the natives still held out in their swamps

---

[1] Pirenne in *The Tides of History* (trans. George Allen & Unwin, 1963) vol. II, p. 306, noted that 'Every winter great Slav-hunting expeditions were organised to which the Teutonic Knights invited the seigneurs of the West'. The same writer considered the brethren's Baltic crusade to be 'the beginning of what was later to be known as "the Prussian Spirit" '. Ibid., p. 157.

[2] '... une secte que après leur mort ils se font ardoir en lieu de sepulture, vestus et aournez chascun de leurs meilleurs aournemens, en ung leur plus prochain boi ou forest qu'ilz ont, en feu fait de purain bois de quesne ...' See *Guillebert de Lannoy et ses voyages en 1413, 1414 et 1421*, ed. J. Lelewel (Brussels, 1844), p. 38.

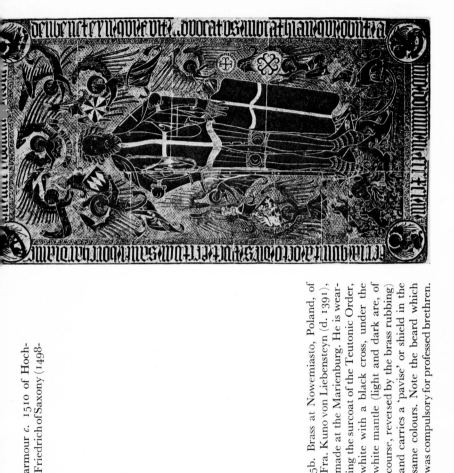

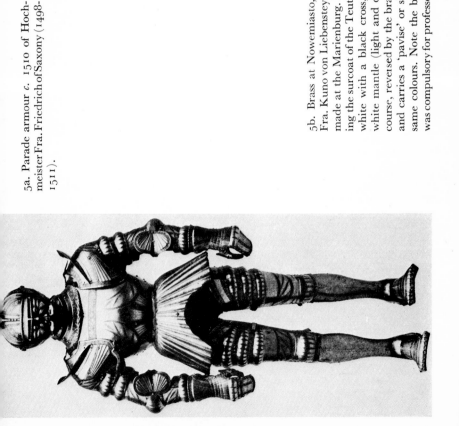

5a. Parade armour c. 1510 of Hoch-meister Fra. Friedrich of Saxony (1498-1511).

5b. Brass at Nowemiasto, Poland, of Fra. Kuno von Liebensteyn (d. 1391), made at the Marienburg. He is wearing the surcoat of the Teutonic Order, white with a black cross, under the white mantle (light and dark are, of course, reversed by the brass rubbing) and carries a 'pavise' or shield in the same colours. Note the beard which was compulsory for professed brethren.

6. Frey Don Juan de Zúñiga, Master of Alcántara (1478–94), attending a
lecture by Elio Antonio de Nebrija, author of the first Spanish grammar.
Both Frey Juan and the *frey-caballero* seated at bottom right are wearing the
Order's habit—white with a green cross on the left breast. From the
frontispiece to Nebrija's 'Institutiones Latinae'.

and forests. Fra. Konrad von Juningen, Hochmeister from 1394–1407, was an able statesman. He saw clearly that the Polish-Lithuanian Empire would only be united by opposition from the Order, and encouraged Vitautas to expand eastwards. In 1399 the grand-duke rode against the Golden Horde, over the Russian plains, with a great army of Lithuanian and Ruthenian boyars. Amongst them, oddly assorted, were the exiled Tartar Khan, Toktamish and a detachment of 500 men from the Teutonic Order. Tamberlane's lieutenant, Edegey Khan, met them on the river Vorskla, a tributary of the Dnieper. He used the tactics employed at Liegnitz and slaughtered two thirds of Vitautas' army, pursuing him mercilessly over the steppes. This ended 'Mad Witold's' hopes of conquering the lands of the Golden Horde. He turned on the *Ordensstaat*. Desperately Konrad tried to keep the peace, besides attempting to secure an alliance with the Khan of Kazan. The brethren possessed fifty-five towns and forty-eight fortresses, and their subjects were prosperous and contented. The *Ordensstaat* could triumph, so long as it avoided a general war on a large scale.

The untameable Samogitians overran Memel in 1397, occupying the fortress-town, which linked the *Ordensstaat*'s two halves, but the brethren recaptured it in 1406. This was the limit of their territorial expansion. They had purchased the Neumark of Brandenburg from Emperor Sigismund in 1402, and their control of the Baltic coastline was not to be equalled until the Swedish empire of the seventeenth century. In 1398 the brethren had landed an army on the island of Gotland, occupied by Swedish pirates, the 'Sea Victuallers', who preyed on the Hansa ships. These were driven out and the seas patrolled. The island was then seized by the Danes, and so the knights returned in 1404 with 15,000 troops and retook it, as well as 200 Danish ships, installing the Hansa in Visby, the capital. Finally, in 1407, the new Hochmeister, Fra. Ulrich von Juningen, gave it back to Margaret of Denmark in return for a guarantee to protect the Hansa.

King Władyslaw did his best to provoke the Order. Polish merchants were forbidden to trade with the burghers of Prussia and Livland, who were already made restive by the

Hansa's decline and resented the Order's private trading ventures. At Władyslaw's request the Duke of Pomerania blockaded the roads from Germany. Władyslaw also fanned the discontent of Prussian junkers, resentful of their immigrant masters. Konrad's dying words had been a plea not to elect his brother in his place. Fra. Ulrich was proud and foolhardy. In 1409 the smouldering border-disputes broke into war. Władyslaw and Vitautas gathered nearly 150,000 men, the whole muster of their empire, with a large force of Cossacks and Tartars and a detachment of Czech and Hungarian mercenaries under Jan Zizka, the future genius of the Hussite wars. The Order's army, together with levies and mercenaries, numbered 80,000. Apart from the Polish chivalry Władyslaw's army was mainly light horse, while the Order's consisted of heavy lancer cavalry, a few arbalestiers with the new steel crossbow and artillery brought from Marienburg. No Livonian brethren were present, but they were confident of victory.

They met at Tannenberg among the Masurian marshes on 15 July 1410. True to his role of God's champion the Hochmeister spurned the idea of a surprise attack. The Poles sang the battle hymn of St Adalbert whereupon brethren replied with the Easter song 'Christ ist erstanden',[1] the guns spoke briefly, and then the heavy Ordensland cavalry, in plate armour and hounskull helmets, attacked, roaring the old war cry 'Gott mit uns', a hammer-like mass of gleaming steel. It shattered the left wing of Czechs and Lithuanians, nearly smashing the right. However the Poles held stubbornly in the centre, and their allies rallied. His left wing had not yet reformed, but Fra. Ulrich charged with the entire reserve, weakened by the treacherous desertion of Kulmerland junkers. The Poles still held. After many more charges, at the end of a long day, the knights were outflanked and the battle degenerated into a sword and axe melée while Tartars surrounded the brethren. Their grim and stubborn Hochmeister refused to leave the 'Götterdämmerung' he had brought about, fighting on in his gilt armour and white cloak beneath the great battle banner, white

---

[1] 'Crist ist enstandin' – see Johann von Posilge in 'Annalista Thorunensis' III–IV, *S.R.P.*, vol. III, p. 316.

and gold with its black cross and eagle,[1] till he was cut down (when found, his body had been mutilated almost beyond recognition).[2] 18,000 of the Ordensland's army fell, including 205 knights; 14,000 were taken prisoner, many to be tortured or beheaded, and fifty standards were hung in Cracow Cathedral. The battle of Tannenberg was the Order's Hattin.

Fra. Heinrich von Plauen, komtur of Schwetz, galloped from Pomerania to Marienburg with 3,000 men, and to prevent it affording cover burnt the beautiful town to the ground. A vast army surrounded him, the captured guns of Marienburg battered the walls and, worst of all, the Order's subjects, even the bishops, gave the Poles a triumphant welcome while Kulmerland gentry sent him insulting messages.[3] Yet Plauen held on with cold courage. His brethren's morale had collapsed but was miraculously restored by a vision of Our Lady. After two months Władyslaw raised the siege and at the First Peace of Thorn in 1411 the Order lost only the Dobrzyn land (south-east of the Kulmerland) to Poland and Samaiten to Lithuania. But it was the end of the Baltic crusade.

---

[1] See 'Banderia Prutenorum', *S.R.P.*, vol. IV, compiled in 1448 by the Pole Johannes Dlugosz at Cracow where the captured banner was probably still hanging.

[2] However it was identified and brought back to the Marienburg for burial even if '. . . the Tartars and the Cossacks practised their hideous tricks of mutilation upon the Grand Master's body'. Treitschke, op. cit., p. 115.

[3] 'They besieged the castle with every kind of siege engine, bombards and other weapons of great strength and power, day and night for two months or more.' See Conrad Bitschin, the fifteenth-century continuer of Dusburg, *S.R.P.*, vol. III, p. 485.

CHAPTER 7

The Crusaders without a cause

Tannenberg destroyed the belief that 'who fights the Order fights Jesus Christ'; no longer could the brethren count on a martyr's crown if they fell in battle. They accepted God's verdict. This defeat was not merely a political disaster, but also a spiritual cataclysm, for the Ordensland had lost its soul.

Sienkiewicz, in his novel, *The Crutched Knights*, describes the visit of a Polish nobleman to Marienburg and his horror at the cowed, poverty stricken Prussian peasantry. In reality they enjoyed far better conditions than Polish serfs, many of whom fled to the Ordensland, where masters were not allowed to flog them. However, as the century progressed the shortage of agricultural labour worsened. Holdings were deserted and both Order and junkers found it hard to cultivate their own lands, while rents decreased. The brethren could impose forced labour service, but not the gentry, which exacerbated junker dissatisfaction with their south German rulers, and as early as 1397 the Kulmerland gentry had formed the *Eidechsenbund*, the League of the Lizard, to voice their grievances. Plauen, now Hochmeister, understood that the character of the *Ordensstaat* must be radically altered. His policy at home was to bring laymen into the administration, and abroad peace at all costs. In 1412 he summoned an assembly of the estates of Prussia, twenty junkers and twenty-seven burghers. In future no taxes were to be imposed or wars declared without their agreement. His brethren were deeply distrustful of this revolution. Fra. Heinrich's harshness had already made him many enemies. Several leading Danzigers had been executed for their treachery in welcoming the Poles after Tannenberg, while brethren who had fled to Germany were brought back in chains. He could not afford to provoke further antagonism.

King Władyslaw sent a stream of raiding parties into Prussia and eventually the young Hochmeister, goaded beyond endurance, ordered the Ordensmarschal to attack the Poles, but consulted none of his great officers, as he was bound by the constitutions. The Ordensmarschal refused to march, forcing Plauen to summon a chapter. This met in October 1413 and deposed the tyrannical Hochmeister.[1] During his brief rule he antagonised all his subjects, knights and laymen. He saw his role as that of a visionary prince, not as the governor of an ecclesiastical corporation, and his arrogance cut at the roots of the Order's discipline. It is significant that his supporters were mainly Rhinelanders, his opponents north Germans. Regional prejudices were already sapping the Order's vitality.

His destroyer and successor, the elderly Grossmarschal, Michael Kuchmeister von Sternberg, who led the brethren in the war of 1414–22, knew the Order could not risk a pitched battle. The knights stayed in the impregnable Ordensburgen, riding forth on vicious raids by night. The Poles counterattacked, and whole districts of the Ordensland were starved to death and depopulated.[2] The brethren were further demoralised by the favourable ear the papacy lent to their enemies' complaints. Finally the war of attrition broke them down and when a vast army invaded Prussia in 1422 they begged for peace, ceding Samaiten and also Nieszawa, the first town given to them long ago by Duke Konrad. In these days of ruin Vitautas fulfilled a lifelong ambition; he was admitted to the Order as a *halbbruder*, and Fra. Winrich must have turned in his grave. The Landmeister of Germany was appalled, bitterly reproaching the Hochmeister.

In 1430 Hochmeister Paul Bellizer von Rusdorf made a final attempt to break the Polish-Lithuanian alliance. There were two claimants to the Lithuanian throne: Svitrigaila, supported

---

[1] The former Hochmeister was accused of scheming to regain power with Polish assistance in 1414 and imprisoned for nine years. Even Treitschke (op. cit., I), p. 125, believed this charge to have been unjust.

[2] Though written over 400 years later, the epic 'Konrad Walenrod' by the great Polish Romantic poet Adam Mickiewicz reflects his countrymen's traditional hatred of the Order. The Hochmeister is made to say of *Litwa*:

> Burned are its towns, a sea of blood is spilled:
> These are my deeds, my oath I have fulfilled.

by the Orthodox boyars of the east, and Zigmantas, backed by
the Poles who led the Catholic magnates of the west. Fra. Paul
allied with Svitrigaila and in 1431 attacked Poland. In 1433
the Livonian Landmeister and his new friends carried all
before them, only to be destroyed by plague,[1] while in 1455
the supporters of Zigmantas wiped out Svitrigaila's army,
together with most of the Livonian brethren. It took years for
the Order to recover its strength in the north.

Bohemia, convulsed by religious war, was not the ally
against Poland she had been in the previous century. The
Hussites were angered by the brethren's part in Emperor
Sigismund's disastrous Crusade against them. Hussite armies
raided the Ordensland from Bohemia, their strange battle
wagons rolling deep into Prussia. They sang a grim war song,
'We, warriors of God', which ended 'slay, slay, slay, slay them
every one' – perhaps they brought too their war drum whose
skin was the skin of their blind and terrible leader, the dead
Zizka. In 1433 Jan Czapko sacked Dirschau and Oliva.[2] The
wagenburgs, laagers of armoured farm carts linked by chains,
from behind which the peasant brigands shot with small hand
guns before sallying out with flails and scythes, proved as
effective as modern tanks. Taborite heretics, the Bohemian
scourge, enjoyed ravaging this clerical state, laying waste,
torturing priests and junkers to death, carrying the common
people away to captivity. Then came plague, bad harvests and
famine. The roads were left to brigands. In any case trade was
dying, for the Hansa was already in decline when the Scanian
herring fisheries failed in 1425. Medieval currency was based
on a bi-metallic standard and a growing scarcity of silver
brought about a steady debasement of the coinage. The
Livonian staple in Novgorod was undermined while Prussian
towns were ruined by imports. Restrictions imposed by the
brethren, customs' dues and a monopoly of the grain trade,
infuriated the bankrupt burghers of the Ordensland. Flat sandy
Prussia with its mournful mists had always been a gloomy

---

[1] The plague was dysentery – one casualty was the Livonian Landmeister
himself, Cysus von Rutenberch. See Dyonisius Fabricius, 'Livonicae
Historiae compendiosa series', *S.R.L.*, vol. 2, p. 460.
[2] See Conrad Bitschin, op. cit., p. 502.

land, but now, afflicted by God, it was becoming a desert.[1]

Comic songs about the brethren's wenching were sung in the Ordensland yet there were still religious who tried to live their difficult vocation. In the fifteenth century an anonymous chaplain of the Order's Frankfurt house wrote the *Theologica Germanica*, a handbook of mysticism based on Meister Eckhart, which enjoyed great popularity.[2] Even in the bewildering days of the Reformation, brethren were to remain faithful to their vows. It is probable that in most *komtureien* the rule was kept with a fair degree of regularity and much respect for tradition.

By 1430 the Emperor Sigismund II, whose domains included Hungary and Croatia, was increasingly alarmed by Osmanli attacks. He therefore proposed to Hochmeister Bellizer that the brethren transfer their headquarters to Transylvania. A *komturei* was set up at Severin (on the Yugoslav border of modern Roumania) under Fra. Klaus von Redwitz to defend the Danube. Unfortunately Sigismund then killed a project, which might have revitalised the Order, by foolishly suggesting that its Prussian lands be shared out among neighbouring princes. Immediately the whole plan became suspect, and after a few years the brethren abandoned Severin.[3]

The foreign policy of Livonian Landmeisters had always differed from that of Prussia, as their opponents were the Russian princes rather than the Lithuanians. During two centuries they fought no less than thirty wars with the land of Russ. The Order had never ceased to covet Pskov and Novgorod the Great, especially the latter's vast commercial empire. In 1444, Livonian brethren began a skilful campaign against the republics. Small raids, whose primary purpose was psychological, were launched across the river Narva. In 1445 able diplomacy nearly succeeded in bringing the Danish king into the war to overawe Novgorod. The merchant state was

---

[1] Conrad Bitschin was so heartbroken that he composed a lament filling nearly a page of his chronicle and entitled 'Exclamacio dolorosa contra maliciam Hussitorum'.

[2] A work which would one day have great influence on Martin Luther.

[3] There is a brief account of this episode in the late Professor R. W. Seton-Watson's *History of the Roumanians* (C.U.P., 1934), p. 35.

blockaded, cut off from its trade with the Livonian towns. The Order made use of its monopoly to forbid the import of grain to Novgorod. However, though well conceived, the campaign failed and in 1448 the knights made peace with the Russians. The war had disastrous consequences, ruining the Livonian staple and harming the Prussian ports.

In 1440 junkers and burghers met at Marienwerder to found the *Preussische Bund*, which became a real state within a state, levying its own taxes. The Order was powerless to suppress the *Bund*, and the Hochmeister tried to reach a *modus vivendi*. It was impossible, for he could not share political power with the Prussian nobility without undermining the whole concept of the *Ordensstaat*, while it was equally difficult to alleviate the burghers' troubles. An explosive situation developed. Hochmeister Ludwig von Erlichshausen appealed to Frederick III in 1453, who solemnly declared the *Bund* dissolved. He could not enforce his decree.[1] In February 1454, after the mysterious murder of their emperor's ambassador, the *Bund* – which included twenty-one towns – renounced allegiance to the Hochmeister, and the country rose. Within two months fifty-six castles were in rebel hands and a ringleader of the revolt, a renegade knight, Fra. Hans von Baisen, journeyed to Cracow to offer the 'crown' of Prussia to Casimir IV. The real object was to win the anarchic freedom possessed by the Polish upper classes.

King Casimir came to Prussia, but instead of a welcome found a war which was to rage for thirteen years. The Ordensland tore itself to pieces, junker fighting junker, burgher warring with burgher. In Königsberg sailors and townsmen battled mercilessly in the narrow streets and along the quays while the merchant princes of Danzig, bitter haters of the Order, sent its supporters to the galleys. Casimir had few troops. However, the *Bund* gave him plenty of money, as did the Danzig oligarchy, and he hired mercenaries, Czechs, and Heyducks – wild

---

[1] 'The Emperor and the Empire looked on inert while the impotence of a theocracy that had been too rigid and the lawless arrogance of the mercantile patriciates and the squires were betraying New Germany to the Poles.' Treitschke, op. cit., p. 135.

Hungarians or Croats – who harried and burnt the wretched Ordensland.

Yet the Order could still produce another Plauen, the Spittler Heinrich Reuss von Plauen, a cousin of the tragic Hochmeister.[1] In September 1454 he marched to the relief of Könitz, besieged by King Casimir with an army 40,000 strong, of Poles, mercenaries and Prussian Leaguers. The Spittler had only 9,000 men, but narrowed the front by a skilful use of marshy ground and, finding a point where the enemy's light troops were exposed, charged in with 1,000 heavy cavalry. Casimir's army disintegrated and the king himself barely escaped, leaving his banner in the brethren's hands.

There were now few sergeants and the ratio of brethren to levies or mercenaries in the squadrons was probably about the same as that of officers and senior non-commissioned officers to other ranks in a modern infantry regiment. Crossbowmen were being replaced by foot soldiers with hand guns, and war carts were used by the Bohemian troops. There were none of the romantic adventurers of Winrich's day. Tannenberg had destroyed the Order's prestige while the Lithuanian wars had ceased to be crusades. There was little point in travelling to northern Europe to obtain experience which could be found nearer home. Only the wolfish freelances came, with scavenging camp-followers, greedy for pay and plunder. This 'Thirteen Years War' was one of sieges and raids, but few pitched battles. Towns were sacked and burnt, villages destroyed, cornfields laid waste, peasants massacred in droves.

The mercenaries, always open to a good offer, changed sides frequently. To pay them, the Hochmeister attempted to sell castles and manors, even towns, without success. Landed property was no longer profitable and capital was scarce. Rents and taxation had ceased to exist. The German Land-meister, Fra. Ulrich von Lentersheim, came to fight at the Prussian brethren's side and gave some financial help, but his advances were soon swallowed up. The desperate Fra. Ludwig guaranteed his troops' pay with twenty towns and castles,

[1] The enthusiastic author of the near contemporary 'Historia Brevis Magistrorum Ordinis Theutonici . . .' calls Fra. Heinrich 'alter Hector et Achilles'.

5*

which they promptly occupied. The Livonian Landmeister tried to buy back Marienburg, but failed[1] and in 1457 the Bohemians sold it to Casimir. The miserable Hochmeister escaped in a small boat to Königsberg, whose sympathetic burghers sent him a barrel of beer, but no money. The Spittler persuaded the loyal Burgomaster of Marienburg, Bartholomaus Blumen, to open the gates to him. Together, with a small band, they defended it desperately against the Poles who surrounded the city and occupied the citadel. Finally in 1460 they were overwhelmed and Burgomaster Blumen was beheaded. But Plauen escaped to fight on.

The brethren's defeat at Zarnowitz (Puck) in August 1462 by a smaller force has been described as the turning-point of the war.[2] The composition of the Order's troops is of interest: 1,000 fully-equipped heavy cavalry, 600 light cavalry, 1,300 militia and 400 foot soldiers. Much more important was the sea battle the following year at the mouth of the Vistula. The brethren sent forty-four ships against the Danzigers, whose own fleet was paid for by the jewels of the merchant's ladies. But the Elbingers, the allies of Danzig, arrived and the Order lost all its ships and 1,500 men. It was a strategic disaster, for it blocked the water route into West Prussia. Yet the brethren still resisted without troops, without money, without hope, their fortresses holding out, with no possibility of relief and falling one by one.

When the Hochmeister finally surrendered in 1466 he had spent sixteen million Hungarian florins, and both sides had lost over 100,000 men. At the Second Peace of Thorn it was agreed that Poland should take Danzig and the western *balleien*, henceforth to be known as 'Royal' Prussia. The Order kept the east while in future no less than half the Teutonic Knights were to be Poles. The Hochmeister had to pay homage for his Prussian lands to the Polish king, a humiliating ceremony which the unhappy Fra. Ludwig performed in the Guildhall at Thorn, 'weeping, and with torn garments'. The *Grosskomturei* was now at Königsberg.

[1] 'The rough fellows broke into the cells, tied up the knights, and proceeded to cut off their beards.' Treitschke, op. cit., p. 133.
[2] Boswell, *C.M.H.*, vol. VIII, p. 578.

The treaty divided the Order. It was difficult for the brethren outside Prussia to obey a Polish vassal who sat in the *Sejm* at the king's left hand. The Livonian Knights were confirmed in the habit of electing their own Landmeister while the German Landmeister adopted the title *Deutschmeister* and became more independant. Livland remained formidable. In 1471 Ivan III, Grand-Prince of Moscow, annexed Novgorod, whereupon the brethren tried to seize Pskov as a counter-stroke, waiting until 1480 when Ivan was fully occupied by the last invasion of the Golden Horde. Landmeister Bernhard von der Borch led a large and well-equipped force[1] through the snow and sacked the small town of Visgorod on 1 January 1480, returning at the end of the month to encircle Pskov with one army, and systematically devastate the countryside with another. Fra. Bernhard retreated when a Muscovite army raided Livonia, but on 1 March he chased the men of Pskov off the ice of Lake Peipus and then sacked and burnt the town of Kobyle, killing nearly 4,000 inhabitants, before withdrawing. The Land-meister's raids had profoundly shaken Pskov's morale. In August he returned without warning at the head of '100,000 men', threatening Pskov. The republic was desperate, but Fra. Bernhard again withdrew. Unfortunately the Golden Horde's invasion failed and Ivan was now free to protect Pskov.

Prussian brethren were determined to regain their independence. In 1498, they elected a powerful prince as Hochmeister, Friedrich of Saxony, the elector's brother. Königsberg was transformed into a semi-regal court administered by Saxon officials, and the Hochmeister-Duke's wealth provided an illusory splendour. He refused to pay homage to the Polish king, demanding the return of west Prussia.

By the end of the century Livland was ailing, split into three camps, bishops, towns and brethren, the latter distracted by feuds between Rhinelanders and Westphalians. Riga, Reval and Dorpat had lost their staple rights at Novgorod when Ivan III expelled the Hansa and all Germans. In any case the bur-ghers of both Livland and Prussia had abandoned the Hansa

---

[1] 'He gathered together a vast army for the purpose, up to 100,000 men, such as none of the Masters before him in Livonia had been able to do.' See Dyonisius Fabricius, op. cit., p. 461. This figure is hardly credible.

after 1467. The Order always maintained good relations with the Tartars, sending ambassadors to Kazan and Astrakhan, but the Golden Horde was in its final decline. Ivan had married a Byzantine princess and Moscow was quickly becoming the third Rome. Its grand-prince wanted an outlet to the Baltic and threatened Narva from his fortress of Ivangorod. Yet Marienland was to enjoy an Indian summer, often called its Golden Age. Fra. Wolther von Plettenberg, born in Westphalia in 1450 and elected Landmeister in 1493, was a ruler of Kniprode's calibre. A handsome man of distinguished manners, a gallant soldier and a gifted diplomatist, he seems to have stepped from the Order's heroic age into its twilit dusk. He restricted admission in Livland to Westphalians and controlled the cities and bishops by playing one against another, taking care to cultivate a special relationship with the Archbishop of Riga. Caspar Linde, archbishop from 1509–24, was a close friend and sympathiser. Even burghers were grateful for Fra. Wolther's benevolent rule, which lasted nearly half a century.[1]

In 1499 Muscovy and Mengli Gerei, Khan of the Krim Tartars, declared war on Grand-Duke Alexander of Lithuania, who allied with the Tartar Khan of the Volga, Sich Achmed, and the Order. In 1501 the Russians defeated and massacred the Lithuanian army, invading Livonia. Alexander sent no help and Sich Achmed was delayed. On 27 August, Plettenberg attacked the Russians alone on the Seritsa river. He had 8,000 foot and 4,000 cavalry. The Russians – Muscovites and the army of the Prince of Pskov – numbered 40,000. Using a murderous combination of artillery and heavy cavalry Fra. Wolther practically wiped them out. The Landmeister fought like a devil, though twice surrounded and once beaten to his knees. According to the chronicler, Balthasar Russow, his 12,000 soldiers killed most of the 40,000 Russians, the remainder fleeing to Pskov. But a severe outbreak of dysentery forced him to withdraw.

In November 1501 the Russians returned: 100,000 Mus-

---

[1] Two hundred years later he was still remembered. 'Walter Plettenberg is the Man, whom those Nations prefer to all their other Heer-Meisters for Valour, Wisdom and Good Fortune.' Blomberg, *An Account of Livonia*, p. 11.

covites and 30,000 Tartars[1] commanded by Ivan's best general, Prince Daniel Shchenya. They joined battle with the Order's main army, based on the fortress of Helmed outside Dorpat and, despite the knights' superior artillery, annihilated them. Not even a messenger got through to warn Plettenberg. Then the Muscovites devastated eastern Marienland, 40,000 Livonians being killed or dragged into captivity. The Landmeister was undismayed. In the spring of 1502 he launched several swift raids into the Pskov country, culminating in September with the siege of Pskov itself. He retreated before the relieving Muscovite army, luring his pursuers into a deathtrap at Lake Smolino. Again he used cavalry and skilled gunners to terrible effect. Many brethren died too, but Plettenberg's army was allowed to withdraw without further challenge. Shortly after, Grand-Duke Alexander made peace with Ivan and in May 1503 the Order's ambassadors concluded a fifty years' truce with the Russians. Russian and German chroniclers differ about the honours of the war, claiming the same battles as victories.[2] Whatever the truth the brethren did remarkably well to tie down a much larger army for so long and to emerge with their territory intact. The achievement is comparable to that of the Finns in the Winter War of 1940.

In 1512 another prince of the empire was elected Hochmeister, the twenty-one-year-old Albrecht von Hohenzollern, Margrave of Brandenburg-Anspach, poor, ambitious and without scruples. He refused to admit Poles to the Order and in 1517, after allying with Denmark and Grand-Prince Vassily III, demanded not only the return of Royal Prussia but also compensation for fifty years' occupation. Finally, in 1519, he attacked his uncle, King Sigismund of Poland, in a campaign of sieges, forays and burnings, but no pitched battles. Only the ravening *Landsknechts* profited, and in 1521 Fra. Albrecht, an indifferent general, agreed to a four years' truce.

But a new foe, Protestantism, now confronted the Order. In

---

[1] 'The Livonians waged a fierce and famous war against the Russians . . . against the hereditary enemies of pious Catholics . . .' Levenclavius, 'De Moscovitarum belli adversus finitimos gestis', *H.R.S.E.*, vol. I.

[2] There is a good summary of the war in J. Fennell's *Ivan the Great of Moscow* (Macmillan, 1961).

1523 Martin Luther wrote to Hochmeister Albrecht: 'Your Order is truly a strange order and especially because it was founded to fight against the infidels. For this reason it must make use of the worldly sword and must act in a worldly manner and yet it should be spiritual at the same time, should vow chastity, poverty and obedience and should keep these vows like the members of other monastic orders.' With habitual invective Dr Luther went on to describe the Order as an hermaphrodite institution. On Christmas Day 1523 the Bishop of Samland publicly accepted Lutheranism in a sermon at Königsberg Cathedral: 'This day Christ is born anew.' The doctrine had already spread among the burghers, even among the knights.

Fra. Albrecht met Luther at Nuremberg during the Imperial Diet of 1524 and was converted. On 8 April 1525 the Hochmeister signed the Treaty of Cracow. Henceforth he held Prussia from the Polish king as an hereditary duchy. Next day he did homage to King Sigismund in Cracow market place.[1] His subjects welcomed the revolution. 'Duke' Albrecht reigned prosperously until 1568, and his heirs until 1618, when the Hohenzollerns of Brandenburg inherited the duchy and their destiny. The black eagle replaced the black cross. A Lutheran source says that only five knights kept their vows: a historian belonging to the Order claims that very few turned heretic. Certainly some married and founded Prussian noble families, but it is also true that many left for Germany.[2]

Fra. Walther von Cronberg was elected Deutschmeister at Mergentheim in 1527 – the year after the Peasants' Revolt when this new *Grosskomturei* had been sacked by a rabble – then Hochmeister in 1530. The following year Charles V created the *Hoch-und-Deutschmeister* a Prince of the Empire. The brethren gave the emperor help, if on a small scale, during the religious wars of the Schmalkaldic League. Plettenberg, the obvious choice, was not chosen, because of his Westphalian bias, certainly not because of a leaning towards Lutheranism suggested by one historian of the Order. He was indispensable in Riga and seventy-five years old. In 1526 Charles V made him a Prince of the Empire.

[1] There is a dramatic account in Wal, op. cit., vol. 6.
[2] Wal claims that very few turned Lutheran.

Luther's teachings spread quickly among Livonian burghers, though not, apparently, among the brethren. To a man of Plettenberg's diplomatic temperament an understanding between Lutheranism and the papacy then seemed far from unlikely and he arranged public debates between Catholics and Lutherans. At the Diet of Wolmar in 1522 Lutheran burghers and even a few brethren protested against Luther's excommunication and in 1524 there were anti-Catholic riots in Riga and Reval. Churches were desecrated, priests and religious expelled from the cities. In 1526, at the second Diet of Wolmar, the assembly asked their ruler to follow Hochmeister Albrecht's example by renouncing his cross and becoming Duke of Livonia. But Plettenberg refused, amicably enough, and his refusal was respected. There was always the shadow of Moscow. In 1533 Fra. Wolther, eighty-three years of age, died a good Catholic at his favourite castle of Wenden after a reign of forty-four years.[1]

For twenty years the Landmeisters remained undisturbed,[2] but at last in 1557 Ivan IV the Terrible denounced the brethren as criminals 'who had deserted the Christian faith and burnt Russian ikons'. The tsar's army was more efficient than his grandfather's, and he had already conquered Tartar Kazan and Astrakhan. In January 1558 Prince Ivan Kurbsky invaded eastern Estonia, burning and slaying. Young people between ten and twenty were dragged off to the Tartar slave markets, goaded on with iron rods, but apart from these every German was put to death horribly, the women having their breasts cut off, the men their limbs. Ten thousand alone were slaughtered before the gates of Dorpat. In May 1558 Kurbsky captured Narva; in July, Prince Shuisky stormed Dorpat. The Russians occupied twenty towns by September, but then retired for the winter, leaving garrisons.

The ailing Furstenberg abdicated and the komtur of Dunaburg, Fra. Gotthard Kettler, was elected Landmeister. The last

[1] For Plettenberg's campaigns see Levenclavius, op. cit.

[2] Westphalians continued to dominate the Order, even during this period. One of the last Landmeisters was Fra. Heinrich von Galen whose family also provided a Prince-Bishop of Munster and, in our own day, Count Clemens von Galen, Bishop of Munster, notable for his defiance of the Nazi régime.

army of the Ordensland marched out to war, to the music of
trumpets and kettledrums, under the battle banner of the
Blessed Virgin. Yet though brethren still wore the black cross
piped with silver on their tunics, with a black enamelled silver
Ritterkreuz hanging from each neck, and though everyone was
ready to roar 'Gott mit uns', they had only 2,000 cavalry besides
a few arquebusiers and pikemen. Kettler took advantage of the
winter weather to overrun several garrisons. Ivan reacted swiftly
and in January 1559 the Russians returned, in the snow, with
130,000 men. This time not even babies were spared.

Twenty years later Sir Jerome Horsey, travelling through
Livonia on his way to Moscow for the Russia Company, spoke to
eyewitnesses. He wrote: 'Oh, the lamentable outcries and cruel
slaughters, drowning and burning, ravishing of women and
maids, stripping them naked without mercy or regard of the
frozen weather, tying and binding them by three or four at their
horses' tails, dragging them some alive, some dead, all bloodying
the ways and streets full of carcases of the aged men and women
and infants.'[1] Ivan, however, now feared an invasion by the
Krim Tartars and gave the Order an armistice, demanding that
the Landmeister come to sue for peace in person.

When the Poles asked the tsar to end his war with the knights,
Ivan replied, 'by the all powerful will of God since the days of
Rurik, Great Prince of Russia, the Livonian lands have been
part of the realm.'[2] In 1560 the Russians invaded Livland once
more, inflicting further atrocities and devastation. To add to the
bloody confusion the wretched Estonian peasantry rose. The
brethren, bankrupt, almost without troops, defended their
fortresses grimly, to no avail. Fellin, the residence of Fra. von
Furstenberg, was stormed by Prince Kurbsky in August, though
garrisoned by a strong detachment of knights with a train of
heavy artillery, and the former Landmeister was carried off to
Moscow. Ivan seriously considered restoring him as puppet head
of a vassal state. But it was too late. The golden age of

[1] See *The Travels of Sir Jerome Horsey, Kt.*, ed. A. Bond (Hakeluyt Soc.,
1856).

[2] Ivan was merely treating Livland in the way that he was accustomed to
treat his own rebellious subjects. For the Russian point of view see I. Grey,
Ivan the Terrible (Hodder & Stoughton, 1964).

Marienland was over in a smoking holocaust of the sort which four centuries later marked the end of the Third Reich.

The Ordensland fell to pieces. In 1562 one last victory was won in the style of Balke and Plettenberg; at Weissenstein after a siege of five weeks a young brother, Fra. Caspar von Oldenbock, with only 2,000 men beat off a Russian force of 30,000.[1] But now, at the urgent request of the merchants of Reval, the Swedes occupied northern Estonia, while the Danes took the offshore islands. Fra. Gotthard gave up the hopeless struggle, ceding all lands of the Order to Poland at the Treaty of Vilnius in November, though he kept his title of Landmeister until 1562. Poles, Swedes, Danes and Livonians united to drive out the Russian tsar. The brethren were disbanded. Some departed sadly for Germany, others stayed, turning Lutheran and marrying, including Kettler himself, who retained the south-west of Livand, becoming Duke of Courland (now Kurzeme), a charming coastal province, which he held as an independent fief from the Polish king (which his descendants ruled until the eighteenth century). So perished the *Ordensstaat*, that strange amalgam of military dictatorship, colonialism and theocracy, the most aggressive interpretation of the kingdom of heaven the world has ever seen. It was the end of a very grim song indeed.

Beyond doubt the Ordensland contributed to the repellent concept of the Herrenvolk. Reading Treitschke's *Das deutsche Ordensland* one immediately recognises his interpretation's influence on the architects of the Third Reich. He spoke of 'the formidable activities of our people as conqueror, teacher, discipliner of its neighbours',[2] of 'those pitiless *racial* conflicts whose vestiges live on mysteriously in the habits of our people',[3] believing that the brethren anticipated 'the two main trends of colonial policy, which were subsequently to guide Britain and Spain'.[4]

Yet these medieval storm troopers escaped Nazi canonisation;

---

[1] For Fra. Caspar von Oldenbock see Balthasar Rüssow, 'Chronica der Provintz Lyfflandt', p. 65. Also Dyonisius Fabricius, op. cit., p. 476, who says that the Russians retired 'cum ignominia'.

[2] Treitschke, op. cit., p. 18.

[3] Ibid., p. 19.

[4] Ibid., p. 55.

they were Catholic noblemen, not Aryan guttersnipes. Without them the colonisation of the Ostland could never have taken place. For all the bloodshed, all the cruelty, it was a glorious saga. Their kingdom has been described with justice as medieval Germany's greatest achievement. But though the knights were German their work was only incidentally national. The Ordensland was another Outremer. Their wars, their government, were for Christianity and not an attempt to build a German Utopia.

IV

THE RECONQUISTA
1158–1493

Spanish and Portuguese orders:
Calatrava – Santiago – Alcántara – Aviz – Knights of Christ –
Montesa

To avoid confusing our warriors with that soldiery which
belongs to the Devil rather than God we will now speak
briefly of the life these Knights of Christ lead on campaign or
in the Convent, what it is they prize, and why soldiers of God
are so different from those of the world.

> Bernard of Clairvaux
> 'De Laude Novae Militiae'

When ye encounter the infidels strike off their heads till ye
have made a great slaughter among them and of the rest make
fast the fetters.

> *The Koran*

CHAPTER 8

The Reconquista

The Reconquista was Outremer's story in reverse, when Christian natives drove out Moslem invaders, though one which lasted eight hundred years. In Spain, military brotherhoods evolved by a long process, not being created to meet the needs of the moment as in Syria; yet their sonorous names – Calatrava, Alcántara, and Santiago – were even more celebrated among Spaniards than those of the Temple or St John. They were the perfected instrument of five centuries of warfare with Islam, given their final shape by the Templars' example.

The Moslem invaders, Arab, Syrian, and Berber, crossed the Straits of Gibraltar in 711; within five years they had conquered the whole peninsula, except a few barren mountains in the north. In 753 the Umaiyad, Abd al-Rahman, arrived in Spain to create a unified Cordoban monarchy whose northern frontier ran from the Ebro to the Tagus, from Coimbra to Pamplona. By the eleventh century five Christian kingdoms had appeared: Galicia (with Portugal), León, Castile, Navarre and Aragon, whose people lived in dread of razzias. Every year the Christian territories were devastated, crops burnt, fruit trees cut down, buildings razed, livestock driven off and the inhabitants herded back to the slave markets. Those who escaped were cowed by ingenious atrocities, the victims' heads being salted as trophies to impress the caliph's unruly subjects. Yet the barbarous princes with their puny kingdoms never forgot they were rightful lords of Spain. The Reconquista was a holy war. The body of St James had been discovered in Galicia and, as *Santiago Matamoros* (St James the Moor Killer), came down from heaven to lead the faithful – his shrine at Compostella becoming the greatest pilgrim centre in Western Europe and his war a crusade long before the Franks marched on Jerusalem.

'Castilian' conjures up patrician pride, but the first Castilians were rough pioneers who colonised the southern lands, protecting

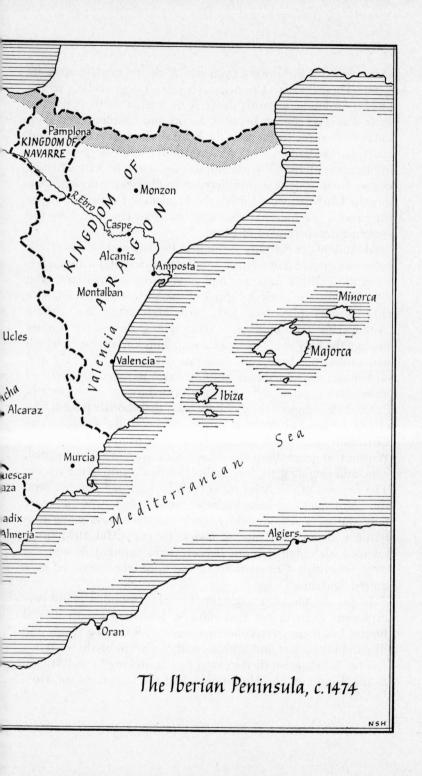

The Iberian Peninsula, c. 1474

themselves by the towers from which their kingdom took its name. These Spanish Cossacks were often refugee rebels, whose hunger for land constantly drove them further south. Naturally there was close contact between Moors and Castilians and even today Arab traits are found in the Spanish character: dignity and courtesy, the sacred duty of hospitality, fantastic generosity, intolerance, an inability to compromise, and a ferocity which is not so much cruelty as indifference to physical suffering. One day the Christian would drive the Moslem out of Spain, but in the process the national character was half conquered by the extremist temperament of Islam.

Al-Andalus could only be united by a despot. In 1031 the caliphate broke up into *taifas* (small city states) and within a few years the military initiative had passed to the Christians, who took Toledo, the ancient capital of the Visigoths, in 1085. The *taifa* princes played a last card and asked the Berber 'Almoravids' (*al-murabbitun* – 'those who gather in the fortress to wage the holy war') to rescue them. This fanatical sect, which had united the barbarous Saharan tribes, came quickly and al-Andalus was added to its empire. *Ribats* were set up – fortified 'monasteries' where tribesmen performed ascetic exercises and fulfilled the religious duty of holy war; their border patrols, the *rabitos*, became as dreaded as the razzias of the caliphs. The Christians nonetheless managed to hold the frontier of the Tagus. Within two generations the Almoravids succumbed to Spanish wine and singing girls, but again 'Ilfriqiya' came to the rescue. The Berbers of the Atlas mountains had formed another sect, the 'Almohads' (*al-muwahhidun* – 'unitarians'), who also saw holy war as a religious duty, their caliphs always going into battle with an entourage of fakirs. In 1147 Abd al-Moumin invaded al-Andalus; more Berbers were brought in and the cities refortified. Christian Spain was once more menaced by a united Andalusia.

In the decade after 1130 the Templars founded many preceptories. Even before that date St John had set up several houses but these were concerned only with nursing work, and dispatching money and supplies to their Syrian brethren. When Alfons, *lo Batallador*, died in 1134 he left his kingdom of Aragon to the Templars, the Hospitallers and the Canons of the Holy

Sepulchre. The Poor Knights were installed in the royal palace
at Sanguera, and obtained many castles. No doubt they were
aided by the Count of Barcelona, Ramón Berenguer IV, a
Templar confrère. In 1143 the Poor Knights were given a great
stronghold at Monzon, while in 1146 they established headquarters at Punta la Reyna, but they were less powerful in
Castile. They had a castle in Portugal at Soure as early as 1128,
setting up outposts in the wild country near Pombal and Ega.
However, the Reconquista required a native solution.

Armed brotherhoods had long existed in Christian Spain. At
first these *hermangildas* were little more than small bands of local
farmers, rather like Boer commandos in the old Transvaal.
Later, however, emulating the Almohad *rabitos*, they acquired
a quasi-religious character and their members may have taken
certain vows such as temporary celibacy and an oath to protect
Christians. It has been suggested that the Iberian peninsula, not
Syria, was the true birthplace of military Christianity. This is a
misleading exaggeration, though the *hermangildas* undoubtedly
contributed to the rise of purely Spanish orders.

Toledo, the Castilian capital, was protected by mountains,
but between this range and the Sierra Morena, which guarded
Cordoba, lay the open plains of the *meseta*. Razzias could gallop
swiftly over the tableland and attack Toledo without warning.
It was essential to hold an advance post on the far side of the
Montes de Toledo. The fortress of Calatrava (*Qalat Rawaah*,
'the castle of war'), sixty-five miles south on the marshy banks of
the upper Guardiana, was ideal. The Emperor Alfonso VII
captured it in 1147, the year of the Almohad invasion, entrusting
it to the Templars. Later, *rabitos* grew more formidable and the
brethren began to doubt if they could hold the castle. In 1157
rumours that African generals were planning an advance finally
decided the Poor Knights, who informed Sancho III that they
were evacuating Calatrava. The king was appalled. He had
nothing to take their place.

A Cistercian abbot, Ramón Sierra, from the Navarrese
monastery of Santa María de Fitero, was in Toledo on business
accompanied by the monk Diego Velásquez, a nobleman and a
friend of Sancho. As both were disgusted by the Templars' lack
of trust in God, the abbot went to the king and offered to defend

Calatrava. There was no alternative; in 1158 the castle and its lands were given to the community of Fitero. Ramón immediately transferred all his monks to Calatrava, preaching a crusade. He was joined by many Navarrese soldiers, and Diego Velásquez organised laymen and brethren into an effective fighting unit, compiling a simple rule. From a *ribat* garrisoned by monks and an *hermangilda* Calatrava was transformed into the first commandery of an entirely new type of military order.[1]

When Ramón died in 1164 Calatrava had still not been attacked. The choir monks elected a new abbot, but the knights and lay brethren chose a Master, Don García. The monks withdrew to Cirvelos, though Diego stayed, recruiting secular priests to serve as chaplains, while Frey García swore to observe the Cistercian rule and asked Citeaux to affiliate his brethren to the white monks.[2] Citeaux responded favourably, accepting these *freyles* of Calatrava into full communion as true brethren, not just as *confratres*, Abbot Gilbert expressing pleasure that they were 'not soldiers of the world, but soldiers of God'. The same year a bull of Pope Alexander III gave them canonical status as a religious order.

The basic organisation of the knights of Calatrava was complete within twenty years, though its constitutions were not finalised until the fifteenth century. The mother house was staffed by *freyles clerigos*, who prayed for success in battle, but the normal *encomienda* contained twelve *caballeros freyles* and a chaplain. The election of the Master resembled a Cistercian abbot's, with a certain flavour of the Visigothic war-band. When he died, his lieutenant, the *comendador mayor*, summoned all knights and chaplains to Calatrava within ten days to choose a successor.

---

[1] For Calatrava see J. F. O'Callaghan, 'The Affiliation of the Order of Calatrava with Citeaux', a series of articles in *Analecta Sacri Ordinis Cisterciensis*, which is the only comprehensive study of this brotherhood.

[2] Ibid., vol. 16, p. 285. 'There should be no hesitation in affirming that it [the spirit of Calatrava] was essentially a Cistercian spirit based not only upon the fundamental texts of the Benedictine Rule and the *Carta Caritatis*, but also upon the less tangible principles of twelfth-century chivalry, seen by the Cistercians as another means of reforming and purifying the lives of men . . .'

The new *Maestre* was raised on high, and given the Order's seal, sword and banner, while his *freyles* sang the *Te Deum*. Then, after swearing loyalty to the King of Castile, he was seated in the magistral throne to receive his brethren's homage amid the pealing of bells, after which there was a High Mass in thanksgiving. As Calatrava was attached to Morimond in Burgundy (the mother house of Fitero), like any dependent priory of white monks the latter's abbot confirmed each Maestre's election, performing an annual visitation. The Maestres' headquarters were in one of the larger commanderies, the castellan of Calatrava being the third great officer, the *Clavero*, who was assisted by a *sub-Clavero* and an *Obrero*, the latter a kind of quartermaster responsible for the house's maintenance. Next came the order's senior clerical officer, the *Gran Prior*, supported by a *Sacrista* or procurator. Always a French Cistercian from Morimond, as heir to Ramón, the *Gran Prior* wore a mitre and carried a crozier, residing at Calatrava where he held a chapter of the house's *freyles clerigos* each day. These lived a life almost indistinguishable from the white monks', using the Citeaux breviary.

Their habit was a hooded white, later grey, tunic. That of the *caballeros* was shorter than that of the *clerigos*, to facilitate riding. On active service knights wore a long sleeveless mantle like a Templar's, but with no cross and sometimes a fur-lined cloak. Armour was always black. Indoors both *freyles caballeros* and *clerigos* donned the full habit of a Cistercian choir monk, including his 'cowl', a pleated over-tunic with wide sleeves.[1] Professions were made to the Prior, later to the Master 'as though he were abbot' after a year's novitiate, who 'clothed' the brethren; there was a single vow of obedience in which those of chastity and poverty were implicit. Each brother was constantly reminded of a Christian's seven obligations, '*comer, bever, calcar, vestir, visitar, consolar, enterrar*' (to feed, give drink to, shoe, clothe, visit, console and bury, the sick, poor or afflicted). Meat was eaten only three times a week, and such offences as fornication were punished by flogging. Silence was kept in chapel, refectory, dormitory and kitchen, while every *caballero* recited the psalter ten times each year. However, knights sometimes sang the whole

[1] See O'Callaghan in *Analecta*, vol. 16., pp. 33–8.

Office with the chaplains, and after 1221 were allowed to sit with the choir monks in any monastery of the Citeaux obedience, entering refectories and chapterhouses forbidden to lay brethren.[1] On campaign they recited a specific number of 'paters' and 'aves'.

A chapter general was held at Calatrava, at Christmas, Easter and Pentecost, when all *caballeros* were bound to attend and receive the sacraments. Each *encomienda* was inspected annually by a knight and a chaplain to ensure that the rule was kept and fortifications maintained. These commanderies, manned by twelve experienced *freyles*, served as a blockhouse for their district, all able-bodied fighting men rallying to the *comendador* in times of danger. In 1179 an *encomienda* was founded in Aragon, at Alcañiz, to fight the Moors of Valencia. This became one of the Order's great houses, with many chaplains, and its conventual life resembled that at Calatrava.

Shortly after Abbot Ramón began his great enterprise, an *hermangilda* near Cáceres had offered its services to the Canons of St Eloi in León for the protection of pilgrims travelling to Compostella. About 1164 the knights of Cáceres were given Uclés to defend on the Castilian frontier south of the Guardiana, and in 1171 the papal-legate, Cardinal Jacinto, presented them with a rule while Alexander III recognised them as the Order of St James of the Sword in 1175.[2] By 1184, when their first Maestre, Frey Pedro Fernández de Fuente Encalato, was killed during the siege of Cáceres, the new brethren had made rapid progress. In Portugal they received several castles from Sancho I, including Palmela, and later acquired lands in France, Italy, Palestine, Carinthia, Hungary and even England. Alfonso IX, '*el Baboso*' (the Slobberer), endowed it with a tenth of all money coined in León. There were five *comendadores mayores* for León, Castile, Portugal, Aragon and Gascony. The priors of Uclés and San Marcos (León) were mitred, ranking as abbots.

Santiago based its rule on St Augustine's, evolving a structure of remarkable originality. Canons looked after the spiritual

---

[1] Ibid., vol. 16, p. 31.
[2] The definitive modern work is Lomax, *La Orden de Santiago 1170–1275*.

Fig. 4. A *frey-caballero* of Alcántara *c.* 1300 in the original habit of the Order. It is the same as that of a Cistercian monk save that the skirts have been shortened to facilitate riding. From Helyot.

welfare of the knights, who took vows of poverty, chastity and obedience,[1] while canonnesses tended pilgrims in separate guesthouses and hospitals. Each *encomienda* contained thirteen brethren, representing Christ and his apostles, as did the Great Council, the *'trezes'*, all celibate *comendadores* who elected the Maestre; in chapter these wore the black habit of their canons. What made Santiago so unusual was its incorporation of married knights, not just as *familiares* or confrères, but as full members who gave up their *patria potestas* and whose goods and families became technically part of the Order.[2] At certain times of the year they made retreats in the *encomiendas* and during Lent and Advent slept apart from their wives, but otherwise lived a normal married life.[3] Knights wore a white habit with a red cross on the shoulder, the bottom arm of which resembled a sword blade. This distinctive cross, the *espada*, was nicknamed the *Largetto* or Lizard. The *Santagnistas'* ferocious motto was 'Rubet ensis sanguine Arabum' (May the sword be red with Arab blood) and they appropriated the old battle cry, *'Santiago y cierra España'*, (St James and close in Spain!).[4]

Before 1170 a small *hermangilda* was operating on the Leónese frontier 'in the jaws of the Saracen'. This brotherhood, 'the Knights of San Julián de Pereiro', would one day become the Order of Alcántara. The brethren's historians afterwards concocted a legend that it was an earlier foundation than that of Calatrava; a certain Suero Fernández Barrientos was supposed to have come from Salamanca in 1156 to San Julián (about twenty-five miles from Ciudad Rodrigo) where a hermit showed him a site for a fortress, his ambition being to save his soul by fighting Moors, but soon after he was killed in battle. Certainly

---

[1] A thirteenth-century Castilian translation of the Rule of Santiago is printed in Lomax, op. cit., p. 221.
[2] See Lomax, p. 238 for a deed of 1190 in which Vitalia, wife of Frey Vitalis de Palombar, is received into the Order.
[3] Chastity was interpreted as 'coniugal castidad': the Rule comments that 'It is a better thing to marry than to be burnt in the flames'. (Clause 1.)
[4] The Rule states that 'The intention of all shall be to defend the Church of God, in order to give souls to Jesus Christ and to go against the Moors not for plunder but for the increase of the Faith of God'. (Clause 34.)

the brotherhood existed a decade later.[1] In 1176 their leader, Frey Gómez Fernández, was granted lands by Ferdinand II of León, and Pope Alexander recognised them as an Order with the right to elect a prior. Frey Gómez received the title of Maestre in 1183 from Lucius III. By 1187 the *Sanjuliánistas* had placed themselves under the protection of Calatrava, developing similar constitutions, though their prior was elected and was not a Cistercian. Brethren were divided into *caballeros* and *clerigos*, wearing a plain white habit.

The Portuguese 'brethren of Santa María' claimed to have been founded by the first king of Portugal's brother, Dom Pedro Henriques.[2] There is evidence that an *hermangilda* of this name guarded the open plains of the Alemtejo province in 1162. Four years later the brethren obtained a house at Évora, a hundred miles south of Lisbon, adopting the Benedictine rule suitably modified by a Cistercian abbot, João Zirita. But although the brethren took the title 'Knights of St Benedict' their inspiration was from Citeaux, and they accepted the Abbot of Tarouca's visitation. Later they too came under Calatrava's control, copying its constitutions. However, Évora was so weak that King Afonso returned to the Templars, who in 1169 were promised a third of any land they might conquer. Through this grant they obtained their famous stronghold at Thomar.[3]

New Orders proved effective in the Leónese and Castilian *estremadura*. The second Master of Calatrava, Frey Fernando Escaza, was a good frontiersman. On one occasion, after raiding Muradel and storming the castle of Ferral, the Moors caught up with him and he was besieged in the keep for ten days. However, the *freyles* galloped from Calatrava to his rescue, and he returned home in triumph with many prisoners and a great herd

[1] See J. F. O'Callaghan, 'The Foundation of the Order of Alcántara', *Catholic Historical Review*, vol. 47.

[2] See Joseph da Purificaõ, 'Catalogo dos Mestres e administradores de illustre e antiquissima Ordem Militar de Aviz', *C.A.R.H.P.*, vol. 2.

[3] The Master of the Portuguese Templars, Gualdim Paes, who reigned for nearly half a century and died in 1195, achieved almost folk hero status by his exploits against the Moors. See 'Catologo dos Mestres da Ordem do Templo Portugueza, e em outras da Hespanha', *C.A.R.H.P.* which credits him with 'immortal gloria'.

of cattle. Border warfare consisted mainly of razzias and skir-
mishes, often degenerating into mere horse-stealing and rustling.
His successor, Frey Martín Pérez de Siones, an Aragonese,
launched several savage expeditions. His most famous exploit
was after the Moors had captured the fortress at Almodovar and
killed seventy knights. He pursued them and took 200
prisoners, promptly cutting their throats. Santiago suffered a
temporary setback, losing Uclés to the Moors in 1176, but
recovering it the same year whereupon its Maestre made a
pilgrimage of thanksgiving to the Holy Land.[1] Nor was San
Julián idle, despite scanty resources. Frey Gómez gave valuable
assistance to Ferdinand II of León, and the next Maestre,
Benito Suárez, captured Almeida. Later, led by the Archbishop
of Toledo, the *Sanjuliánistas* carried out a particularly destructive razzia on the district between Jaén and Córdoba.

In 1194 King Alfonso VIII of Castile challenged Caliph
Yakub ibn-Yusuf to come to Spain and fight. The Almohad, a
fine soldier, marched out from Marrakesh the following year
with an enormous army accompanied by a pack of slave
dealers and, crossing the straits to al-Andalus, advanced north.
Alfonso hastened to meet them, but the kings of León and
Navarre failed to join him, supposedly insulted by his boast that
Castilian Knights could do the job alone. However, the Masters
of Calatrava and Santiago, Nuño Pérez de Quiñones and
Sancho Fernández de Lemos, who had sworn a pact of brotherhood, rode with him. Hopelessly outnumbered they advanced
to meet the caliph.

Spanish weapons and armour were those used throughout
Europe: sword and lance, steel helmet, chain tunic and shield.
Tactics were based on the single, decisive charge, though there
was a tendency to wear lighter equipment and ride Arab horses.
Auxiliary cavalry had little more than a bull-fighter's lance,
javelins and a knife. Infantry consisted of spearmen, slingers and
archers carrying swords or axes. A rich man's arms were often

[1] As in other military brotherhoods *caballeros* who sought a more contemplative life could, with their Master's permission, transfer to a house of
clerigos or to another Order. Lomax (op. cit., p. 94) cites the examples of
Maestre Fernando Díaz who became a canon of Santiago and of a brother
who joined the notoriously severe hermit Order of Grandmont.

7. The commandery of the Order of Santiago at Segura de la Sierra, Jaén.

8. The tomb of 'El Doncel', Frey Martín Vasquez de Arce, a *frey-caballero* of Santiago who was killed before Granada in 1486, in the cathedral at Siguenza. Note the Order's mantle and *espada*.

jewelled and damascened in the Saracen fashion, especially the superb swords from Toledo, while Andalusian mantles were worn and some knights preferred to use Moorish scimitars.

Almohad cavalry, Berber or Andalusian, wore mail shirts and spiked onion helmets, charging with spears held overarm or hurling javelins. Their swords were light scimitars, their shields heart-shaped, their armour often gilded or silvered and they used lassos or hooked lances to pull opponents from the saddle. The infantry were Negroes with broad-bladed stabbing spears and enormous hide shields, supported by archers and slingers, who could discharge lethal clay bullets from a surprising distance, while to demoralise the enemy there was always a band with drums, trumpets and cymbals. Moorish horsemen frequently swamped Spanish cavalry by sheer numbers, preventing them from choosing suitable ground or assembling their elaborate formations. If the Christians did manage to launch a charge its impact was often absorbed by a dense mass of Negro infantry sometimes roped together.

On 18 July 1195 Alfonso's army met the Berber horde outside the Moorish castle of Alarcos near Ciudad Real. Yakub made skilful use of his numbers and amid shrill war cries and the throbbing of drums the Castilians were annihilated; 25,000 were killed or taken prisoner, among them Frey Sancho and many brethren, though the King and the Master of Calatrava escaped, hotly pursued by Berber cavalry, to the *encomienda* of Guadalherza which they just managed to hold. Another group including some *freyles* tried to make a stand in a pass near La Zarzuela and were slaughtered to a man. Yakub advanced slowly north; within two years he had captured Guadalajara, Madrid, Uclés and Calatrava – whose chaplains were put to the sword. But he failed to take Toledo and his triumph would prove only a temporary setback for the Christians.

CHAPTER 9

The Great Advance

Alarcos must have seemed an irreparable disaster, for by 1197 two Orders had lost their mother houses and most knights were dead or slaves. When Calatrava's brethren set up a new head-quarters at Salvatierra nearby, calling themselves 'Knights of Salvatierra', they nearly succumbed to an Aragonese plot. Though Frey Nuño, a Leónese, had survived, the brethren of Alcañiz tried to secede, electing their *comendador*, García López de Moventi, as *Mestre;* Innocent III forced them to end this abortive schism, but Aragonese discontent still simmered, and in 1207 Maestre Ruy Díaz de Anguas was to recognise the *comanador* of Alcañiz as his Order's special representative to the King of Aragon.[1] The brotherhood was strong enough to endure both defeat and internal dissension. Islam was faced by a really effective fighting machine which knew how to fall back on prepared positions and which still held the *meseta.*

Kings were learning to depend on the *freyles*, and even on the international Orders, though probably these could seldom put more than twenty brethren in the field. Local Templar Masters and Hospitaller Priors had to be approved by the king, who frequently appropriated revenues intended for *Ultramar.*[2] Apart from the priory of Castile the territorial boundaries of the *caballeros de San Juan* never corresponded to those of the king-doms, the Portuguese priory including Galicia and the Navarrese northern Aragon, while Valencia was to become a separate unit under the castellan of Amposta. Though a bailiff was sometimes styled 'Grand Commander in Spain' his over-all jurisdiction was only theoretical. For promotion caravans against

[1] Rades, 'Discordia y scisma en la Orden', *Chrónica de Calatrava*, p. 21.
[2] Iberian Hospitallers frequently failed to send Responsions (revenues) to the convent and often ignored the Grand Master so occasionally one of their priors was nominated 'Grand Commander in Spain', with authority over all peninsular brethren of St John. See Riley-Smith, op. cit., p. 369.

the Moors were reckoned equal to those served in the Holy Land.

When the Almohads had invaded southern Portugal in 1190 and only Évora and Gualdim Paeis' Templars at Thomar held out, King Sancho I learnt a valuable lesson, afterwards erecting many *comendas* on the far side of the Tagus for the brethren of St Benedict. In 1211 Afonso II was to give the town of Aviz to the fourth recorded *Mestre* at Évora, Fernaõ Rodrigues Monteiro, whose brethren became known as Knights of Aviz.[1]

Meanwhile, frontier warfare continued with unflagging ferocity. The news of Salvatierra's evacuation in 1211 warned the pope that a massive Almohad offensive was imminent, and he proclaimed a crusade while Rodrigo Jimenez de Rada, Archbishop of Toledo, preached the Holy War. Next summer a large army assembled with detachments from all Iberian kingdoms save León, the Orders contributing many squadrons. There was also a large number of French and Italian crusaders, the Archbishop of Narbonne bringing 150 knights. Everyone, including the Kings of Aragon and Navarre, placed themselves under the command of the same Alfonso who had been defeated at Alarcos. They marched out from Toledo in June 1212, Archbishop Rodrigo riding at their head, carrying his cathedral's great silver cross. On 1 July, Calatrava was recaptured and restored to the brethren. Then a temporary shortage of provisions disgusted the foreign crusaders, who turned back. Weakened and discouraged, the Christian army continued its advance.

The Moorish army, both African and Andalusian, was thought to number 460,000, and though this figure is impossibly high it must still have been enormous. The young Caliph Muhammad III ibn-Yakub, melodiously named 'Miramamolin' by the Spaniards, selected a position at Hisn al-Uqab, afterwards known as Las Navas de Tolosa, which could only be approached through a narrow mountain pass, where he hoped to ambush the *Nasrani*. However, on the night of 15 July they succeeded in forcing the pass and reaching open ground suitable for heavy cavalry. Next morning they assembled their battle order. The

[1] See Cocheril, 'Essai sur l'origine des Ordres Militaires dans la Péninsule Iberique'.

centre was commanded by King Alfonso, the right wing by
Sancho VIII of Navarre, the left, which included the Orders,
by Pere II of Aragon. Here the Hospitallers were led by the
Prior of Castile, Frey Gutierre de Armildez, the Templars by
their Castilian Master, Frey Gómez Ruiz and Calatrava by
Frey Ruy Díaz. Santiago's Master, Frey Pedro Arias, rode with
the centre as the host's standard bearer. The fight began badly.
The Christians' charges were beaten back, the Moors concentrating on the centre and left, encouraged by their caliph who
directed operations from a great red velvet tent, wearing his
ancestor's black cloak, scimitar in one hand, *koran* in the other,
surrounded by fakirs and hedged by a bodyguard of gigantic
Negroes linked with iron chains. When Frey Pedro was slain
Alfonso began to lose heart. The Aragonese *Templarios* were
killed to a man and their Castilian brethren suffered ghastly
losses, but covering themselves with glory, the *freyles* of
Calatrava in blood-stained white habits refused to budge. They
were decimated and Frey Ruy lost an arm. However, the
Almohad onslaught was halted, whereupon King Sancho
smashed the Africans with a final decisive charge, breaking
through to the caliph's pavilion and cutting down his guard.
Muhammad fled, followed by the remnant of his host. It was
Islam's bloodiest defeat.[1]

Al-Andalus was doomed, for the victory opened up the valley
of the Guadalquivir exposing the Córdoban heartland. Military
Orders were the shock troops of the inevitable offensive, the
Masters acting as strategic advisers. Their scouts and spy service
gave them an unrivalled knowledge of the terrain and enemy
fortifications. Not only did the kings use *freyles* as panzers, but
they employed them to consolidate the advance, endowing the
brethren with vast tracts of land. Before it had been difficult to
attract settlers to the south. All too often frontier life ended in
red ruin. Moorish razzias on border villages were conducted
with great slaughter, men being impaled or crucified, women
raped and disembowelled, their babies tossed on spearpoints.
To desperate peasants holding out in the village church against
a *rabito* the brethren's arrival must have seemed like divine

[1] There is a colourful account of this battle in Rades, *Chrónica de Calatrava*,
pp. 28–30.

intervention – *freyles* had the glamour of Texas rangers rather than the chilly halo of pious crusaders. Now colonists were protected by their patrols and blockhouses while chaplains converted resentful *mudéjares*.[1]

Encomiendas tended to be priory towns rather than isolated strongholds, the actual commandery usually being centred on a rectangular Spanish keep, or *torre del homenaje*, with extravagantly machicolated corner towers to facilitate arrow fire and oil pouring. Often there was a watchtower outside the walls, a *torre alberrano*, connected only by a plank bridge with the *encomienda*, as at Zorita de los Canes (Calatrava). Chapels were always of particular magnificence, like that of Calatrava la Nueva with its great rose window (see pl. 11). Built of stone or yellow brick the architecture frequently reflected Moorish influence, though the *encomienda*-castle of Maqueda (Calatrava), north-west of Toledo on the road from Madrid to Extremadura, was in the French style – a square bastille with massive round towers. At Calatrava la Vieja a castle of this sort with rectangular bastions overlooked the town flanked by the conventual buildings and another smaller fortress; the style was plain and typically Cistercian though, later, *mudéjar* arcades with horse-shoe arches were added while the chapel was a converted mosque. At Aviz a town grew up beside the castle and priory, which were separate in the peninsular fashion. Iberian Orders never evolved a specific pattern of *domus conventualis*, even if a few *encomiendas* were fortress monasteries like Alfama in Valencia and Osuna (Calatrava) near Seville, but usually castle and conventual buildings were separate as at Alcañiz, a compound enclosed by a curtain wall.

In 1217 Alfonso of León gave Alcántara, which guards the great Roman bridge (*al-Cantara* – the bridge) over the Tagus near the Portuguese border, to Frey Martín Fernández de Quintana, the new Master of Calatrava, but next year Frey Martín made a pact with the Master of the Sanjuliánistas, Frey Nuño Fernández, ceding the town and all possessions of Calatrava in León. San Julián, sometimes called the Order of Trujillo, was renamed Alcántara. Its second house was

[1] This point, that brethren protected colonists and aided agriculture, is made by Almeida, *Historia da Igreja em Portugal*, vol., I, p. 552.

Magazella, also a priory-commandery. In 1218 Calatrava transferred all Portuguese properties to Aviz, preferring to consolidate its main territory, which eventually ran from Toledo to the Sierra Nevada, including La Mancha and the upper waters of the Guardiana and Guadalquivir. In 1216 the mother house was moved to Calatrava la Nueva in the Sierra de Atalayo, as Calatrava la Vieja had lost its strategic value. Here the crippled Maestre Ruy Díaz who had abdicated on the battlefield of Las Navas spent his last days with great saintliness.

The *freyles* not only cultivated their estates with *mudéjar* slaves but also exploited the barren *mesetas* in true Cistercian style, ranching cattle, horses, goats, pigs and, in particular, sheep, all half-wild, driving them into the high sierras during the summer. They owned some of the best pastures in Spain. Directed from the *encomiendas* their serving brothers made excellent herdsmen, and the wool, meat and hides fetched good prices. Business became still more profitable when Merino sheep were introduced from Morocco about 1300. Spanish landowners were to copy the knights' *haciendas* and bring them to the New World, and so the monkish frontiersmen could claim to be the first cowboys.

In 1217 the Spanish St Louis became King Fernando III of Castile. *Fernando el Santo* resembled the Frenchman in his grim orthodoxy and hatred of infidels. A Franciscan tertiary who wore a hair shirt, fasted and spent long hours in prayer, he claimed to fear the curse of a single poor Christian woman more than the anger of a whole Moorish host. But the Castilian was also a ruthless statesman and brilliant general. He saw the Reconquista as a war no less holy than the Syrian crusade, and when Louis asked him to come to Outremer, Fernando replied, 'There is no lack of Moors in my own country.' He spent the night before each battle in prayer and his character was typical of those who entered military Orders.[1]

Now that African rule in Andalusia had collapsed, *taifas* reappeared. The king promised the brethren new lands. They raided ceaselessly, returning with severed heads dangling from their saddles, for they had learnt Moorish ways. It was the

[1] 'In fine, he acted the part of a good Man and a Just Prince' – John Stevens, *The General History of Spain* (London, 1699).

Moslems' turn to complain of butchered women and children. By 1225 rival claimants were squabbling bloodily for the Almohad throne, and the Castilian army, whose real objective was Córdoba, raided Jaén, while the *freyles* of Calatrava captured Andújar. Fernando then intervened in the Almohad succession, sending an army to Morocco which gained Marrakesh for his ally Mamoun. The king's strength was doubled by his succession to the Leónese throne in 1230. Each year he conquered more territory. In 1231 he took Trujillo with assistance from the Master of Alcántara, and though Frey Pedro González, Master of Santiago, was killed in 1232 besieging Alcaraz it fell to his successor. Next year the king faced a capable opponent at Jerez de la Frontera, ibn-Hud, Emir of Murcia: only ten Christians died in the battle, but Moors were slain by the thousand, fleeing in terror. In 1234 Fernando drove the infidels out of Ubeda, where the *freyles* of Calatrava and Santiago distinguished themselves. When at this time the king summoned the Master of Alcántara he came with 600 horse and 2,000 foot; his Order was growing steadily more formidable. Meanwhile the Castilians were enlarging their bridgehead near Córdoba.

The Aragonese Reconquista was entirely separate from the Castilian struggle. The Moorish war had been neglected until the Albigensian crusade put an end to aspirations north of the Pyrenees. Then Jaume the Conqueror stormed the pirate's nest of Majorca. Minorca surrendered four years later while Ibiza was taken by the Archbishop of Tarragona in 1235. Aragonese were as different from Castilians as Portuguese. Catalan, the official tongue, was closer to Provençal than Castilian; 'brethren' were *'els frares cavallers i clergues'*. Although the kings endowed Templars and Hospitallers generously, especially the latter's convent at Sigena, their attempts to found an Aragonese brotherhood failed dismally.[1] The obscure Brothers of St George of Alfama were founded about 1200, following the Augustinian rule and sporting a white habit, but they achieved little. By 1233 a Provençal nobleman, Pere Nolasco, had organised a confraternity of 'Mercedarians' to ransom penniless Christian slaves,

[1] In 1221 King Fernando ordered that Monfrac – the rump of Montjoie – should be incorporated with Calatrava.

and as these must be rescued by every means including war the new Order was given a military organisation. Its habit was white, like all Iberian military orders, while a small shield bearing the royal arms of Aragon hung from the neck. Clerical brethren had gained control by 1317, when the Order ceased to be military, though honorary knights continued to be appointed. In practice these Mercedarians were probably never more than supernumerary troops.

In 1236 Christian troops raiding the suburbs of Córdoba discovered that it was almost undefended. Immediately the king was informed. He arrived quickly with reinforcements, including a detachment from Calatrava. The Murcian ibn-Hud tried to save the ancient capital of Abd al-Rahman and al-Mansur, but dared not face the Castilian army and rode off in despair. Fernando ordered those who would not accept the true faith to leave Córdoba and then marched into the deserted city. He turned the still glorious mosque into a cathedral, dedicating it to the Blessed Virgin.

Meanwhile the Aragonese were proving equally successful. King Jaume burst through the Valencian mountains in 1233, reaching the Sierra de Espadan, and was soon in front of the capital. The only brethren present were twenty Templars. After a long siege Moorish Valencia, the city of the Cid, surrendered in September 1238, 'King Zayne' recognising Jaume as the kingdom's ruler north of Xuxcar; but by 1253 the latter controlled the whole country. The Reconquista of the east coast was complete.

These spectacular advances had a tactical explanation. The Almohad collapse took away the Moors' numerical superiority, so that enveloping tactics became impossible. Now the Christians used their own light cavalry to hold down the Moors and, having chosen the terrain, each charge achieved the maximum impact. Almost invariably this broke the Moorish battle order, rolling over their small Arab horses and riding the infantry into the ground.[1]

A determined attack was made on Murcia in 1243, and,

[1] Fighting did not make them forget religious duties; in 1245 the Cistercian Chapter-General described Calatrava as 'membrum nobile et speciale Ordinis Cisterciensis'. See O'Callaghan, op. cit., vol. 16, p. 287.

seeing no hope, the wali of the capital surrendered. Fernando went on to capture Jaén and Carmona before investing Seville in 1247. Surrounded by hills covered with olive orchards, with its beautiful mosque, the pink *Giralda*, its libraries, pleasure gardens, orange groves and luxurious baths, and guarded by the river Guadalquivir, flanked each side by lighthouses with gilded roofs, the former capital of the Almohads recalled the splendours of Córdoba under the caliphs. Its junta had neglected to ally with other *taifas* and found itself isolated. Wisely the junta entrusted its beautiful city's defence to the brave wali of Niebla, Abu Ja'far. Ramón Bonifaz, Castile's 'emir of the sea', destroyed the Moorish fleet in the Guadalquivir, cutting off all hope of African relief. An Andalusian army gathered in the hills among the villages, 'which gleamed like white stars in a sky of olives', but was cut to pieces by Fernando and Muhammad ibn-al-Ahmar, ruler of Granada; Abu Ja'far must have watched the rout from the great tower-minaret. Assault parties in which *freyles* of Santiago and Calatrava were prominent hammered at the Sevillanos night and day. The city's once-crowded wharves, divided by the river, were joined by a bridge of boats, but during a storm the Christians broke it in two, ramming the light craft with heavy-laden ships. Then they burst into Tirana, the northern suburb, whose inhabitants fought to the death. Finally, after a siege of sixteen months, Seville surrendered. Many of its grief-stricken citizens departed to Granada or Africa. First to enter were 270 *Santaguistas* whose Master planted the red damask standard of St James and the white horse high on the city walls.[1] Fernando rode in to dedicate the mosque to Our Lady and celebrate Christmas. It was here that the noblest Spaniard of the Middle Ages chose to be buried, in a Franciscan habit, when he died in 1252.

There were many new *encomiendas* and priories to pray for his soul, including convents of nuns. Those of Calatrava followed the Cistercian rule. However, some sisters of Santiago were married; these did not have the white cloak, but wore a black

---

[1] Significantly this Master was long remembered in his Order as 'el Josue español'. See Lomax, 'A Lost Mediaeval Biography: the Crónica del Maestre Pelayo Pérez' in *Bulletin of Hispanic Studies*, XXXVIII (1961).

6*

habit like the Order's chaplains who ranked as canons regular.
Mother superiors were known as *comendadoras*.

Fernando's successor Alfonso X had ambitions of playing
'Solomon' to his father's 'David'. Learned rather than wise,
el Sabio was a patron of lawyers and astronomers but was no
politician, reigning with great pomp and singular ineptitude.
Nonetheless, the early years of his reign saw the destruction of
what remained of western Andalus. By 1251 the Orders (notably
Portuguese Santiago under Gonçalo Péres, *Comendador-Mor* of
Palmela) had finally conquered and subdued the eastern
Algarve, while in 1262 Castile captured the strong city of Niebla
and then the port of Cádiz and, a year later, Cartagena.

There were urgent problems of administration and resettle-
ment. The only solution was to grant large estates to the nobles
and the Orders. As early as 1158 Abbot Ramón had brought
peasants from his domain at Fitero. Maestres and *ricos hombres*
attracted colonists by *fueros*, charters which offered both townsmen and peasants more freedom than elsewhere. Soon the south
flourished again, though the crown derived scant profit. The
great lords' sole obligation was to provide troops, and they ruled
their vast *latifundios* like independent princes. *Freyles* benefited
most of all.[1] Eventually Calatrava's lands reached to the Sierra
Nevada while Alcántara owned half Extremadura. Santiago's
possessions equalled those of both Orders put together. Hebrew
stewards ran these estates very profitably indeed. In 1272 Frey
Gonzalo Ruiz Girón, Master of Santiago, farmed his rents in
Murcia, Toledo and La Mancha to Jewish bankers Don Bono,
Don Jacobo and Don Samuel.[2] Nonetheless brethren themselves
spent much time in estate management.

The *mudéjares* must have been heartened by the Mameluke
victory in Syria at Ain-Jalud in 1260. Grasping settlers had
goaded the Moorish landowners of Murcia beyond endurance,
and suddenly in 1264 they rose without warning to massacre the
Christians. Hundreds of towns and villages repudiated Castilian

[1] There was of course some rivalry, with inevitable wrangling over lands
and jurisdiction. See Lomax, op. cit., ch. VI under 'La rivalidad con
Calatrava' and 'disputas territoriales y fiscales'.
[2] An agreement between these bankers – don Bono, don Jacobo and don
Samuel – and the Master of Santiago is printed in ibid., pp. 270–1.

rule and it took Alfonso two years, even with help from Aragon, to crush this desperate revolt. The Reconquista had ground to a halt.

Al-Andalus was now confined to the kingdom of Granada. The creator of this last *taifa* was a border chieftain, Muhammad ibn-Yusuf ibn-Ahmed ibn-Nasr, called al-Ahmar, who realised that, since the Sierra Morena and the Guadalquivir had been lost, Spanish Islam must find new frontiers. The mountainous region around Granada – where he installed himself in 1238 – was ideal, extending from the sea to the Serranía de Ronda and the Sierra de Elvira, with the Sierra de Nevada as a backbone, while its ports gave access to Africa. Al-Ahmar came to terms with the Reconquista. When Ferdinand was besieging Jaén in 1246 the sultan suddenly rode into his camp to pay homage, and as Ferdinand's vassal he intervened decisively at Seville. His most remarkable innovation was European armour, and Granadine troops began to wear Spanish mail and ride heavier horses, attacking in dense formations. Supported by *jinetes*, the traditional light cavalry, this new army proved most effective. Granada was a microcosm of al-Andalus. Refugees had fled to it from all over the peninsula; many Granadine labourers were supposedly descended from Moorish noblemen. Its capital's glories are well known, especially the Alhambra with its Court of Lions and Court of Myrtles, red towers, delicate pavilions, flower gardens and cool fountains, but the seaports of Malaga and Almeria were even richer. Peasants tilled and irrigated every inch of fertile soil, famous for wheat and fruit. Merchants exported silks, jewellery and slaves, returning with African and Asiatic spices, while a vigorous intellectual life produced many poets and historians. With its exotic luxury and in the certainty of ultimate doom, Granada had some affinities with Outremer.

When al-Ahmar died in 1273 a new Berber dynasty was established at Fez, the *Banu Marin* under the gifted Yakub, a philosopher-warrior. Muhammad II, of Granada, offered him Tarifa, north-west of Gibraltar. Yakub arrived in 1275 with his Berber '*Guzat*', fanatical troops similar to the rabitos. The Moroccan horde swarmed up to Jerez in the old style, killing and burning. Yakub then retired but launched another raid in 1279.

Christian Spain lived in dread of another Moslem invasion.

The Reconquista made small progress during the reigns of Sancho IV (1284–94) and Ferdinand IV (1294–1312), though the former took Tarifa and the latter Gibraltar, attacking from the seaward side. The rock was too exposed to attract settlers, so Ferdinand granted it a *fuero* giving asylum to all criminals, robbers, murderers and even women who had run away from their husbands. Then it was the turn of Islam. In 1319 the two Castilian regents perished in 'the disaster of the Vega' and the frontier towns were so horrified that they formed a league to make peace with Granada at any cost. Five years later the Berbers took Baza and Martos, and then in 1333 recaptured Gibraltar.

All this time the brethren continued to raid. Like their opponents the Spaniards slew and laid waste, torturing prisoners to discover treasure, just as later they would do with Incas or Aztecs. The background was the hot yellow plains, their monotony broken only by rocks, olive orchards and the sheep which grazed on the parched dusty scrub, the bleak sierras with deep valleys and high passes, or the carefully tilled Granadine *vega*. Towns were built of whitewashed mud brick, their narrow streets resembling a Moroccan souk. Despite its dangers the military vocation had become an attractive career; a *comendador* was a rich landowner. Before, a desire for spiritual perfection had been the sole requirement for a postulant, but by the end of the thirteenth century Orders stipulated that he must show all four grandparents to have been of noble birth.[1] Every race has a patrician ideal and the Spanish *hidalgo* was distinguished by aloof dignity and really diabolical pride, a type particularly common in Castile, that land of *caballeros y piedras* ('knights and stones'). Spaniards were notorious for bloodthirsty tempers in a violent age; Sancho IV, *el Bravo*, murdered a favourite with his own hands while several Castilian kings stabbed their enemies to death. Iberian Orders were continually rent by vicious

[1] At the Chapter of 1259 Santiago reserved castellanries for *freyles* of noble blood, limited profession to candidates of knightly birth and reserved many privileges to brethren – lay and clerical – of knightly birth. Lomax (op. cit p. 88) believes that before this date many *freyles caballeros* must have been of plebeian origin.

quarrels.[1] Nonetheless, they were proud of their history. A *frey-caballero* of Santiago, Pere López de Baeza (fl. c. 1329), *comendador* of Mohernando, wrote a brief chronicle of his brother-hood's origins. No doubt this was read in the refectories.

By this date Maestres were transformed into princes with rich *encomiendas* in their gift, who could not only command the Orders' troops but hire mercenaries. Half of Calatrava's revenues, the *mesa maestral*, went to the Master, who on one occasion brought 1,200 lances to the field. A magistral palace was built near Ciudad Real at Almagro in the centre of Calatrava's enormous domains, which became the administrative capital and which, though its Gothic splendours have not survived, was probably the nearest approach to a Spanish Marienburg. At Alcántara *freyles* kept their court in a palace next to the castle. Maestres now spent too much time with the king and the Chapter of Calatrava had to stipulate that their Master must visit Calatrava at least three times a year. Instead of the Gran Prior, the Maestre of Calatrava began to profess knight brethren themselves, an innovation copied by Alcántara and Aviz. Masters were exposed to many temptations, for it was easy to defy authority. The feudal levies' disorderly appearance made the *freyles'* discipline all the more alarming and the spectacle of silent squadrons trotting past, superbly-mounted cavalrymen in black armour and hooded white habits, must have been extraordinarily impressive. Inevitably they became involved in politics.

In 1287 the Portuguese Master of Alcántara took his *freyles* to the aid of King Dinis of Portugal, whose brother the Infante Dom Afonso was in revolt. By this date Portuguese Saõ Thiago (Santiago), under pressure from Dinis, had become a separate order, electing its own *Mestre* at the headquarters in Palmela, though it was many years before Castile recognised the secession.[2] Aviz had received the visitation by Frey Martín

---

[1] In 1297 there was a fierce struggle for the Mastership of Calatrava between Frey Gutierre Pérez, the *comendador mayor*, and Frey García López de Padilla, the *clavero*, which the abbot of Morimond's visitation failed to solve. See O'Callaghan, *The Affiliation* ... etc., vol. 16, p. 256.

[2] Saõ Thiago was not properly independent until John XXII's bull of 1317. See F. de Almeida, op. cit., vol. I, p. 330.

Ruiz of Calatrava as late as 1238 but was, in practice, independent. Lack of strong authority and employment on purely secular campaigns weakened the vocation.[1] In 1292 Frey Ruy Pérez Ponce, Master of Calatrava, demanded payment from Sancho IV when asked to garrison Tarifa.

Unrest was perhaps highest at Alcántara. In 1318 some brethren, both *caballeros* and *clerigos*, complained to Master Garcia López de Padilla of Calatrava that their own Master, Frey Ruy Vásquez, was ill-treating them. Calatrava had the right of visitation, so Frey Garcia arrived at Alcántara with two Cistercian abbots, whereupon Ruy, his *comendador mayor* and the *clavero*, barricaded themselves in the conventual buildings, protesting that the privilege had lapsed. However, a chapter of only twenty-two knights declared Frey Ruy deposed and stormed the *encomienda*; Suero Pérez de Maldonado was elected Master in his place. Ruy Vásquez escaped to Morimond and appealed but the abbot recognised the deposition's legality, forbidding Frey Ruy to leave France. This lamentable incident indicates spiritual decline, though the Master of Alcántara still remained a power in the land, and in 1319 Frey Suero attended the wedding of Ferdinand's sister to the King of Aragon, making an *hermandad* with the Masters of Calatrava and Santiago the same year.[2]

The suppression of the Templars gave the peninsula two new brotherhoods. King Dinis did not wish St John to become overmighty in Portugal, and, as the pope would not agree to the crown's acquisition of the Poor Knights' property, the king created the Order of the Knights of Christ, simply deleting the words 'of the Temple' from their title. In 1318 the new brotherhood was installed in all former Templar preceptories, though it is unlikely that any Poor Knights were admitted. The first *Mestre* was a brother of Aviz, Dom Gil Martins, who by 1321 had sixty-nine knights, nine chaplains and six sergeants, with

---

[1] 'Thus, the Reconquista degenerated into a series of tournaments between Christian and Moorish knights, while the ideal of the monk-warrior "religioso-guerrero" which had inspired the brethren changed slowly into the courtier knight of the romances.' Lomax, op.cit., p. 99.

[2] See Rades, 'Deposicion del Maestre', *Chrónica de Alcántara*, p. 15.

constitutions modelled on those of Aviz and Calatrava.[1] Under the *Mestre* was the *Prior Mor* – who summoned brethren to the castle-convent at Castro Marim for magistral elections – the *comendador mor*, the *claveiro*, and the *alferes* or standard-bearer.

The Aragonese Order of Montesa was erected on the ruins of the Temple, with Fra. Guillem d'Eril as *Mestre*; several Mercedarian Knights enrolled now that their own brotherhood had ceased to be military. Like the Knights of Christ, the Order of Montesa was based on a headquarters house staffed by knight and chaplain brethren with a prior and *clavero*, and affiliated to the White Monks. Its first members, including Fra. Guillem, were mainly Aragonese *frares* of Calatrava, whose *comanador major* presided over its inauguration, assisted by Hospitallers, Mercedarians and Knights of Alfama. The brethren retained the white mantle, but unlike the Portuguese exchanged their red cross for a black one. They took their name from their headquarters, a former Templar preceptory in Valencia where more Moslems remained than anywhere in Spain. Here they could deal with *mudéjar* revolts or pirate raids. Soon the new brethren numbered four or five times as many as their predecessors, which resulted in severe impoverishment, and they seem to have had difficulty in recruiting chaplains. Though rich and respected, the three orders – Montesa, Calatrava at Alcañiz, and Santiago at Montalbán[2] – never dominated Aragonese politics.[3]

Alfonso XI (1312–50) was the leader who met and broke the Moslem resurgence. His subjects feared him even more than the Moors, for he used treachery and murder to intimidate the nobles, killing rebels without trial. They called him 'the avenger'

[1] Almeida, op. cit., vol. I, p. 340.

[2] Montalbán – confusingly spelt Montalaun by Rades – was the *comanadoria major* in Aragon and was accompanied by a priory which was the only house of *Santeaguista* canons in that kingdom.

[3] During the many revolts in fourteenth-century Aragon '. . . among the few who firmly supported the king were the Castellan of Amposta, the Master of Montesa and the *comendador major* of the Order of Santiago in Aragon'. See Luttrell, *The Aragonese Crown and the Knights Hospitallers of Rhodes 1291–1350*. The same authority makes the point that by the mid fourteenth century the Aragonese Hospitallers firmly controlled by the king had almost become a national as well as an international Order, pp. 17–18.

or 'the implacable' but admired his grim courage. In the end
they named him after his finest victory, '*el rey del Río Salado*'.
He was determined to be a strong king and as he could not merge
the brotherhoods into a single royal military Order he brought
them firmly under his control. The beginning of his personal rule
coincided with a peculiarly unedifying display on the part of
Calatrava.

Since 1325 the aged Maestre of Calatrava, Garcia López,
had been quarrelling with his *comendador mayor*, Juan Núñez de
Prado, who disputed the *maestrazgo*, alleging that Frey Garcia
had shown cowardice in the battle of Baena, abandoning the
Order's standard.[1] After a pitched battle, the old man agreed to
abdicate in return for the rich *encomienda* of Zorita de los Canes.
Frey Juan was duly installed in 1329 but then refused to honour
the bargain. The indignant Frey Garcia thereupon set himself
up as Master in Aragon and though he died in 1336 the schism
lasted until 1348, when En Joan Fernández, the *comanador major*,
recognised the Castilian Maestre, though Alcañiz remained
semi-autonomous. Soon the *comanadoria major* had the authority
of a separate *mestrat*.

Alfonso needed crack troops led by good generals, not a
squabbling rabble under fractious grandees, and in 1335 he
forced the abdication of Alcántara's Master, Ruy Pérez de
Maldonado, precipitating a bitter struggle within the Order
which lasted for over two years until, after a short but bloody
siege, Valencia de Alcántara was stormed by royal troops and
the Master, Gonzalo Martínez, beheaded and burned. Alfonso[2]
then installed the obedient Nuño Chamiro. There was even

[1] See Rades, *Chrónica de Calatrava*, pp. 50–1 – 'vn llano cerca de Vaena'.
Also O'Callaghan, op. cit., vol. 16, p. 260.

[2] See Rades, *Chrónica de Alcántara*, p. 23 – '. . . le hizo degollar y aun hizo
quemar su cuerpo'. Also Stevens, op. cit., p. 261 – 'D. Gonzalo Martínez
or Núñez of Calatrava was impeach'd of several hainous Crines and
being Summon'd to appear and answer for himself, fled to the King of
Granada. . . . Nevertheless in the Spring the King went into *Andaluzia* and
besieg'd the Master of *Calatrava* in *Valencia* a Town within the Bounds of
the Antient Lusitania. He was taken, condemn'd as a Traytor, Beheaded
and Burnt for a Terror to others.' (Here Mariana has confused Calatrava
with Alcantára.)

greater interference with Santiago. When Maestre Vasco
Rodríguez Coronado died in 1338, Alfonso ordered the *trezes*
to elect his eight-year-old bastard by Leonor de Guzmán, Don
Fadrique. Instead they chose Frey Vasco López, whereupon the
king advanced on Uclés and Frey Vasco fled to Portugal.
Alfonso forced the brethren to depose him and accept Leonor's
brother, Alonso Méndez de Guzmán, promising the succession
to Fadrique. Frey Alonso was killed two years later, upon which
the ten-year-old boy was solemnly installed as Master of
Santiago.

Alfonso was faced by an alliance between the able Sultan
Yusuf of Granada and the formidable Marinid Abul Hassan,
'the Black Sultan'; both dreamt of recovering their 'lost land'
just as did Henry V of France or Louis IX of Outremer. In 1340
the African fleet defeated the Castilian navy off Gibraltar,
sinking thirty-two warships, whereupon Abul Hassan of Fez
landed at Algeciras with the largest Moorish army seen in Spain
since the Almohads. Granadine troops hastened to join the
Marinids and Tarifa was invested. It took Alfonso six months
to gather his army, which assembled at Seville by October. By
northern standards Spanish troops were old-fashioned, their
armour too light. The king had one modern asset – cannon,
thick tubes of cast iron bound with iron bands, firing large stones;
frequently these blew up, killing their brave gunners. Alfonso
himself commanded the centre, accompanied by the Archbishop
of Toledo, and all three Maestres, Nuño Chamiro of Alcántara,
Juan Núñez of Calatrava and Alonso Meléndez de Guzmán of
Santiago. Alfonso IV of Portugal arrived with 1,000 lances and
sent ships to the joint Castilian-Catalan fleet commanded by the
Hospitaller Prior of Castile, Alfonso Ortiz Calderón. Tarifa still
held out.

Though a few Granadines had European armour, most
Moorish horsemen were lightly equipped *jinetes* and Abul
Hassan relied on numbers and speed. On 30 October Alfonso
attacked him at the river Salado, the Portuguese taking the
Granadines, the Castilians the Moroccans. Suddenly a sortie
from Tarifa burst into the unguarded enemy camp. The Moors
panicked and the Christians proved heavy enough to break
them, Berbers and Granadines fleeing with ghastly losses.

Christian casualties were relatively light, though Frey Alonso died a glorious death. Santiago and the Hospitallers had ridden with the Castilians, Calatrava and Alcántara with the Portuguese. It was the end of the Marinid threat.

Alfonso invested the port of Algeciras in 1342, beginning a long siege during which two Masters of Alcántara died; one drowned fording the river Guadarranque at night, whilst his successor succumbed to wounds.[1] The straits of Gibraltar were again blockaded. Early in 1344 the Earls of Derby and Arundel arrived in Alfonso's camp, and he used them to impress a Moorish embassy, who were intrigued by the Englishmen's ornate crests – animals and perhaps even an odd Saracen's head modelled in boiled leather. Chaucer's knight was present at this siege, possibly in the earls' retinue.[2] The starving town surrendered the same year, in March.

One last Moroccan foothold remained – Gibraltar. In 1350 Alfonso advanced on the rock with a large army, but the Black Death came to its rescue and he died of bubonic plague. The Moors admired their savage enemy and a number joined the black-robed mourners of his funeral procession as it crossed the sands. This cruel, brilliant soldier was the last king of Castile able to unite his subjects in Holy War. Unfortunately he had involved the brethren even more deeply in secular politics. Now kings would use them to fight barons instead of Moors.

[1] Torres y Tapia, *Crónica de la Orden de Alcántara*, vol. II, p. 50.
[2] See Russell, *English Intervention in Spain and Portugal in the time of Edward III and Richard II.*

Kings and Masters

Alfonso's son, the boy Pedro III, inherited a kingdom which was almost impossible to govern. 'Bastard feudalism' was in full, noxious flower: great lords hired troops, keeping these private armies on a permanent footing, and even the townsmen's *cofradias* – municipal leagues – had their own soldiers. Alfonso had left a *maîtresse en titre* the haughty Leonor de Guzmán, with five sons, the eldest being Enrique, Count of Trastámara, and Fadrique, Master of Santiago.[1] She was dangerous and ambitious for her children, and King Pedro murdered her in 1351. Next year Enrique rebelled, beginning a long and terrible struggle for the crown. The king's problem was to survive at all for he had little money, few troops, no obvious allies and an uncontrollable nobility. Pedro therefore turned to treachery and murder so that a chronicle of his reign reads like a Gothic novel, his courtiers in their fantastic clothes appearing as tragic players against a background of perpetual pageant with the rich tones of a Catalan altarpiece in the royal palaces at Seville or Valladolid. *Freyles caballeros* in woollen tunics and white mantles stood out among this living tapestry for they had to spend much time at court with their Maestres.

Enrique of Trastámara schemed with implacable hatred. In 1354 a second rising was very nearly successful and the Maestre of Santiago joined his brother, but was reconciled with Pedro the following year. The king had to make sure of the Orders. Frey Fernán Pérez Ponce de León,[2] Alcántara's Maestre, would not submit and was deposed, as was his successor, Diego

---

[1] Doña Leonor de Guzmán retained the seal of Santiago on behalf of her son, after the death of her brother, the Master Alfonso Meléndez de Guzmán. See Ayala, *Crónica del Rey Don Pedro* (1779), vol. I, p. 22. A footnote cites the Bullarium of Santiago.

[2] Rades, *Chrónica de Alcántara*, p. 25 – Don Fernán Pérez Ponce was Dona Leonor's cousin.

Gutiérrez de Zavallos, who proved equally unsuitable, the *freyles* being forced to take Suero Martínez as their superior. Old Juan Núñez of Calatrava had tactlessly criticised the royal mistress, Blanche de Padilla, and then intrigued with Aragon; he was arrested at Almagro and taken to the commandery of Maqueda, where his throat was cut.[1] He left two bastard sons but it was his nephew who avenged him, the *Comendador Mayor*, Pedro Estevañez Carpenteiro. The brethren elected Frey Pedro, whereupon the king ordered them to install Blanche's brother, Diego García de Padilla. The *Comendador Mayor* proclaimed himself Master at the *encomienda* of Osuna, mustering 600 lances and occupying Calatrava. The Order was split. When the anti-Master finally surrendered at Toro in 1355 he was brought to the royal palace, where the king personally butchered him in the presence of the queen-mother.[2] Finally in 1358 King Pedro lured Frey Fadrique of Santiago to Seville. The Master was hunted through the Alcázar by the arbalestier guards who clubbed him to death with maces;[3] he was still breathing, and Pedro gave his own dagger to a Moorish slave to finish the job. Santiago then elected García Álvarez de Toledo with royal approval. The king now controlled the only real armies in Castile.

His power was at its zenith in 1362 when Pere IV, '*lo Ceremonios*', of Aragon, was all but defeated. Since Castile was now allied with England, the despairing Enrique had to take refuge in France. The Moors had become friends. When in 1359 the emir Abu Said seized power, the deposed Muhammad V fled to Fez, but, receiving no help from the Marinids, tried Seville. Pedro welcomed him, lent him troops and money, and set him up at Ronda from whence he recovered Granada in 1362. In his turn Abu Said, 'the Red King', took refuge

---

[1] See Rades, *Chrónica de Calatrava*, p. 54 – 'Don Iuan Núñez de Prado degollado'.

[2] Ibid., p. 56 – 'El Rey mato a don Pedro Estevañez'. Rades says that King Pedro 'le dio de estocadas delante de la Reyna su madre, y fue luego muerto'. However, Ayala (op. cit., p. 208) says that he was clubbed to death with a mace by the squire of his rival as Master, Diego García de Padilla, outside the castle.

[3] Ayala, op. cit., pp. 240–2. – the slave was 'un mozo de su camera'.

with Pedro, who promptly murdered him.[1] No doubt Diego García of Calatrava mourned him, as he had once been taken prisoner by Abu Said and released after a most hospitable entertainment.[2] Though Pedro kept the Nasrid crown jewels brought by his rash visitor he maintained excellent relations with the Alhambra.

Martín López de Córdoba, to whom the king gave the *maestrazgo* of Alcántara in 1365, was *contador mayor* (royal treasurer) and from the same mould as the period's politician Prelates, though nonetheless unswervingly loyal to Pedro. That year Enrique invaded Castile, having hired French mercenaries by making huge promises. The French *gens d'armes*, veterans of the English wars, commanded by the great captain, Bertrand du Guesclin, proved invincible in their heavy plate armour, riding down the lightly armed Spaniards. Soon the Castilian nobility began to desert and all three Orders divided into Pedro or Trastámara factions. Yet their blood was still stirred not only by cymbals, nakers and kettledrums but also by the timeless bell-like cadences of the plain chant. Having neither wives nor children they were each other's family, a surprisingly strong tie even in the most relaxed communities. It gave *freyles* a basic solidarity which increased their effectiveness as a fighting unit, but it also gave internal quarrels a quality of peculiar bitterness.

Meanwhile, as Enrique continued to advance, the king sent Frey Martín, now Master of Calatrava,[3] to Edward III to beg for help; and then in 1366 fled to Bordeaux – murdering the Archbishop of Santiago *en route*. Next year he returned with Edward, Prince of Wales, whose seasoned companies could cope with the best French troops. On 3 April 1367 he met the Trastámara army at Nájera. Calatrava, Santiago and Alcántara had brethren fighting on both sides. As usual the Black Prince

---

[1] 'El Rey Bermejo' and his court seem to have been shot to death with javelins. See Ayala, op. cit., p. 347 – '. . . E el Rey don Pedro le firio primera de una lanza. . . '

[2] In 1362. Ibid, p. 336, also Rades, *Chrónica de Calatrava*, p. 57 – 'El Rey Moro [Abu Said] hizo el Maestre muy amoroso recibimiento y le trato muy honrradamente' because he was a brother of Blanche de Padilla.

[3] Diego García de Padilla had been asked to advocate. Rades, op. cit., p. 58.

routed his opponents, though Enrique escaped to Aragon. However, despite Pedro's considerable charm and the gift of the Red King's great ruby (actually a garnet), Prince Edward was infuriated by his inability to pay for the expedition, and left Spain.

Then the Trastámara came back with du Guesclin, accompanied by *his* Masters of Santiago and Calatrava. Pedro's army was mainly *mudéjar* and Granadine *jinetes* and he dared not face the French cavalry. In the end he lost patience and marched to meet his enemies. In 1369 du Guesclin easily routed the Moors at Montiel. After the battle the two rivals met in the Frenchman's tent. On entering, Pedro the Cruel rushed at his halfbrother, but a page tripped him and as he lay on the ground Enrique pulled up the king's belly armour and stabbed him in the stomach. The Maestre Martín López, legal guardian of Pedro's daughters, held out for them at Carmona until May 1371. He was beheaded in the market place at Seville despite Enrique's sworn word.[1] Helped by his Frenchmen, Enrique II (as the Trastámara was now called) overcame all opposition by recklessly mortgaging the *realengo* (the royal domains), granting lands, privileges and titles in wild profusion.

Between 1355 and 1371 no less than sixteen Masters or antiMasters had occupied the three Castilian *maestrazgos*, of whom six died a violent death, three being murdered. Not only had they waged purely secular battles, but brethren had fought brethren. The last quarter of the fourteenth century saw a series of visitations which attempted to restore discipline. Calatrava was the daughter house of Morimond, whose abbot possessed the right of visitation. Similarly Alcántara, Aviz and Montesa were subject to Calatrava's visitation; either the Master came in person or sent a deputy. Pride was the *freyles'* worst vice but fornication followed close. Ballads often refer to beautiful Mooresses, and since Christian Spain had taken over slavery from the Moors there were many temptations. In 1336 Abbot Renaud forbade suspicious-looking women to be admitted at Alcañiz after nightfall, ordering that a reliable man act as porter. The Order's statutes contained savage punishments for lapses of

[1] Ayala, op. cit., vol. 2, pp. 21, 22 – 'que el Rey Don Enrico le guardaria al seguro que le avia fecho'.

chastity,[1] including flogging, which meant 'the discipline' every Friday, besides eating one's food off the floor for a year. In practice concubinage seems to have been common and in 1418 Abbot Jean IV of Morimond ordered that brethren who kept mistresses must forfeit their offices; nonetheless several Masters left bastard children.

In Portugal the brethren's power had increased steadily, even if the Cortes complained of their rapacity. Hospitallers were frequently employed as ambassadors to Rome. Their priory of Crato, which included Galicia, had its headquarters at Belver.[1] Towards the middle of the fourteenth century Prior Álvaro Gonçález Pereira built a castle at Almiéria which still stands, its donjon, the largest of four square towers, serving as keep. The Portuguese Knights of St John enjoyed greater power than their Spanish brethren, but it was the brothers of Aviz who had the most decisive impact on domestic politics.

In 1383, King Fernando died. His heir was Beatriz, wife of the Castilian Juan I. The Portuguese, especially the merchants and peasants, after countless atrocities, had a real loathing for their neighbours, so with much popular support a bastard half-brother of the late king was proclaimed Governor and Defender of the Realm. This new ruler was a brother-knight, João, Mestre of Aviz, his supporters being led by 'the Holy Constable' Nun' Álvarez Pereira, one of the Hospitaller Prior's thirty-two sons. Their cause was described by a contemporary as 'a folly got up by two cobblers and two tailors', opposed by the majority of ricos-homems who included the claveiro of Aviz and the Constable's brother, Pedro, Prior of Crato.[2] The first Castilian invasion, in 1384, was a failure and two successive Masters of Santiago died of plague besieging Lisbon. After João, dispensed from his vows, had been proclaimed King of Portugal, King Juan returned in 1385 accompanied by 20,000 cavalry and 10,000 foot, among whom were detachments from Alcántara, Calatrava and Santiago. More nobles had now joined the

---

[1] Yet a contemporary critic of Juan Núñez of Calatrava had written 'Fué este maestre muy disoluto acerca de las mujeres'. O'Callaghan, op. cit., vol. 16, p. 25.

[2] See 'Catologo dos Grampriores de Crato da Ordem de S. João de Malta' in Collecçam etc., vol. 4.

popular cause including Fernão Afonso de Alburquerque, Mestre of Saõ Thiago, the new king's ambassador to London and original architect of the Oldest Alliance. Nonetheless, João had pitifully few troops.

On 14 August 1385 the royal Mestre and the Holy Constable met the Castilians at Aljubarrota as they were advancing on Lisbon. The Portuguese army was mainly infantry, with 4,000 spearmen and slingers, 800 crossbowmen and a small company of English archers. Though some brethren were present, João had only 200 horse. Nun' Álvarez employed classical tactics, his foot soldiers giving way in the centre before the Castilians, who pressed in towards the young king's banner. This allowed archers and crossbowmen a clear field of fire, shooting point blank at the enemy, till the Portuguese cavalry broke the demoralised rabble of cursing men and screaming horses. Juan's forces were completely routed with very heavy casualties, among them the Master of Calatrava, and the king fled to Seville. Shortly afterwards Nun' Álvarez invaded Castile and smashed the army of Alcántara at Valverde, killing Pedro Múñiz of Santiago. Thus began the dynasty of Aviz.

Castile suffered another disaster ten years later. The Master of Alcántara, Martín Yáñez de Barbudo, once *claveiro* of Aviz, proclaimed a crusade in 1394 and led an expedition into Granada. The Nasrid kingdom was difficult country to invade, mountainous and without water. The *vega* was rich enough, but there were only small areas under extensive cultivation so that cattle had to be imported from north Africa or rustled from the infidels. An enemy would find his supply lines cut in this in-hospitable land and the Moors' favourite tactic was to ambush raiders in the mountain passes. Muhammad VI's soldiers surrounded Frey Martín's over-confident troops, then massacred them.[1]

Calatrava was undergoing radical reforms. Though Gonzalo Núñez, a former Master of Alcántara, was not untouched by scandal – there were stories of a secret marriage – he was a gifted administrator. By now the offices of *Comendador Mayor* and *Clavero*

[1] See Torres y Tapia, *Crónica de la Orden de Alcántara* vol. II, p. 179 – '. . . eran tantos los dardos, saetas, y lanzas que los Moros arrojaban, que se escaparon pocos de sus manos, y á ellas murio el Maestre.'

had become elective, but the Maestre could still allot benefices. Frey Gonzalo introduced *priorados formados* for the chaplains, whose incumbents ranked as priors. Life in the new houses reflected that at Calatrava and Alcañiz, though there were no resident *caballeros*. In 1397 the visiting Cistercian abbot confirmed this innovation. The reason was financial rather than spiritual, as religious needed funds to support themselves, being no longer content with bare necessities. Calatrava now possessed about forty commanderies. The number of *freyles caballeros* is not known, though Abbot Martin, who visited Calatrava in 1302, noted that over 150 knights were present. At its peak Santiago, the largest order, may have numbered – without its Portuguese offshoot – nearly 250 *freyles*. However, with no more than four *caballeros* to every *encomienda* – communities of twelve had long been abandoned – each military brother had a reasonable chance of obtaining a commandery.

The Aragonese Brotherhood of Montesa was exceptionally poor and its brethren were advised to obtain financial assistance from relations while waiting for a commandery; on one occasion ten gold *libras* was stipulated.[1] Less rigorous qualifications for admission may be attributed to this poverty: only two proofs of nobility, whilst sometimes candidates of ignoble birth were accepted. The problem was partly solved by union with Alfama in 1400. The joint order was henceforth known as that of Our Lady of Montesa and St George of Alfama, its *freyles* wearing a red cross.

Afonso IV had obtained papal permission for Aviz to bear a green cross, while Knights of Christ bore a double one of red and silver.[2] Saõ Thiago's cross was red like that of its Spanish parents, but the bottom arm ended in a fleur-de-lis, not a sword. In 1397 Calatrava adopted a red cross fleury which evolved into a curious and distinctive shape, the petals of the lis bending back until they touched the stem to form a Lombardic 'M' – for

---

[1] In 1444 abbot John VI of Morimond conducted a visitation of Montesa and found novices so poverty stricken that he ordered all future postulants to obtain this sum from their relatives, to maintain them until they acquired a *comanadoria*. O'Callaghan, op. cit., vol. 16, p. 14, n. 6.

[2] 'Their Badge a Red Cross with a white Twist in the middle.' Stevens, op. cit., p. 248.

María. Shortly afterwards Alcántara began to use a green cross
of similar design.

Modifications in dress reflected the decline of primitive ideals.
In 1397 the chapter general at Calatrava obtained papal permission for *freyles caballeros* to stop wearing hood and scapular.
From 1400 the cut of a brother's clothes resembled an ordinary
nobleman's – a short grey tunic with a cross embroidered on the
breast. He was clean-shaven and wore linen, though he continued to sport the great white mantle. Later Santiago
brethren adopted a black tunic with a prominent red *espada*
on the chest. Despite sartorial indulgence the Cistercians
watched carefully over their military brothers' spiritual welfare, their visitations continuing with much fulmination against
fornication.

Sometimes the brethren proved bad lords. Lope de Vega has a
play, based on an incident in Rades y Andrada's *Chrónica de
las tres Órdenes,* which is called 'Fuente Ovejuna' after the
remote Extremaduran town of that name near Córdoba. Here,
in 1476, the townsmen rose against a tyrannical *comendador* of
Calatrava, Frey Fernán Gómez de Guzmán, who was too fond
of their wives and daughters and even of their brides. After his
servants had been killed, the *comendador* was hurled from his
castle window on to spears and pikes held by women waiting
below.

In the red palace beneath the perpetual snow of the Sierra
Nevada Nasrid sultans still reigned in splendour. Granada both
repelled and fascinated its neighbours by its beauty, luxury and
exotic vice; every Spanish lady lusted after Granadine silks
despite those magnificent robes with which the sultan was
believed to poison his enemies. Embassies from the north wandered under the coral turrets and through the strange courts of
the Alhambra and the Generalife, past fountains and date
palms, through gardens of mimosa and almond blossom or
lemon groves and orangeries, shaded by cypresses. Many
brethren had visited Granada as captives, ambassadors or even
guests and acquired a taste for such oriental luxuries as sherbet,
soap, carpets and steam baths. They were taught to fight in the
Moorish way, as *jinetes* or on foot with axes and to ride Arab
ponies, and they employed *mudéjar* turcopoles and secretaries.

Muhammad VI's attack on Murcia in 1406 provoked a furious Christian reaction. In 1407 the Regent of Castile, Don Fernando, led the royal army into western Granada accompanied by many *freyles* including Enrique de Villena, the eccentric Master of Calatrava. After a siege of only three days the brethren of Santiago stormed Zahara, then Ayamonte, but Ronda proved too strong, even though the Regent had brought St Ferdinand's sword with him. However, he returned in 1410 to invest the rich town of Antequerra.[1] A relieving party came down from the hills in May and attacked a Christian division, mistaking it for the whole army, whereupon the Castilian vanguard charged the Moors from behind and cut them to pieces. Sultan Yusuf III abandoned all hope of saving his beleaguered subjects, who tried to assassinate the Regent. But on 18 September, Christian troops scaled the walls, though the citadel was not taken for another week. Don Fernando came back to Seville in triumph, with Moorish prisoners in chains. Yusuf made peace, ceding Almería, a valuable salient for future raids.

It has been claimed that by 1400, because of the decline of feudal cavalry, the brotherhoods were no longer a military asset, while the new mercenary companies had by now acquired a higher degree of discipline. But brethren knew how to adapt themselves and *freyles*, besides hiring troops, left their squadrons to officer crossbowmen, artillery or infantry. The fifteenth century saw them more formidable than ever. Each Maestre controlled one of the three most numerous, best equipped, best organised, best paid, best led and most dangerous professional armies in Castile.

The sons of *ricos hombres* or *escuderos*, most brethren had a natural bent for estate management, though they were assisted by the indispensable Jews. Probably conventual life was ill-observed in the smaller houses as some of them were left to stewards.[2] High officers were magnates who dominated local

---

[1] See MacDonald, *Don Fernando de Antequerra*.
[2] 'The increasing laxity in the Order of Calatrava must be traced chiefly to the admission to the ranks of men unworthy and unsuited to wield the spiritual and temporal swords in defence of Christendom. . . . There were two major inducements; the opportunities for satisfying both personal ambition and greed.' O'Callaghan, op. cit., vol. 16, p. 285.

society while the Master of Santiago was *ex officio* treasurer of the *Mesta*, a confederation of sheep ranchers which constituted the richest and most powerful corporation in medieval Spain. Many noble families owed their wealth and prestige to a relative's tenure of a *maestrazgo*; the Figueroa dated their rise to fortune from Lorenzo Suárez's mastership of Santiago, as did the Sotomayor from Juan and his nephew Gutierre's occupation of Alcántara.[1] A Master could bring massive patronage to his kinsmen's aid, obtain 'mercies' for them from the king, including lordships and lucrative posts, win friends by granting benefices, intimidate their enemies with his soldiers, and in general give them unlimited opportunities of advancement. Fifteenth-century Maestres either came from great families like that of Guzmán, the most powerful in Spain, or founded new houses.[2]

Though an excellent steward to young King Juan II, the regent coveted these princedoms for his sons. In 1409 Alcántara became vacant. Its brethren elected their *clavero* as Master despite Ferdinand's known wishes, but the election was quashed on a technical hitch. The regent wrote two letters to each *comendador* and in January 1409, with papal dispensation, his eight-year-old son was solemnly clothed with the habit and then installed as Maestre.[3] The same year Ferdinand obtained the mastership of Santiago for his even younger son Enric. However, Don Ferdinand himself found promotion in 1410, being elected to the throne of Aragon. The coronation at Saragossa, postponed until 1414, was organised by the king's friend and cousin, Enrique, Marqués de Villena, Maestre of Calatrava.

In 1404 King Enrique III of Castile forced the election of this twenty-year-old dilettante who was not even a member of the Order, and was married. His wife Doña María conveniently announced that her husband was impotent and that she would enter a convent. Rome granted an annulment, together with a dispensation from the novitiate and 'Frey Enrique' was enthroned. After King Enrique died in 1407, a group of *freyles* hopefully elected Frey Luís de Guzmán, the *Comendador Mayor*, but seeing the regent's determined support for his relative, he

[1] See Múñoz de S. Pedro, *Don Gutierre de Sotomayor, Maestre de Alcántara*.
[2] See Highfield, *The Catholic Kings and the Titled Nobility of Castile*.
[3] See MacDonald, op. cit.

fled to Alcañiz, that haven of dissident Castilian *caballeros*. The 'impotent' Master had now resumed living with his wife; he seems to have had little taste for the military vocation, with intellectual interests and women taking up all his time. The Guzmán faction persisted and eventually in 1414 the Chapter-General at Cîteaux declared Enrique's election invalid. Luís became Maestre, Villena retiring happily enough with his wife to Madrid, where he died in 1434. He is the supreme example of an intellectual Master, his interests including literature, alchemy, medicine and gastronomy. Popular tradition also credits him with practising Black Magic.[1] He made the first translation of *The Aeneid* into a vernacular language and the first Castilian translation of Dante. He also wrote on verse form, astrology, leprosy and the evil eye, and compiled the first Spanish cookery book, the *Arte Cisoria*. So bizarre are the latter's recipes that some historians believe they hastened his early demise. If his writings are pompous, his interests eccentric and superstitious, Villena was nonetheless one of Spain's earliest humanists.

Maestres have an admirable record of patronage. Villena's supplanter himself, Luís de Guzmán, commissioned a Spanish translation of the Hebrew Old Testament (now known as the *Alba Bible*) from Rabbi Moshe Arragel of Guadalajara, which is also a triumph of the illuminator's art; its frontispiece shows the Master seated on his throne, holding the Order's sword, wearing a grey tunic and a great white cloak with the red cross, while below him his brethren in grey, red-crossed but without cloaks, are depicted fulfilling the seven duties of a Christian. The Rabbi had toiled at his task for ten years, in the *encomienda* of Maqueda. Like all grandees each Master kept 'his Jew' who combined the roles of financial adviser, land agent, accountant and even tutor.

It was the Portuguese Orders who made the most use of science. King João, once Master of Aviz, procured the Knights of Christ's *mestrat* for his third son Dom Enrique, that of Aviz

---

[1] Rades, *Chrónica de Calatrava* p. 66. 'This don Enrique de Villena, Master of Calatrava, was greatly learned in the human sciences, that is to say in the liberal arts, astrology, astronomy, geometry, arithmetic and the like; in law and necromancy so much so, as is said and written with such admiration by so many people, that he is thought to have made a pact with the Devil.'

for his youngest Dom Fernando.[1] In 1414 Enrique persuaded his father to revive the Holy War and the following year, in July, an expedition sailed for Ceuta; incredibly this strong seaport, which had so often menaced the Reconquista, fell within five hours, the young Mestre fighting throughout in full armour beneath the terrible sun with unflagging determination. The chronicler Zurara wrote that Enrique the Navigator's object was 'to extend the Holy Faith of Jesus Christ and bring it to all souls who wish to find salvation'. The Master was not concerned with the expansion of Europe but with the expansion of Christendom.[2] To this end he sought for 'a Christian kingdom that for love of Our Lord Jesus Christ would help in that war'. His whole life shows that the military vocation was still a living ideal; like a Carthusian he wore a hair shirt and his devotions were almost excessive. However, he exploited every modern method. At Sagres his staff included geographers, shipwrights, linguists, Jewish cartographers and Moorish pilots. The team studied map making and how to improve navigational instruments, the astrolabe and compass. Islam had conquered the Spains; Christianity would conquer Africa, then Asia. By 1425 his brethren had colonised Madeira and the Canaries. In 1445 they settled the Azores. The systematic exploitation of the west African coast began in 1434, made possible by the new caravels, the most seaworthy ships of their day. Rigged with many small sails instead of one or two huge spreads of canvas as hitherto, these new ships were much easier to handle – a smaller crew made provisions last longer.

Juan II of Castile reached his majority in 1419 but for most of his reign the real ruler would be his favourite, Álvaro de Luna. Poor, a bastard of a great family and greedy for possessions, he was nonetheless a brilliant statesman. First he had to overthrow Enric, Master of Santiago, Don Fernando of Antequerra's son This wild adventurer had abducted Doña Catarina, Juan's sister, with 300 troops, forcibly married her, then seized the king who gave him the lands that had once been Enrique de

---

[1] Before sailing for Ceuta King João appointed Dom Fernando Rodrigues de Sequeira, Mestre of Aviz, to be Regent of the Realm.

[2] Strictly speaking Dom Enrique was the Order's *Regidor*, or administrator, to which office he had been appointed in 1418.

Villena's. In 1422 Álvaro persuaded Juan to escape and imprisoned the Master for three years until his brothers, Alfons, King of Aragon, and Joan, King of Navarre, obtained his release. The Constable of Castile made the grand gesture of invading Granada in 1421. The Orders went with him, including Frey Luís de Guzmán, and a base was set up in the Sierra Elvira, whence the Castilian army raided the *vega* outside the Nasrid capital. The incensed Muhammad VII attacked them, but was heavily defeated in a memorable battle at Higuerela, after which a young *comendador* of Santiago, Rodrigo Manrique, took the town of Huéscar, where no Christians save captives had entered for seven centuries. The glory was saddened by an ambush in which fifteen *comendadores* of Alcántara and many *caballeros* were slaughtered.

In 1437 the Orders of Christ and Aviz sent an expedition against Tangier, led by the latter brotherhood's Master, Dom Fernando. It landed in August and was quickly surrounded by the Moors. The Mestre surrendered, yielding his banner of Our Lady carrying the Order's green cross. Dom Enrique went to the Sultan of Fez, offering Ceuta for his brother, but the '*infante santo*' died in captivity. Enrique returned to his ships. Lagos was reached, serving as a base for further explorations. Soon African gold, Negro slaves, ivory, monkeys, parrots and strange animals filled Lisbon's markets and swelled the Order's coffers. Trading posts were established, defended by brethren, while the Templars' red cross continued to sail south. In 1452 an Ethiopian ambassador visited Portugal. The Order of Christ grew steadily richer. Dom Enrique obtained the Cape Verde Islands, and his brethren introduced sugar cane to their Madeira estates. In 1460 Afonso V granted them a levy of five per cent on all merchandise from the new African discoveries. If Knights of Christ were busy overseas, at home Saõ Thiago proved no less politically minded than Castilian Santiago: in 1449 its Mestre, the Count of Ourem, was largely responsible for the battle of Alfarrobeira, when his supporters killed the Regent, Dom Pedro.

Castilian Orders were as fractious as ever. Luís de Guzmán, growing old, virtually abdicated his responsibilities in 1442, whereupon the Order's *Comendador Mayor*, Frey Juan Ramírez de Guzmán, advanced on Calatrava with 500 horsemen and 1,200 foot. The *Clavero*, Fernando de Padilla, acting on the Master's instructions, met the attacking force at Barajas with 1,200 cavalry and 800 infantry, and inflicted a complete rout, taking Frey Juan prisoner. When Luís died, shortly after, the brethren chose Frey Fernando, but the constable wished to install En Alfons of Aragon, and so the Master-elect withdrew from Almagro to Calatrava where, besieged by the royal army, he was killed with a missile thrown by one of his own supporters. However, the constable turned against Prince Alfons in 1445 and Calatrava now had three aspiring superiors: Alfons in Aragon, Juan Ramírez de Guzmán supported by the Andalusian commanderies, and at the mother house itself a new contender, Pedro Girón.[1] Then Enric of Santiago returned to Castile with his nephew, Alfons of Calatrava, hoping to make the *maestrazgo* of Santiago into a hereditary duhy, but was crushed by the constable at Olmedo. Enric was mortally wounded though Alfons escaped. The *Trezes* elected Rodrigo Manrique, *comendador* of Segura (see pl. 7), but Luna took this greatest of masterships for himself; a contemporary portrait shows 'Frey Álvaro' at prayer in his white cloak and gilt armour (see pl. 9). Meanwhile Pedro Girón made good his claim to Calatrava, Juan Ramírez yielding while Alfons remained helpless at Alcañiz. In 1450 the latter raided Castile with 300 cavalry only to retreat hastily before the formidable Frey Pedro, who crossed the Aragonese border, burning and slaying.

Don Álvaro's arrogance had made him many enemies, including Juan Pacheco, Marqués de Villena, and his brother Pedro Girón. Suddenly they united and seized the constable in the summer of 1453, executing him on a charge of bewitching the king. Pacheco now became the strongest magnate in Castile and his power grew even greater when the remorseful Juan II died the next year. He had been young Enrique IV's tutor and remained his friend and favourite. *El Impotente* was weak, stupid and unstable. The monarch was probably not a homosexual (a smear intended for Pacheco, who was alleged to have perverted his foul-smelling, ape-like pupil) for he rutted with ladies of the

[1] See O'Callaghan, 'Don Pedro Girón, Master of the Order of Calatrava 1445–66', *Hispania*, vol. 21, 1961–2.

9. Frey Don Álvaro de Luna, Master of Santiago (1445–53), kneeling at prayer, with St Francis. Over the gilded armour of a Master, Frey Álvaro wears the Order's habit—a white mantle with the red *espada* and a red bonnet. From the retable by Sancho de Zamora in the chapel of Santiago at Toledo Cathedral.

10. The façade of the Priory of the Order of Christ at Thomar, 1510–14.

court despite his supposed impotence.[1] His time was spent shambling after favourites through the Alcázar of Segovia with its silver walls, marble floors and gilded statues or at his beloved, obscure *mudéjar* Madrid, or on endless hunting parties. Dressed like a Nasrid emir and wearing the Granadine fez, Enrique received audiences cross-legged on a carpet ringed by Moorish crossbowmen. Soon Pacheco filled Álvaro de Luna's position, supported by a clique which comprised his Caltravan brother, his uncle Alonso Carillo, Archbishop of Toledo, and three young men: Juan de Valenzuela, later Castilian Prior of St John; Gómez de Cáceres and the Andalusian Beltrán de la Cueva – the last two future Maestres. Although the king's brother, Alfonso, was appointed Master of Santiago, Pacheco increased his strength, remorselessly extracting huge grants from the crown.

In 1462 the queen gave birth to a daughter, Juana. In view of the king's impotence this was something of a surprise, and so, as the queen doted on Beltrán de la Cueva, the child was popularly named *la Beltraneja*. Yet Don Beltrán became royal favourite. An armed opposition, among them Frey Pedro Girón, demanded full recognition of the king's brother as heir to the throne. But the infante's deprivation of Santiago, which was given to Beltrán, made even Pacheco join the rebels. Enrique compromised, restoring Alfonso to his *maestrazgo*, Don Beltrán being compensated with a duchy, but the revolt continued. Frey Pedro Girón occupied Toledo, whence he ravaged the royal lands. The monarch was universally execrated, not least on account of his Granadine arbalestier guard who 'forced married women and violated maidens and men against nature'. In 1465 at Ávila de los Caballeros Enrique's crowned effigy was enthroned outside the walls, then solemnly stripped of its regalia by a group of nobles, and hurled to the muddy ground amid the vilest abuse.[2] The Master of Alcántara, Gómez de Cáceres y

---

[1] 'His Manners and course of Life were wholly addicted to Debauchery and Lewdness.' Stevens, op. cit., p. 381.

[2] 'Then a Cryer proclaimed Sentence against the King, laying to his Charge many horrid Crimes. While the sentence was reading they leasurely stripped the statue of all its Robes, and at last with Reproachful Language threw it down from the Scaffold.' Ibid., p. 407.

7

Solís, a former favourite, had a prominent role in the macabre ceremony. The infante Alfonso, Master of Santiago, was proclaimed king. Deadlock ensued until Pacheco made a surprising offer which the king eagerly accepted. Pedro Girón was to be dispensed from his vow as a *frey-caballero* and given Alfonso's sister, the Infanta Isabella, as wife. In return he and Pacheco would kidnap Alfonso, join the royal army and break the revolt.

The Master of Calatrava had few qualms about marriage; his reputation for womanising was well earned – on one occasion he had tried to seduce Isabella's mother. The future Isabella the Catholic, sixteen years old, was so appalled by the news that she spent a day and a night in prayer. But once the papal dispensation arrived the former Frey Pedro set out from the magistral palace at Almagro, escorted by a strong troop of his former brethren. The wedding was to be in Madrid. However, the bridegroom was alarmed on his journey by a strange omen – an uncanny flock of white storks hovering over a castle where he was to rest. Next day he took to his bed with a quinsy and three days later he was dead.[1]

Much nonsense has been written about the death of 'this middle-aged debauchee' – of his furious resentment that God was cheating him – but in fact the Master seems to have made a pious and resigned end, dictating a will full of admirably devout sentiment. He had built a splendid chapel at Calatrava for his tomb, which bore a proud but simple inscription.[2] Indeed the last twelve years of his life had been mainly spent in battle against the Moors. The Granadine wars of Enrique IV were discredited by the king's antics, particularly by the ludicrous *promenade militaire* of 1457 when the queen and her disreputable ladies dressed as 'soldiers'. Yet Pedro and his brethren took part in

---

[1] 'Not long before the Master's Death, in the Territory of Jaén, there appeared such a multitude of Locusts that they hid the sun.' Ibid., p. 408.

[2] Rades, *Chrónica de Calatrava*, p. 78. 'Aqui yaze el muy magnifico y muy virtuoso Sennor el noble don Pedro Girón, Maestre de la Cauallería de la Orden de Calatrava, Camerero Mayor del Rey de Castilla y de León, y del su conseio: el qual en veynte annos que fue maestre, en mucha prosperidad esta orden rigio, defendio, y acrescento en muy grand puianza. Desta presente vida fallescio a dos dias de Mayo, Anno del Sennor De. MCCCCLXVI.'

serious expeditions every year from 1455 to 1457 and from 1460 to 1463, six raids being launched between 1455 and 1457 alone, while in 1462 the Master captured Archidona, though this success was eclipsed by the Duke of Medina Sidonia retaking Gibraltar the same month. Pedro was succeeded as Master by his bastard son, Rodrigo Télles Girón, only eight years old, Morimond stipulating that the Order must be ruled by four guardians until the boy came of age. These had little power, as Pacheco became coadjutor in 1468 but, even so, Abbot Guillaume III took the opportunity to revise the *freyles'* statutes, issuing definitive constitutions in 1467 and conducting a visitation the following year.

In 1458 Afonso V, 'the African', of Portugal revived the Holy War in North Africa. Landing 25,000 men with contingents from all Orders the king quickly captured the little town of Alcacer-Seghir, a valuable base for further operations. Tangier was attacked three times in 1463 and 1464, while Portuguese troops even raided mountain villages. When the Marinids of Fez finally collapsed in 1471 Afonso brought up 30,000 men to storm Arzila and, at last, Tangier itself. Triumphantly he proclaimed himself 'King of Portugal and the Algarves on this side and beyond the sea in Africa'.

The second bloody battle of Olmedo in 1467, when the *Clavero* of Calatrava commanded a rebel division, did little to resolve Castilian strife, but in the following summer 'Alfonso XII' died. Pacheco then reconciled the two factions. For himself, this brilliant schemer obtained the *maestrazgo* of Santiago, remaining virtual dictator of Castile for the rest of his life. The remainder of King Enrique's sad reign was distracted by the *freyles'* noisy quarrels. In 1472 the Maestre of Alcántara, Gómez de Cáceres, insulted his *Clavero*, Alfonso de Monroy, at a wedding breakfast. The infuriated brother struck his Master, who promptly imprisoned him. Frey Alfonso managed to escape, gather supporters and seize Alcántara.[1] Gómez speedily returned to retrieve his headquarters, accompanied by 1,500 horse and 2,500 infantry, but was ambushed and killed. Monroy was elected to the *maestrazgo*, though he still had to contend with

[1] Rades, *Chrónica de Alcántara*, p. 45. 'Ocasion de las discordias entre el Maestre y el Clauero.'

the late Master's supporters led by his nephew, Francisco de Solís, who held the priory-fortress of Magazella. The latter eventually agreed to surrender the great *encomienda*. Unwisely Frey Alfonso came to take possession with an inadequate body-guard and was arrested at dinner, whereupon Francisco proclaimed himself Maestre.[1] Then the Duchess of Plasencia set up her son Juan de Zúñiga as a rival candidate.[2] In 1474 Alfonso de Monroy escaped from captivity – after breaking his leg in a previous attempt – and there was war between the three contenders, an unedifying conflict which continued for the rest of the decade. Juan Pacheco died the same year; the Master of Santiago and coadjutor of Calatrava had used his two Orders to dominate the Castilian state, the climax of the *freyles'* political influence. Three brethren now claimed Santiago: young Diego Pacheco, Alonso de Cárdenas chosen by San Marcos, and the valiant old warrior, Rodrigo Manrique, elected at Uclés. The third and certainly the worthiest candidate soon became un-disputed Master. Enrique IV expired in December 1474, to be succeeded by Isabella the Catholic who with her husband, Prince Ferdinand of Aragon, was to unite Spain. However, Afonso of Portugal was betrothed to his niece, *la Beltraneja*, and claimed the Castilian throne. Amongst those who recognised Juana as queen was the young and popular Frey Rodrigo Télles Girón. His *Clavero*, Frey Garci López de Padilla, stood with Isabella, as did Rodrigo Manrique of Santiago and Francisco de Solis of Alcántara. In February 1476 the decisive battle was fought at Toro, when the Portuguese were annihi-lated. Isabella was firmly established and Ferdinand became King of Aragon in 1479.

When the veteran Rodrigo Manrique died in 1476 his succession was disputed between the Conde de Paredes and the *Comendador Mayor* of León, Alonso de Cárdenas. Paredes, how-ever, died suddenly, and Frey Alonso marched on Uclés. The *Trecenazgo* assembled for his election. Isabella, hearing the news at Valladolid 150 miles away, rode to Uclés, hardly leaving the saddle for three days, and burst in upon the astounded *Treces*,

[1] Ibid., p. 49. 'Dan al Maestre unos grillos de hierro por principio de la cena.'
[2] Ibid., p. 47. 'Duquesa de Plasencia pretende el Maestradgo para su hijo.'

beseeching them to leave the choice to her husband. They
consented but Ferdinand allowed them to elect Cárdenas. Juan
de Zúñiga became undisputed Master of Alcántara in 1487.
Francisco de Solis had been murdered during the Portuguese
wars; lying wounded on the battlefield he was recognised by a
former servant of his old rival, Monroy, who promptly cut his
throat. Frey Juan proved the most intellectual of all Maestres,
a keen humanist who attended lectures at Valladolid. The
revival of classical Latin in Castile was inaugurated by Antonio
de Nebrija, whom he installed in his palace at Zalamea, while a
Jewish scientist, Abraham Zacuto, was employed to teach the
Master astronomy and advise him on the less reputable science
of astrology, as Juan was writing a treatise on the subject for
the guidance of Alcántara's physicians. Though Calatrava's
schism lasted until the end of the Portuguese wars Rodrigo
Télles Girón, who possessed all his family's charm and ability,
was then confirmed in the *maestrazgo* by Ferdinand and
Isabella, and reconciled with his *Clavero*, Frey Garci López. He
served the crown loyally during the remainder of his short life.

Something of Castilian brethren's mentality may be learnt
from the elegy which Jorge Manrique wrote on the death of his
father, the Master of Santiago, '*tanto famoso y tan valiente*'. In 1474
Frey Jorge, *comendador* of Montízon, had himself become one
of the *trecenazgos*, or great officers of the Order, because of his
prowess and bravery. His melancholy and haunting poem is
one of the best loved in all Spanish literature:

> What became of the King, Don Juan?
> And the Infantes of Aragon,
> what became of them?
> What became of the gallants all?
> What became of the feats and deeds
> that were done by them?
> The jousts and the tournaments,
> the trappings, the broideries,
> and the plumes,
> were they vanity alone,
> no more than springtime leaves
> of the gardens?

He speaks of '*la dignidad dela grand cavalleria del Espada*' and, significantly, of how lasting joy can only be obtained by monks through prayer and weeping or by knights through hardship and battle against the Moors. The tone is one of aristocratic pessimism:

> *Nuestras vidas son los rios*
> *Que van a dar enla mar*
> *que es el morir . . .*[1]

Three years later, in March 1479, Frey Jorge, fighting for Queen Isabella against *la Beltraneja*, was mortally wounded in a skirmish before the fort of Garci-Muñoz. He was buried at Uclés. One would like to think that he resembled his brother knight in religion, el Doncel, killed in battle against the Moors in 1486, of whom there is a striking effigy in the cathedral at Siguenza (see pl. 8).

The military orders had reached their ultimate political development during Enrique IV's reign, but even under Ferdinand and Isabella they at first retained their dominant position, possessing armies far beyond royal resources. During all the decades of weak central government they had acquired a stranglehold over the administration which was consciously exploited by ambitious politicians. Since Álvaro de Luna's day, Santiago was a perquisite of the chief minister, dispensations by-passing the novitiate, and a determined faction could even appropriate the celibate masterships of the other Orders. Military brethren were no longer an asset to the state, but a liability. Yet there was to be one last blaze of glory.

[1] '*Coplas que fizo por la muerte de su padre*'. See 'Oxford Book of Spanish Verse' (1965), p. 43. The translation is from Gerald Brenan's 'The Literature of the Spanish People' (O.U.P. 1951), p. 99.

CHAPTER 11

Triumph and Nemesis

In 1476 Muley Hassan, the aged but ferocious sultan of Granada, refused to pay tribute to Castile, telling its ambassador that 'Granadine mints no longer coin gold – only steel'. Isabella asked the pope for a crusading indulgence in 1479, but the Moors moved first. On the night after Christmas 1481, during a blinding storm, they broke into Zahara, massacring most of its population. It was more than a century since a frontier town had been captured by Moors. Isabella immediately sent the Master of Calatrava to Jaén and the Master of Santiago to Écija, ordering all *adelantados* and *comendadores* to reinforce their garrisons. In February 1482 a small Castilian force surprised and stormed the rich town of Alhama, holding it against furious attempts at recapture by the enraged sultan, who slew the messenger who brought the news. It was the turn of the Granadines to be horrified. The Christians had thrown their victims' corpses over the walls for dogs to eat the rotting remains. Muley Hassan retreated, to find his son, Abu Abdullah, proclaimed sultan. The humiliated old man took refuge at Málaga, where his brother, az-Zagal – the Valiant – was alcalde. A popular ballad made '*el rey Moro*' – Muley Hassan – lament

> *Que Christianos, con braveza*
> *Ya nos han tomado Alhama,*
> *Ay de mi Alhama!*

King Ferdinand was so encouraged that he attacked the city of Loja, in mountainous country perfectly suited to the Moors' style of fighting. The *cadi*, Ali-Atar, surrounded the Castilians on the heights of Albohacen, driving them into a ravine – a tangle of maimed screaming horses, rearing and lathering blood, their equally crazed riders bellowing with rage or pain under the hail of poisoned javelins. Moorish cavaliers rode in and out cutting down the unhorsed. Frey Rodrigo of Calatrava was killed by two arrows; many brethren had their heads taken to adorn Granadine saddles. Losing his siege train, Ferdinand managed to withdraw over the rocky hills but only with the greatest difficulty.

Fortunately there were men who knew how to repair Castilian morale. The *Clavero* of Calatrava, Garci López de Padilla, elected to take Rodrigo's place, was a flesh and blood testimony to the military vocation's survival, who said his Office in choir every day and really lived the rule; noted for his devotion to the Order's founder, St Ramón Fitero, he spent much of his time in prayer before his relics. In battle Frey Garci was a skilled and popular soldier.[1]

After defeating the Master of Santiago in the Axarquia in March 1483 the Moors launched a counter-raid by Sultan Abu Abdullah himself. 'Boabdil' rode out with nearly 10,000 hand-picked cavalry, including his gallant father-in-law, Ali-Atar, to attack the town of Lucena but was ambushed by a force of only 1,500 lances. In the rout Ali-Atar was slain and the sultan taken prisoner. Immediately Muley Hassan's supporters, led by az-Zagal, seized the kingdom. After much deliberation Ferdinand and the royal council decided, with inspired cunning, to release Boabdil; the Granadines were divided against each other and eventually Boabdil took Alméria, his father retaining the capital. Yet until 1484 the war seemed no more than another incident in the Reconquista. The Christians employed the traditional tactics of the *cavalgada*, with heavy cavalry and lightly armed *escaladores* – footmen carrying ladders and grappling hooks, knives and axes in their belts, whose task was to scale castle walls quickly and silently. The Moors too retained their customary style of fighting. Even if hand gunners were replacing slingers, their favourite soldiers were still *jinetes* on Arab ponies or Berber footmen including savage Negro *gomeres*, while even the poorest Granadine kept his crossbow. Two thirds of Granada was mountainous, protecting the coastal plain, whose strong towns were supplied by sea from the Maghrib. The sierras were inhabited by pugnacious mountaineers who

[1] Rades, *Chrónica de Calatrava*, p. 81. 'En tiempo de paz siempre residio en al Convento de Calatrava; y alli continuava el Choro y guardara en todo la vida reglar come buen reglar.'

cut Castilian supply lines climbing the misty passes. Armies could not live off waterless rocks and even in the *vega* invaders starved when the Moors deliberately destroyed their own crops. Winter made conditions impossible. This little Spanish kingdom was the jewel of Islam and its people had no sense of doom.

However, with the resources of a united Spain Ferdinand and Isabella hired specialist mercenaries from all over Europe. German and Italian gunners brought 'bombards' firing iron or marble cannon balls weighing up to 160 lbs as well as fire balls, lumps of tow soaked in oil, gunpowder and stone shells which were not so primitive as they sound, splintering on impact with an effect like shrapnel. Siege engineers came from Italy to train corps of sappers. In 1485 'Switzers', the first pikemen, appeared in Spain, carrying the great eighteen-foot spear and using the hollow square. French crusaders, *gens armerie* – heavy cavalry in plate armour – came too, though the English Earl Rivers brought archers and billmen, 300 veterans from the Wars of the Roses. New troops were accompanied by new tactics. Campaigns were directed at each of the three chief cities in turn, Malaga in the west, Almería in the east and finally Granada itself. Captured towns became bridgeheads, garrisoned during the winter, so that no ground had been lost when the advance was resumed the following spring. Light troops systematically devastated the *vega* on a scale hitherto unknown, while the Castilian and Catalan fleets blockaded the coast, their war galleys chasing Barbary merchantmen away from Granadine ports.

By 1484 Muley Hassan was near death. His brother, az-Zagal, rode into Granada, with the heads of Calatravan *freyles* dangling from his saddle, and seized the throne. Again Boabdil fled to the Christians and again he was released to fight his uncle. However, in the spring of 1485 King Ferdinand set out from Córdoba with 29,000 troops, accompanied by the Masters of Santiago and Alcántara. Their objective was Ronda, the second city of the western province. Hitherto it had been thought impregnable, built on a hill top and surrounded by deep ravines. But sappers dragged the new artillery up the mountains facing Ronda, until the great lombards were trained

7*

on the city. The inhabitants were not at first alarmed. Then on
5 May the bombardment began with gunners firing down into
the city. The Rondeños were terrified by the fire balls with their
blazing tails but, on seeing their ramparts splinter and crumble,
towers collapse and houses demolished, were more appalled
by the cannon shot. To reply they had nothing heavier than
arquebuses. After only four days the outer walls fell and the
suburbs were stormed, whereupon guns were brought up to
hammer the inner ramparts at point-blank range, while more
traditional weapons, stone-throwing catapults and battering
rams, set to work. Soon Ronda was a mass of flaming rubble,
its defenders cowering deafened and terrified in the ruins. On
15 May the garrison surrendered unconditionally.

The bombardment of Ronda doomed the Granadines. Nearly
100 strongholds surrendered. By the end of the year half of
western Granada, as far as the mountains guarding Málaga, was
in Christian hands. Desperately the *Ulema* tried to make peace
between the sultan and his uncle, but neither would agree.
Meanwhile their supporters fought savagely. Loja, Boabdil's
residence, was the target selected by Ferdinand in May 1486;
his artillery battered it into submission. It was soon followed by
the towns of Mochin and Illora, the 'shield and right eye' of
Granada, controlling the western roads to the capital. Once
more Boabdil was released. The following year, 1487, the
Castilian army concentrated on Málaga 'the hand and mouth of
Granada' and second city of the kingdom. In the spring they first
took Vélez Málaga and then, with 70,000 men, besieged the
great port itself. A fierce emir, Hamet el Zagri, and a strong
Berber *guzat* were in command of the city, which had two vast
keeps, the Gibralfaro and the Alcazaba. The Christians were in
larger force than ever before with bigger and better artillery.
As an ultimate refinement of psychological warfare they
brought carillons of bells which played havoc with devout
Moslem sensibilities. Yet Málaga almost defeated its besiegers.
The sheer size of the immense city's fortifications daunted the
crusaders. The Málagueños, who shuddered amid the roar
of cannons and the crash of falling masonry, were cut down by
saker shot or stone shell splinters and cowed by fireballs. But
Hamet, who had already experienced one such siege, ordered

his Berber knifemen to cut any defeatist throats. Only in August did starvation force the brave Moors to capitulate. They were sold into slavery, their city and province settled by Christian Spaniards.

The surrender of Malaga meant that the Nasrid capital would become untenable. The dying kingdom was now split in two, the North ruled by Boabdil from the Alhambra, and the eastern province of Almería ruled by az-Zagal at Baza, Granada's other great artery. In the summer of 1488 Ferdinand attacked Almería unsuccessfully. The Moors were filled with joy, for at last they had beaten back the Christians. But in the following year the king returned with an army of nearly 100,000 men. This city, protected by woods and a network of canals, held a garrison of 20,000 carefully chosen warriors who were commanded by a redoubtable general, cidi Yahya. The siege, which was drawn out for five months, cost the Spaniards 20,000 casualties through plague and sorties. In August the rains turned the battlefield into a Passchendaele, the Lombards being bogged down in mud. By November, though the cidi wished to carry on, the Moors were near breaking point. A high officer of Santiago, the *Comendador* of León, negotiated a truce and Yahya sent to az-Zagal, asking leave to yield. The old emir gave way to pious resignation. In December Yahya surrendered Baza. Az-Zagal then gave up his strongholds of Guadix and Almería, and retired to the Maghrib, where he was blinded by the Sultan of Fez. Moslem Spain's last great warrior ended a beggar in the souk.

Boabdil never believed his terrible uncle could fail and had promised to surrender Granada, in return for a vassal principality. But even this degenerate could not abandon the city of his ancestors. He refused and once again Moors raided La Frontera, inciting their enslaved brothers to rise. King Ferdinand led two savage *cavalgadas* into the *vega* during 1490, but the Moors gained a victory, by annihilating a small force of English bowmen at Alhendin. Finally in April 1491 the beautiful Moslem capital, filled with refugees, was invested by the Christians, for the last time, with 50,000 men. The Granadines foresaw their own doom, yet like the poulains at Acre they fought magnificently. The crusaders nearly lost heart, but then Queen

Isabella arrived to build the city of Santa Fé (Holy Faith). The town was built of stone, not wood or canvas, opposite Granada as a sign of invincible determination. In November Boabdil despaired. Negotiations were concluded principally through Frey Gonsalvo de Córdoba, a commander of Santiago who spoke fluent Arabic.[1] Weeping, the last Sultan of al-Andalus greeted his destroyers on 2 January 1492 before riding off to a small domain in the desolate Alpujarras. Then the Christian army entered.

On the Torre de la Vela of the red Alhambra, Frey Diego de Castrillo, *Comendador Mayor* of Calatrava, erected a crucifix, and when the Master of Santiago set up the crimson banner of St James with the Moor slayer on his white horse, the whole army greeted it with a roar of 'Santiago y cierra España'. The holy land of the apostle James was cleansed of Babylonians, its captivity brought to an end. The brethren had consecrated the Reconquista and now it was complete. The entry into Granada was their apotheosis.

The Catholic sovereigns had no wish to destroy the military Orders; they simply wanted to control them. The Portuguese expedient of nominating infantes to the masterships had been successful. By careful pressure on the curia the Aragonese Pope, Alexander VI Borgia, was persuaded to ratify the Crown's assumption of the *maestrazgos*, of Calatrava (when Garci López de Padilla died in 1487) and of Santiago (when Alonso de Cárdenas died in 1493). These were not extinguished, but merely administered by the king as a provisional measure. Then, in 1494, Juan de Zúñiga of Alcántara was persuaded to abdicate. The next step was the nomination, instead of election, of *claveros* and *comendadores mayores*, the latter becoming royal lieutenants. But although the *mesa maestral* was appropriated to purposes of state, life in the *encomiendas* changed little.[2] Juan de Zúñiga retired to a commandery with three knights and three chaplain brothers to observe the rule properly, and, if Alexander VI dispensed *all* Spanish military brethren from celibacy, it was

---

[1] This *frey-caballero* later became one of Spain's greatest generals in the Italian wars.

[2] Pope Sixtus IV allowed *freyles caballeros* to wear clothes of whatever colour they wished but they retained the white cloak with its distinguishing cross. O'Callaghan, op. cit., vol. 16, p. 37.

a dispensation rather than a reform and merely brought them into line with Santiago. Alexander VI had given as reason the need 'to avoid the scandal of concubinage', but many brethren remained celibate.

No strong government could tolerate these immense corporations. Soon after 1500 it was estimated that Santiago possessed 94 commanderies with an annual revenue of 60,000 ducats, and Alcántara 38 commanderies with 45,000 ducats. Estimates for Calatrava vary, but there seem to have been between 51 and 56 *encomiendas* with 16 priories, yielding an income of between 40,000 and 50,000 ducats, the Orders' estates comprising not less than 64 villages with 200,000 inhabitants.[1] For the Renaissance mind such wealth was better used as an instrument of royal rather than clerical patronage. Now that the Reconquista was complete, the Spanish Order's decline became inevitable. The new centralised monarchies took over the brotherhoods with royal councils to administer their masterships. This decline, however, was only gradual; in 1508 Cardinal Ximenes proposed that Santiago's headquarters be moved to Oran while as late as 1516 the *Trecenazgo* at Uclés attempted to elect a Maestre. Then in 1523 Charles V officially embodied administration of the masterships of Santiago, Alcántara and Calatrava in the Crown, and in 1527 he pledged their revenues to the Fuggers. By mid century military Orders were hardly more than civil lists to provide royal favourites with titles, places and pensions, even if canon law regarded them as religious. The Iberian military vocation was dead, though it remained a splendid ghost for many years.

Nonetheless, in 1500 it seemed that military Christianity had a future in Portuguese Africa and the Indies, although brethren of Aviz and of Christ were allowed to marry after 1496 'on account of concubinage' and in 1505 were dispensed from their vows of poverty. Aviz had 48 *comendas* and 128 priories, but this was nothing in comparison to the riches of the Knights of Christ. King Manoel reassumed his mastership, encouraging members of other Orders to transfer. His brethren possessed 454 commanderies by the end of his reign, in Portugal, Africa and the

[1] These figures, which are often quoted, are those given by Marineo Siculo in *Obra de las Casas Memorables de España*.

Indies. Their wealth was reflected in the Order's headquarters.
Built on a hill overlooking Thomar the priory's size and
splendour make it easy to believe that the Knights of Christ was
the richest corporation in Europe. It has sixteen cloisters with
vast conventual apartments. The chief glories are, however, the
church and chapter-house, both built by João de Castilho in the
exotic *Manuelino* idiom with luxurious carving – curiously
nautical as well as oriental in feeling. Motifs of stone ropes and
sails, bosses and spirals like sea shells, all with a quality of
marine encrustation, are repeated throughout on walls, pillars
and window tracery. Though odd, the effect is undeniably
dazzling, and Thomar is the most magnificent of Iberian
commanderies, perhaps the supreme architectural achievement
of military Christianity.

Unfortunately, an attempt to reform the Order was too
extreme. The Hieronimite priest Antonio de Lisboa made
impossible conditions, restoring all the old vows, while chaplains
had to resume conventual life at Thomar, following the arduous
Cistercian rule. The innovations for knights proved impracticable and were soon discarded. When Prior Antonio began to
observe the new constitutions in 1530 he had only twelve
Thomaristas with him. The reform drove a wedge between
knights and chaplain brethren, destroying any sense of vocation
which remained to the former.

Yet as late as 1536 Santiago rebuilt its second *encomienda*, San
Marcos at León. This Renaissance Ziggurat, its massive court
surrounding an elaborate conventual church, was a palace
barracks rather than a fortress and a witness to the brethren's
staggering wealth as well as to their confidence in the future.
By the middle of the century Santiago, Calatrava and Alcántara
all possessed university colleges at Salamanca and a real
attempt was made to reform chaplains, not drastically as in the
purging of Thomar, but as a rational improvement. The
brethren produced their greatest writer, a *frey clerigo*, Rades y
Andrada, whose *Chronica de las tres Ordenes*, published in 1572,
still remains the standard work on Spanish military Orders.[1] He

[1] This deals only with Santiago, Calatrava and Alcántara but in the
following year Rades published a little book containing the Statutes of
Montesa, though it does not include a chronicle.

was an excellent historian, conscientious and methodical, who carefully collated charters and compiled lists of Masters and *comendadores*. Every military Order produces chroniclers, but Rades was outstanding. Unfortunately, as in Portugal, the chaplains' revival cut them off from the *caballeros*.

Much of Spanish history cannot be understood without some knowledge of the brethren. They had become the Reconquista itself and helped form their country's military tradition, that compound of unspeakable ferocity and incredible gallantry, expressed in the modern *Tercio Extranjero*'s motto – 'Viva la Muerte'. It was this spirit and the techniques of the Reconquista which overcame Aztecs and Incas, creating the Spanish Empire, while Portuguese brethren transformed the crusading ideal into a movement of colonisation which ended with Europe dominating the world. At home, Castilian *freyles* captured the State. Admittedly this was a dubious achievement, but no one can dispute the value of the great advance under St Ferdinand when failure meant the postponement of the Reconquista for centuries; al-Andalus, a menace to the Christian west, might well have revived under Turkish rule. The brotherhoods harnessed the anarchic Iberian temperament with their pride, dynamism, inflexible determination and refusal to compromise in a fashion unparalleled by any other institution save the Jesuits. Indeed, for a time these brethren personified their countrymen's character. In order to devote himself to the defence of Spain and Catholicism, Philip II built the Escorial, his monastery palace, and unconsciously the Maestre of seven Orders was building the last and greatest of the *encomiendas*.[1]

[1] King Philip had acquired three more with the crown of Portugal, while the last Mestre of Montesa, En Luys Borja, had died in 1589.

V

READJUSTMENT
1291–1522

The end of the Templars and the Hospitallers' new role:
Secularisation in Europe – Rhodes – the later Crusades

Never do they idle or wander where fancy takes them. If not
campaigning – a rare occurrence – instead of enjoying a well
earned reward these men are busy repairing their weapons and
clothes, patching up rents or refurbishing old ones and making
good any shortcomings before doing whatever else the Master
and the Community may command.

Bernard of Clairvaux
'De Laude Novae Militiae'

Ye shall do battle with them unless they profess Islam.

The Koran

CHAPTER 12

Readjustment and the Templar dissolution

In 1303 the island of Ruad was captured by Mamelukes and its Templar garrison taken in chains to Cairo to be shot to death with arrows before an appreciative crowd. The brethren had raided Alexandria unsuccessfully in 1300, while two years later they had tried and failed to re-establish themselves at Tortosa; now the last toehold on the Syrian coast had been lost. Burdened by exorbitant taxes, Europe was reluctant to donate yet more money for Holy Wars and its kings were too busy to go on crusade. Nonetheless, the military orders were blamed for losing Outremer.

St John's new headquarters were the Hospital at Limassol; the Grand Commandery of Cyprus at Kolossi, a formidable stronghold six miles away, had always been their richest house in the Levant. As the island's chief seaport, Limassol made an excellent base for war galleys – in 1299 the Admiral became a great officer of the Order.[1] However, in 1302 the total strength of this Cypriot convent was only sixty-five brother knights, five of them English.[2] The Poor Knights also transferred their headquarters to Limassol; apart from the Grand Preceptory their main house in Cyprus seems to have been Templos near Kyrenia and they had nearly fifty estates on the island. Naturally the two great brotherhoods squabbled. Nor was it long before Templars began meddling in Cypriot politics. Forbidden by King Henry to acquire more land they plotted to replace him with his brother Amalric; Henry was seized by the brethren and imprisoned in Armenia, an unwilling guest of King Oshin.[3] St Lazarus soon abandoned military activities

[1] This was Fra. Foulques de Villaret, later Master. Riley-Smith, op. cit., p. 330.
[2] Ibid., p. 328.
[3] Ibid., pp. 210–13.

as too expensive for a poor brotherhood, while it is far from
clear whether the Master was the prior of Capua or the
preceptor of Boigny, though the latter was recognised by
English and Scottish brethren. Probably it had never been
an exempt Order – i.e. free from episcopal control – like the
Templars and Hospitallers, and local bishops may well have
been anxious to make use of what revenues it possessed,
reducing the role of knight brethren. The Hospitallers of
St Thomas suffered a similar decline but managed to maintain a preceptory in Cyprus throughout the fourteenth
century.

The European strength, however, of all Orders was un-
impaired. In England, St John possessed thirty commanderies,
each commandery, often occupied by a steward with a
church patterned on the Holy Sepulchre. Such houses usually
contained three brethren – knight, chaplain and sergeant – and
novices; postulants entered at sixteen but could not serve in the
East until reaching the age of twenty. Conventual life was
observed, the Office said in choir every day. Occasionally a
lesser commandery was given to a chaplain, more rarely to a
sergeant. Several smaller houses or manors were attached
to each commandery, often occupied by a steward with a
secular priest. In all there were probably forty-five establish-
ments. The senior officer was the prior at Clerkenwell. His
territory included Wales, which had a single commandery,
Slebeche, in Pembrokeshire. The Prior of Ireland – whose
grand commandery was Kilmainham – came under Clerkenwell's jurisdiction, though this was never very effective as Irish
brethren had a lamentable tendency to embroil themselves in
tribal warfare. Scotland had only one commandery, Torphichen
in Midlothian, though its incumbent was always known as
Prior of Scotland. He too was subordinate to London. The
Prior of England, 'My Lord of St John's', given precedence
before all lay barons, was an important figure in English
life, not least because of his magnificent residence with its
household of knights and chaplains. Clerkenwell was the
second richest monastic establishment in London, owning
the great wood of St John's and the manor of Hampton
Court.

Like St John the Poor Knights had houses from Sicily to Scandinavia, grouped in provinces; all obeyed the Temple of Jerusalem – now at Limassol – but were also subordinate to the Master of the Paris Temple where the 'Chapter of the West' was held. Under the Provincial Masters, usually known as Grand Preceptors, came the priors who commanded groups of preceptories. The Grand Preceptor of England – second senior officer in Europe – was in charge of the Grand Preceptors of Scotland and Ireland but had little control in practice. Life in British preceptories was very like that in Hospitaller commanderies, though apart from houses for elderly brethren they did not maintain hospitals. 'Red Friars' took an even more prominent part in public life than St John, and Temples always outshone Hospitals in splendour. The London house derived an income of £4,000 from its preceptories, an enormous revenue for the period. However, avarice earned the Templars much unpopularity; the most notorious incident was the Eperstoun affair. A husband had bought a corrody (board and lodging annuity) at the preceptory of Balentrodach with his life interest in his wife's property. When he died the Poor Knights claimed the widow's house. She refused to leave, clinging to a door post, so a brother hacked off her fingers with a knife. Edward I restored the unfortunate woman's property, but later her son was murdered by Templar troops, whereupon the brethren took possession. They also took part in civil wars, Irish brothers joining in the local chieftains' squabbles while Scots brethren helped Edward I defeat Wallace at Falkirk.

By contrast St John maintained many hospitals, dispensing food and accommodation to pilgrims and the sick poor. There were also nearly 200 leper hospitals in medieval England, perhaps twenty of them administered by the Burton Lazars' preceptory where there was provision for a Master and eight brethren as well as leper brothers. Usually houses dedicated to St Lazarus or Mary Magdalene belonged to this Order but not all have been identified. Its London house was at St Giles-outside-the-City. The preceptor of 'La Mawdelyne' at Locko in Derbyshire depended directly on Boigny.[1] St Thomas had

[1] See 'The Preceptory of Locko', *V.C.H.*, *Derbyshire*, vol. 2, pp. 77–8.

its Master and twelve brethren at the headquarters in Cheap-side[1] besides hospitals at Doncaster and Berkhamsted.[2]

For many years there had been strange rumours about the Templars, who had developed a mania for secrecy. Minds darkened by hostility were only too ready to credit sinister accusations; 'suspicions among thoughts are like bats among birds – they ever fly by twilight', and the brethren became enveloped in a miasma of poisonous gossip. In France the Poor Knights were especially pretentious. Their Master, Fra. Jacques de Molay, was godfather to Philip IV's son and though in 1287 Philip had declared forfeit all Templar property acquired since 1258 he did not implement the decision. They supported him against Pope Boniface VIII, confirming a secret treaty of alliance in 1303 while in 1306 the king took refuge for three days in the Paris Temple to escape a furious mob. This sanctuary was also the royal treasury. Perhaps Philip's enforced sojourn aroused his cupidity; he had already organised a vicious pogrom against the Jews, seizing their property, besides extracting forced loans from the Lombards. Indeed he had good reason to appreciate the brethren's wealth, having borrowed large sums (on special terms), including a dowry for his daughter Isabella, the 'she-wolf', when she married the future Edward II. The Paris Temple constituted something like a European money market. Pre-ceptories were the safest banks available and credit rates compared favourably with those of Jews or Lombards, Templar bills of exchange being accepted everywhere. It seems that the brethren preferred money to landed property; about 1250 Matthew Paris estimated the Hospitallers' wealth at 19,000 manors, the Poor Knights at 9,000. Yet the latter was un-doubtedly the richer order. All orders had *confratres* who led an ordinary life, but spent certain periods in the houses, coming to the brotherhoods' assistance in a crisis. Both Templar and Hospitaller rules made provision for married

[1] See 'St Thomas of Acon', *V.C.H., London*, vol. 1, pp. 491–5.
[2] It has been said that the abbey of St Thomas in Dublin belonged to the Order but the editor of this house's cartulary believed that the abbey was one of Victorine (Augustinian) Canons from its foundations. See *The Registers of the Abbey of St Thomas, Dublin*, ed. P. Gilbert (London, 1889).

confratres to live at preceptories with their wives in special quarters, though in practice this was very rare. All *confratres* received valuable privileges, and consequently there were several thousand honorary Templars in Europe, many of them rich men.

Philip 'le Bel' was famous for extraordinary good looks, but beneath the thick yellow hair his pale blue eyes reflected a chilly inhumanity. Secretive by nature, he was an enigma to his courtiers. His ambition was that France should take the empire's place; for this he needed a subservient papacy and money. There is a certain resemblance to Henry VIII, despite the Frenchman's icy puritanism; both were strikingly handsome, intellectually brilliant and entirely without scruple.

Several writers had produced plans for the Holy Land's recovery; the most practical came in 1305 from the Aragonese Dominican Fra. Ramon Llull: European kings were to pool resources under a single 'war-leader king', the *Rex Bellator*, who would organise the campaign, while military brethren were to be combined in a single order 'the Knights of Jerusalem'. This scheme received very serious consideration and the papacy contemplated the appointment of Fra. Foulques de Villaret, Master of St John, as head of the new brotherhood. An earlier project had been Pierre Dubois' *De Recuperatione Terrae Sanctae* written about 1300, also advocating the union of military Orders; a secret appendix showed how the king might obtain control of the whole Church through the cardinals. Philip solemnly proposed to Rome that he himself should become *Rex Bellator*, that the French kings be appointed hereditary Masters of the brethren of Jerusalem, that the surplus revenues of *all* Orders be placed at the *Rex Bellator's* disposal, and that the new Master should have four votes at the conclaves which elected popes. The brethren, however, firmly rejected any suggestion of amalgamation.

The fall of the imperial monarchy had opened the way for national monarchies; never again could a pontiff depose princes, arbitrarily summon Europe to a crusade or protect clergy against an irate king. Philip's destruction of Boniface VIII marked the final collapse of papal pretensions. They

quarrelled over clerical dues, the conflict ending with Boniface's death after his seizure by French troops. Clement V, a
former archbishop of Bordeaux, who became pope in 1305,
moved the papal court to Avignon where it remained for over
seventy years – 'the Babylonish captivity'. This new Vicar of
Christ, weak, racked by ill health, was desperately afraid of
his former sovereign who had secured his election by heavy
bribes.

The decision to destroy the Templars was probably made by
Philip's chancellor, Guillaume de Nogaret, a lawyer whose
parents had been burnt at the stake as Albigensian heretics.
He had little love for Rome and during the struggle with Pope
Boniface was the king's chief instrument. He was also responsible for the royal finances. Suggestions that Philip feared a
Templar *coup d'état* are unrealistic; the Order's combat troops
were in Cyprus. Nogaret needed 'evidence'. His first source was
Esquiu de Florian of Beziers. This medieval Titus Oates, once
Templar prior of Montfaucon, had been expelled for irregulari-
ties and during his efforts to obtain 'justice' had committed
at least one murder. In 1305 Esquiu offered to sell King Jaume
of Aragon his former brethren's 'secret', accusing them of
blasphemy and horrible vices. The king was unimpressed, but
French agents saw possibilities in Esquiu, who was asked to
make a legal deposition. Next year royal officials recruited
twelve spies to join the Order. By 1307 Nogaret had sufficient
material – of a sort – on which to base a prosecution.

Clement was weak and credulous but not dishonest. A
crusade was being considered and on 6 June 1306 the pope
wrote in all sincerity to the Masters of the Temple and the
Hospital: 'We wish to consult you about a crusade with the
kings of Cyprus and Armenia.' The Templar Master, Jacques
de Molay, answered with a detailed memorandum, announcing that he would visit Clement to discuss the matter in detail;
no doubt he hoped to wrest the crusade's leadership from the
Hospital. He landed at Marseilles in early 1307 with sixty
knight brethren and rode to Paris in great state. Among their
baggage were twelve pack loads of gold and silver, including
150,000 gold florins; later they were to regret this ostentation.
King Philip gave them a warm welcome, but the Grand

Preceptor of France knew something was in the wind. However, after seeing the pope at Poitiers, and asking for a papal commission to investigate and dispel any hostile rumours about his Order, Fra. Jacques returned to the Paris Temple. On the night of Thursday, 12 October 1307, Philip's troops broke in to arrest Molay with sixty brethren, incarcerating some in royal prisons, others in the Temple's own dungeons. By the morning of Friday, 13 October, 15,000 people had been seized: knights, chaplains, sergeants, *confratres*, and retainers – even labourers on the Order's farms. Probably not more than 500 were full members, less than 200 were professed brethren. By the weekend popular preachers were denouncing the Poor Knights to horrified crowds all over France.

The arrest was illegal; the civil authority could not arrest clerics responsible only to Rome. But Philip hoped to substantiate certain charges: denial of Christ, idol worship, spitting on the crucifix, and homosexuality – unnatural vice was a practice associated with the Albigensians and all these accusations were the stock in trade of heresy trials. The French Inquisition staffed by Dominicans, 'Hounds of the Lord', was expert at extracting confessions. The brethren, unlettered soldiers, faced a combination of cross-examining lawyers and torture chambers whose instruments included the thumbscrew, the boot, and a rack to dislocate limbs. Men were spread-eagled and crushed by lead weights or filled with water through a funnel till they suffocated. There was also 'burning in the feet'. Probably the most excruciating torments were the simplest – wedges hammered under finger nails, teeth wrenched out and the exposed nerves prodded. The Templars would have resisted any torment by Moslems but now, weakened by confinement in damp, filthy cells and systematic starvation, they despaired when the torture was inflicted by fellow Christians.

It is not surprising that thirty-six brethren died, or, that out of 138 examined 123 confessed to the least nauseating charge, spitting on the crucifix, for medieval man was accustomed to swearing oaths under duress and then obtaining absolution once he was safe. Even Jacques de Molay stooped to this stratagem, humiliated by a charge of homosexuality which he furiously denied. However, though his 'confession' may have been politic it unnerved the brethren, while Fra. Hugues de Peyraud frightened them still more by admitting *every* accusation; 'made of the willow rather than the oak' the wily Treasurer cooperated with gusto, declaring he worshipped an idol in chapter. At Carcassonne two brethren agreed they had adored a wooden image called 'Baphomet' while a Florentine Templar named it 'Mahomet' and another brother said it had a long beard but no body. Royal agents hunted frantically for Baphomet and 'discovered' a metal-plated skull suspiciously like a reliquary. These avowals of idolatry only served to discredit other evidence for in extremities of pain and anguish men will say anything. Yet only three brethren would confess to homosexual practices, a refutation of 'indecent kisses'. It was alleged that in the rite of profession, postulants were required to kiss their superior on the navel or the base of the spine – possibly a few preceptors indulged in mumbo-jumbo but it is highly unlikely. And intensive searches failed to find 'the secret rule'.

When one considers how the Templars fought and died throughout the crusades it seems hard not to believe in their innocence. Yet until the discovery of documents relating to the trial of Aragonese brethren most historians were inclined to find them guilty. Even today no less an authority than Sir Steven Runciman remains suspicious. At the end of his *History of the Crusades*, referring to the charges against the Order, he writes: 'It would be unwise to dismiss these rumours as the unfounded invention of enemies. There was probably just enough substance in them to suggest the line along which the Order could be most convincingly attacked.'[1] In *The Medieval Manichee* Sir Steven suggests the possible influence of Dualist ideas and usages. This indeed may be the clue. It is surely more than coincidence that the most strident accusations came from the heartlands of the Albigensian heresy; Nogaret was a Provençal, Fra. Esquiu a Catalan. Local brethren in these regions could well have turned isolated preceptories into Cathar cells during the previous century when the heresy was at its height, while the Order's bankers would have been quite

[1] Runciman, *History of the Crusades*, vol. III. p. 436.

capable of protecting fugitive heretics to obtain the Cathar treasure which disappeared just before their last stronghold fell in 1244. Admittedly Catharism was almost extinct by 1307. But vague memories from years before of heresy hunts within the Order, kept secret to avoid scandal, may have been the origin of tales of devil worship, secret rites and sodomy which were all charges which had been made against the Cathars. Perhaps Pope Clement's confusion is not so surprising after all.

Surely the King, the Chancellor, the Grand Inquisitor, the bishops and the archbishops could not all stoop to false witness? At first the pope had protested vigorously, suspending the Inquisition in France on 27 October 1307. But by now Philip was announcing sensational 'discoveries', including a letter of confession from Fra. Jacques, and so, at the end of November, Clement issued a second bull ordering the arrest of all Templars. Courts of enquiry were set up throughout Christendom. In January 1308, with some reluctance, England arrested its Templars. There were not more than 135 in the country – 118 sergeants, 11 chaplains, and only 6 knights. The Grand Preceptor, Fra. William de la More, was immured in the Tower of London, his brethren in various prisons, though there was no interrogation for eighteen months. Irish and Scottish Templars were also rounded up. All but two Scottish brethren escaped; shrewd politicians, they may well have found refuge with the Bruce's guerillas – certainly King Robert never legally ratified the Scottish Temple's dissolution.

Aragonese *Templarios* were not numerous, but they were front-line troops and far too proud to surrender tamely;[1] Monzon only capitulated in May, and Castellat held out until November, while other peninsular fortresses resisted even longer. The Aragonese commission found the brethren innocent and the Archbishop of Compostella pronounced the Castilian brothers blameless too, as did the Portuguese bishops their Templars. Prince Amalric, the Cypriot regent who had been

[1] In 1309 the Count of Armagnac would write to the King of Aragon '. . . I have just learnt that the King of Granada proposes to invade and ravage your kingdom with a vast multitude of Saracens, Jews and Templars converted to the Saracen creed'. See Finke, op. cit., vol. 2, p. 188 (no. 105).

installed by the Poor Knights, delayed until May before acknowledging receipt of the papal letter; his country too could ill afford to lose valuable fighting men. He seems to have warned the brethren, who surrendered on terms. Even when King Henry escaped from Armenia to recover his throne with Hospitaller aid, his courts acquitted the Templars.[1] With an arrogance worthy of Wilhelm II's army, German brethren exploited their countrymen's love of soldiers; Wild-und-Rheingraf Hugo, *Pfleger* (preceptor) of Grumbach and twenty ritter all in full armour, and carrying swords strode into the Archbishop of Metz's council.[2] The *Pfleger* roared that not only was the whole *Tempelherrenorden* innocent of such vile insults and his Grossmeister a man of piety and honour, but Pope Clement was an evil tyrant, unlawfully elected, whom he, Hugo, with his ritter, declared deposed. Further, all brethren would welcome ordeal by battle; all challenges would be accepted. The council dispersed hastily. Similar scenes occurred throughout the Reich, commissions finding their 'honoured prisoners' not guilty. Pfleger Hugo's bluff and honest approach proved more effective than any Gallic subtleties.

In France the situation had changed radically at the end of June 1308. In May Philip came to Poitiers to discuss the affair with Clement, finally agreeing to surrender the Templars to a papal commission. In return the pope withdrew his suspension of the Grand Inquisitor – Philip's confessor – Guillaume de Paris. In fact Clement left the brethren's enemies in full control for the French Church was packed with royal agents. Philip forced the appointment of one of his creatures, Philip de Marigny, to the archbishopric of Sens. As his suffragan, the Bishop of Paris had to obey the new archbishop. Immediately seventy-two Templars were brought to Poitiers, where they repeated their 'confessions' *en masse* before a horrified Clement. The pope interrogated Fra. Jacques and the Grand Preceptors of Cyprus, Normandy and Aquitaine, who admitted their guilt. All were gagged by dread of reprisals as they knew that Clement was weak and were

[1] See Schottmueller, vol. 2, for documents of the investigations in Cyprus.
[2] See Schottmueller, *Der Untergang des Templer-Ordens*, vol. 1, p. 441. *Wild-und-Rheingraf* was a title signifying 'Count of the Forest and the Rhine'.

already appalled by his failure to rescue them. Only when safe in the commission's hands would they dare tell the truth; it is possible that most brethren had received instructions from their superiors. Unfortunately these first confessions left an indelible impression on Clement, who always remained convinced of the brethren's guilt. Most historians credit the pope with a total lack of scruple. But Clement was not only frightened, he was also ill and tired; not only vacillating by nature, but cursed with a weak man's obstinacy. One cannot accept that he sacrificed the Temple to save the papacy yet one can understand how a bewildered, impulsive opportunist, forced into a decision, would be reluctant to change his mind. The pope may not have credited *all* charges, but he was sure *something* was wrong. He was not Machiavellian, merely a weakling.

From Spain and Cyprus came news that the Templars were innocent, while investigations in the empire too found them guiltless. Pressure could be brought to bear on England, but here many prisoners had escaped, and when the remaining fifty were interrogated nothing could be extracted; a second enquiry in 1310 examined 228 brethren with no more result. Finally Clement ordered Edward II to use torture. Eventually King Edward agreed, stipulating that there must be no 'mutilations, incurable wounds or violent effusions of blood'. Torture had been employed before – in Henry III's reign – but the *Ecclesia Anglicana* always opposed its use. Out of more than 200 Templars including *confratres* and retainers, examined in 1310 and 1311 all of whom were subjected to excruciating agonies, only four admitted to spitting at the cross. The Grand Preceptor begged his examiners 'for the love of God and as you hope for salvation judge us as you will be judged before God'. But there was no mercy.

The commission finally assembled in August 1309. The seven members sat in the Bishop of Paris's palace; their chairman, the Archbishop of Narbonne, was Philip's man. At first the Templars were uncertain that it really was the commission for which they waited. Then the Preceptor of Paris retracted his confession and on 26 November the Master came before the commissioners. Suddenly this stooped, broken old man, in rags reddened by rusty chains, drew himself erect and addressed the court like a parade ground. Vehemently he retracted his confession, rejecting categorically 'wicked and false accusations by the Order's enemies'. Later the Master growled how he wished France had the custom 'as among Saracens and Tartars' of beheading perjurers'[1] He declared that no other Order had such rich churches or beautiful relics, or priests who celebrated mass with more dignity and devotion, adding that 'no Order has fought more determinedly, more bravely, given its blood more generously in Palestine for Christianity'. Fra. Jacques also made a simple, but moving declaration of faith. Nogaret interrupted: 'the Order's corruption is notorious . . . a chronicle at St Denis states that when the Templars were beaten Saladin blamed the defeat on their vice and sodomy, on betraying their own religion.'[2] The Knight answered that he had heard no such tale before; of course there had been alliances, to save Outremer. The court was impressed. Yet the commissioners could not credit false witness of such magnitude. On the other hand this man seemed so sincere – he had begged to be shriven and for communion. Jacques de Molay was asked if he would conduct his Order's defence. Then the Master made two fatal mistakes.

First he demanded to see Pope Clement, for now that the commission had assembled he could speak without fear. Unfortunately Fra. Jacques had been *too* subtle; after that first shattering interview Clement had made up his mind once and for all. Molay's second error was refusing to undertake the brotherhood's defence. To begin with he told the court he would be a 'poor creature' if he did not, but he needed money and lawyers. However, on reflection, Fra. Jacques declined, realising that royal agents might intimidate the defending counsel. Alone it was impossible as Molay, who was unlettered,[3] was entirely dependent on secretaries. He staked everything on

---

[1] Michelet, op. cit., I, p. 34, '. . . quod observatur a Saracenis et Tartaris contra tales perversos'.

[2] Ibid., p. 44, '. . . quod in cronicis, quae erant apud Sanctum Dionisium, continebatur quod tempore Saladine. . . . Templarios fuisse dictum adversitatem perpessos, quia vicio Sodomitico laborabant, et quia fidem suam et legem prevericati fuerant . . . '

[3] Ibid., p. 42, '. . . miles illiteratus . . .'

the pope; with really free access he could convince Clement and save his brethren. But the pope had no intention of seeing him. Cunningly the chairman adjourned the commission until February 1310; by then the Templars would have heard of their Master's refusal and be entirely demoralised. In March, at his final appearance before the commission, Molay again refused and asked to see the pope.

Probably Philip and his advisers anticipated no more trouble. Yet though dispersed and confined for two night-marish years there is a strong likelihood that somehow brethren, though gyved and bound, had managed to communicate and agree on a common policy. Suddenly in April brother after brother retracted his confession, over 500 of them offering to defend the Temple. The court had to take them seriously; the prisoners were assembled in the garden of the commissioners' palace to choose four representatives – two chaplains and two knights – the most capable being the priest Fra. Pierre de Boulogne, once Preceptor of Rome. On 7 April he appeared in front of the commission and produced a statement for the pope, affirming the Order's innocence. The preceptor demanded that his brethren be removed from royal custody, that laymen – Philip's agents – be excluded from the court and that the accused be supplied with funds. He showed a remarkable grasp of the legal situation, pointing out that if his brethren agreed to plead before the court this did not mean they recognised its legality. Pierre argued his case with fluency and logic. How could Templars deny Christ when so many had died in Palestine rather than do this very thing? The commission were visibly shaken.

But Philip's creature, the Archbishop of Sens, controlled the ecclesiastical machinery of Paris; fifty-four Templars were handed over to the secular authority to be burnt as relapsed heretics. More torture, bribes, the pleading of relatives, could not cow them. All met an agonising death with determination, shrieking that they were guiltless. Even so, one brother, Amaury de Villiers-le-Duc, 'pale and terrified', broke down in front of the papal commissioners. Fifty years of age and thirty years a Templar, he may well have been a Palestinian veteran.[1]

[1] Ibid., p. 275, '. . . dictus testis, palidus et multum exterritus'.

Shaking, Fra. Amaury cried that his tortures had been so terrible he would have confessed anything and begged the tribunal
not to tell his jailers what he had said – faced by the fire he 'would
swear to murdering God himself'[1] if necessary – whereupon the
pitiful object was carried back to its cell. As the account occurs
in the official report, available to royal agents, one prefers not
to speculate on his subsequent fate. By the end of May, 120
Templars had been burnt. The Archbishop of Sens demanded
that Reynaud de Pruino, Pierre de Boulogne's colleague, be
handed over for examination. The commissioners were beginning to panic; on 30 May they adjourned, surrendering Reynaud
and Pierre to the council of Sens. Every brother withdrew both
his retraction and his offer to defend the Order.

Perhaps the Templars' worst anguish was spiritual – it must
have seemed that God Himself had died – and probably many
brethren went mad. Yet the wildest rumours circulated, for
French public opinion undoubtedly believed in the brethren's
guilt. They were supposed to have summoned devil women from
hell and slept with them, while bastards were roasted in front of
images smeared with children's fat, and cats were worshipped.
The commission reassembled to examine witnesses who offered
no defence.

Philip was apprehensive of the General Council of the Church,
soon to assemble. The propaganda campaign against Clement
was resumed. He was forced to try Boniface posthumously, the
late pontiff being accused of every imaginable iniquity, including black magic. This preposterous charade had the same object
as the Templar plot – to tarnish the papacy, bringing it more

---

[1] Ibid., p. 276, '... et quod eciam interfecisset Dominum, si peteretur
ab eo'.

11a. The main façade of the chapel of Calatrava La Nueva, mother house of
the Order of Calatrava from 1216, showing the great rose window.

11b. Frey Don Luís de Guzmán, Master of Calatrava (1414–43). This
miniature, c. 1430, shows the Master seated on the magistral throne and
holding the sword of Calatrava. He wears the Order's white mantle and red
cross. Beneath him, seven of his brethren are depicted fulfilling the seven
basic duties of a Christian, while others applaud a new translation of the
Bible. All wear black or grey tunics with the red cross. From the Alba Bible.

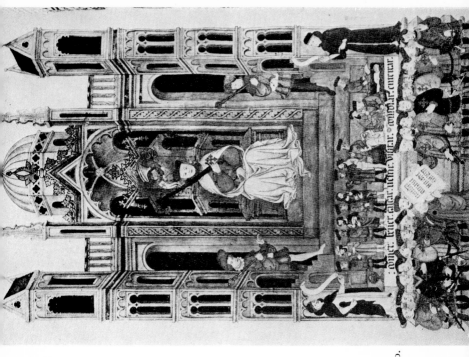

11a. 11b.

12a Monastery of the Order of Santiago at San Marcos, León, begun in 1536.

12b. Rhodes in 1486. Note the war galley in the foreground.

firmly under French control. However, the prosecution was discredited by its own absurdity and the trial was abandoned in return for papal condemnation of its former Praetorian Guard. When the council met at Vienna in October, however, it invited the Templars to defend themselves once again. Seven Poor Knights, bearded, wearing full armour and the red cross habit, appeared from nowhere. Clement was appalled; such monsters of guile might well convince foreign bishops of their innocence. Hastily he adjourned the council. These trusting brethren were arrested, and a massive hunt was started for their comrades, 1,500 of whom were supposed to be concealed in the neighbouring Lyonnais.

In February 1312 the French Estates' General demanded the Order's condemnation. Finally, in March, Clement, in private consistory (that is, with his advisers *in camera*) formally pronounced the Poor Knights of the Temple of Solomon to be guilty of all charges made against them. When the council reassembled on 3 April they were presented with a *fait accompli*, the bull, *Vox in excelso*, declaring the Order dissolved. The pope explained his reasons; canonically the Templars could not be convicted on the evidence, but he himself was convinced of their guilt and had therefore exercised his prerogative to condemn them. The General Council accepted his decision without demur. On 2 May a further bull disposed of the brotherhood's lands which were given to the Hospitallers. Those brethren who had retracted confessions – or refused to confess at all – received life imprisonment, while those who had stuck to their confessions were released on a minute pension, most of them ending up as beggars. Clement waited before sentencing the high officers, Jacques de Molay (still pleading for an interview), the Treasurer and the Preceptors of Maine and Normandy.

The brethren of St John watched their rival's destruction with mixed feelings. They could not altogether repress their pity for men who had so often been comrades-in-arms; English Hospitallers always referred to Grand Preceptor de la More, who died in the Tower, as 'the Martyr' and their Prior William de Tothale drew up a list of the Temple's Masters to pray for their souls. However, even the most sympathetic looked forward to getting his hands on their wealth. But the kings had seized the

8

preceptories and were reluctant to disgorge; Philip kept all revenues till his death, claiming the Templars had owed him the cost of their trial, while in England Edward II had already shared out the spoils, and the Order of St John found itself faced by countless lawsuits from the occupants and the descendants of the original donors. Even when an Act of Parliament recognised the Hospitallers' title in 1324 it took years before this was properly implemented – the Strand Temple was only recovered in 1340, the remainder being let to lawyers. In Europe one half of the Poor Knights' possessions was lost to the laity.

None the less, this was an immense accession of wealth for the Hospitallers.[1] In Germany the vast estates of the Templars enabled the *Herrenmeister* of the Brandenburg *Ballei* of the '*Johanniterorden*' to become semi-autonomous. English commanderies had to be drastically reorganised to absorb new lands; sometimes the commandery itself was transferred to a former preceptory, as at Egle in Lincolnshire. Scotland was in such chaos that the Apostolic Decree dissolving the Scots' Temple was never ratified, but it is untrue that the Templars continued as part of a combined Order, even if a few Poor Knights may have been received as Hospitallers. Some English brethren were taken in as pensioners; in 1338 a former Templar was still living at Egle.[2] Finally after years of litigation the number of St John's English houses rose to fifty-five. In 1338 their brothers numbered thirty-four knights, forty-eight sergeants and thirty-four chaplains.

Even the greediest Hospitaller must have been shaken by the last act. On 14 March 1314 the four Templar great officers were paraded on a scaffold outside Notre-Dame to hear their sentence – life imprisonment. Then Molay spoke from this macabre rostrum, the Templars' ultimate battleground: 'I think it only right that at so solemn a moment when my life has so little time to run (he was nearly seventy) I should reveal the deception which has been practised and speak up for the truth. Before

---

[1] Even in Aragon, after sufficient had been taken to found the new Order of Montesa, enough Templar property fell into the hands of the kingdom's *Hospitalarios* to make it necessary to divide the Castellanry of Amposta (i.e. priory of Aragon) and erect a new priory of Catalunya.

[2] See Larking & Kemble, *The Knights Hospitallers in England*.

heaven and earth and with all of you here as my witnesses, I admit that I am guilty of the grossest iniquity. But the iniquity is that I have lied in admitting the disgusting charges laid against the Order. I declare, and I must declare, that the Order is innocent. Its purity and saintliness is beyond question. I have indeed confessed that the Order is guilty, but I have done so only to save myself from terrible tortures by saying what my enemies wished me to say. Other knights who have retracted their confessions have been led to the stake; yet the thought of dying is not so awful that I shall confess to foul crimes which have never been committed. Life is offered to me but at the price of infamy. At such a price, life is not worth having. I do not grieve that I must die if life can be bought only by piling one lie upon another.' Two of his brethren listened fearfully, but the Preceptor of Normandy, Fra. Geoffroy de Charnay, rallied to the Grand Master, speaking with equal defiance. Next morning the two brothers in religion were burnt alive over a slow charcoal fire on an island in the Seine, shouting their innocence through the flames. The crowd was inclined to think them martyrs. A legend grew up that Fra. Jacques had summoned Philip and Clement to come before God for judgement; certainly the pope was dead within a month, the king by the autumn, and his three sons and successors all died young.

One must not see the attack on the Templars as an isolated incident. Such vicious accusations were made against the Teutonic Knights that they transferred their headquarters from Venice to Prussia, while the crisis confirmed St John's decision to move to Rhodes, hastening their development into a federation of national brotherhoods; Philip attempted, unsuccessfully, to stop this reorganisation, which made a French takeover impossible. It also perpetuated the Leper Knights' division; in 1308 King Philip took Fra. Thomas de Sainville, the Master General of the Knighthood of St Lazarus, and all his Order's possessions under royal protection, but when Thomas died in 1312 his successor was not recognised by Naples and in 1318 Pope John XXII gave the priory of Capua full independence – henceforth there were two distinct branches of St Lazarus – Burton Lazars supporting Boigny.

Sometimes the Roman Church has proved an unnatural

mother, savaging those who love her best – like the eighteenth-century Jesuits – but seldom so gullible or so cruel as in the bull *Vox in excelso*. As Hilaire Belloc said, 'When one remembers how the Catholic Church has been governed, and by whom, one realises that it must be divinely inspired to have survived at all.' Some Castilian Templars were so horrified that they fled to Granada[1] and turned Moslem. The Poor Knights' most lasting achievement, their contribution towards the overthrow of the Church's attitude to usury, was economic. No medieval institution did more for the rise of capitalism. Yet the Templars deserve to be remembered not as financiers but as the heroes of Acre, that strange fellowship of death who died for Christ with such disturbing courage.

[1] Occasionally fugitive *freyles* of Santiago turned Moslem – see Lomax, op. cit., p. 95 on Chapter of 1251.

CHAPTER 13

Rhodes and the Sea Knights

Unlike the Templars the Hospitallers responded brilliantly to the challenge of new conditions. Rhodes had become a nest of pirates, Greek, Italian and Saracen, a Levantine Tortuga disrupting Christian trade throughout the Aegean. Initially the brethren occupied the island for this reason alone, but the attack on the Templars shocked them into making it their headquarters. In 1306, after spies had brought glowing reports, Master Foulques de Villaret, formerly the Order's first Admiral, sailed for Rhodes in June with two galleys and some transports carrying only 35 knights and 500 infantry. *En route* he was joined by a Genoese adventurer, Vignole de' Vignoli, who brought two more galleys. The great port beat off their first assault, but in November the key fortress of Philermo was taken and the brethren invested Rhodes in earnest. Though Greek troops joined the outlaw garrison, for the Byzantine emperor had no wish to forfeit his nominal sovereignty, the little army hung on grimly, Fra. Foulques borrowing money to hire more soldiers. Finally the city was stormed and its defenders fled to the hills. This probably took place in early 1307, the convent being transferred two years later.[1]

This hilly island, forty-five miles long, twenty-two miles wide and divided by mountains, was famed for an idyllic climate and fertile crops, though there was no town other than Rhodes itself, which the brethren had made the safest trading base in the Levant, its landlocked harbour fortified by chains, booms and moles. Egypt and the Anatolian emirates would have to suffer endless raids; not without reason did they name the Hospitaller lair 'stronghold of the hounds of Hell'. Crusading states are usually limited to six but Rhodes has some claim to be the seventh.

Sweeping reforms dealt with new maritime duties; from 1299

[1] Riley-Smith, op. cit., p. 216.

the admiral ranked as a conventual bailiff while the Turcopolier, now responsible for coastal defences, was similarly promoted. Then the threat of Philip IV acted as a catalyst for a structural revolution; even in the thirteenth century there had been an embryonic division into *langues*, those speaking the same tongue. The Order was now divided into seven of these *langues*, each comprising several priories under a Grand Priory and with its own *auberge* (hall of residence) at Rhodes; Provence, Auvergne, France, Italy, Spain, England (with Ireland) and Germany (including Scandinavia and Bohemia-Poland). Because of the large number of Gallic brethren France was given three *langues*, while in the fifteenth century Spain would be divided into Aragon (with Catalonia and Navarre) and Castile (with Crato, i.e. Portugal). Though he ranked lower than his nation's Grand Prior, at Rhodes a brother commanding a *langue* was one of the conventual bailiffs, and styled a *pilier*: Provence was under the Grand Commander, the Master's lieutenant administering the brotherhood's properties; Auvergne had the Marshal, senior military officer; France the Hospitaller; Italy the Admiral; Spain the Drapier; England the Turcopolier; Germany the Grand Bailiff.

The Chapter General included all brethren from the Master to the humblest serving brother, but as its meetings were stormy and often riotous it met less and less. Day-to-day government was administered by the Venerable Council, a quorum of senior officers, though the most important constitutional body was the Sacred Council, an assembly of bailiffs – conventual, Syrian (nominal except for Armenia), and European. Italy possessed seven priors, the Iberian peninsula five (the castellan of Amposta ranking as prior of Aragon). England had four members: the Turcopolier, the priors of England and Ireland, and the commander – styled bailiff – of Egle. All *langues* shared the Syrian posts and the seven Cypriot commanderies. To become a bailiff it was necessary to spend fifteen years at Rhodes. As great officers they were distinguished by a larger cross and called 'bailiffs grand cross', receiving especially rich commanderies – the English prior, for example, occupied four besides Clerkenwell.

The fourteenth century was to prove a difficult one for the Order of St John, for the concept of the crusade was dying, while

Italian merchants were strangling the Latin East with their capitalist tentacles, averse to alienating Moslem business interests. Despite the Templar properties there was a steady decline in revenues and the Order was hard hit by the Black Death. It had already suffered severe financial losses when the Florentine banks had failed in the 1340s. There were also severe internal dissensions, even at Rhodes. Fra. Foulques, able and charming but overbearing, became increasingly dictatorial and then went to pieces, womanising and drinking. In 1317 angry brethren led by an elderly, embittered commander, Fra. Maurice de Pagnac, tried to murder him but he escaped to the castle on the acropolis of Lindos.[1] In 1319 John XXII confirmed Fra. Foulques' deposition and he retired to a commandery in Languedoc.[2] Pagnac had died, and so the brothers elected Fra. Elyon de Villeneuve as their superior.

Yet life on Rhodes remained sufficiently monastic. Brethren ate and slept in their *langue*, saying Office in its chapel. Altogether the *auberges* constituted one Convent, and all brothers attended chapters in the magistral palace, keeping important feasts in the Order's church where novices made their solemn profession to the Master. Several hundred knights lived on Rhodes – two hundred in 1330, twenty-eight of them English – so a single house was impracticable. Rhodian coins show the Master kneeling before a crucifix, proclaiming both his religious status and his role as 'Guardian of the Poor'. All brethren worked in the great hospital, with its 1,000 beds where the sick slept between linen sheets and ate off silver plates, drinking wine from silver cups. Patients included casualties in battle, merchants, pilgrims and the island's poor. Every evening at sunset in the 'Palais des Malades', chaplain brethren recited the great prayer for 'Our Lords the sick': 'Seigneurs Malades, pries pour pais que Dieu la mande de ciel en terre. Seigneurs Malades, pries pour le fruit de la terre que Dieu le multiplie en telle manière que saincte église en soit servie et le peuple soutenu. Seigneurs Malades, pries pour l'apostell de Rome et pour les

[1] The *Cronica Magistrorum Defunctorum* (XXIV) says that these brethren would have murdered Foulques in his bed ('in suo lecto interfecissent') had not his chamberlain helped him to escape.

[2] He died in poverty – 'Obiit frater simplex et egenus'. Ibid.

The Levant c. 1480

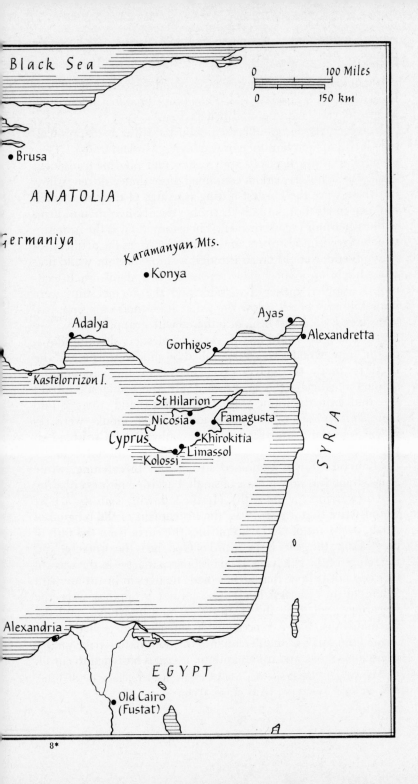

cardennaus et pour les patriarches et pour les arcevesques et pour les evesques et les prelats. . . .' They prayed too for all Christian kings, pilgrims, captives and benefactors.[1]

However, the Hospitallers' chief business was at sea, protecting Christian merchantmen or waylaying Moslem traders. They themselves ran a fleet of cargo vessels and pilgrim transports. Their battle flotilla seldom contained more than a dozen galleys but these were the hardest-hitting warships of their day, small but extremely fast, usually carrying twenty-five men-at-arms with rather more crossbowmen. Their torpedo was the iron ram which stoved into timbers, and mangonels were the artillery – a heavy boulder could crash through a ship's bottom while fireballs, naphtha or incendiary arrows set her alight. Such techniques crippled rather than sank and the enemy ships were immobilised – holed below the water line, their oars smashed, transfixed by a metal beak or tethered with grappling hooks – so that the knights could board, their arbalestiers shooting down on the crew. Rhodes was often lashed by sudden storms and the brethren made themselves excellent sailors, the best fighting seamen of their age; in Edward Gibbon's majestic prose: '. . . under the discipline of the Order that island emerged into fame and opulence; the noble and warlike monks were renowned by land and sea; and the bulwark of Christendom provoked and repelled the arms of the Turks and Saracens'.

Mameluke Egypt remained strong and threatening, while Asia Minor was now a mass of small Turkish emirates ruled by *ghazis* (warriors for the faith). (In the following century a poet would write that a *ghazi* was 'the instrument of the religion of Allah, a servant of God who purifies the earth from the filth of polytheism; the *ghazi* is the sword of God, he is the protector and the refuge of the believers. If he becomes a martyr in the ways of God, do not believe that he has died; he lives in beatitude with Allah, he has eternal life.') The largest groupings were the Karamans, ruled by the Grand Karaman at Konya, and the Germaniyans, but a succession of superb leaders had transformed the small Osmanli clan into the dominating tribe, under whose horsetail standard all ambitious *ghazis* hastened to enroll.

[1] L. Le Grand, 'La Prière des Malades dans les Hôpitaux de St Jean', *Bibl. de l'Ecole des Chartes*, LVII (Paris, 1896).

In 1326 Orhan – 'Sultan, son of the Sultan of the Ghazis, Ghazi son of the Ghazi, Marzuban of the Horizons, Hero of the World' – captured Brusa, and, in 1329, Nicaea. It was only a matter of time before Osmanli *spahis* conquered the Balkans.

Of Christian neighbours Greece – 'Romania' – was a mosaic of small, violently inimical states. The Palaeologan revival waned until the Byzantine Empire entered its final decline with the civil wars of the mid fourteenth century. Every hilltop and island was ruled by an independent lord – Greek, French, Spanish or Italian – while Genoese and Venetians possessed a multitude of trading posts. The Order of St John had several commanderies, the Teutonic Knights a few isolated *komtureien*. Cyprus was Rhodes' chief neighbour. Hugh IV (1324–58) and his descendants were each crowned King of Cyprus at Nicosia, King of Jerusalem at Famagusta nearest the mainland and their sons styled Prince of Antioch or Tyre. Despite nostalgia for *la douce Syrie* – Frankish ladies always wore black in mourning for the lost kingdom – Cypriot nobles with names evocative of Outremer – Ibelins, Gibelets, Scandelions – led a sybaritic existence in delightful villas amid rose gardens and vineyards. To Hospitallers the Cypriot monarch was the most important sovereign in Christendom but, as Jacques de Molay had written to Pope Clement, his army was too small. Then there was Armenia, hard pressed by Mamelukes. When the last Hethoumid died in 1342 the Cilicians chose Hugh IV's nephew, Guy de Lusignan, as their king. But these ferocious mountaineers were unreliable; not only did they quarrel – Guy was murdered in 1344 – but they reacted violently at tactless attempts to Romanise the Gregorian Church with its hooded prelates, crowned *vartapets* (archpriests) and dramatic liturgy. Even when their country was reduced to its capital, Sis, with a string of coastal fortresses and a few mountain strongholds inland, the proud, warlike barons held out among their wild glens and clifftops. Yet for all their courage 'Erminie' was doomed.

The sea-knights won victory after victory. Those of their victims who escaped, limped home with horrific tales of these fiendish dogs from Gehenna. In 1319 the Grand Commander Albrecht zu Schwarzenberg was escorting the Genoese governor of Chios to his island when he was attacked by a Turkish fleet, which he routed. Only six enemy vessels escaped, by night, while most of the Faithful were drowned. The *ghazis* wanted revenge, and in June 1320 Rhodes was blockaded by eighty warships. But the pugnacious Fra. Albrecht sailed out to meet them with the Order's battle squadron of four galleys and twelve other vessels. Most of the enemy's ships were boarded or sent to the bottom, while their entire assault force, which had landed on a nearby island, was captured.[1] In 1334 a fleet of Hospitaller, papal, Cypriot, French and Venetian crusaders ambushed Yakshi, emir of Marmora, off the island of Episkopia on the Negropont coast, and during a running battle which lasted nine days outsailed and outfought the Turks, who lost over 100 vessels.[2]

In 1334 Clement VI, learning that Umur of Aydin was building an armada of landing craft, formed the Latin League comprising Cyprus, Venice and Rhodes. Their combined fleet of twenty-four galleys commanded by the Prior of Lombardy, Fra. Gian de Biandra, stormed Umur's stronghold of Smyrna in October, burning his entire navy of 300 ships at anchor. All Christendom rejoiced and a crusading army of 15,000, mainly French, arrived in 1346. Another victory was won, off Imbros, in 1347 by the Catalan prior, Pere-Arnal de Peres Tortes, where the Turks lost 100 galleys, while the following year, Umur himself was killed during a gallant attempt to retake his beloved Izmir. Now the brethren held it for the pope.[3] This crusading resurgence, however, was checked by bubonic plague. In Cyprus only the fortress of St Hilarion – where the royal family took refuge – was immune, and the mortality was so terrible that for years afterwards visitors were deterred by the island's reputation for disease and poisoned air.

The fighting brethren were tending to secularisation, careerists being heartened by the practicability of concubinage in remote houses. After the Templar dissolution the Order of St John was weakened by brethren hurrying back to Europe in hope of some rich commandery. The General Chapter of 1330 ordained that before promotion all brothers must serve five years 'in the

[1] Delaville le Roulx, *Les Hospitaliers   Rhodes*, pp. 78, 79.
[2] Ibid., p. 89.
[3] Ibid., pp. 94, 95, 108, 109.

convent', including three *caravans*, each constituting a year's active service. In 1342 the pope had complained to Fra. Elyon about his Order's laxity, threatening to create a new brotherhood with its surplus revenues. By the end of the fourteenth century few European commanderies contained more than one brother, the commander himself. In England conventual life ceased, save at Clerkenwell, postulants entering the novitiate at Rhodes. The St Lazarus and St Thomas brotherhoods were moribund. After the Black Death there was a remarkable decline in leprosy. Formerly houses like Burton Lazars, with separate cells for each leper, and medicinal baths, only took in those suffering skin disease; now ordinary sick were admitted, though the 'Governor, Warden and Master of Burton Lazars' conducted visitations until well into the fifteenth century, sometimes acting as Lieutenant in Scotland for the Master at Boigny.[1] The last known Knight of St Thomas, Fra. Richard de Tickhill, was professed and given the habit by the preceptor of Cyprus, Fra. Hugh de Curteys, in 1357 at the Church of St Nicholas of the English in Nicosia.[2]

Rhodes, a Levantine Carcassonne, must have seemed surprisingly familiar to western visitors. There were two ports, the outer or 'Harbour of the Galleys' formed by a long curving neck of land, the inner a landlocked bay whose narrow entrance was guarded by moles on which stood the towers of St Jean and St Michel. The city was built in a semi-circle around this inner port, protected by a double wall with thirteen towers and five projecting bastions – one of which was allotted to the English brethren – and also by a rampart along the harbour front. Though the great cathedral of St Jean, begun in 1310, had been built in a hybrid Catalan-Italian style, other churches such as St Catherine's were flamboyant with ogee arches and wild tracery, while the rich merchants' houses next to the *collachium* were both imposing and luxurious and, like the brothers', swamped in a sea of flowers – roses, oleanders, bougainvillea, Turkish tulips, mimosa and jasmine. Inland, as far as the eye could see, was a rich green vista of gardens, orchards, vineyards, farms, with an abundance of fig, nectarine and peach

[1] *V.C.H.*, *Leicestershire*, vol. 2, p. 36
[2] Stubbs, *The Mediaeval Kingdoms of Cyprus and Armenia*.

trees. Everything in the city, even its ramparts, was built of
honey-coloured stone. The markets sold every luxury known –
silks, spices, scent, sandalwood, damascene metalwork, precious
stones, jet, furs, amber and slaves – for this embattled port
commanded the Levant trade routes. In its narrow, cobbled
streets, through the Gothic gateways, swarmed not only Greeks
and westerners but Christian Copts from Egypt, Armenian
refugees, Syrians of Poulain or Jacobite origin and even
Georgians, besides Jews from the ghetto. Yet Rhodes was their
home and they were loyal to their lords, the sons of country
gentlemen in Yorkshire, the Limousin or Westphalia, the
Campagna, Castile, or any other land in western Europe.

The *collachium* was the compound which cloistered the
'convent' proper including the Magistral palace, the Order's
church, the Sacred Infirmary and the *auberges* in the '*rue des
Chevaliers*'. By now every *langue* owned one, though in the
previous century the Catalan prior Pere-Arnal de Peres Tortes
recorded that when he arrived he 'had to beg his lodging in the
streets', after which he erected a fine Aragonese *auberge*. Naturally
some *langues* were better represented than others, particularly the
French, while Poles and Scandinavians must have felt lonely in
the German house. The total strength of knights in the convent
was raised from 200 to 350 in 1466, to 400 in 1501 and finally in
1514 to 550,[1] but the number of English brethren never rose to
more than twenty-eight. Despite this disparity the system worked
well enough, apart from occasional squabbles over precedence.
Many were stationed outside the convent. On the island itself
there were fortresses inland protecting little country towns, and
a castle on the bay of Trianda, a few miles west of Rhodes, as
well as the acropolis of Lindos, a fortified table mountain whose
garrison included twelve brothers under a commander. The
Order ruled the entire Dodecanese archipelago, Kos – or Lango –
being the most important with a flourishing town often described
as a miniature Rhodes. Symi and Leros were defended by strong
towers while a hundred miles to the east, just off the Anatolian
mainland, was Kastelorizon or 'Châteauroulx'. All had har-
bours where the brethren's galleys could shelter and revictual.
No doubt knights posted to these isolated outposts pined for the

[1] King, *The Knights of St John in the British Empire*, p. 52.

convent, where not only did they eat off silver but their diet, included nutmeg, cinnamon and pepper in quantities unknown in Europe save at the greatest tables, while sugar was a commonplace. Persimmons, dates and pomegranates were served in that age when oranges and lemons were an exotic luxury to the West, as well as those sweet wines beloved by the medieval palate. Brethren returning from the stench of bilge and galley slaves knew the pleasure of hot baths. For relaxation there was hawking and buck hunting, and no doubt sailing and fishing. Visitors were always welcome and occasionally there was the excitement of royal guests, Byzantine or Cypriot, besides Turkish and Egyptian embassies. Yet the *collachium* made Rhodes a real monastery, spiritual duties being enforced with a heavy hand, and sometimes wilder spirits, who found it too severe, fled to the fleshpots of Cyprus.

Hugh IV of Cyprus abdicated in 1358 to make way for his son, Pierre I, a visionary who was determined to win back Jerusalem. His reign began with a series of spectacular victories. As Armenia had appealed to Rome for help, in 1361 Pierre garrisoned the hard-pressed *Haiot* port of Gorighos, after which, assisted by the crew of four Hospitaller galleys, he stormed the pirate city of Adalia.[1] Soon the Turks learnt to dread this fierce king, who dragged captured *ghazis* 'at the horse's tail', but Pierre left for Europe to plead for a crusade, travelling to Venice, Avignon, France, England, Germany, Bohemia and Poland. By 1364 it was time he returned; Cyprus had been laid waste by Turkish raiders, and hitherto friendly emirs were growing menacing. In June 1365 the king sailed with his crusaders from Venice to Rhodes, where the Cypriot fleet joined him in August.

Together with the Hospitaller flotilla of sixteen galleys carrying 100 brothers and their mercenaries under the Order's admiral, Fra. Ferlino d'Airasca, this armada – 165 vessels in all – set out for Alexandria.[2] It included flat-bottomed landing craft from which horsemen could ride out on to the beach. The destination was kept secret and the Mamelukes were taken by surprise. Pierre de Thomas, the papal legate, harangued his flock: 'Soldiers of Christ take comfort in the Lord and his Holy

[1] Delaville le Roulx, *Rhodes*, p. 141.
[2] Ibid., p. 152.

Cross and fight His War bravely – have no fear of the enemy and
pray to God for victory. The gates of Paradise are open.'[1] The
Egyptians defended their walls vigorously with cannon, vats of
boiling oil and molten lead, flame throwers – wooden tubes
discharging jets of naphtha – and even gas bombs, inflammable
discs which emitted dense fumes of sulphur and ammonia to
drive blinded attackers reeling back, vomiting and choking. At
first the Christians were beaten off, their scaling ladders thrown
down, then some sailors crawled through a drain to open a gate
and the besiegers swept into the great city. Many brethren fell
during the assault and Fra. Robert Hales, Bailiff of Egle, performed prodigies of valour.

> O worthy Petro, king of Cypre, also
> That Alisaundre wan by heigh maistrye . . .

The glory was tarnished by massacre: 20,000 men, women and
children died in the sack.

Unfortunately the crusaders, gorged with plunder, exhausted
from rape, refused to march on Cairo, and Pierre, heartbroken,
was forced to evacuate hard-won Alexandria. A tyrannical
disposition and a vigorous private life had made him many
enemies at home, including the queen (although Pierre spread
her nightdress over his bed every night he spent away from her!).
One evening in 1369, as the king lay asleep with his favourite
mistress, some dissident noblemen burst in and killed him. Then
the kingdom's Turcopolier castrated the royal corpse; the
Lusignan vitality died with Pierre.

An old comrade suffered a worse fate. European kings had
begun to employ Hospitaller priors as ministers and in 1380
Robert Hales, the hero of Alexandria and Prior of England,
became Richard II's treasurer. Alas, 'Hob the Robber's' poll
tax provoked the Peasant's Revolt. After burning Clerkenwell
the mob prised Fra. Robert and the Archbishop of Canterbury
out of the Tower, hacked off their heads, which were then stuck
on poles, and nailed the archbishop's mitre to his skull.

Juan Fernández de Heredia became Master in 1374. Born in
1310, this penniless scion of a great Aragonese family entered
religion after being widowed twice. Hitherto his career had been

[1] Luttrell, *The Crusade in the Fourteenth Century.*

a scramble for power – and money to leave to the children adopted by his brother. Ingratiating himself with successive popes, he became Captain of the papal Guard. He fought at Crecy in 1346 – questionable conduct for the Pontiff's envoy, even if he saved the French king's life – and was regarded with deep disapproval by many brethren. However, Avignon friends bought him promotion and ultimately the Mastership. As soon as he was Master he leased Achaia for five years, paying its pretender 4,000 ducats. After leaving Rome in 1377 he helped the Venetians storm Patras, where he was first over the wall and personally beheaded its emir in single combat, an extraordinary feat for a man of sixty-seven. He then retook Lepanto, on the other side of the Gulf of Corinth, recently captured by Albanian tribesmen, but was ambushed by them and sold to the Turks to spend a year in captivity. When Navarrese mercenaries invaded Achaia shortly after, he decided to evacuate the Order's troops.

Juan's later years were troubled by the papal schism, with Urban VI reigning at Avignon, 'Clement VII', the anti-pope, at Rome. The Master, with the French and Spanish kings, supported the latter, and Urban therefore nominated an anti-Master, Fra. Ricardo Carracciolo, Prior of Capua. Some brethren turned pirate, like Fra. Guillaume de Talebart who, in 1391, boarded two Aragonese merchant ships off the Sardinian coast and seized a valuable cargo of coral.[1] However, the convent remained loyal to Heredia, who had become a much loved superior, until his death at Avignon in 1396.

As a keen humanist Heredia commissioned the first translation of Plutarch into a vernacular language – Aragonese – as well as part of Thucydides' *Peloponnesian War*, Marco Polo's *Travels* and some oriental works.[2] Indeed the Hospitallers did include intellectuals, such as Jean Hesdin, dean of the theological faculty of Paris, an enthusiastic classicist and the spokesman for the French party during the controversy over the papal return to Rome,

---

[1] Delaville le Roulx, 'Deux aventuriers de l'Ordre de l'hòspital – les Talebart', *Melanges sur l'Ordre de St Jean de Jerusalem*.

[2] For his career see Delaville le Roulx, *Les Hospitaliers à Rhodes*, and Herquet, *Juan Ferrandez [sic] de Heredia, Grossmeister des Johanniterordens*. The latter work has an appendix dealing with his literary activities.

who was attacked by Petrarch.[1] Several brethren were masters of canon law, a necessary qualification for dealing with the Roman bureaucracy.

Brother knights were called, of course, to be Men of God – 'that with this rule of life we may merit the reward of eternal life'. Every day these tough pirates recited the Little Office, the Office of the Dead or 150 'Pater Nosters'. Their habit remained the black tunic and cloak, and though it is unlikely that knights joined in singing the full Roman Office like Spanish *freyles caballeros*, on great feasts they attended Canonical Hours at the Conventual church, where non-military brethren acted as canons, the Master presiding from an abbatial throne. Even on caravans the sea-knights chanted their 'Pater Nosters', led by the ship's chaplain, while the galley was halted to say the 'Angelus', while, thankfully, slaves rested on their oars. It was not enough for Hospitallers to substitute 'the defence of the Holy Catholic faith against the infidels and the enemies of the Christian religion' in place of 'the defence of the Holy Land'; there must be a double profession. The Church had hallowed secular knight-hood with a ritual in which sword, belt and spurs acquired a quasi-sacramental quality. St John made this ceremony a preface to the old, non-military rite of profession when the candidate received the habit, to stress the dual vocation. Those who found the life difficult faced Draconian penances. A brother guilty of negligence or calumny could incur the *septaine*; one week's confinement to the *auberge* where he ate bread from the floor – fighting off the dogs – and drank water, while every twenty-four hours he was scourged 'with thongs' before the High Altar of the Conventual church. Graver offences, gambling and dining in low taverns, earned forty days of the same treat-ment – the *quarantaine*. 'The crime of fornication', concubinage, duelling or simony were punished by incarceration in the con-vent's prison *and* flogging. All brethren had to confess to the Order's priests of whom there were two grades, chaplains at Rhodes under their conventual prior, and priests-of-obedience in Europe – an inferior class who did not have to furnish proofs of nobility and rarely obtained commanderies. The brother-hood's real spiritual superior was the Reverend Grand Master,

[1] See Luttrell, *Jean and Simon de Hesdin – Hospitaller Theologians*.

'servus pauperum Christi et custos Hospitalis Hierusalemis'.

Often the crew of an Egyptian carrack, becalmed off some exquisite Aegean island, would wake at sunrise to see beneath the violet sky a galley darting out from a silent cove. The noise in itself was terrifying: huge oars beating the water in a rhythmic stroke sounded by shrill, whistle blasts or banging on a gong. There was a jarring crash when the prow's iron beak buried itself in ship's timbers followed by deafening explosions as bowchasers raked the decks and then, through the smoke, along the ram or over a boarding bridge, swarmed the steel-clad brethren.

All knights were anxious to complete the caravans necessary for promotion. A voyage lasted several months, and they lived in acute discomfort, fitting themselves into the machinery of an instrument built for speed and fighting. Brethren and their *patrons* slept huddled together under a tent on the stern platform and their provisions were restricted to oil-soaked biscuit and watered wine. The real horror was the stench of rowers, and brothers sometimes plugged their noses. These poorly fed oarsmen, criminals or Saracen prisoners, were chained to their benches, lashed by overseers and only when in port were sheltered by a sailcloth awning. Yet shipmasters saw to a bare minimum of health, as starved or scurvy-ridden rowers could not produce an adequate rate of knots. Ships now mounted guns – breech-loading lombards, unreliable and dangerous but effective enough at short range. The Order's sea-going hierarchy consisted of the Admiral; the Captain of the Galleys on permanent duty with the battle squadron; and the *patrons* or ships' captains, who were frequently bailiffs. A fixed complement of brethren manned the guardship which patrolled outside Rhodes night and day.

The whole of the Latin East was failing, even Cyprus. After the coronation banquet of 1372 several Genoese were killed in a brawl, whereupon the republic invaded the island. Eventually a bitter peace was concluded, with Genoa retaining Famagusta. Jacques I, released from imprisonment in an iron cage, isolated the port with a ring of fortifications, but the monarchy was ruinously weakened despite his coronation as King of Armenia in 1393, for the last Haiot strongholds had been overrun by the Mamelukes. The Turks were swallowing Greece; Adrianople became their capital in 1366. The kingdom of Bosnia, the empire of the Serbs and the tsardoms of the Bulgars were soon conquered. In 1394 Bayezid proclaimed himself 'Sultan of Rum' (Rome). His army was invincible, its key troops being *spahis* (bowmen equipped with steel helmet, mail shirt, shield, lance and yataghan) who were supported by similarly armed feudal troops under beys. Tactics were still the arrow storm and lightning charge. Though cruel and greedy for plunder these soldiers went to war without whores, shunning wine and gambling.

The pope succeeded in launching the greatest expedition since the days of St Louis. Philippe de Mézières, once Pierre I's chancellor, had wandered all over Europe for nearly half a century preaching Holy War. The Balkans could be reached without a dangerous sea voyage while at hand there were powerful allies, Hungary-Croatia and Wallachia. Jean de Nevers brought 10,000 Burgundians and Frenchmen, the Earl of Huntingdon 1,000 English. From Germany came 6,000 men, and there were also Czechs, Poles, Spaniards and Italians. All met at Buda in July 1396, where King Sigismund of Hungary had assembled 60,000 Magyars and Transylvanians with 10,000 Vlachs under their Prince, Mircea the Old. Most of the western contingents were *gens d'armes* in grotesque *hounskull* helmets with 'pig face' visors and *jupons* (short cloth tunics worn over mail shirts). However, the majority of eastern Europeans were light cavalry or spearmen. By September, besides whoring and drinking bad wine, they had invested the Bulgarian city of Nicopolis and spent a fortnight trying to starve its Osmanli garrison into surrender. They were joined by the Venetian, Genoese and Hospitaller contingents, the latter under Master Philibert de Naillac, whose galleys had sailed up the Danube from the Black Sea.

On 25 September 1396 Bayezid *Yilderim* ('Lightning') appeared with an equally large army, 100,000 men, including a force of Christian Serbs under their despot, Stefan Lazarović. The sultan's first line of battle was light auxiliaries – *akinjis* (horse) and *azebs* (foot) in front of rows of pointed stakes. These sheltered his real infantry of archers and axemen. Behind them, completely hidden by a range of low hills, were the *spahis* and feudal cavalry. The French chivalry hurled themselves at the Turks' light troops. After killing at least 10,000, they dismounted to pull out the stakes and get at the bowmen, who fled up the hill. The knights pursued on foot, climbing the steep incline in their heavy armour. Suddenly '40,000' *spahis* galloped over the crest, charging down on the sweating men-at-arms still toiling up towards them. It was a massacre, and even the unwounded rolled down the hill to lie prostrate at the bottom. Sigismund and his Magyars, with the Germans and the brethren, rode forward to meet the Turks, though their Roumanian allies had fled. They slew 15,000 infidels and for a moment it seemed Bayezid might be defeated, but then the Serbs came to his rescue with a ferocious charge. Sigismund and Philibert escaped in boats down the Danube, while archers galloping along the bank shot at them until they were picked up by a Venetian galley. Most Hungarians, however, died beside their German comrades and many brethren fell with them. Next day, apart from 300 great nobles rich enough to pay extortionate ransoms, the captured knighthood was slaughtered 'from morning till Vespers'. Nicopolis was the Latin East's death sentence.[1]

Bayezid then besieged Constantinople for seven years, but the Hospitallers were needed elsewhere; in 1400 they bought Mistra and Acrocorinth from the despot of the Morea, who had fled to Rhodes. Mistra refused to admit the brethren, as the Turks had now withdrawn from the Peloponnese, but Acrocorinth, which was more exposed, welcomed them. However, after four years the Master sold these Greek possessions to the empire. Bayezid had indeed intensified his siege of Constantinople in 1402, uttering threats of massacre and extermination, but was himself overwhelmed the same year by Tamberlane at Chibukabad.

Yet Tamberlane was a *ghazi* too and invested Smyrna on 2 December 1402. The first day a white flag flew over the Khan's tent signifying that if the city surrendered the lives of all would be spared; the second day the flag was red, promising mercy for the common people but not their rulers; the third day it was black – no man, woman or child would be spared. The besiegers numbered tens of thousands and had brought every conceivable

[1] See Atiyah, *The Crusade of Nicopolis*.

siege engine. The captain of Smyrna, Fra. Iñigo d'Alfara,[1] his
200 brethren and their few mercenaries had to man the ramparts
under a sky black with missiles, while sappers tunnelled ceaselessly beneath their feet. Even so a contemporary Persian historian wrote that the Tartars, victors from Delhi to the Don,
thought that they fought 'like a band of enraged devils'. After a
fortnight a Hospitaller fleet was sighted but the besiegers re-
doubled their efforts and breached the city walls. The remnants
of the garrison cut their way through to the jetties and swam out
to the galleys. In the ensuing orgy of extermination the
triumphant horde fired the heads of fallen brethren at the
Christian ships.

Smyrna had protected Black Sea shipping, and a few years
later, therefore, Fra. Philibert occupied the Turkish castle of
Bodrun on a mainland peninsula opposite Rhodes, building a
great stronghold, Fort St Pierre, with seven lines of fortification
and a secure harbour.[2] He was an unusually able Master who
reunited the brethren, even though the papal schism continued.
Probably his worst problems were financial, as receipts from
European commanderies dwindled alarmingly. He travelled to
many western capitals on fund-raising expeditions, visiting
London in 1410. The brethren increased their commercial
activities, investing in Italian enterprises or trading direct with
Alexandria and Damietta. But even if they negotiated treaties
with Egypt their caravans continued to sweep the Levantine
seas.

Fortunately for Rhodes, Cairo regarded Cyprus as its chief
enemy. The island was weakened by recurrent outbreaks of
plague, by swarms of locusts and by the declining authority of
an impoverished monarchy. Yet King Janus saw himself as
another Pierre. Frequent raids were made on the Egyptian coast
and Moslem merchantmen attacked without mercy, for Janus
would not restrain his privateers. In Pierre's day the
Mamelukes had been crippled by a shortage of ships' timber,
but now they possessed the Cilician forests. In 1426 Sultan
Barsbei dispatched an armada of 180 galleys, carrying cavalry

[1] See Delaville le Roulx, 'L'Occupation Chrêtienne à Smyrne, 1344–1402',
Melanges.
[2] Delaville le Roulx, *Rhodes*, p. 309.

and Turcoman regulars, which landed in late June. The king, woefully incompetent, was surrounded and routed at Khiro-kitia;[1] his horse was killed under him and he proved too fat for any remounts available. The Mamelukes then burnt Nicosia to the ground and laid the whole kingdom to waste. In Cairo the wretched Janus was paraded through the streets on a donkey, his bare feet shackled beneath its belly save when jeering guards made him dismount to kiss the ground. After a year the king 'who never smiled again' was released on payment of the enormous ransom of 200,000 ducats, to which the Order contributed 30,000.[2]

Henceforth Cypriot kings were the sultan's vassals and almost overnight an aggressive crusader state had changed into a harmless trading base. Royal authority all but disappeared and the estates of both king and magnates never recovered. Indeed, the Order of St John, the largest landowner in the country, found its houses nearly bankrupt: in 1428 Grand Commander Hermann von Ow leased Kolossi to two brethren for seven years at a nominal rent of four ducats on condition they put the commandery on its feet – the normal income was 12,000 ducats.[3] In 1440 the Order reached an agreement with Cairo whereby Cyprus would not be involved in any future hostilities. The brethren could expect little help from the shattered kingdom's scanty forces and could certainly not afford to defend it, while both sides were anxious to safeguard their mercantile interests. Now Rhodes was the sole heir of crusader Jerusalem.

[1] Ibid., vol. 2, pp. 478–80. There was a Hospitaller commandery at Khirokitia.
[2] Bosio, op. cit., vol. II, p. 146.
[3] Ibid., p. 147, and Hill, *A History of Cyprus*, vol. 2, p. 487.

CHAPTER 14

The Three Sieges

The convent's growing peril heightened its brethren's sense of dedication. Significantly Hospitallers began to use the term 'our holy Religion' more often when referring to their Order, and the official adoption of the style 'Grand Master' by Fra. Antonio Fluvian, elected in 1421, reflects renewed purpose as much as worldly grandeur. Rhodes was the new kingdom of Jerusalem where warriors guarded a consecrated citadel under the patronage of the Holy Virgin of Philermo whose icon they had brought from Acre. Brethren could die in some peace of mind, sending as many of Christ's enemies to hell as possible before they themselves ascended to eternal glory. No doubt they were conscious of being the only fighting brotherhood outside Spain and the Baltic lands.

For even the last vestiges of St Lazarus were disappearing. In England there was no mention of Locko after 1351, though its revenues continued to be enjoyed by Burton Lazars, and Chosely had gone by 1458. In 1450 the pope granted the petition of Master William Sutton that no further confirmation was needed once Burton Lazars had elected its superior. Scotland stayed loyal to Boigny a little longer, though in France too preceptories were degenerating into sinecures. The Leper Knights of Outremer would have had difficulty in recognising their incumbents as brethren.[1]

Rhodes was always ready for an attack. The guardship patrolled the coast ceaselessly, there was a tall watchtower on Simi, and not only were Hospitaller consuls active in Egypt but Rhodian merchants knew every rumour circulating in Cairo or Alexandria. Fortunately the brethren's seamanship often enabled them to outsail and outfight far larger forces. This was dramatically evident in 1440 when Sultan Jakmak of Egypt, increasingly incensed by the pirate monks' depredations,

[1] *V.C.H., Leicestershire*, p. 37.

sent a fleet against them. After destroying the villages on
Kastelorrizon his eighteen galleys, 'extremely well furnished
with soldiers, oarsmen, cannon and ammunition', went on to
attack the convent itself. As soon as they were sighted, the
marshal of the Order, Fra. Louis de Saint Sebastien, led out
his entire battle squadron, eight galleys and four armed cargo
vessels, firing his guns and playing martial music. So unnerved were the Egyptians by this unexpectedly aggressive
reception that they ran close in to the shore, laying alongside
each other and turning their poops seaward. Here they held
off the brethren with a barrage of cannon shot and Greek fire
until nightfall. They then hurriedly set sail – apparently bound
for Turkey. But Fra. Louis learnt from a captured Mameluke
that their real destination was Lango. Sailing hard throughout
the night, he managed to intercept them. Again the horrified
Egyptians refused battle, taking refuge in an uninhabited
harbour 'which the Turks call Carathoa'. They thought themselves safe enough in its sandy shallows, for the Hospitaller
carracks shipped too much water to follow. Swiftly Fra. Louis
transferred the latter's men-at-arms aboard his galleys and then
went into the attack. A 'great and bloody battle' ensued in
which the Mamelukes lost 700 men against 60 Rhodian
casualties. Only nightfall and a rising sea saved them from
annihilation.

The wasps' nest was never disturbed with impunity. In the
summer of 1444 an Egyptian armada landed 18,000 men, who
devastated the island before investing the city and its convent.
Luckily, small reinforcements had just arrived from Burgundy
and Catalonia. After six weeks the Mameluke guns breached
the massive curtain walls and the Grand Master, Jean Bonpars
de Lastic, realised that a general assault was imminent. Before
dawn on 24 August he assembled his troops silently in the
darkness, outside the ramparts, with knights and pikemen in
the centre, arbalestiers on the wings. In these days brethren
fought on foot in brigandines (leather coats sewn with metal
studs) and steel hats or *sallets* (while, as seamen, their favourite
weapon seems to have been the boarding pike). Among
Englishmen present was the Turcopolier, Fra. Hugh Middleton. At first light the charge was sounded, whereupon, with

trumpets braying, kettledrums and cymbals clashing, the
formidable little army smashed its way into the sleeping
Mameluke camp roaring the old battle cry 'St Jean, St Jean'.
It was over quickly: the enemy bolted to their ships, though not
before hundreds had been cut down by exulting brethren, who
captured the entire siege train. Jakmak was so disheartened
that he made peace in 1446.[1]

But if the convent had weathered its first great siege it would
soon be confronted by a far more terrible foe. The Turks were
steadily overrunning Greece; the Latin lords of the archipelago and the mainland frequently sent desperate appeals
to the bailiff of the Morea, while the empire itself was very
near the end, reduced to Constantinople, and a few towns. In
1451 the most ferocious of all sultans ascended the Osmanli
throne – Mehmet II, who on several occasions swore he would
conquer Rhodes after Constantinople. Probably the fall of
Byzantium and the hero death of the eighty-first Roman
emperor in 1453 were more keenly mourned by the knights
than anyone, if only as apocalyptic confirmation of the Latin
East's doom. Grand Master Jacques de Milly launched a series
of highly successful raids on the Turkish coast while Mehmet
was busy subjugating the remnants of Roumania. Then in 1462
Pius II's crusade failed to materialise. Broken-hearted, the
pope died: Holy War was dead. Although the brethren foiled
an Egyptian attempt to conquer Cyprus the kingdom's affairs
were deteriorating, and it was no doubt a growing sense of
isolation which caused the increase of the convent to 400
knights in 1466. Careful thought had been given to their
deployment; in 1460 the garrison of Bodrun was raised to
fifty and that of Kos to twenty-five, while forty were assigned
to guardship duty. Fortunately the Turks were distracted by
a long war with Venice, which continued until 1479.

The Grand Commander of Cyprus in 1467 was Fra. John
Langstrother, an English brother of boundless ambition whose

[1] Belabre, p. 28, gives this account but does not quote his sources. Bosio,
op. cit., pt. II. pp. 162, 163 – gives few details save that after forty days the
Egyptians, having done much damage with their artillery, were then
driven back to their ships by a sortie. It is also known that Lastic and
Middleton were in the convent.

early history was a good example of a successful career in the Order. Born in 1416, by 1448 he was a commander and Lieutenant-Turcopolier, castellan of Rhodes in 1453, Bailiff of Egle in 1464 and Grand Prior of England in 1469. Fra. John had already been appointed the kingdom's treasurer by the Earl of Warwick, who had taken over the government from Edward IV. Edward later dismissed Langstrother, but in 1471 'My Lord of St John's' supported Henry VI, commanding part of the Lancastrian van at Tewkesbury. After the defeat he took refuge in the abbey, but was dragged out and beheaded.[1]

The case of Ireland shows just how anarchic and unprofitable were some European priories. Here most commanderies were farmed out to laymen, while Irish brethren were never seen at Rhodes, being far too involved in tribal politics. The nadir was reached during the lordship of Edward IV, when Fra. James Keating became prior. Little better than a bandit, on one occasion he seized Dublin Castle. He ignored the General Citation of 1480 and in any case never sent Responsions (revenues) to the convent. Grand Master d'Aubusson declared him deposed in 1482 but when Fra. Marmaduke Lumley came to take his place Keating promptly imprisoned his unwary brother. Fra. James was still disastrously active in Henry VII's reign.[2]

Most brothers were *petite noblesse* – in England, gentry. English brethren rarely bore great names though even if their fathers had been merchants who purchased land and arms or their brothers were apprenticed to a trade there was a very real gap between knight and burgess. Perhaps the fifteenth century had not evolved the meticulous stratification of *seize quartiers*, but in that strange pageant world a man's occupation had almost mystical symbolism, and all military brethren enjoyed the glamour of aristocracy.

Chivalry still flourished in northern Europe, but as an aesthetic cult, whose devotees belonged to court orders such as the Golden Fleece, the Star, the Porcupine, the Garter. Living an Arthurian dream and taking fantastic vows, their

[1] See King, *The Knights of St John in the British Empire*.
[2] See R. Bagwell, *Ireland under the Tudors* (London 1885).

arena was the tournament rather than the battlefield. If these exotic fraternities met at 'Chapters' clad in 'habits' and attended corporate services in their own churches their ideals were those of the 'Morte d'Arthur', not the cloister. Brethren at Rhodes living hard, simple lives bore small resemblance to the weird *incroyables* of the Burgundian court.

If there were sinners amongst them, weak 'from the strength of evil passions', they remained essentially men of God. In the *Liber Missarum ad usum Ecclesiae Hospitalis Sancti Johannis* compiled at Rhodes in 1465 the feast of St John was celebrated with three masses – the last pontifical – at midnight, at dawn and at full light; a liturgical distinction normally reserved for Christmas Day.[1] Before the end of the century a Cardinal Master would preside in the conventual church wearing cope and mitre. Even today a modern chaplain of the Religion can write, 'for the knight the poor are nothing less than Christ, incarnate in their suffering and in them he takes care of Christ'.[2]

The net, however, was closing. In 1463 the Lord of Lesbos sent a desperate appeal for help, but, though the brethren rushed to defend his capital, Mytilene, it fell by treachery. In 1470 the Turks descended on Euboea (Negropont), whereupon the Order sent a flotilla under Fra. Pierre d'Aubusson to relieve its Venetian garrison – without success, as the republic's admiral lost his nerve. The knights concentrated on strengthening their own island. They had to face formidable new troops, the *yeni cheri*. These Janissaries were recruited from a compulsory tribute of Christian boys, but developed into a crack unit employed for assaults or forlorn hopes; before 1500 they never numbered more than 2,000. Not only did they forgo wine, gambling and whores but they were forbidden to marry and slept in dormitories, being affiliated to the Bektashi sect of dervishes whose originator, Haji Bektash of Khurasan, had blessed their foundation. Armed with spear and yataghan they presented a strange, disturbing appearance when attacking, led by their chief officers the *Chorbaji* (soup-maker) and

[1] See Ducaud-Bourget, *The Spiritual Heritage of the Sovereign Military Order of Malta*, p. 153.
[2] Ibid., p. 154.

the *Kaveji* (coffee-maker) in an odd minuet-like marching step; three paces forward, a pause, then three paces forward again, to the sound of a braying military band, the *Mehtar*. Over mail shirts they wore a uniform of green and yellow cloaks with white ostrich plumes and tassels hanging from high white mitres; their standard was a flowing banner of white silk hung with horsetails. But their performance was no less remarkable than their appearance.

By 1479 Mehmet was ready to settle accounts. He had a worthy opponent in the Grand Master, Pierre d'Aubusson. Born in 1423 this fifth son of a great Limousin family had entered the Order in his late twenties, having already seen military service against the English.[1] Despite his northern origins, he probably by now had more in common with the princes of Renaissance Italy than those of late medieval France or ducal Burgundy – he was enough of a *Quattrocento* intellectual to employ the humanist poet Gian Maria Filelfo as Latin secretary. Remarkable as soldier, administrator and diplomat Fra. Pierre's greatest gifts were realism and leadership, and he combined magnetic appeal with a magnificent appearance. Both brethren and Rhodians were devoted to him. Mehmet sent an ambassador to lull the brethren's suspicions, but Pierre was not deceived. In all he could muster perhaps 600 brethren with 1,500 mercenaries, Rhodian militia and privateer sailors, while since his election he had been strengthening fortifications, deepening ditches, demolishing buildings close to the city walls, installing artillery and laying up stocks of food and ammunition.

Turkish agents, however, considered the garrison hopelessly inadequate. Mehmet appointed an apostate member of the Byzantine imperial family, Misac Palaeologus Pasha, as Vizier and commander of the expedition. In April 1480 lookouts on Rhodes sited enemy warships, and on 23 May '70,000 men' landed at the bay of Trianda while the port was blockaded by fifty galleys. Misac pitched camp on the hill of St Etienne, overlooking Rhodes. The key to the siege was Fort St Nicholas on the promontory flanking the outer harbour: once it had fallen Rhodes could be starved into surrender. A large Turkish

[1] See Bouhours, *The Life of the renowned Peter d'Aubusson.*

battery was built on the opposite shore, mounting three brass 'basilisks', the period's howitzers, discharging stone balls over two feet in diameter.

These guns were directed by Meister Georg, a German artillery expert, who suddenly appeared before the walls claiming sanctuary 'for the sake of conscience'. In fact he was a double agent spurred on by bribes to discover where artillery fire would do most damage, and tried to panic the garrison by describing the besieging army's vast size and ferocity. All believed that if Rhodes fell they would be impaled alive, for the Turks had brought large quantities of sharpened stakes. But the Grand Master saw through this feigned deserter and later hanged him.[1]

When his guns had battered a wide breach in the fort's walls, the Vizier ordered the first assault. Turkish galleys sailed in to land troops on both sides of the mole. Wading ashore their feet were impaled on ships' nails and old knives set in baulks of timber laid on the sea bed.[2] Halting in agonised confusion they made excellent targets for hand gunners and arbalestiers, while in the breach they were decimated by cross fire from flanking batteries, before meeting a counter-charge led by d'Aubusson. His helmet knocked off by a cannon ball, Fra. Pierre joked about improving prospects of promotion and then returned to the fight. Eventually the enemy galleys fled before a flotilla of fire ships, whereupon Misac called off his thoroughly demoralised men, leaving 600 dead.

The distance between Fort St Nicholas and the opposite shore was hardly 150 yards. The Turks therefore constructed a pontoon, and one night a small boat fastened an anchor in the rocks under the mole round which a cable was passed to haul the floating bridge across. However, an English sailor dived in and removed the anchor. Next came an assault by night, on 18 June, the Turks attacking all along the mole in a swarm of light craft and towing their pontoon into position, galleys pounding away at the fort. The darkness was lit up by the

[1] '. . . a diabolical hypocrite . . .' – see Taafe, op. cit., vol. 3, p. 50.
[2] See Caoursin, *Obsidionis Rhodiae Urbis Descriptio*, trans. Kay, p. 14, '. . . and thereabout the sea is at every tide, flow and ebb, wherefore there were thrust down pipes and tuns and tables full of nails. . . .'

weird glow of naphtha and molten lead, flickering gun-fire and the flames of incendiary ships; several enemy galleys were set alight, garrison artillery sinking at least four. The battle raged from midnight until ten o'clock the following morning. It was reported that the Turks lost 2,500 – including the officer who had led the storming party, a son-in-law of the sultan. Misac was so discouraged that he did nothing for three days but sit brooding in his tent.

He had ordered a general bombardment at the beginning of the siege before concentrating on the south-eastern section of the ramparts, which contained the Jewish quarter. Even if the Master's palace was in ruins, strategically the building was unimportant – though the destruction of the magistral wine cellar upset some brethren – but here the walls were old and not too solid. The enemy's batteries thundered ceaselessly, protected by earthworks and timber shelters, the largest mounting eight brass basilisks, while their sappers undermined the foundations. As the walls soon began to crumble, d'Aubusson built a ditch and a brick wall behind them. Everybody took a hand at the work, citizens and knights toiling day and night, the Master himself setting an example. A rain of incendiary arrows and grenades started fires all over Rhodes, so he sent women and children into the cellars or a primitive air raid shelter roofed with baulks of timber. He also ordered the construction of a good old-fashioned trebuchet:[1] sardonically christened 'the tribute' this devilish machine threw rocks so large they splintered wooden battery shelters like matchwood and opened up mines.

Some Italian brethren lost their nerve and found a spokesman in the magistral secretary, Filelfo, who begged d'Aubusson to negotiate. The Master called them together, saying coldly that it was still possible for a galley to run the blockade and they could leave at once, then bullied and coaxed them into a tougher mood. Misac resorted to Byzantine methods; two 'deserters', an Albanian and a Dalmatian, were sent into the city with the cheerful news that Mehmet was on his way with

[1] Ibid., p. 24, '. . . an engine called a Trebucher, like a sling, which was great, high and mighty and cast great and many stones'. Bosio, op. cit., pt. II, p. 331.

100,000 men. D'Aubusson refused to believe it, and they attempted to enlist Filelfo in an attempt to murder him. Immediately the Italian informed his Master and the wretched men were lynched by the garrison.

All this time the bombardment of the south-east wall continued. One battery was stormed under cover of darkness by the Italians who returned with Turkish heads on their pikes, but the vizier had the moat filled with rubble. After six weeks only a heap of collapsed masonry with a breach wide enough for cavalry to ride through stood between the brethren and their enemies. Misac's envoy, Suleiman Bey, came to the breach, declaring a good defence had earned good terms; by surrendering, the garrison could become Sultan Mehmet's allies, by resisting they would be annihilated – the breach was open, 40,000 crack troops waiting. Fra. Antoine Gautier, castellan of Rhodes, answered that if the walls were down there were fresh defences behind them, that attackers could only expect the same reception they had had on the St Nicholas mole, that the sultan had an odd way of making friends and that anyway his brethren were ready for an assault. For a day and a night every Turkish gun available pounded the breach. After the bombardment had stopped, an hour before dawn on 28 July, a single mortar was fired as signal and scaling parties crept forward silently. The exhausted, deafened garrison was asleep and the few guards easily rushed – within minutes the Turks had captured not only the breach but the bastion of Italy, sending word to the Pasha to bring up more troops.

Fra. Pierre was there at once, gripping a half-pike, shouting to his brethren they must save Rhodes or be buried in its ruins. First up the ladder on to the mound of rubble, he was knocked down twice but climbed back. Soon knights and Turks were at each other's throats all along the shattered rampart. Usually armour made up for lack of numbers; great elbow guards could catch and snap a sword and at close quarters a man-at-arms would rip his lightly-armed opponent to shreds. However, now it seemed that the defenders, reeling from fatigue, would be pushed off the walls. Elbowing forward in his gilt armour[1] followed by three standard bearers and a handful

[1] See Bosio, op. cit., pt. II, p. 338.

13b. A late-fifteenth-century knight of St John, Fra. Alberto Aringhien. Note the galleys in the background. From a painting by Pinturicchio.

13a. The siege of Rhodes in 1480. The brethren are wearing the *sopravest* of the Order of St John, a red surcoat with a white cross. From Caoursin's 'Relation du siège de Rhodes'.

14a. A Venetian galley of the type used by the Order of St John at Rhodes and at Malta.

14b. The *gran galleone* of the Grand Master of the Knights of St John at Malta. Note the lateen rig. The sails were red and white and the hull painted in black and gold.

of brethren the Master used himself as a living banner to rally the convent, whereupon Misac sent in a squad of Janissaries with orders to kill him.

Beneath his battle banners of the Virgin, the Baptist and the Crucifixion, he faced them. Soon the Grand Master was almost down, wounded in three places; the tide turned as brethren rushed to his rescue, but not before he collapsed with two more terrible wounds including a punctured lung. As he was carried to the rear, blood pouring from his armour, Fra. Pierre muttered 'We die here – we *don't* retreat'. Brethren hurled themselves on the astonished Turks, who suddenly broke; not only were they swept off the ramparts and out of the breach – where many were jammed in and killed – but the vizier's camp was stormed and his standard captured.

Misac gave up in despair. The garrison claimed that 3,500 Turks who had fallen swelled his casualties to 9,000, the defenders having killed more than twice their own number, not to mention 30,000 wounded. Even if the vizier had known that more than half the brethren had died, including most bailiffs, the news that the Master's wounds were not mortal was sufficient disappointment.[1] His army's spirit was broken and when a Neapolitan carrack and a papal brigantine ran the blockade the humiliated Turks burnt their stores and set sail, three months after investing the port.

Plainly the Turkish defeat was a miracle, and as at Marienburg the brethren had seen Our Lady with a host of angels, all wearing good fifteenth-century armour, accompanied by a familiar figure in camel hair – John the Baptist; the vision was gratifyingly corroborated by tactful prisoners. Pierre d'Aubusson recovered to find himself the hero of Europe.[2]

Mehmet, infuriated, began preparations for a fresh expedition, but died in May 1481. Though he had intended his

[1] Caoursin, op. cit., p. 30. 'But the Lord Master had five wounds of the which one was jeopardy of his life ... but through the Grace of God and help of leeches and surgeons.'

[2] The Master wrote a letter with a lively account of the siege to the Emperor Frederick III which is printed in Taaffe – the Latin original is in bk. 4, app. CLXXII and a translation in bk. 3, p. 53.

younger son Djem to succeed him, the elder Bayezid was more
popular and reduced his brother to hiding in the Karamanian
mountains. Djem took the desperate step of begging d'Aubusson
for refuge and a galley was sent to collect him; he arrived at
Rhodes in mid-summer to be received with the honours due
to a reigning sovereign. Cruel, treacherous and a born soldier
this Osmanli was as formidable as his father, and had he gained
the throne would have turned on his hosts without compunc-
tion. Bayezid II was the best sultan the brethren could hope
for, a pious Moslem preoccupied with building mosques, and
naturally peaceable. Understandably the Grand Master
expected diplomatic capital and shortly afterwards sent Djem
to France where he stayed in distinguished confinement at
the larger commanderies. Pierre obtained a pension for him
from Bayezid of 30,000 gold ducats – besides an annual
indemnity of 10,000 for the Religion. Finally in 1488 this
fainéant sultan was handed over to Pope Innocent VIII, and in
1495 died, reputedly poisoned by the Borgia pontiff Alexander
VI.

In 1485 Fra. Pierre was made cardinal and papal legate.
Not only did he build a church in thanksgiving for his
miraculous victory but he tightened the religion's discipline.
Some brethren had begun to dress in silks and velvets with
gold chains and jewelled scabbards; these were rigorously
proscribed and they had to wear their habit, black cassock,
cloak and skullcap, with a small white cross on the cloak's
left breast. European commanders may have lived as rich
country gentlemen yet the visitor to Rhodes knew he was in a
monastery; contemporary illustrations show a habited, monkish
community in chapter, listening to the scriptures in the
refectory or working in their hospital. Meanwhile the city's
walls were rebuilt and new towers added. Fort St Nicholas
became a great star-shaped bastion, its angled gun emplace-
ments making frontal assault impossible. Heavier cannon were
installed, while the convent raised its permanent garrison to
450 brethren in 1501. That year all Jews were expelled as constituting a potential fifth column. Pierre's criterion was survival,
and for the same reason that he expelled Hebrews he courted
Rhodians, admitting them to the Religion, even to bailiwicks.

The convent was on good terms with most European sovereigns, who tended to nominate grand priors. Clerkenwell escaped this fate, though the English priory had its troubles: in 1515 the great house of canonesses at Buckland severed its connection with the Order,[1] while Cardinal Wolsey prised a lease of their richest manor, Hampton Court, out of Prior Docwra. But on the whole relations with England were excellent. Henry VII was named 'Protector of the Religion' and English grand priors continued to attend parliament and head embassies to Rome or Paris.

In 1494 Charles VIII of France, who idolised d'Aubusson, invaded Italy with the avowed object of going on to conquer Constantinople and Jerusalem. Next year he was crowned at Naples as Emperor of the East and King of Jerusalem, while Pope Alexander VI organised a Holy League against the Turk with Pierre as generalissimo; it included Emperor Maximilian, and the kings of Spain, Portugal and Hungary, as well as Charles's successor, Louis XII, and the Doge of Venice. The convent made extensive preparations but the crusade never materialised. Fra. Pierre 'died of chagrin' in 1503, eighty years old and worn out by ceaseless vigilance. Rhodes gave him the funeral of a great monarch; a grieving procession marched through the silent city led by four brethren carrying his personal banners while two more bore his Red Hat and legate's cross. Greek as well as Latin bishops and clergy walked in the cortège.

To the conquerors of Rum the very existence of Rhodes was an insult and in 1503 the corsair Jamali raided the island to terrorise its inhabitants. The brethren, however, placed squadrons of cavalry at strategic points, and the raiders moved on to Leros. This islet-rock had only two knights in its tiny castle – the elderly bed-ridden commander and a young brother, Paolo Simeoni, eighteen years of age. The latter and their few servants manned the guns but by the first evening enemy artillery brought part of the walls crashing down. Next morning the infidels were astonished to see a large contingent of brethren waiting for them in the breach and hastily they set sail; Fra. Paolo had dressed the island's entire population,

[1] See Knowles & Hadcock, *Mediaeval Religious Houses*.

men and women, in the Order's red surcoats.[1] In 1506 seven
Egyptian 'flutes' – extremely fast and unusually long and
narrow galleys with very large sails – attacked Kos. A pair
were sent ahead as scouts but two Rhodian warships suddenly
appeared from behind a promontory, cutting them off, whereupon the Mamelukes beached their vessels and fled inland.
The brethren put a crew on board the flutes, who decoyed the
remainder of the flotilla into a bay where the Order's galleys
lay in wait; all five were captured and the prisoners sold as
slaves.[2] Even more spectacular was the taking of 'the great
carrack of Alexandria' in 1509. Every year this treasure ship,
named 'Queen of the Seas', plied between Tunis and Constantinople with wealthy merchants bringing fabulous luxuries
from India. The 'Mogarbina' was a gigantic vessel with seven
decks, whose main mast 'needed the arms of six men to circle
it' and, defended by '100 guns and 1,000 soldiers', the traders
confidently ventured their richest wares, for the carrack had
repulsed the brethren on several occasions. Commander de
Gastineau, a wily Limousin, waylaid the leviathan off Crete.
Under pretence of parleying he laid the Order's own great
carrack alongside and then mowed down the captain and
officers on the poop with one murderous salvo of grapeshot.
The leaderless crew struck their colours and the knights boarded
to find a staggering consignment of silver and jewellery as well
as bales of silk, cashmere and carpets, and quantities of pepper,
ginger, cloves and cinnamon. On the way home the gleeful
brethren captured three smaller cargo ships and the entire
treasure was eventually sold in France, its owners being held
to ransom or sent to the slave market.[3]

In August 1510 Sultan Qansuh al-Ghawri of Egypt sent his
nephew with twenty-five sail to 'Laiazzo' – Ayas near Alexan-
dretta on the coast of Asia Minor – to bring back a badly
needed consignment of ships' timber. The Order's spies sent
word of the expedition to Rhodes. Suddenly, out of the blue,
the brethren appeared before Ayas with four galleys under Fra.
Andrea d'Amaral and eighteen armed carracks and feluccas

[1] Bosio, op. cit., pt. II, p. 488.
[2] Ibid., p. 489.
[3] Ibid., p. 491.

under Fra. Philippe Villiers de l'Isle Adam (a shared command
which one day would bear bitter fruit). The Mamelukes rashly
sailed out to meet them, in order of battle. After a particularly
bloody hull-to-hull fight the brethren won a glorious victory,
capturing four war galleys and eleven other vessels. It was the
greatest of all their Rhodian sea battles and a triumph for their
espionage system. In addition there were political overtones.
The timber had been intended for a new Egyptian fleet which
was to have joined the Turkish navy in driving the Portuguese
out of the Red Sea – the abortive alliance was the last between
Mameluke and Osmanli, who soon turned on each other. In
1516 the Turks defeated and killed Qansuh al-Ghawri, hanging
the last Mameluke sultan the year after. Above all, the battle
off Ayas had been an uncomfortable reminder to the Porte that
Rhodes was an increasingly formidable sea power.

The gentle Bayezid was made to abdicate in 1512 and was
poisoned by his own son Selim I, 'the Grim', in whom blood-
lust and treachery reached manic intensity. He was a brilliant
soldier and won many victories, equipping his Janissaries
with arquebuses. The convent trembled, but fortunately Selim
was occupied with wars in Hungary, Persia and Egypt. Then
in 1517 he added Cairo and the caliphate to his possessions;
the convent was encircled. However, just as he was about to
set out for Rhodes in 1521 Selim died. His successor, Suleiman
the Magnificent, most attractive and most formidable of
Turkish emperors, inherited a campaign-hardened army
accustomed to victory. Anatolia was now the Osmanli heartland yet only a few miles off its coast lay that hornet's nest of
idolatrous pirates, described by the contemporary chronicler
Kemal Pashazade as 'this source of sin and gathering place of
twisted religion'. Until it was extinguished Turkey needed all
warships for home waters and could never be a great maritime
power herself.

The magistral election of 1521 was contested by Fra.
Thomas Docwra, Prior of England; by the Portuguese Prior
of Castile, Fra. Andrea d'Amaral; and by Fra. Philippe
Villiers de l'Isle Adam, Prior of Auvergne. The third was
chosen, to the noisy dismay of Amaral, who shouted 'This will
be the last Grand Master of Rhodes'. Receiving a letter from

the new sultan congratulating him on his election Fra. Philippe wrote a sardonic reply tantamount to a challenge, for his spies had infiltrated Suleiman's seraglio and he knew that an attack was imminent.[1] Europe ignored his appeals for help but a resourceful serving brother managed to hire 500 Cretan arbalestiers, despite their Venetian rulers' prohibition, disguising them as merchants or deckhands.[2] Best of all he recruited Gabriele Tadini de Martinengo, the greatest military engineer of the day, who evaded frenzied attempts to stop him reaching Rhodes. Once there the devout Martinengo was so impressed that, being unmarried, he asked to join the Order. Delighted, Philippe not only accepted this gifted postulant as an unprofessed brother 'of Magistral Grace' but also made him a Knight Grand Cross, whereupon the new bailiff enthusiastically set about strengthening defences: ravelins – arrow-shaped double trenches – were dug in front of each bastion and 'fascines and gabions' – wooden bundles and baskets of earth – heaped near any danger point, while every battery, protected by mantelets of wood or rope, was sited to command maximum fire. Philippe's garrison was little bigger than d'Aubusson's – he had 500 brethren, 1,000 men-at-arms and some militia – but his fortifications were stronger and his fire power immeasurably superior.[3]

On 26 June 1522, two days after the feast of St John, a Turkish armada of 103 galleys with 300 other vessels was sighted. Every Rhodian flocked to the Conventual church where, 'when the sermon was done a ponthyficall mass was celebrate with all solempnytees,' and 'the reverent lorde grete mayster'[4] laid the city's keys on the altar, entrusting them to St John. Finally he personally elevated the Host, blessing the

[1] Suleiman's letter is printed in Vertot, op. cit., II, p. 456.
[2] Bosio, op. cit., pt. II, p. 525.
[3] Bosio gives a complete list of the names of brethren present, many misspelt – pt. II, p. 533 *et seq.*
[4] See 'The begynnynge and foundacyon of the holy hospytall, & of the ordre of the knyghtes hospytallers of saynt Iohan baptyst of Ierusalem. (Here foloweth the syege, cruell oppugnacyon, and lamentable takynge of the cyte of Rodes.) Imprynted by Robert Coplande: London, the xxiii of Iuly 1524.'

island and its garrison. Then in gilt armour he rode through the streets, whilst brethren stood to their posts. He had already allotted sectors, as well as inspecting each langue's contingent in full battle order outside their respective auberges.

Contemporaries believed that the besiegers numbered 140,000 soldiers and a labour force of 60,000 Balkan peasants.[1] Their commander was Suleiman's brother-in-law, Mustafa Pasha, brave but inexperienced – 'plus brave soldat qu'habile géneral'.[2] Even though his chief of staff, Pir Mehmed Pasha, was a seasoned old aga, scarred veterans of Selim's campaigns had small confidence in this young courtier. Pir wrote to Suleiman stating that morale was low, that the sultan must come himself if the faithful were to take Rhodes, and on 28 July the Grand Signor arrived with 15,000 troops.

Throughout August the Turks concentrated on the ramparts between the bastion of Aragon and the sea. Their bombardment was more scientific than that of 1480 and the artillery included mortars for vertical fire. Mines now used gunpowder, besides being dug more quickly – with the greater number of pioneers available – though Martinengo detected many by means of drum parchment seismographs with little bells.[3] Methodically, guns demolished carefully selected areas and two huge earth ramps – 'marvellous great hills' – were built as high as the walls, to shoot down into the city. On 4 September two great gunpowder mines exploded under the bastion of England and twelve yards of rampart came crashing down, filling the moat – a perfect breach. The Turks assaulted at once and soon held the gap. Philippe was saying office in a nearby church. Taking its opening words 'Deus in adjutorium meum intende' for inspiration he seized his half pike and rushed out to see seven horsetail standards waving from the ruined wall. Mercifully the English brothers under Fra. Nicholas Hussey held an inner barricade from which Philippe led a counter-charge to such effect that the Turks deserted both breach and standards, though Mustafa slashed with his own sword at those who fled. The magistral standard bearer,

[1] These are Bosio's figures – op. cit., pt. II, p. 544.
[2] Vertot, op. cit., vol. II, p. 482.
[3] Bosio, op. cit., pt. II, p. 558.

the English Fra. Henry Mansell, was mortally wounded, but the besiegers had lost many men, including three sanjak beys.[1]

Twice more Mustafa repeated his assault on the badly damaged bastion of England. Columns of the Children of the Prophet, a thousand deep, came roaring over the barricades, but the Turcopolier Fra. John Buck counter-charged from the rubble. The enemy gave ground, and Mustafa himself rushed to their support. However, the English now had formidable help – German brethren under Fra. Christoph von Waldner – while cannon arrived, easily transportable sakers and falconets (six and three pounders), to cut bloody swathes at close range. The Pasha fought like a lion until his men dragged him away. The convent's casualties were high too, including Buck and von Waldner with many English and German brothers.[2] Mustafa decided to risk everything in a general assault on 24 September, which Sultan Suleiman watched from a convenient hillock. Four bastions, those of Aragon, England, Provence and Italy, were pounded mercilessly, and then through the smoke came the *yenicheri* racing for the walls. The Aragonese began to fail – they faced the Aga of the Janissaries – but the Grand Master came up with 200 fresh troops and the Aga was hurled back. Suleiman sounded the retreat; his warriors were about to break. Never had they met men like these, fanatics fiercer than the wildest dervish. Over 2,000 Turkish corpses remained.

Burning with shame the sultan paraded the entire army to see his brother-in-law shot to death with arrows, only sparing him after old Pir Mehmed had pleaded for mercy. Suleiman was about to raise the siege when an Albanian deserter claimed that so many brethren had been killed that Rhodes could not face another assault, whereupon he appointed a new commander-in-chief, Ahmed Pasha, an elderly engineer general with great experience. 'Hakmak Bashaw's'[3] strategy was one of attrition.

Philippe's powder was running short, and though a makeshift

[1] Ibid., p. 559.

[2] Ibid., pp. 560 and 563; Vertot, op. cit., vol. II, p. 482.

[3] Fra. Nicolas Roberts' rendering of his outlandish name – see below, p. 252.

mill was built there was insufficient saltpetre. Steadily Ahmed's guns demolished the walls; every day fewer fighting men were on their feet. Winter storms prevented the priories' contingents from leaving Messina; an English ship carrying the Bailiff of Egle was overtaken by a tempest in the Bay of Biscay and sank with all hands. Then a Turkish girl slave persuaded fellow slaves to fire the city, but they were caught and executed. A Jewish doctor was found shooting messages into the enemy camp. Even more alarming, Andrea d'Amaral's servant was discovered communicating with the Turks by the same means. Under torture he implicated his master, Prior of Castile and Grand Chancellor. 'Put to the question' Amaral denied the charge though he may have attempted to negotiate privately. Nonetheless, if not a turncoat this bitter old man's defeatism had unnerved the whole garrison. He was solemnly degraded from his vows and then beheaded.[1]

The Turks, protected by huge wooden shields, had dug trenches up to the walls. During an attack on the bastion of Aragon the invaluable Gabriele Martinengo was shot in the eye – the bullet passing through his head. The Master moved into the crumbling tower, which he did not leave for five weeks, sleeping on a straw mattress amid the rubble. Desperate watchmen scanned the horizon for relief. Finally, Philippe ordered the garrison of the archipelago and Bodrum to run the blockade in feluccas, with twelve knights and 100 men.[2] By the end of November bombardment had so destroyed the bastion of Italy that two churches were demolished to build barricades, while the bastions of England and Aragon had hardly one stone standing on another. When the next general assault came Martinengo was on his feet again and he and Philippe were everywhere, urging on their exhausted troops. Fortunately it rained and the Turks' ramps became a sea of mud, their powder useless, with the Janissaries beaten off once more with heavy casualties.

Verlot, who knew his Order, comments: 'On est bien fort et bien redoutable quand on ne craint point la mort.' Suleiman despaired. He had lost over 50,000 men – so the brethren

[1] For the Amaral affair see Bosio, op. cit., pt. II, pp. 576, 577.
[2] Ibid., p. 578.

9*

believed – besides thousands dead from plague and cold. An
officer was sent to the walls offering good terms, telling the
garrison it was doomed. 'Brethren of St John only do business
with their swords' shouted a commander. The English brother
Nicholas Roberts afterwards wrote '. . . Most of our men were
slain, we had no powther nor . . . manner of munycone nor
vitalles, but all on by brede and water; we wer as men
desperat determyned to dye upon them in the felde rather than
be put upon the stakes, for we doubted he would give us our
lyves considering ther wer slain so many of his men . . .'[1]
Winter set in, howling gales and snowstorms. The Grand
Master, although determined to die fighting, summoned the
council.

An eye-witness account of this dramatic meeting survives.
It was written by an elderly commander who had been caught
in Rhodes by accident, having come there on business, not to
fight. 'Frère Jacques, Bastard de Bourbon' as he engagingly
styled himself – he was a natural son of the Prince-Bishop of
Liège – says that all senior officers reported disastrous losses.
Martinengo was particularly blunt. 'Le capitaine frère Gabriel'
reported to the very reverend Master and very reverend lords
of the council that 'having seen and considered the great
pounding the town has suffered, having seen how large the
breach is and how the enemy's trenches are inside the town to
a depth of 100 feet with a breadth of more than 70 feet, having
also seen that they have broken through the wall in two other
places, that the greater part of our men-at-arms – both knights
and all the others – are dead or wounded and supplies
exhausted, that mere workmen are taking their place, it is
impossible to resist any longer unless some relief force comes to
make the Turk strike camp'. The Bastard adds that an excited
debate followed as to which was better – 'die to the last man
or save the people'. Many argued that 'ce fut bien et saincte-
ment fait de mourir pour la foy' though others pointed out
that the sultan's terms did not require them to deny Christ.[2]
Suddenly the Greek bishop and a delegation of weeping
citizens appeared, begging the brethren to capitulate. Fra.

[1] Roberts' letter is printed in Taaffe, op. cit., bk. 4, app. CCIV.
[2] Bourbon, op. cit., p. xxxviii.

Philippe 'fell downe allmost ded'.[1] Recovering, he and the bailiffs finally agreed 'it would be a thing more agreable to God to sue for peace and protect the lives of simple people, of women and children'.

A truce was arranged, but within a week it was broken. Then on 16 December Fra. Nicholas Fairfax ran the blockade in a brigantine, bringing all he could find – a cargo of wine and 100 Cretan arbalestiers.[2] By now the city's walls were mounds of rubble, the brethren's remnant living in muddy holes where they sheltered from snow and sleet. On 17 December the Turks attacked, and again the day after. Powderless, weak from cold and hunger, reeling brethren still managed to hurl them back. Perhaps it was during this last ghastly struggle that a slain English brother's Greek mistress cut their two children's throats, donned his armour, took his sword and went to the trenches, where she fought until killed. But other Rhodians were deserting, despite summary executions. On 20 December the Grand Master asked for a fresh truce.

Suleiman's terms were generous: in return for Rhodes, its archipelago with Bodrun and Kastelorrizon, the brethren were free to leave with all their goods. The Turks would even supply ships. No churches would be turned into mosques and Rhodians would have freedom of worship, besides being dispensed from all taxes for five years. After the Grand Master had been entertained in the sultan's 'red pavilion', Suleiman, disdaining an escort, visited the ruined city, where Philippe showed him the pathetic barricades. Asked to enter Turkish service, he replied, 'a great prince would be dishonoured by employing such a renegade'. Later the sultan remarked how sorry he was to make 'that fine old man' leave his home.[3]

On the night of 1 January 1523 a single trumpet sounded and then, to the besiegers' amazement, the brethren marched out

---

[1] Taaffe, op. cit., bk. 4, app. CCIV.

[2] Bosio describes Fairfax as 'Huomo molto spiritoso e prudente'. Op. cit., pt. II, p. 578.

[3] Ibid., pt. II, pp. 589, 590; Baudoin, op. cit., vol. I, pt. 267; Taaffe, op. cit., bk. 3, p. 25.

in parade order, armour burnished, banners flying and drums beating. Yet though the Emperor Charles V might comment 'nothing in the world was so well lost as Rhodes', the Hospitallers who sailed away into the snowy darkness knew that Jerusalem had fallen once again.

VI

THE LAST CRUSADE
1523–1571

Malta, Lepanto and the Counter-Reformation:
St John – St Lazarus – San Stefano

So they are seen to be a strange and bewildering breed, meeker
than lambs, fiercer than lions. I do not know whether to call
them monks or knights because though both names are correct
one lacks a monk's gentleness the other a knight's pugnacity.

> Bernard of Clairvaux c. 1128,
> 'De Laude Novae Militiae'

Possessor of men's necks.

> A title of the Turkish sultan

CHAPTER 15

The battle for the Mediterranean

It seemed unlikely that the Order of St John would survive, its homeless brethren wandering anxiously from refuge to refuge – from Messina to Cumae, from there to Civita Vecchia, thence to Viterbo, then Cornetto, and Villefranche and finally to Nice. In 1524 the Emperor Charles V offered Malta and Tripoli, but the religion had not yet abandoned all hope of Rhodes. Then in 1527 Henry VIII announced that the English Langue would become a separate brotherhood with the task of defending Calais, and the alarmed Grand Master came to England; Henry was upset that he had not been consulted about the Order's future. However, Fra. Philippe flattered him with the title 'Protector of the Religion' besides agreeing to retain the Turcopolier designate John Rawson[1] as Irish prior because of his success 'in civilising the natives', whilst in return the king allowed Fra. William Weston to be installed as Grand Prior of England.[2] The Master held deep misgivings about the emperor's offer, which entailed swearing fealty, but, after his captain-general failed to hold Modon in the Morea despite its capture, was compelled to accept in 1531. Many years would elapse before the brethren were reconciled to Malta.

This new kingdom, even smaller than Rhodes – seventeen miles by eight – was arid and treeless, its thin soil criss-crossed by dry stone walls and bare ravines. There were no rivers, not even streams. Gozo was no better, Comino and Cominetto hardly more than rocks. Most of the 20,000 inhabitants spoke 'a sort of Moorish' though their nobles were Aragonese or Sicilian. Neither the capital, Citta Notabile – modern Mdina – 'an old, deserted town', or the few mean villages held any charm for Aegean exiles. Inside Grand Harbour two rocky spits divided by a deep creek project from the eastern shore.

[1] For John Rawson see *D.N.B.*
[2] For William Weston also see *D.N.B.*

On the northern one was a fishing village, Birgu, guarded by a
ramshackle tower mounting three old cannon, Fort St Angelo.
Later the creek would become the Harbour of the Galleys,
the southern spit Senglea. A hilly peninsula, Monte Sceberras,
separated Grand Harbour from another large bay, Marsamxett.[1]

The convent was established in Birgu, protected by earthworks rather than ramparts. Auberges, installed in little houses
were for reasons of economy occupied only by young knights,
who slept in dormitories. Commanders were expected to buy
their own houses with revenues or prize money, though they
must say office and hear mass every day, dining 'in hall' four
times a week. Outside, brethren retained the habit only for
formal or conventual occasions, but their new dress was clerical
enough – a white linen cross sewn on the black doublet and a
white enamelled cross hanging from their necks. The makeshift convent's scattered buildings were uncloistered by a
collachium, and whoring and duelling were rife. Serious crime
earned incarceration in the peculiarly grim dungeons of St
Anthony, or loss of the 'habit'. When an English brother
murdered his Maltese mistress at the same time as a chaplain-
novice was caught pilfering jewels from Our Lady of Philermo's
shrine, the miserable pair were tied in sacks, rowed out to sea
and thrown overboard. In 1532 a gentleman-in-waiting of the
Prior of Rome killed a Provençal knight in a duel; uproar
broke out with a pitched battle in the streets between the
French, Italian and Spanish langues. Nomadic life had
unsettled the Order.

In 1534 Grand Master de l'Isle Adam, who was over seventy-
five and quite worn out, died, still homesick for Rhodes. He left
a formidable fleet. Its warship continued to be the galley, best
suited for a small navy's hit-and-run tactics. The great carrack
of the Religion, bluff-bowed, four-masted and square-rigged,
sometimes accompanied caravans, though her purpose was
essentially defensive, to convey a valuable cargo or important
embassy. Sailing from Candia to Messina in 1523 Fra. William
Weston had commanded such a vessel, capable of carrying 500

[1] For the unenthusiastic report of the commissioners whom the Order had
sent to investigate Malta, see Vertot, op. cit., vol. III, p. 41 *et seq.*

men with provisions for six months, her hull lead-plated against gunfire like the six-decked 1,700 ton *Santa Anna* built for the Order in 1530. Other ships included brigantines – light, deckless square-rigged two-masters useful as troop carriers – besides a swarm of feluccas and tartans, the *saettas* ('arrows') who nosed out prey for galleys. Despite vows of poverty brethren were allowed to keep a portion of their prize money, the *spoglio*, though, except for one-fifth which could be willed away, their fortunes reverted to the Religion when they died. In its straitened circumstances the convent now sold knights the privilege of fitting out their own galleys.

In 1535 the emperor attacked Tunis, recently seized by Khair ed-Din Barbarossa, Dey of Algiers; his ships were commanded by the redoubtable Andrea Doria, while the Religion sent four galleys, the great carrack and eighteen brigantines under its Vice-Admiral, Fra. Ottavio Bottigella, Prior of Pisa. Though garrisoned by 6,000 Turks Goletta was quickly stormed, the knights leading the assault, while as soon as Barbarossa marched out from Tunis some brethren among his prisoners led by Paolo Simeoni, the hero of Leros, overpowered their jailers and captured the citadel whereupon the Moslem army outside the walls fled and Simeoni opened the gates to the imperial troops. The brethren entertained Charles to a victory banquet on board the *Santa Anna*; finding the splendour of their table *equipage* and air of magnificence unedifying, he muttered sarcastically 'What do they do for God?' Bottigella broke in '*They* go before God without weapons or uniform, but in sandals, a plain habit and a hairshirt – they do not stand, they prostrate themselves. If your Majesty joined them you'd be given a choir stall, a black cowl and a rosary.'[1]

The Reformation was beginning to sap the brethren's strength. In 1545, when the Margrave of Brandenburg turned Protestant, the *Johanniterorden* was lost. Ironically the indirect architect of the English Langue's destruction, Clement VII, had once been Fra. Giuliano de' Medici, Grand Prior of Capua. At first Henry VIII considered establishing an Anglican order, but in May 1540 the English priory was dissolved and its brethren pensioned

[1] Schermerhorn, *Malta of the Knights*, p. 108, who takes the story from *La Soberana Orden Mil. de S. Juan de Jer; por Un Caballero de la Orden.*

off. Irish houses, most of which had been held by Prior Rawson himself, were also confiscated. Only the Scots priory remained, with its single commandery at Torphichen. The ten English brethren at Malta obtained funds from the common treasury, but English bailiwicks were not refilled as they fell vacant.[1] In 1539 Fra. Thomas Dingley, commander of Baddesley, had been beheaded together with a Knight of Honour, Adrian Fortescue,[2] for denying the Royal Supremacy; then in 1541 another professed brother, Fra. David Gunstone, was hanged and quartered. Two more brethren, William Salisbury and John Forest, died in prison. Their Langue numbered less than fifty and Knights of Honour were even fewer, and therefore St John gave more lives for the papacy than any Order in England save the Carthusian. In Fuller's words, 'The Knights Hospitallers, being gentlemen and soldiers of ancient families and high spirits, would not be brought to present to Henry VIII such puling petitions and public recognitions of their errors as other Orders had done.'[3]

At Burton Lazars, 'a very fair hospital and collegiate church' with a Master and eight brethren, St Lazarus' statue and holy well still attracted pilgrims. In 1540 Dr Thomas Legh, 'of a very bulky and gross habit of body', an agent of Cromwell in the Dissolution of the Monasteries, became its last Master; the Duke of Norfolk wrote 'alas what pity it were that such a vicious man should have the governance of that honest house' – by 1544 Burton Lazars was dissolved.[4] St Lazarus continued a shadowy existence in France. Its few commanderies enjoyed enviable incomes and a Hospitaller attempt to appropriate one in 1544 was stubbornly resisted, the *Parlement* of Paris deciding in favour of 'the Order of St Lazarus' in 1547. Fra. Jean de Levis of Malta was elected Master General in 1557, fiercely opposed by François Odet, commander of Villeray, who only submitted

---

[1] By 1548 English brethren in Malta were reduced to pawning their plate. See Scicluna (ed.), *The Book of Deliberations of the Venerable Tongue of England 1523–1527.*

[2] For Adrian Fortescue see *D.N.B.*

[3] Fuller, *The Historie of the Holy Warre* (Cambridge, 1640).

[4] For Thomas Legh see *D.N.B.*; for the houses' surrender, *V.C.H. Leicestershire,* vol. 2, p. 38.

after extracting a promise to preserve the Order's independence.[1]

Each year more *korsanlar* raided the Mediterranean coast, almost within sight of the Eternal City itself. Tripoli was in particular danger and as late as 1551 St John considered transferring the entire convent to this cluster of oases hemmed in by burning sand and stony hills. Torghut was now the most dreaded corsair and installed himself at Mahedia between Tunis and Tripoli, where he became such a nuisance that in 1550 the emperor sent an expedition, including 140 brethren, to burn out this wasp's nest. Torghut, 'Sword of Islam', swore vengeance. In July 1551 he cast anchor in the Marsamxett. Birgu was too formidable so he besieged Mdina, devastating the island. The Turcopolier Fra. Nicholas Upton, optimistically appointed on the death of Henry VIII, rode out with thirty knights and 400 local horse to inflict casualties; the victory was marred by Upton, an immensely fat man, expiring from heat stroke. The corsair then set sail for Tripoli, where an inadequate garrison sweltered in a rickety castle. Its governor, the Marshal Gaspard de Vallier, fought bravely, but no relief, not even a messenger, came, and he surrendered. He returned to a grim welcome. There had been criticism in the convent of Grand Master d'Omedes, who gave way to senile rage, and the marshal was deprived of the habit and imprisoned; had not a courageous brother remonstrated the infuriated old man would have beheaded him.[2]

Yet caravans were increasingly successful. The Religion's naval hierarchy had taken on its final form with a Grand Admiral – sometimes represented by a Vice-Admiral – and a Captain-General of the Galleys. *Les Patrons*, now called captains, were each assisted by a lieutenant and a ship-master, the latter a hired mariner. Moslem traders dreaded Strozzi and Romegas no less than Christian merchantmen feared Torghut. Leone Strozzi was appointed captain-general when young but left the Order to fight Charles V, after his father, a prisoner of the emperor, had committed suicide. A bitter, quarrelsome man, he had eventually to leave France, but Omedes refused to take back this stormy

---

[1] Bertrand de la Grassière, *L'Ordre Militaire et Hospitalier de Saint Lazare de Jérusalem*.

[2] See Vertot, op. cit., vol. III, p. 291 *et seq.*

petrel, who set up as corsair, calling himself 'the Friend of God alone'. Strozzi's little fleet became a byword, for he was a superb seaman who feared nothing and the religion gladly reinstated him when he next applied; but Fra. Leone resigned once again to wage a vendetta on the Medici, dying in an obscure raid on the Tuscan coast. In his *Memoirs* Benvenuto Cellini says of Strozzi, 'That excellent officer was one of the greatest men of the age in which he lived and at the same time one of the most unfortunate', while that fierce old soldier Blaize de Montluc described the Prior of Capua as 'one of the bravest men that these hundred years have put to sea'.[1] The most famous of the Order's sailors was Mathurin d'Aux de Lescout Romegas, who never attacked an enemy ship without taking or sinking it, frequently engaging half-a-dozen Turkish vessels singlehanded. He was indestructible. On the night of 23 September 1555 a terrible storm struck Malta, sinking every ship in Grand Harbour. Next morning knocking was heard from the keel of Romegas's galley floating bottom up; planks were prized loose whereupon out crawled the ship's monkey followed by the redoubtable captain.[2]

Omedes decreed that postulants must show four proofs of nobility, though the Order admitted aspirants with insufficient quarterings, the usual fault being a rich mother of plebian origin, as Knights 'of Grace'; later these inferior brethren were barred from promotion to bailiff, though many became Knights 'of Justice' (i.e. by right of birth) by papal dispensation. The Religion's sisters had also to produce proofs of nobility, Sigena in Aragon attracting the daughters of the greatest families in Spain, while a convent was established at Malta. Their red habit was replaced by a black one in mourning for Rhodes, though the white cross was still worn; at Sigena the cross was red and the coif white, nuns carrying silver sceptres in choir on great feasts.[3]

---

[1] Cellini, p. 396; Montluc, *Commentaries* p. 288. For Strozzi's career see Brantôme, *Les vies des hommes illustres et grands captains françois*, vol. 2, p. 352.

[2] For Romegas see Vertot, op. cit., vol. III, p. 411 *et seq.* For his miraculous escape see Bosio, op. cit., pt. III, p. 367.

[3] There is a colourful account of Sigena in modern times – before its sack and destruction in 1936 by Spanish Republicans when the entire community was murdered – in Sir Sacheverell Sitwell's *Monks, Nuns and Monasteries* (Weidenfeld & Nicolson, 1965).

Confratres, or Knights of Honour, had to have the same qualifications as professed knights, but Donats formed two classes, the
plebian being indistinguishable from serving brethren, those of
noble birth aspirant Knights of Justice. Even chaplains and
servants-at-arms must never have worked with their hands or
engaged in shop-keeping and usually belonged to the haute
bourgeoisie or the obscurer ranks of the *petite noblesse*. Serving
brethren were non-commissioned officers, 'demi-chevaliers',
rather than orderlies; some of the bravest being promoted to
Knights of Grace. Many brothers came to Malta as pages, no
more than twelve years old, though they had to be fifteen before
entering the novitiate, which lasted a year and was undergone
in a special house supervised by the Novice Master. However,
professions were always made at home to a knight of the local
priory.

Fra. Claude de la Sengle became superior in 1553 and devoted
himself to fortifying the convent. The star-shaped Fort St Elmo
was built on Monte Sceberras commanding the entrances to
Grand Harbour and the Marsamxett, though Fra. Claude
concentrated his chief efforts on the peninsula opposite Birgu,
Fort St Michel being strengthened and bastions erected; grateful
brethren surnamed the promontory 'Senglea'. In 1557 Fra.
Jean Parisot de la Valette was elected Grand Master. A devout
Gascon from Quercy born in 1494 this tall nobleman, bearded
like a patriarch, silver-haired and burnt brown by the sun, 'in
temperament rather melancholy',[1] possessed complete self-
control, invariably speaking in a low voice. 'Fra. Jehan' had
never left the convent since his solemn profession – normally
knights who had completed four caravans (eight cruises) and
spent three years at Malta could expect to retire to their commandery for a well-earned holiday. This was not the case with
Valette, who sailed on caravan after caravan. In 1541 his galley,
the *St Jean*, was taken by the Turks and he survived a terrible
year at the oars. Now that he was Master, duelling, gambling
and whoring were rigorously punished and conventual
observance enforced, brethren being required to hear Mass and
say office daily besides attending Matins and Vespers at the
Convent church on important feasts. Financial administration

[1] Balbi, op. cit., p. 27.

was thoroughly overhauled. But Fra. Jean's main reforms were defensive, as befitted a veteran of Rhodes; Birgu's buildings were strengthened while a boom of steel links 200 metres long was forged at Venice to bar the Harbour of the Galleys.

Queen Mary had revived the English Langue in 1557; Clerkenwell was restored under Grand Prior Thomas Tresham with ten commanderies, the three bailiffs – Turcopolier, Prior of Ireland and Bailiff of Egle – reappointed and the little auberge in Birgu reoccupied by five brethren.[1] But Elizabeth became queen and by 1559 the Langue had again broken up. In 1564 the last Scots prior, Fra. James Sandilands,[2] turning Protestant, was given his commandery by the Crown and was created Lord Torphichen. The only English brother left in Malta was Oliver Starkey, Lieutenant Turcopolier and commander of Quenington, a quiet scholarly man who lived alone in a house in Majjistral Street next to the deserted auberge. Later he was made Latin Secretary to La Valette, a post which entailed drafting all diplomatic correspondence.

The Religion was heartened by the advent of a new brotherhood. In 1561 Cosimo I of Tuscany founded the Knights of San Stefano, their rule 'Benedictine', their mission war on corsairs. There were four classes: knights with four proofs of nobility who took vows of poverty, *charity*, and obedience, wearing a white cloak lined with rose, a gold-edged red Maltese cross on the left breast; chaplains in white soutane and cape, their cross edged with yellow; serving brethren in white serge with a plain red cross; and canonesses. The Grand Dukes were hereditary Masters, knights could marry, and conventual duties were part-time – bailiffs, comprising Constable, Admiral, Grand Prior, Chancellor, Treasurer, Conservator and Conventual Prior being elected for three years.[3] Cosimo endowed his brethren magnificently, engaging the painter-architect Giorgio Vasari to build an ornate church and convent at Pisa, the first hung with Turkish trophies, the latter adorned with frescoed ceilings

[1] For Thomas Tresham see *D.N.B.*
[2] For James Sandilands see *D.N.B.*
[3] See Helyot, 'De l'Ordre Militaire de Saint Etienne Pape & Martyr en Toscane', *Histoire des ordres religieux*, vol. VI, p. 248.

commemorating Lepanto.[1] However, these knights of the latter day Renaissance were not only ornamental; many bachelor brothers lived in the convent, and their galleys cooperated enthusiastically with Malta.

In 1564 Romegas waylaid a great Turkish carrack on her way from Venice to Constantinople with a cargo valued at 80,000 Spanish ducats.[2] As this ship belonged to the Kustir Aga, Chief of the Black Eunuchs, and the 'imperial odalisques' had shares in her cargo, there was great uproar in the seraglio. Meanwhile an aged Turkish 'lady of high rank', who had previously been captured, was sending piteous letters from Malta. Suleiman, old now, saddened by a son's rebellion and the death of his favourite wife, was easily angered; 'Allah's Bestower of Earthly Peace' could no longer tolerate pirate unbelievers in the Turkish *Mare Nostrum*. Torghut, the brethren's implacable foe, exaggerated their weakness, so the sultan sent his generals to attack Malta with less than 30,000 men. They were, however, the cream of the imperial army: headed by 6,000 hand-picked Janissaries trailing long damascened muskets, there followed 9,000 crack Spahis in vivid contrast, feudal levies, who probably resembled the regiments maintained by the Porte, clad in crimson, yellow or dark blue brocade, horsemen using the horn bow though they had guns too and knew how to fight on foot. There were 6,000 corsairs and sailors, less luxuriously armed, and 3,500 rapacious *akinjis*, volunteers who served for plunder. Grimmest of all were 4,000 dervish Ghazis, berserk with hashish.[3]

This force had two commanders: the aged Mustafa Pasha – a veteran of Rhodes – and the young Piyale, a Serbian foundling who had married an Osmanli princess and become *Kapudan Pasha*, admiral-in-chief of the Turkish navy. Their staff included Ali el-Uluji, the future hero of Lepanto, and many famous corsairs, but despite such talents and the presence of Suleiman's personal standard – a great silver disc with its gold ball and crescent surmounted by all-conquering horsetails – the expedi-

[1] Einar Rud, *Vasari's Life and Lives; the first art historian*, trans. Spink (Thames & Hudson, 1964), p. 74.
[2] See Balbi, op. cit., pp. 28–31, and Vertot, op. cit., vol. III, pp. 421, 424.
[3] Balbi, op. cit., p. 36 – I have accepted Balbi's figures.

tion was to be handicapped by this divided command. However, the cannon of 1565 were more effective than before and musketry had improved, for Janissaries had become skilled marksmen; their long-barrelled wheel-locks made at Constantinople by German gunsmiths could not be so quickly loaded as the shorter European arquebus but were more accurate. Spies reported that artillery would blast Malta's makeshift defences out of existence within a few days.

The Religion's agents could not fail to notice the seething activity in Constantinople's dockyards and arsenals. Brethren were summoned from Europe and large supplies of food and powder stored in cellars dug in the rock beneath St Angelo. Malta was not a country off which besiegers could live; peasants stripped it of crops, poisoning the wells with hemp and rotting offal. Mdina, well fortified and garrisoned by militia, was left to fend for itself. Fra. Jean had 600 brethren – the resident community of 474 brother-knights and 67 serving brethren and, in addition, new arrivals – with 1,200 Italian and Spanish mercenaries and 3,000 Maltese militia. Other troops available, including galley slaves and Greeks resident in the island, numbered 1,300. In all his total strength was 6,000 men of whom less than half were professionals.[1] Furthermore, the Sicilian Viceroy had given Philip II's word that 25,000 men would relieve the convent.

Militia and mercenaries fought as pikemen or arquebusiers, though all carried swords. The mercenaries, as professionals, were armoured with high-crested morion helmets, 'breast-and-back', and tassets (articulated thigh plates). Militia had only helmets and leather jerkins. Their knight officers carried sword and dagger, the former a broadsword or rapier, though some brethren preferred the great German two-hander. A few may have had the hand buckler, a small shield with a spike. On the walls many wielded hooked halberds or boarding pikes. 'Harness' was still an advantage in hand-to-hand combat; most brethren must have worn *armatura de piede*, half-armour for fighting on foot, while some wore a thickened 'bullet proof' breast plate, others the brigantine of metal-studded cloth. Over all was the scarlet sopravest, the battle habit, something like a herald's

[1] Ibid., p. 41.

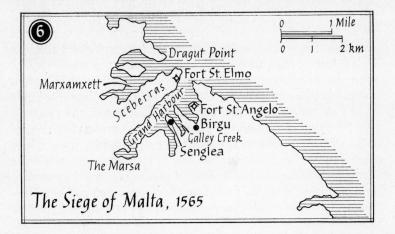

The Siege of Malta, 1565

tabard, its great white cross square ended instead of eight pointed. The Grand Master's sopravest was of cloth-of-gold.

The Religion was not an ordinary army but a monastery at war which followed its *reverendissimus magister*, his leadership resting on spiritual foundations – brethren who disobeyed him disobeyed Jesus Christ; they were still convinced that by dying in battle against the infidel they gave their lives for the Saviour as He had for them. La Valette understood his children perfectly. In the spring they were assembled in chapter to hear him preach a noble sermon: 'Today our Faith is at stake – whether the Gospel must yield to the *Koran*. God is asking for the lives which we pledged to Him at our profession. Happy are those who may sacrifice their lives.'[1] Then he and his habited brethren went in solemn procession to the Conventual church where all renewing their vows, confessed, attended High Mass and took Communion; this was the corporate Communion of a religious community re-dedicating itself to God as its members must soon fulfil their vocation – to die for Christ in defence of Christians.

The convent was largely protected by water. Ramparts were inadequate but earthworks – moats, trenches, ramps – excellent, covered by well-sited artillery. St Angelo, at the tip of the

[1] Vertot, op. cit., vol. III, p. 436.

northern peninsula, was garrisoned by 500 troops with fifty brethren under La Valette himself who made it his command point, and had two tiers of batteries. The rest of the peninsula was guarded by the walls of Birgu and several small bastions linked by trenches, though the landward side was weak, dependent on earthworks manned by the French Langues, the German taking the shores, while the Castilian held the vulnerable angle to the south. Between this bastion of Castile and the Hospital was 'the Post of England' – knights from several nations under Oliver Starkey. Senglea, the southern peninsula, even better served by the sea, had four bastions in Italian charge, while the Aragonese manned Fort St Michel on the landward approach. Fort St Elmo, at the foot of Monte Sceberras, shaped like a four-pointed star, was built of poor quality stone but strengthened by a raised gun emplacement (or 'cavalier') on the seaward side and an outwork of trenches, a 'ravelin' facing the Marsa. Normally manned by only eighty men its garrison was raised to three hundred, Fra. Luigi Broglia, the old bailiff in command being joined by a brother scarcely less aged, Fra. Juan de Eguaras, Bailiff of Negropont.

On 18 May 1565, the infidel armada was sighted: 180 warships besides cargo vessels and transports, with nearly 30,000 eager troops, and a floating arsenal of cannon.[1] It anchored in the exposed bay of Marsaxlokk. Mustafa was in favour of storming Mdina but Piyale feared for his ships and insisted that St Elmo, which commanded the entrance to Marsamxett, a perfect haven, must first be taken. The little fort was invested and on 25 May batteries opened fire; their guns included ten 80-pounders and a basilisk hurling balls of 160 lbs. Jean rushed in 64 brethren and 200 mercenaries under Fra. Pierre de Massuez Vercoyran – 'Colonel le Mas'. Old Broglia, suffering heavy casualties, soon asked La Valette for more reinforcements; his messenger, Fra. Juan de la Cerda, told the Sacred Council that St Elmo would quickly fall.[2] The angry Master announced his intention of taking command himself, but eventually sent Fra. Gonzalez de Medran with 200 troops and 50 knights. By 29 May the Turks had captured the outermost trench. Then, on 2 June,

[1] Ibid., p. 444.
[2] Balbi, op. cit., p. 56.

Torghut, eighty years old, arrived with 1,500 corsairs and more cannon. He deplored Piyale's plan of concentrating on St Elmo yet knew that to abandon it would have a disastrous effect on morale. His guns were mounted on Gallow's Point, subjecting the tiny stronghold to an even fiercer pounding.

On the night of 3 June Turkish sappers found the ravelin unguarded and knifed the sentries; Janissaries nearly succeeded in storming St Elmo itself before the portcullis could be lowered and were only halted by two small cannon. The Turks continued to attack until noon next day. Fire throwers and boiling oil supplemented the fort's cannon while there was a large supply of fiery *cercles* and grenades: the former were huge hoops bound with inflammable wadding set alight and hurled with tongs – a lucky throw could ring three infidels to turn them into flaming torches. Handbombs were earthenware pots packed with combustibles, four fuses projecting from the spout to make sure it exploded. Morale was epitomised by Fra. Abel de Bridiers de la Gardampe who fell shot in the chest; a brother bent over him but he muttered 'Go away – don't think I'm alive – your time's better spent helping the others' and then crawled away to the fort's chapel to die at the foot of the altar.[1] Five hundred Turks were dead as against 20 brethren and 60 mercenaries, but without the ravelin the fort's besiegers could now build a ramp and fire down on the defenders. A sortie failed to retake it. By 7 June the barrage was rocking the fort 'like a ship in a storm', and Gonzalez de Medran brought Fra. Jean the message that the considered opinion of Broglia and Eguaras was that the bastion was doomed; he himself believed that further defence of this outpost would waste good troops.

La Valette disagreed, certain that relief must come if only he could hold on long enough, for the Sicilian viceroy, García de Toledo – a *frey-caballero* of Santiago – considered Malta the key to Sicily. Further, the viceroy's son, 'a promising youth who took the Habit', was in the convent.[2] St Elmo would buy time. He was therefore thunderstruck when on the night of 8 June, after a major assault, Fra. Vitellino Vittelleschi appeared with a round robin signed by fifty-three of his beleaguered brethren –

[1] Vertot, op. cit., vol. III, p. 461.
[2] Ibid., p. 432.

though not by old Broglia or Eguaras – which stipulated that unless evacuated at once they would sally out to die a holy death. Three brothers were immediately sent to investigate. One, Fra. Constantino de Castriota, reported that St Elmo could resist for many days and offered to lead a relief force. Only fifteen brethren with 100 militia, all volunteers – including to the general wonderment, two Jews – were allowed to go but a shrewdly phrased letter told the garrison they were welcome to return to a safer place; all stayed. Meanwhile the bombardment continued; it was not a question of demolishing ramparts but of clearing debris. The Turks assaulted relentlessly, by night as well as by day. On 18 June Torghut and Mustafa ordered a general assault. 'So great was the noise, the shouting, the beating of drums and the clamour of innumerable Turkish musical instruments, that it seemed like the end of the world.'[1] Their troops too were equipped with grenades, limpet wildfire bombs which clung to armour. Four thousand arquebusiers blasted every gap in the rubble with a storm of lead while culverins from Monte Sceberras and Gallows Point hurled cannon balls – iron, bronze or stone. Then the dervishes went in, mad with prayer and hashish, frothing at the mouth, followed by Spahis and finally by Janissaries. This was the chosen élite of an army accustomed to victory from Persia to Poland.

The Grand Master, however, had ferried over quantities of ammunition and barrels of re-invigorating wine and so when the enemy came yelling through what was left of the walls cannon tore into them; as for limpet bombs the knights had great vats of sea water into which to jump.[2] After six hours this assault was called off. One thousand Turkish bodies littered the blood-soaked ground, while 150 defenders had died, including Medran, cut down as he seized a horsetail banner. The wounded were ferried back to that blissful Hospital where the period's best medical skill soon restored them. Torghut began to build new batteries on Monte Sceberras just before he was mortally wounded by stone shrapnel – and soon it became impossible to reinforce or to evacuate St Elmo. On 22 June the faithful launched the fiercest assault yet. The walls, reduced to their

[1] Balbi, op. cit., p. 81.
[2] Bosio, op. cit., pt. III, p. 561.

foundations, were heaped with rocks, earth, palliasses, baggage, corpses, anything that would serve as a barricade. In six hours the attackers lost 2,000 men and then withdrew in amazement. But they had killed 500 Unbelievers. A swimmer got through to St Angelo and Fra. Jean tried unsuccessfully to send one last detachment of volunteers – but it could not pass the enemy's hail-storm of shot.

At midnight on the morning of 23 June – the Eve of St John – mass was said in the tiny chapel, the only surviving building. Two chaplain brethren heard each man's confession, then every-one received the Body of the Lord he was soon to meet. Finally the chaplains buried their chalices and burned the chapel's furnishings; all night long these two priests tolled its bell – as a Passing Bell. Just before first light the soldiers of Christ took up their positions; there were only sixty left. The senior officers, Eguaras, 'Colonel Mas', and a Captain Miranda were too badly wounded to stand, so they sat, Eguaras weak from loss of blood and Miranda horribly scorched by wildfire, in chairs at the main breach, Mas, whose leg was smashed by bullet wounds, sitting on a log.[1] At 6.00 a.m. the entire Turkish army attacked; even galleys sailed in to bombard the stinking mound of rubble and rotting corpses, regardless of fire from St Angelo. Yet for four hours the defenders answered them with guns and grenades, until at last they stormed in. Old Juan de Eguaras, hurled from his chair, jumped up with a boarding pike before a scimitar took his head off, while Mas, sitting on his log, slew several Turks with his great two-handed sword. An Italian knight lit a beacon to tell his Master it was over. Only nine brethren – probably mortally wounded – were taken alive, though a handful of Maltese swam to safety. It had cost an army acknowledged as the best of its time nearly five weeks, 18,000 rounds of cannon shot and 8,000 men to gain this little fort.[2]

'My God,' said Mustafa looking across at St Angelo, 'if this small son cost so much what do we pay for his father?'[3] Each brother's corpse was decapitated, a crucifix hacked in its chest, nailed to a wooden cross and pushed out to sea. Next morning,

[1] Ibid., pp. 572, 573; Vertot, op. cit., vol. III, p. 490.
[2] Balbi, op. cit., p. 91.
[3] Vertot, op. cit., vol. III, p. 492.

on the feast of the Religion's patron, the tide brought in four
mutilated bodies. Fra. Jean burst into tears. At once he ordered
all prisoners to be beheaded; suddenly the Pasha's troops heard
gunfire, then their comrades' bleeding heads were bouncing all
over the camp.[1] Meanwhile the Grand Master reminded his
brethren of their vocation as they renewed their vows on that
Baptist's Day: 'What could be more fitting for a member of the
Order of St John to lay down his life in defence of the Faith' he
preached – the dead of St Elmo 'have earned a martyr's crown
and will reap a martyr's reward'. Nor did he forget the militia
and the mercenaries: 'We are all soldiers of Jesus Christ like you,
my comrades,' he told them.[2] A reinforcement reached the
convent on 3 July, a 'Little Relief' or *piccolo soccorso* consisting of
700 soldiers led by 42 brethren and 'gentlemen volunteers'
under Frey Melchior de Robles of the Order of Santiago.[3]
Two of them were English, John Evan Smith and Edward
Stanley, and no doubt they received a warm welcome from
Fra. Oliver Starkey at the 'Post of England'. Meanwhile
dysentery and malaria had broken out among the Turks, whose
water came from poisoned wells. The Pasha offered terms, to
receive a contemptuous refusal.

Mustafa then had eighty galleys hauled by slaves from
Marsamxett over the narrowest stretch of Monte Sceberras
into Grand Harbour; the Senglea promontory could be attacked
by the army from the landward side, by the navy from the
seaward. Hastily Fra. Jean constructed a coastal boom – iron
chains fastened on stakes set in the seabed – while he built a
pontoon bridge between Birgu and Senglea. On 5 July seventy
Turkish cannon opened fire on Senglea, killing women and
children in the streets. Sappers swam in with axes to destroy the
boom but were driven off by Maltese knifemen who grappled
with them in the water. Hassem, the young Dey of Algiers, now
arrived with 2,500 veteran corsairs who sneered at the Turks'
performance at St Elmo; Mustafa allowed them to lead a
general assault on 15 July. Of the enemy troops, Turkish,
Algerian and Corsair, Balbi, an eyewitness, wrote 'Even the rank

[1] Ibid., p. 492.
[2] Ibid., vol. IV, p. 3.
[3] Balbi, op. cit., p. 101.

and file wore scarlet robes and there were many in cloth-of-gold and of silver and of crimson damask. Armed with fine muskets of Fez, scimitars of Alexandria and Damascus, they all wore splendid turbans.'[1] Hassem, with half his force, tried to rush Fort St Michel where Robles tore them to bloody shreds with grapeshot; his other troops waded ashore on the seaward side but La Valette sent reinforcements over the pontoon. Mustafa then dispatched ten boatloads of Janissaries to land on an unguarded stretch of Senglea. He did not know of a hidden battery under St Angelo. As the boats approached, its commander trained five culverins – loaded with stones, chains and spiked iron balls – at a range of 150 yards and blew them out of the water with a single salvo. The few survivors drowned. This repulse saved the day. Meanwhile, after five hours' fearful carnage the appalled Hassem began to withdraw, whereupon St Michel's garrison sallied out in pursuit; 'remember St Elmo' shouted brethren and Maltese. The infidels left 4,000 dead, including those who drowned.[2] The Grand Master laid up six captured Turkish standards in a church and ordered the singing of a 'Te Deum'.

The Turks would not give up – they knew that the defenders were desperate. The garrison had been decimated, supplies almost exhausted. Relentlessly the enemy hammered away. The heaviest cannonade of the siege began on 2 August – it could be heard in Sicily. Then came another general assault on Senglea; the faithful charged Fort St Michel five times in six hours – Maltese women helped drive them off with tubs of boiling water. On 7 August came another general assault; Piyale attacked Birgu with 3,000 men, rushing into a breach in the bastion of Castile to be decimated by crossfire. Mustafa attacked Senglea simultaneously, cheering on his troops as they finally stormed St Michel. This time the bastion of Castile had been well mined and besiegers poured into the yawning breach. Amid the smoke and confusion many believed it was the end. Snatching a helmet and a half pike Fra. Jean ran to the breach. A grenade exploded, wounding him in the leg, but he refused to leave: 'I am seventy-one – how can it be possible for

[1] Ibid., p. 111.
[2] Ibid., p. 117.

a man of my age to die more gloriously than among my brethren and my friends in the service of God, in defence of our holy Religion?'[1] The storming party was thrown out, but Senglea and Birgu were collapsing. Every casualty at the Hospital who could walk had to man the walls. Suddenly, the retreat was sounded; the Pasha thought that his enemy's relief had come. In fact a few cavalry had ridden out from Mdina to massacre the Turkish wounded. For ten days their enraged comrades attacked daily before launching yet another general assault on 18 August. On 20 August 8,000 Turks were again thrown back from Fort St Michel. Three days later the entire Sacred Council was in favour of withdrawing to Fort St Angelo. But Fra. Jean would not abandon 'his loyal Maltese, their wives and their families', while Turkish batteries in Birgu would soon demolish St Angelo – 'here we die together or drive out our enemies'.[2] Then he blew up the bridge between Birgu and St Angelo.

The assaults and the bombardment continued, mercilessly. Yet if the garrison were desperate so were the Turks: food and ammunition were running out, for supply ships were waylaid by Christian corsairs. This was an excessively hot summer – fever raged among the besiegers and plague was feared. Guns were wearing thin, and so was morale; it was rumoured that *djinn* and *affrit* had been seen at La Valette's side – he was a magician in Satan's pay. The attackers had to be driven on by other officers. Mustafa called off an assault on Mdina, whose governor had manned the walls with townsmen in red sopravests and loosed off every gun available. On 8 September a Christian fleet passed St Angelo, each ship firing a three-gun salute, and Piyale's navy was too demoralised to attack. The relieving force which landed further north was at most 10,000 strong but included knights from all over Europe, even another English brother. When Mustafa, who had set sail, realised how few they were he landed again, at St Paul's Bay. But his men were already beaten: Christian troops smashed into them and total rout was only averted by Mustafa's leadership. Grimly he and Piyale sailed for Constantinople; Osmanli sultans seldom forgave failure – death was the usual penalty. And of the 40,000

[1] Vertot, op. cit., vol. IV, p. 51.
[2] Ibid., p. 61.

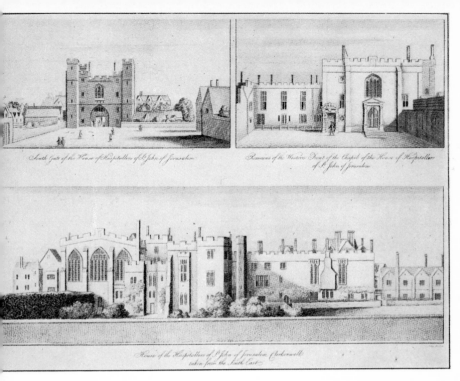

South Gate of the House of Hospitallers of St John of Jerusalem

Remains of the Western Front of the Chapel of the House of Hospitallers of St John of Jerusalem

House of the Hospitallers of St John of Jerusalem Clerkenwell taken from the South East

15a. The Priory of the Hospitallers at Clerkenwell, residence of the Grand Priors of England. From an engraving by Wenceslaus Hollar in 1656.

15b. Effigy of Fra. Thomas Tresham (d. 1559), Grand Prior of the Order of St John in England and Premier Baron. From his tomb at Rushton parish church in Northamptonshire.

16a. The Auberge of Castile in Valetta, remodelled by Grand Master Fra. Manoel Pinto de Fonseca (1741–73). A symbol of the Baroque to Rococo sunset of military religious order.

16b. Fra. Luís Mendez de Vasconcellos, Grand Master of the Knights Hospitaller of St John (1622–3). The habit is still unmistakably monastic.

besiegers – Turks, Algerians, Berbers – only 10,000 survived.
Suleiman was enraged, shouting 'Only with me do my armies
triumph – next spring I will conquer Malta myself.'[1] But he
spared his trembling generals.

La Valette received the dilatory viceroy with every honour.
Only 600 fighting men were on their feet to greet him; over
2,500 mercenaries had died with 250 of the brethren, besides
7,000 Maltese men, women and children.[2] But they were the
heroes of Europe. Pius V offered Fra. Jean a Red Hat, which he
declined gracefully as it meant visiting Rome and he would not
leave the convent. Even the Archbishop of Canterbury ordered
services of thanksgiving. King Philip sent a sword of honour with
15,000 troops to guard the island until it was re-fortified;
Catholic sovereigns gave him many handsome contributions
for this purpose.

Now a real convent could be built. Monte Sceberras was the
site for *Humilissima Civitas Valettae*, work beginning in March
1566. Fra. Jean was refounding Jerusalem, the Rhodes of his
youth; church, hospital, palace and auberges were to be simple,
with a *collachium* as in that lost but still beloved Aegean island. A
portrait of the Very Reverend Grand Master shows a curiously
reflective face, an abbot's face, and indeed Valetta was intended
first and foremost as a monastery, the mother house of a great
Order. He lived another two years, watching his dream – which
he 'loved like a daughter' – take shape, before dying of a stroke
in August 1568. He was buried in his brothers' new home.
Oliver Starkey wrote an epitaph: 'Here lies Valette, worthy of
eternal honour, he that was formerly the terror of Asia and
Africa and the shield of Europe, whence by his holy arms he
expelled the barbarians, the first buried in this beloved city of
which he was the founder.'

Yet the siege had decided nothing and the Turks completed
their conquest of the Levant. Venetian Cyprus fell in 1571,
and even the Serene Republic joined Pius V's Holy League of
Spain, Genoa, Tuscany and Malta. In August of that year its
fleet gathered at Messina under Philip II's bastard brother, the
young Don John of Austria, assisted by Frey Luís Zúñiga y

[1] Ibid., p. 80.
[2] Balbi, op. cit., p. 189.

10

Requesens, Santiago's *Comendador Mayor* of León. Their armada had 202 galleys, 70 small sailing ships and 8 large Venetian galleasses (a kind of galleon with oars). Of the Order's contingents San Stefano's was the biggest – 12 galleys – but Malta's was the most formidable – 3 galleys under the Religion's Admiral, Pietro Giustiniani with Romegas.

By now the galley had reached its final form, as much as 180 feet in length if one includes raked poop and prow; such a vessel might have a beam of less than 20 feet, shallow draughted and rolling horribly. But in calm water, propelled by thirty oars a side and two lateen rigged masts, its average speed was two knots – over four for short distances. Normally a 48-pounder culverin and four 8-pounder sakers were mounted on the prow, with smaller guns elsewhere. Maltese galleys were black-hulled with gilded poop and prow, their oars red-bladed, sails striped red and white, scarlet pennants floating from the mastheads, the Religion's banner at the stern. These ships, invariably named after saints, were floating chapels; their priest brothers said mass two hours before dawn each day on an altar at the poop, office was never missed, and brethren always confessed and took Communion before going into battle.

Crusaders and faithful met in the Gulf of Corinth off Lepanto on 7 October 1571. Ali, the Kapudan Pasha, had 216 war galleys, 37 galliots (small galleys) and various lesser vessels.[1] The crusader line of battle was Venetians on the left flying yellow banners, Genoese on the right flying green, and Don John and his ships with the papal galleys in the centre flying azure, with behind them a reserve – probably including San Stefano's squadron – flying white; Malta's vessels flanked Don John's right. Along his front line he spaced the galleasses, where their big guns' cross-fire could do most damage. Confidently the young Admiral sailed forward to music from his minstrels' gallery, unfurling the blue banner of the Holy League embroidered with the figure of Christ crucified. The Turks were spread out over six miles in poor formation which deteriorated under fire; a galley sank at the third salvo.

Ali Pasha and his red banner emblazoned with the prophet's

[1] Dall' Pozzo, *Historia della Sacra Religione Militare di S. Giovanni Geroso-limitaro*, vol. I, p. 19.

sword went straight for the *Reale*, the League's flagship, guns blazing; his iron ram penetrated to the fourth rowing bench – for a moment her crew feared she would settle. But now Don John's bowchasers raked Ali's own flagship. Then the troops, 300 Janissary marksmen with 100 archers against 400 Spanish arquebusiers, set to; the prince would not shoot until he 'could be splashed with his enemies' blood'. Many Christian oarsmen left their benches and grabbed boarding pikes. The struggle surged from one ship to the other until the papal commander, Colonna, who had just captured the Bey of Negropont, came up, blasting the Turks from stern to stern. Don John's men boarded for the third time; not one enemy soldier survived. Elsewhere the entire Christian centre had been victorious. On the left the issue was more in doubt. Chuluk Ali – 'Sirocco' – had attacked savagely, and though he was killed his ships outflanked the League's line, passing between it and the coast. However, fighting like fiends, the Venetians drove them aground, Christian galley slaves breaking loose to slaughter their masters. It was very different on the right. That superb seaman Ali el-Uluji, Dey of Algiers, made a wide sweep as though to take the Christians in the rear, and the Genoese drew back to forestall him. A galley, by stopping one bank of oars and double stroking the other, could turn in its own length. Suddenly the corsairs swung in, racing for the now isolated squadron of Malta. The brethren fought with habitual ferocity but were hopelessly outnumbered; their flagship was overwhelmed and the great banner of St John torn down, only three knights surviving – an Italian, an Aragonese who lost his arm and half one shoulder from a single sword cut, and the admiral himself found beneath a pile of Turkish dead. The Order's other galleys would have been taken too had not the reserve come to their rescue, followed by Don John and then the Genoese. Surrounded, el-Uluji battled on magnificently for another hour before cutting his way out with twelve ships. His Moslem comrades had lost 210 vessels – 40 sent to the bottom – and 30,000 men, including nearly all senior officers.[1]

Though Constantinople remained a formidable naval power it lost the Mediterranean at Lepanto. Even if a hundred years

[1] Ibid., p. 30.

later the Poles would have to save Vienna, the Holy League was
the last crusade; Islam was no longer a danger to Christendom.
This great victory doomed the Religion of St John as a fighting
force, destroying its *raison d'être*.

VII

EPILOGUE

Heirs of the Military Orders

They shall beat their swords into plowshares and their spears
into pruning hooks.

Isaiah

If Grand Masters are mortal one can say that the Religion of
St John is immortal.

Vertot

CHAPTER 16

Heirs of the Military Orders

The Counter-Reformation rejected the military religious vocation. It is significant that that dedicated soldier Ignatius Loyola never once considered it. Instead he gave the Church new shock troops, the Jesuits. Fighting brotherhoods had served their purpose. Yet they were a long time dying. This survival was due to their aristocratic character which made them bastions of the nobility even in Protestant countries: the Lutheran *Johanniterorden* restored the Brandenburg *Ballei* to such effect that in 1763 Grand Master Pinto recognised them as brethren, and in the Netherlands the Utrecht *Ballei* of the *Duitsridder* continued as an association of Calvinist noblemen, while the first religious order refounded by the Anglican Church was the Venerable Tongue of the Knights of St John. Perhaps the function of these Protestant brotherhoods was purely charitable but their Catholic cousins went into battle until the end of the eighteenth century. There was plenty of campaigning for Baroque paladins, the outstanding episode being the twenty-years' siege of Candia (Crete). When the end came in 1668 St John's brethren fought with all the spirit of La Valette, holding the half-demolished gate of San Andrea for three months amid a holocaust of mortar shells, mines and red shot; when the twenty-nine brothers who remained on their feet withdrew, the Venetian general wrote to the Council at Venice 'I lose more from the departure of those few superbly brave soldiers than from all the rest put together.' The previous year the garrison had been heartened by an apparition from the past, a detachment of white-cloaked Teutonic Knights.[1] Then in 1687 St John helped the Venetians conquer the Morea, while a *Malteserorden* force assisted imperial troops in a campaign which recovered Belgrade in 1688.

[1] For the Teutonic Knights at Candia, see Voigt, *Geschichte des deutschen ritter-ordens in seinen zwolf Balleien in Deutschland* (Berlin, 1857–9), vol. II, pp. 387.

St John even acquired colonies. In 1653 Grand Master
Lascaris bought the Caribbean islands of Tortuga, St Croix
and St Barthélemy, to be administered as a bailiwick, but the
venture proved a failure and in 1665 the colonies were sold to
the French West India Company.[1] Malta grew steadily richer,
its European revenues supplemented by the *spoglio* and by the
corso, which allowed privateers to buy the right to fly the Order's
flag. By now 'The Most Eminent and Most Reverend Lord the
Grand Master of the Sacred Religion and Most Illustrious Order
of the Hospital and of the Holy Sepulchre in Jerusalem, Prince
of Malta, Gozo and Rhodes, and Lord of the Royal Domain of
Tripoli' had a monarch's trappings, for not only did he rank as
equal to a cardinal-deacon at Rome after 1630, but in 1607 he
had been made a Prince of the Empire and could address kings
as 'mon Cousin', receiving ambassadors from Rome, Vienna,
Paris and Madrid.

Valetta possessed an appearance of monumental strength;
the religion's church was low, lest defending guns should have
their field of fire restricted seaward, and auberges were self-
contained barracks with guardrooms, supply depots and slave
quarters. Even the magistral palace was austere – lodgings for
an abbot rather than a prince. Plain too was the Sacred
Infirmary, but on a vast scale, with its great ward measuring
185 feet by 34 feet. The city was a soldiers' cantonment, its
streets on a grid pattern with box-like blocks of white houses.
However, the decision not to build a *collachium* reflected growing
secularisation and the convent's grim exterior hid a wealth of
luxury. Within, its rooms were lined with Gobelin tapestries,
carpeted by Persian rugs, and furnished with rich cabinets, silver,
porcelain, and antique bronzes. The Conventual church was a
Baroque treasure cave of sculpture and mosaic whose gilded
roof framed scenes from the Baptist's life, and whose chapels
were adorned with superb statuary; that of Italy had been
decorated by Caraveggio. Even the floor was magnificent,
marquetried with a mass of exuberant plaques, commemorating
dead knights, inlaid with jasper, porphyry, agate, onyx, lapis

[1] See D. D. Macpherson, *De Poincy and the Order of St John in the New World*
(St John's Gate, 1949).

lazuli and every known marble – a stone kaleidoscope of rainbow hues.[1]

The Order's continuing inspiration produced historians of some brilliance, in particular the Conventual chaplain Fra. René Aubert de Vertot d'Auboeuf, whose *Histoire des Chevaliers Hospitaliers de S. Jean de Jérusalem* was published in 1726. Vertot wrote for the general reader, to glorify his Order and justify a military calling in the age of Newton and Montesquieu. He is often uncritical and inaccurate, but he succeeded in providing a readable and enjoyable introduction to the history of his Order, and was recommended by such an historian as Edward Gibbon.

Even in Vertot's century St John saw plenty of action, and after 1704 ships of the line began to replace galleys. In 1716 Malta, Venice and the papal states joined in a last Holy League in an attempt to save the Morea, and as late as 1760 Grand Master Pinto was only saved from Turkish invasion by French intervention. Caravans continued until the Order's final expulsion from Malta, the most famous of its later corsairs being Fra. Jacques-François de Chambray, who sailed on thirty-one caravans, amassed a *spoglio* of 400,000 livres, captured over 1,000 slaves and took eleven prizes. In his youth Fra. Pierre-André de Suffren captained one of the religion's warships, but serving with the French during the American War of Independence he made himself feared by the entire English navy, while in 1782-3 he aided Hyder Ali and Tippoo Sahib, outsailing and outgunning a British fleet larger than his own; this Vice-Admiral of France ended his days as the Order's ambassador to Paris.

Life at the sleepy Teutonic court of Mergentheim was like that in most German principalities, a round of religious services, card games, hunting parties and formal dinners. This quaint little state on the Tauber river in what is now Wurtemburg consisted of less than forty square miles of farmland, whose 20,000 inhabitants were ruled from the Order's imposing castle. The Hoch-und-Deutschmeister had a handful of lifeguards, but there was small sign of military activity, for his knights had found a new way of fulfilling their military obligation: from

[1] See Scicluna, *The Church of St John in Valetta.*

10*

1695 the Order's revenues financed the *Hoch-und-Deutschmeister* regiment to fight against the Turks, and many brethren served in the Habsburg armies – one great Master was Archduke Karl, Napoleon's adversary. Admission was eagerly sought, as rustic commanderies, with Baroque chapels in the Rhineland or Westphalia, made charming retreats for pious bachelors but were hard to obtain, thirty-two *German* quarterings being required. The Teutonic Order could never forget its lost lands; in 1618 it protested loudly when the Hohenzollern Elector of Brandenburg took possession of East Prussia on the extinction of Duke Albrecht's line, while it again complained when the Elector assumed the title 'King-in-Prussia' in 1701. They too produced a fine historian. In 1784 Fra. Wilhelm Eugen Josef de Wal published the first volume of his great history of the Order, dedicated to the Hoch-und-Deutschmeister, Archduke Maximilian-Franz. Wal, who wrote in French, is the Teutonic Vertot. His purpose was the same, to provide a general introduction to his religion, justifying its calling and glorifying its achievements. However, the *komtur* was more critical than the abbé and went to the sources, Petrus von Dusburg and Pusilge, producing a book even more readable than Vertot's. He realised that articulate brethren had a vital role, a duty to make known their Order's ideals and traditions.[1]

Spanish and Portuguese Orders were now no more than civil lists providing titles and pensions, even if their recipients were in theory committed to certain minimal religious duties such as a simple daily office. Nonetheless, grandees wore the *habito* or

---

[1] An interesting example of an eighteenth-century Teutonic Knight was Count Maximilian von Merveldt. Born in 1764, this scion of a famous Westphalian family served as a hussar against the Turks before entering the Order in 1791. He then fought in the Revolutionary Wars, against the French, winning the coveted Maria-Theresa Cross for his gallantry at Neerwinden. During the Napoleonic Wars, he achieved considerable distinction as a cavalry soldier and a diplomat – he rose to the rank of *Feldmarschall Leutnant* and was Austrian ambassador to St Petersburg. In 1808, after his *komturei* had been secularised by the French, he was dispensed of his vows and married. Von Merveldt died in 1815 as Austrian ambassador to London – his widow declined the British government's offer of a state funeral in Westminster Abbey.

white cloak with pride; Velasquez portrays himself bearing Santiago's red *largetto* on his doublet. The haughty commendatore
in *Don Giovanni* was in fact a comendador of Calatrava in the
seventeenth-century original of Tirso de Molina. *Clerigos* and
comendadoras continued reasonably observant until the eighteenth
century, when they became impoverished and demoralised,
their priories falling into ruin. Iberian Religions had by then
become a mere shell, the military tradition preserved only by
enrolling army officers, including many Irish émigrés.

The Baroque romanticism of the later Renaissance gave birth
to two restorations of St Lazarus, in Savoy as the Order of St
Maurice and St Lazarus and in France as the Order of Our
Lady of Mount Carmel and of St Lazarus. These revivals were
commedia dell'arte rather than Indian summer, even if their
inspiration was genuine enough, a fast waning flicker of the
military vocation. The French venture, begun by Henri IV,
was built up by Louis XIV into a rival of St John. By 1696 it had
over 140 commanderies, maintaining a small squadron of warships to fight English 'corsairs'. In that year Louis XIV appointed the Marquis de Dangeau as Grand Master, whose
supreme achievement was to provide his chevaliers with 'habits';
the Grand Master sported a cloth-of-silver tunic, a mantle of
purple velvet powdered with gold fleurs-de-lis and a white-
plumed purple bonnet, whilst his knights wore white satin
tunics embroidered with a huge cross of orange-tawny and
green, purple mantles, and plumed bonnets.[1] By the Revolution
this 'Religion' enjoyed a relationship with the French crown
analagous to that which exists today between the British
monarchy and the Venerable Order of St John; it is hard to
exaggerate its social standing, for admission had become
rigorously restricted and its Masters were invariably Princes
of the Blood.[2]

Eighteenth-century brother-knights were living ghosts, ex-
posed to the mocking laughter of Voltaire and the *Encyclopédistes*.
It was the age of *Candide* and *Tristram Shandy*, of Gibbon,
Rousseau and Beaumarchais, yet at Malta and Mergentheim

[1] See Bertrand de la Grassière, *Histoire des Chevaliers-Hospitaliers de Saint-
Lazare*, p. 97 *et seq.*
[2] See Helyot, op. cit., vol. I, p. 386 *et seq.*

there were crusaders in clanking armour vowed to fight the infidel. At Malta the magnificent Auberge of Castile, begun in 1744 by the architect Domenicho Cachia, was a monument to defunct asceticism, an *hôtel* for noblemen, not a monastery, even if it contained chapel, refectory and dormitory, Cassar's sober edifice being replaced by a spectacular Italianate showpiece. But the exquisite Manoel Theatre of 1732 offers even more vivid testimony to the waning of monastic ideals, with its gilded boxes and *salons*; that elegant stage was the scene of long-forgotten plays, and operas sung by *Castrati*. Here in the candle-light beneath sparkling chandeliers and painted ceilings knights deigned to mingle with the Maltese aristocracy. The military vocation was a spiritual fossil. From now on critics scorned increasingly this superannuated ideal from the Gothic Ages.

Nonetheless, the Grand Masters' benevolent despotism was effective. Brydone, an English tourist of 1770, wrote of Valetta's streets as 'crowded with well dressed people who have all the appearance of health and affluence....'[1] Bread was cheap, its price carefully controlled, so there were no starving peasants while the bourgeois flourished. Cities were properly policed and streets swept, health regulations were far in advance of their day, and even the penal code was comparatively enlightened. The Sacred Infirmary cared for an average of 350 sick at any one time; food was specially chosen, vermicelli and chicken for the weak, wine and game for the strong, served from silver dishes. A vast staff included doctors, surgeons, nurses, pharma-cists, while there were clinics for outpatients, with one for venereal disease and another for leprosy. An external nursing service tended the old in their own houses. There were free pre-scriptions for slaves and beggars while almshouses for the aged poor and an orphanage were maintained. Yet despite these benefits, and though the cotton industry and Levant trade had made them rich, the Maltese, aristocrats and bourgeois alike, resented the Order's rule.

The French Revolution doomed St John. At the end of 1789 the deputy Armand-Gaston Camus asked the Assembly to sup-press its commanderies; in early 1790 he issued a pamphlet

[1] *A Tour through Sicily and Malta* (London, 1773).

stating that ' "the Religion" has triumphed over its enemies – as a military force the Order of Malta no longer serves any purpose'. A host of other publications derided these 'armed monks' and the uselessness of St Lazarus and St John. In July the former was suppressed, but the latter managed to retain its possessions, as Malta was valuable to French commercial interests, until Louis XVI's flight to Varennes in 1791, which was largely subsidised by the Religion. The loss of its revenues was a grievous blow. Within the convent morale was weakened by freemasonry. Brethren were beginning to doubt their vocation.

Napoleon believed that Egypt was necessary to France. In 1797 he wrote '400 knights and at most a regiment of 500 men, are the only defence of La Valette's city. The inhabitants, who number more than 100,000, are well disposed towards us and are disgusted with the Chevaliers, who can no longer subsist and are dying of hunger. I have purposely had all their Italian property confiscated. With Malta and Cyprus we will be masters of the whole Mediterranean.' It would give the Corsican parvenu, who had once described the Hospitallers as 'an institution to support in idleness the younger sons of certain privileged families', real pleasure to destroy their maritime Bastille. On 9 June 1798 a French fleet reached Malta with 29,000 men on board. Grand Master Ferdinand von Hompesch was timorous and indecisive, his troops an *opéra bouffe* showpiece, and his guns painted dummies. The brethren, unnerved by the new age and many of them old, could hardly be expected to offer much resistance to 'Christian' Frenchmen. On 13 June, Bonaparte marched into the convent, writing to the sultan at Constantinople that 'France has destroyed the Knights of Malta and broken the chains of the enslaved Turks'; within a week the Religion had been expelled from its island.

One group of knights elected Tsar Paul of Russia as Grand Master, an election which had no canonical validity though Pius VI was loath to condemn a friendly sovereign; the Grand Cross was bestowed on Paul's mistresses but the most incongruous recipient was Lady Hamilton, decorated at Nelson's request. After this bizarre interlude the convent's restoration seemed assured in 1802 by the treaty of Amiens; unfortunately

England refused to evacuate Malta. Later attempts to find the religion a new home, such as Metternich's hint of Rhodes in 1824 and Cardinal Lambruschini's chimera of Algiers in 1830, came to nothing.[1] The few knights who constituted the convent wandered through Italy until at last they reached Rome in 1831; since 1805 they had had no Grand Master, only a lieutenant appointed by the pope. Indeed the Revolution seemed to have completed the destruction begun by the Reformation. During the Peninsular War and the subsequent upheavals Iberian military Orders were a particular object of liberal hatred as absentee landlords: by 1846 the last house of *clerigos* had been dissolved. The Teutonic Order lost Mergentheim in 1810 and was reduced to two bailiwicks within the Habsburg Empire.

However, Romanticism and Sir Walter Scott created a more favourable climate. With its aristocratic traditions the Hospitaller vocation had a strong appeal for the nineteenth-century upper classes. Hospitals and associations of honorary Knights of St John were founded all over Catholic Europe, even in England; in 1839 the Priory of the Two Sicilies was restored and the same year a new Priory of Lombardy-Venetia was founded with Austrian help, while in 1879 Pope Leo XIII appointed a Grand Master. In 1852 Frederick William IV of Prussia restored the *Johanniterorden*. In 1874 Pope Pius IX united the four great Spanish brotherhoods under a conventual prior at Ciudad Real, nominated by the sovereign, though each Order retained some autonomy, keeping its distinguishing cross; in 1916 Alfonso XIII took the title 'Maestre of the Four Orders'. St Lazarus survived in suitably exotic fashion: after the fall of the Bourbons a quorum of chevaliers had invested the Melkhite patriarch of Jerusalem with the Mastership and in 1910, with the patriarchate's blessing, a group of enthusiastic Frenchmen reconstituted the Order, obtaining recognition from the occupants of hereditary commanderies. There was even a new 'Order', the Knights of the Holy Sepulchre, founded by the papacy in 1868, whose 'brethren' are still to be seen at Catholic cathedrals on great occasions, each one resplendent in a white cloak, with a red cross with four smaller crosses in its angles, and a black bonnet.

[1] See A. Lavigerie, *L'Ordre de Malte depuis la Revolution Française* (Paris, 1889).

In 1827, during a Hospitaller attempt to raise money for the conquest of Rhodes – a story which reads like a Balzac novel – some French knights persuaded Sir Robert Peat, George IV's Chaplain Extraordinary, to refound the English Grand Priory. Sir Robert recruited both Catholics and Anglicans in the belief that he was supported by a Capitular Commission, but the Lieutenant Masters at Rome would not recognise his 'restored' Langue. Finally, in 1854, the new brethren set up an independent brotherhood on the model of the *Johanniter*: 'the Grand Priory in the British Realm of the Most Venerable Order of the Hospital of St John of Jerusalem'. In 1888 Queen Victoria became the priory's sovereign and since then a royal prince has always been Grand Prior. It acquired the old gatehouse and chapel at Clerkenwell for headquarters and founded many hospitals, but it is best known for its magnificent ambulance service.[1]

Napoleon had nearly destroyed the *Deutschritter*, but in 1834 Emperor Franz I gave them sovereign status within Austrian territory. Knights of Honour were instituted in 1866, recruited from the greatest families of the empire. Their new convent was a splendid castle at Botzen, and they retained the *Deutscheshof* in Vienna with its beautiful Gothic church. Professed brethren, usually twenty in number, were celibate and always serving officers of the *Kaiserliche und Koenigliche Armee*, like their very reverend superior, who was still colonel of the *Hoch-und-Deutschmeister*; his regiment was an honoured ornament of Strauss's Vienna, renowned for a splendid band with its own stirring regimental march. Archduke Eugen, Hoch-und-Deutschmeister from 1887 to 1923, was an able and popular general who played an important part in the Austro-Hungarian victory at Caporetto in 1917, besides being a devout religious. After the fall of the Habsburgs the Teutonic Order transformed itself into a mendicant brotherhood. Power now lay with the chaplains, one of whom was elected Hochmeister, and no more ritter were professed though Knights of Honour – who no longer needed thirty-two quarterings – were still recruited.

During the civil war all Spanish brotherhoods suffered

[1] See King and Luke, *The Knights of St John in the British Realm* (St John's Gate, 1967).

ruinously. Two of Calatrava's convents were sacked, though fortunately its third house of *comendadoras* was safe in Burgos. Hitler dispersed the Teutonic Order and all but extinguished the *Johanniter*, twelve of whose brethren were hanged after the July Plot of 1944.[1] Then, in 1945, the latter's Dutch branch seceded to form a separate Order under their sovereign, as the Swedes had done in 1921. Most German hospitals had been destroyed by bombing.

However, since the war the *Johanniterorden* has regained much of its strength with branches in France, Finland and Switzerland, besides restoring good relations with the Dutch and Swedish orders. The present *Herrenmeister* is Prince Wilhelm Carl of Prussia. The *Deutsche Orden* has re-established itself and numbers nearly 100 priest brethren; Dr Adenauer was a Knight of Honour and invested with the black crossed white cloak. Its headquarters are still the *Deutscheshof* in Vienna. Knights of St Lazarus also flourish, with the Orleanist prince, Charles-Philippe, Duc de Nemours, as their Grand Master. In France where its headquarters are once more the Grand Commandery at Boigny, besides numbering several French dukes among its knights, it is sometimes regarded as a semi-Royal order. In 1961 a British branch was re-established and the present Grand Prior of St Lazarus in England is Lord Mowbray, Segrave and Stourton, Premier Baron of England and a direct descendant of the crusader Mowbray who first introduced the Order into this country in Henry II's reign. St Lazarus contributes much money to leprosy research, and indeed the late Dr Schweitzer was a commander. Spanish brotherhoods remain a bastion of the Iberian nobility.

After Grand Master Prince Chigi's death in 1951 the Knights of Malta underwent a decade of crisis. A group of cardinals believed that their immense resources should be controlled by the *Curia*, and there was a long struggle, for the brethren claimed that as a sovereign body they were exempt from curial interference. Eventually John XXIII allowed the order to elect Fra. Angelo de Mojana as Grand Master in 1962, and since then the knights have greatly increased their standing, exchanging diplomatic representatives with over thirty countries

[1] I owe this information to the late Sir Harry Luke, Bailiff of Egle.

and continuing to issue passports. In 1966 the Grand Master visited Uruguay, Argentina and Brazil, whose presidents received him with the honours of a reigning sovereign. The same year Malta and the Order of Malta accepted ambassadors from each other, the knights being given a bastion in the old wall of Valetta as official residence; the island has reason to be grateful to its former rulers for during the Suez crisis of 1956 the Order's envoy in the Lebanon negotiated the evacuation of Maltese subjects from Egypt. Within the Vatican the Grand Master keeps some ceremony at his palace on the Aventine, the smallest sovereign state in the world;[1] on formal occasions brethren wear military uniform, a red tunic with a sword and cocked hat, but the black habit is worn for clerical events. The Grand Master and the bailiffs who govern the Order are still professed Knights of Justice who possess the necessary proofs of nobility, take the vow of celibacy, and address each other as 'Fra.'. Their prestige is based on more than tradition, for over 8,000 honorary knights belong to the brotherhood, which, if a last bastion of aristocracy, nonetheless wields vast wealth and influence in Catholic countries. In the smart Parisian's Proustian world the 'bal des chevaliers de Malte' has semi-regal status, while the Order's gala nights at the Opéra are attended by Bourbon royalty. In England the Order's membership is mainly recruited from the ancient Catholic families, those 'Recusants' who have always resisted the Reformation and remained loyal to Rome.[2] Certainly the knights are likely to have some difficulty in adapting themselves to the Roman Church's *aggiornamento*, but their German associations are doing fine work in Vietnam their hospitaller activities range from Peru to Pakistan.[3]

Hitherto the strength of these remnants of the military orders has been their ability to attract the ruling class. The ideal of

[1] The palace has been in the Order's hands for over 650 years. Originally it was a Templar preceptory while during the Hospitallers' Maltese period it served as their embassy.

[2] In 1970 a British sub-priory was set up, consisting of six 'Knights of Obedience' under a Regent, Lord Robert Crichton-Stuart, Bailiff Grand Cross of Obedience.

[3] The Order publishes a 'Bulletin' which gives details of these activities.

the Christian soldier is not quite dead – in 1945 many German officers on the Russian front sincerely believed they were resisting the forces of anti-Christ rather than defending Hitler, while the late Field-Marshal Alexander was a knight of the Venerable Order of St John, and both a former C.I.G.S. and a recent commander-in-chief of the Rhine army are Knights of Malta. However, this attraction will be weakened by the passing of the 'officer and gentleman' concept, which had meaning between the wars for such writers as Stefan Georg, Antoine de St Exupéry and Henri de Montherlant, whose own message seems nowadays no less anachronistic. Indeed military religious Orders are the only institutions left to keep alive the concept of aristocracy. Everywhere the hereditary principle is looked at askance – even in England the House of Lords has opened its doors to life peers while no hereditary peerages have been created for several years. The Orders alone preserve the mystique of rank and birth in a society which finds aristocracy not merely alien but incomprehensible. They constitute the last defendable bastions of hereditary nobility, especially such international brotherhoods as St John and St Lazarus. Yet the defenders will have to recruit their knights from socialist meritocracies or managerial élites in that 'ant heap of the future' so much dreaded by St Exupéry.

But this book is only concerned with soldier monks, who went into battle and died for Christ, not with the future. Other forms of Christianity besides Catholicism have promoted war: the Taborites of Bohemia and Cromwell's Independents slew Romish idolaters with pious gusto; British Protestantism produced such Old Testament warriors as Gordon and Orde Wingate, while Russian Orthodoxy has proclaimed Holy Wars. But not even the latter evolved monks whose life's work was battle. Indeed this concept has been restricted to Western Europe. The Buddhist monasteries which raided tenth-century Kyoto were decadent and unrepresentative, while the Shias' monkish state of Ardabil in fourteenth-century Iran was an aberration; the prophet himself declared that Islam had no room for monasticism. Ghazis and Janissaries were merely *dévots* who waged war on idolaters as a pious duty. Alone of all religions Catholic Christianity produced the monk-warrior.

The Roman Church evolved its religious Orders to deal with specific problems: Benedictines to save learning and agriculture, Dominicans to fight heresy, Franciscans to contain popular mysticism, Jesuits to combat the Reformation and military brethren to give Christendom troops and tame warrior lords. Paradoxically the military vocation's greatest triumph was to rid itself of militarism. The brothers' achievements had been extraordinary. As soldiers they were the first European professional armies. The endurance of Outremer, the Reconquista, the forest campaigns in Lithuania, the sieges of Rhodes and Malta, are epic testimony. At sea, brethren of St John had no equals until the seventeenth century. Politically these Orders controlled Jerusalem and Castile, won the crown of Portugal, and, on the Baltic, successfully opposed Poland and Moscow. As administrators, Iberian Knights made good the Reconquista, while the Ordensland anticipated Hohenzollern Prussia. As colonists they ranched the *meseta*, civilised the Lithuanian wilderness, and explored the African and Indian coasts. This restless energy was generated by the internal conflict between monk and knight. Everything about them was a strange contradiction: monks booted and spurred, armour glinting beneath their habits, trumpet and kettledrums mingling with the plain chant, battle banners jostled by processional crosses, a clash of swords ringing above the convent bell. They at least were sure they did the will of God. 'We gat not this by our own sword, neither was it our own right arm that saved us . . .,'

APPENDICES
GLOSSARY
BIBLIOGRAPHY
FURTHER READING
INDEX

APPENDIX I

Lists of Masters

1 Grand Masters of the Poor Knights of Christ and the Temple of Solomon
2 Grand Masters of the Sovereign Military Hospitaller Order of St John
3 Hochmeisters of the Teutonic Knights
4 Masters of Calatrava
5 Masters of Santiago
6 Masters of Alcántara
7 Masters of the Knights of St Lazarus

1. GRAND MASTERS OF THE POOR KNIGHTS OF CHRIST AND THE TEMPLE OF SOLOMON

1118	Hugues de Payens	1193	Gilbert Erail
1136	Robert de Craon	1201	Philippe du Plaissiez
1146	Everard des Barres	1208	Guillaume de Chartres
1152	Bernard de Tremelai	1218	Pierre de Montaigu
1153	André de Montbard	1230	Armand de Perigord
1156	Bertrand de Blanquefort	1244	Guillaume de Sonnac
1169	Philippe de Milly	1250	Reynald de Vichiers
1170	Eudes de St Amand	1256	Thomas Berard
1179	Arnold de Torroge	1272	Guillaume de Beaujeu
1185	Gerard de Ridefort	1291	Tibald Gaudin
1191	Robert de Sable	1295	Jacques de Molay

2. GRAND MASTERS OF THE SOVEREIGN MILITARY HOSPITALLER ORDER OF ST JOHN

1099–1120	Gerard	1120–60	Raymond du Puy

1160–2 Auger de Balben
1162 Arnold de Comps
1162–70 Gilbert d'Assailly
1170–2 Cast de Murols
1172–7 Jobert de Syrie
1177–87 Roger des Moulins
1188–90 Armengaud d'Asp
1190–2 Garnier de Naples
1193–1202 Geoffroy de
    Donjon
1203–6 Afonso de Portugal
1206–7 Geoffroy le Rat
1207–28 Garin de Montaigu
1228–30 Bertrand de Thessy
1230–6 Guerin
1236–9 Bertrand de Comps
1239–42 Pierre de Vieille
    Bride
1242–58 Guillaume de
    Châteauneuf
1258–77 Hugues Revel
1277–85 Nicholas Lorgne
1285–93 Jean de Villiers
1293–6 Eudes des Pins
1296–1305 Guillaume de
    Villaret
1305–19 Foulques de Villaret
1319–46 Elyon de Villeneuve
1346–53 Dieudonné de Gozon
1353–5 Pierre de Corneillan
1355–65 Roger des Pins
1365–74 Raymond Béranger
1374–6 Robert de Juilly
1376–96 Juan Fernández de
    Heredia
  (1383–95 Ricardo
    Caracciolo)
1396–1421 Philibert de
    Naillac

1421–37 Antoine Fluvian de
    la Rivière
1437–54 Jean Bonpar de
    Lastic
1454–61 Jacques de Milly
1464–7 Pedro-Ramón
    Zacosta
1467–76 Gian-Battista Orsini
1476–1503 Pierre d'Aubusson
1503–12 Eméric d'Amboise
1512–13 Gui de Blanchefort
1513–21 Fabrizzio del
    Caretto
1521–34 Philippe Villiers de
    l'Isle Adam
1534–5 Pietro del Ponte
1535–6 Didier de Saint Jaille
1536–53 Juan d'Omedes
1553–7 Claude de la Sengle
1557–68 Jean Parisot de la
    Valette
1568–72 Pietro del Monte
    San Savino
1572–81 Jean l'Evêque de la
    Cassiere
1581–95 Hugue Loubenx de
    Verdalle
1595–1601 Martín Garzes
1601–22 Alof de Wignacourt
1622–3 Luís Mendez de
    Vasconcellos
1623–36 Antoine de Paule
1636–57 Jean Paul de Lascaris
    Castellar
1657–60 Martin de Redin
1660 Annet de Clermont de
    Chattes Gessan
1660–3 Rafael Cotoner
1663–80 Nicolas Cotoner

1680–90 Gregorio Carafa
1690–7 Adrien de Wigna-
      court
1697–1720 Ramón Perellos y
      Roccaful
1720–2 Marc'Antonio
      Zondadari
1722–36 Antonio Manoel de
      Vilhena
1736–41 Ramón Despuig
1741–73 Manoel Pinto de
      Fonçeca
1773–5 Francisco Ximenes de
      Texada
1775–97 Emmanuel de
      Rohan Polduc

1797–1803 Ferdinand von
      Hompesch
(1799–1803 Emperor Paul I
      of Russia)
1803–5 Giovanni Thomasi

(1805–79 LIEUTENANT
      MASTERS)
1879–1905 Gian-Battista
      Ceschi a Santa
      Croce
1905–31 Galeas von Thun
      und Hohenstein
1931–51 Ludovico Chigi
      Albani della Rovere
1962– Angelo de Mojana

3. HOCHMEISTERS OF THE TEUTONIC KNIGHTS

1198 Heinrich Walpot von
      Bassenheim
1200 Otto von Kerpen
1206 Herman Bart
1206 Hermann von Salza
1239 Conrad of Thuringia
1241 Gerhard von Malberg
1244 Heinrich von Hohenlohe
1253 Poppo von Osterna
1262 Anno von Sanger-
      hausen
1274 Hartmann von
      Heldrungen
1283 Burchard von
      Schwenden
1291 Conrad von
      Feuchtwangen
1297 Gotfried von
      Hohenlohe

1309 Siegfried von
      Feuchtwangen
1312 Karl von Beffart
1324 Werner von Orselen
1331 Luther, Duke of
      Brunswick
1334 Theodor, Burgrave of
      Altenburg
1342 Ludolf Koenig von
      Weitzau
1345 Heinrich Dusener von
      Arfberg
1351 Winrich von Kniprode
1382 Konrad Zolner von
      Rotenstein
1391 Konrad von Walenrod
1394 Konrad von Juningen
1407 Ulrich von Juningen
1410 Heinrich von Plauen

1414 Michael Kuchmeister
von Sternberg
1422 Paul Bellizer von
Rusdorf
1441 Konrad von Erlichs-
hausen
1450 Ludwig von
Erlichshausen
1469 Heinrich Reuss von
Plauen
1470 Heinrich Refle von
Richtenberg
1477 Martin Truchses von
Wetzhausen
1489 Johann von Tieffen
1498 Friedrich, Duke of
Saxony
1511 Albrecht, Margrave of
Brandenberg-Anspach
1526 Walther von Cronberg
1543 Wolfgang Schuzbar
1566 Georg Hund von
Wenckheim
1572 Heinrich von
Bobenhausen
1595 Archduke Maximilian
1619 Archduke Karl

1625 Johann-Eustasius von
Westernach
1627 Johann-Caspar von
Stadion
1641 Archduke Leopold-
Wilhelm
1662 Archduke Karl-Joseph
1664 Johann Caspar von
Ampringen
1684 Ludwig-Anton,
Pfalzgraf von Neuburg
1694 Franz-Ludwig,
Pfalzgraf von Neuburg
1732 Duke Clemens-August
of Bavaria
1761 Duke Karl-Alexander of
Lorraine
1780 Archduke Maximilian-
Franz
1801 Archduke Karl-Ludwig
1804 Archduke Anton-Viktor
1833 Archduke Maximilian-
Josef
1863 Archduke Wilhelm-
Franz-Karl
1894 Archduke Eugen
(abdicated 1923)

4. MASTERS OF CALATRAVA

1164 García
1169 Fernando Escaza
1180 Martín Pérez de
Siones
1182 Nuño Pérez de
Quiñones
1199 Martín Martínez

1206 Ruy Díaz de Anguas
1212 Rodrigo Garcés
1216 Martín Fernández de
Quintana
1218 Gonzalo Yáñez de
Novoa
1238 Martín Ruiz

1240 Gómez Manrique
1243 Fernando Ordoñez
1254 Pedro Yáñez
(formerly Master of
Alcántara)
1267 Juan González
1284 Ruy Pérez Ponce
1295 Diego López de
Sansoles
1296 García López de
Padilla
1329 Juan Núñez de Prado
(*de facto* from 1323)
1355 Diego García de
Padilla
1365 Martín López de
Córdoba
(formerly Master of
Alcántara)

1371 Pedro Múñiz de Godoy
(anti-Master 1369,
Master of Santiago
1384)
1384 Pedro Álvarez de
Pereira
1385 Gonzalo Núñez de
Guzmán
1404 Enrique de Villena
1414 Luís González de
Guzmán
(*de facto* from 1407)
1443 Fernando de Padilla
1443 En Alfons de Aragón
1445 Pedro Girón
1466 Rodrigo Téllez Girón
1482 Garci López de
Padilla
(d. 1487)

5. MASTERS OF SANTIAGO

1170 Pedro Fernández
1184 Fernando Díaz
1186 Sancho Fernández de
Lemos
1195 Gonzalo Rodríguez
1204 Suero Rodríguez
1206 Ferrán González de
Marañón
1210 Pedro Arias
1213 García González de
Arauzo
1217 Martín Peláez
Barragan
1222 García González de
Candamio
1224 Fernando Parez Chacín

1227 Pedro González
1238 Rodrigo Yñiguez de
Mendoza
1242 Pelayo Pérez Correa
127? Gonzalo Ruiz Girón
1280 Pedro Núñez
1287 Gonzalo Pérez Martel
1287 Pedro Fernando
Mate
1293 Juan Osorez
1311 Didaco Moñiz
1318 García Fernández de
Truxillo
1327 Vasco Rodríguez
Coronado
1338 Vasco López

1338 Alfonso Meléndez de
Guzmán
1342 Don Fadrique
1358 García Álvarez de
Toledo
1359 Gonzalo Mexia
1370 Fernando Osorez
1382 Pedro Fernández
Cabeza de Vaca
1384 Rodrigo González
Mexia
1384 Pedro Múñiz de Godoy

1385 García Fernández
Mexia
1387 Lorenzo Suárez de
Figueroa
1409 En Enric
1445 Álvaro de Luna
1453 Don Alfonso
1468 Juan Pacheco
1474 Rodrigo Manrique
1477 Alonso de Cárdenas
(d. 1493)

6. MASTERS OF ALCÁNTARA

Anti-Masters are given in brackets

Priors:

1165 Suero Fernández
Barrientos
fl. 1176 Gómez Fernández

Masters:

1183 Gómez Fernández
1200 Benito Suárez
1218 Nuño Fernández
1219 García Sánchez
1223 Arias Pérez
1234 Pedro Yáñez o Períañez
(later Master of
Calatrava)
1254 García Fernández
1284 Fernán Paez
1292 Fernán Pérez Gallego
1316 Ruy Vásquez
1318 Suero Pérez
1335 Ruy Pérez de
Maldonado

1335 Fernán López
1335 Suero López
1337 Gonzalo Martínez de
Oviedo
1340 Nuño Chamiro
1343 Pere Alfons Pantoja
1343 Pedro Yáñez de
Campo
1346 Fernán Pérez Ponce de
León
1355 Diego Gutiérrez de
Zavallos
1365 Gutiérrez Gómez de
Toledo
1365 Martín López de
Córdoba
(later Master of
Calatrava)
1365 Suero Martínez
(1365 Pedro Múñiz
de Godoy, anti-Master
of Calatrava 1369,

Master of Calatrava
1371, Master of Santiago
1384.1365 Pedro Alfonso
de Sotomayor)
1369 Ruy Díaz de la Vega
(1369 Melen Suárez)
1369 Diego Martínez
1369 Diego Gómez Barroso
1385 Gonzalo Núñez de
Guzmán
(later Master of
Calatrava and then of
Santiago)

1394 Martín Yáñez de
Barbudo
1394 Fernán Rodríguez de
Villalobos
1409 Don Sancho
1416 Juan de Sotomayor
1432 Gutierre de Sotomayor
1455 Gómez Cáceres y Solís
1472 Alonso de Monroy
1473 Francisco de Solís
1478 Juan de Zúñiga
(abdicated 1494)

7. MASTERS OF THE KNIGHTS OF ST LAZARUS

1120 Roger Boyant
1131 Jean
1153 Barthélemy
1154 Itier
1155 Hugues de Saint-Paul
1157 Raymond Dupuis
1164 Rainier
1168 Raymond
1169 Gérard de Montclar
1185 Bernard
1228 Gautier de Neufchatel
1234 Raynaud de Flory
1267 Jean de Meaux
1277 Thomas de Sainville
? Adam de Veau
1342 Jean de Paris
1354 Jean de Couraze
1355 Jean Le Conte
1368 Jean de Besnes
1424 Pierre des Ruaux
? G. Desmares

1469 Jean Cornu
1493 François d'Amboise
1500 Agnan de Mareul
1519 François de Bourbon,
Duc d'Estouteville
1521 Claude de Mareul
1524 Jean Conti
1557 Jean de Levis
1564 Michel de Seure
1578 François Salviati
1586 Michel de Seure
1593 Aimard de Clermont
de Chastes
1603 Jean-Charles de
Gayand
1604 Philibert, Marquis de
Nerestang
1620 Claude, Marquis de
Nerestang
1639 Charles, Marquis de
Nerestang

1645 Charles-Achille,
Marquis de Nerestang
1673 François-Michel Le
Tellier, Marquis de
Louvois (Grand Vicar,
d. 1691)
1693 Philippe, Marquis de
Dangeau
1720 Louis d'Orléans, Duc de
Chartres
(abdicated 1752)
1757 Louis de France, Duc de
Berry
(later Louis XVI)
1773 Louis Stanislas Xavier
de France
(later Louis XVIII)

1814–1930 Council of
Officers, under
the protection of
the Kings of
France until 1830,
and then under
that of the
Melkhite Patri-
arch of Jerusalem
until 1930
1930 Don Francisco de
Borbon, Duke of
Seville
1952 Don Francisco de
Borbon y Borbon
1967 Charles Philippe, Duc
de Nemours

Key Dates

1115 Hugue de Payens recruits 'Poor Knights' to protect pilgrims.

1128 Council of Troyes – St Bernard compiles the Templar rule and writes 'De Laude Novae Militiae'.

1137 The Hospitallers of St John are given the castle of Gibelin.

1158 Abbot Ramón de Fitero and his monks garrison Calatrava.

1197 Foundation of the Teutonic Order.

1230 Fra. Hermann Balke and the Teutonic Knights arrive in Prussia.

1291 Acre falls – the end of Latin Syria.

1307 Philip IV of France arrests the Templars.

1309 The Hospitallers transfer their headquarters from Cyprus to Rhodes.

1410 Hochmeister Ulrich von Juningen and his brethren are defeated by the Poles at Tannenberg.

1434 Enrique the Navigator, Master of the Order of Christ, sends out his first expedition to explore the African coast.

1468 Frey Juan Pacheco, Master of Santiago, becomes coadjutor of Calatrava – zenith of the military Orders' political role in Castile.

1494 Frey Juan de Zúñiga of Alcántara abdicates and no new Master is appointed – the three Castilian masterships are administered by the crown.

1522 The third great siege of Rhodes which falls to the Turks.

1525 Hochmeister Albrecht of Hohenzollern secularises the *Ordensstaat*, and becomes Duke of Prussia – the *Grosskomturei* is moved to Mergentheim.

1561 Secularisation of the Teutonic Knights in Livland – Landtmeister Gottert Kettler becomes Duke of Courland.

1565 The Turks besiege Malta and are unsuccessful – Military Christianity's most famous feat of arms.

1571 Battle of Lepanto – the Turks lose control of the Mediterranean.

1726 The abbé Vertot publishes his history of the Order of St John.

1798 Napoleon Bonaparte captures Malta and evicts the Order of St John.

1834 Headquarters of the Sovereign Military Order of St John – the former Knights of Malta – are moved to Rome.

1962 The Order of St John summons its first Chapter General since 1776 – Fra. Angelo de Mojana is elected Grand Master.

Chronology

1099 Jerusalem falls to the First Crusade.

1115 Hugue de Payens recruits 'Poor Knights' to protect pilgrims.

1118 Hugue de Payens is given the 'Temple of Solomon'.

1126 The Hospitallers of St John possess a constable – the first suggestion of military activity.

1128 Council of Troyes – St Bernard compiles the Templar rule and writes 'De Laude Novae Militiae'.

1137 The Hospitallers of St John are entrusted with the key position of Beit Jibrin and build the castle of Gibelin.

1144 Edessa falls to the atabeg Zengi.

1147 The Second Crusade – Templars wear the Red Cross for the first time.

1158 Abbot Ramón de Fitero and his monks garrison Calatrava.

1164 Calatrava recognised as an Order of the Church.

1164 The *hermangilda* of Cáceres are given Uclés to defend – origin of the Knights of Santiago.

1166 Foundation of the Order of Évora (the future Knights of Aviz).

1175 The Order of Santiago is given canonical recognition by the papacy.

1176 The Order of San Julián (the future Knights of Alcántara) is recognised by the papacy.

1180 The Castilian Count Rodrigo founds the Order of Montjoie in the Holy Land.

1187 The Franks are defeated by Saladin at the Horns of Hattin and lose Jerusalem.

1191 The Third Crusade captures Acre – establishment of the new kingdom of Jerusalem.

1191 The English Order of St Thomas Acon is founded during the siege of Acre.

1195 The Spanish are defeated at Alarcos – Calatrava is lost to the Moors.

1197 Foundation of the Teutonic Order.

1204 The Fourth Crusade captures Constantinople.

1204 Foundation of the Sword Brethren in Livland.

1210 Hermann von Salza is elected Hochmeister of the Teutonic Order.

1211 The Knights of Évora are given the town of Aviz – henceforth they are known as Knights of Aviz.

1211 King Andrew II of Hungary invites the Teutonic Order to Transylvania to fight the heathen Cumans.

1212 The Spaniards defeat the Almohad caliph at Las Navas de Tolosa.

1217 The Fifth Crusade.

1217 The Knights of San Julián are given the town of Alcántara – henceforth they are known as Knights of Alcántara.

1229 The Sixth Crusade – Frederick II regains Jerusalem.

1230 Hermann Balke and the Teutonic Knights arrive in Prussia.

1233 Foundation of the Mercedarians.

1236 The Castilians capture Córdoba.

1237 Amalgamation of the Sword Brethren with the Teutonic Order.

1240 Alexander Nevsky defeats the Teutonic Knights at Lake Peipus.

1241 The Mongols defeat Boleslav the Chaste and the Teutonic Knights at Leignitz.

1244 The Franks are defeated at La Forbie.

1246 The Castilians capture Seville.

1249 St Louis and the Seventh Crusade surrender to Baibars and the Mamelukes.

1256 War of St Sabas – civil war between the military Orders in Syria.

1260 Battle of Ain Jalud – Baibars of Egypt defeats the Mongol expeditionary force and Islam is saved.

1264 Revolt by the Moors of Murcia – the rising is quelled but the Reconquista is halted.

1268 Antioch falls to Baibars.

1283 The Landtmeister Konrad von Thierberg drives the last native chieftain out of Prussia – all but 170,000 Prussians have been exterminated.

1289 Tripoli falls to the Mamelukes.

1291 Acre falls – the end of Latin Syria.

1304 The Isle of Ruad, last Syrian outpost of the Templars is taken by the Mamelukes.

1307 Philip IV of France arrests the Templars.

1309 The Hospitallers transfer their headquarters from Cyprus to Rhodes.

1309 The Teutonic Order transfers its *Grosskomturei* from Venice to Prussia.

1311 The Templars are officially dissolved by the papacy.

1319 Foundation of the Portuguese Order of Christ.

1321 Foundation of the Aragonese Order of Montesa.

1340 Battle of the Río Salado – Alfonso XI of Castile and the Iberian Orders defeat the Marinids' and Granadines' final attempt to reconquer Spain.

1344 Smyrna is captured and entrusted to the Knights of St John.

1365 Pierre I storms Alexandria – high water mark of the later Levantine Crusade.

1385 King João of Portugal – former Master of Aviz – defeats the Castilians at Aljubarrota.

1386 Grand Duke Jogaila of Lithuania turns Christian and becomes King Władyslaw II of Poland-Lithuania.

1396 Bayezid defeats the crusaders at Nicopolis.

1402 Tamberlane captures Smyrna from the Hospitallers.

1406 The Teutonic Order finally subdues Samaiten, uniting Prussia and Livland – greatest extent of the Order's power.

1410 Hochmeister Ulrich von Juningen and his brethren are annihilated by the Poles at Tannenberg.

1415 King João of Portugal captures Ceuta – beginning of the crusade in North Africa.

1426 King Janus is defeated at Khirokitia – Lusignan Cyprus ceases to be a crusader state.

1434 Henry the Navigator, Master of the Order of Christ, sends out his first expedition to explore the African coast.

1435 Grand Duke Zigmantas of Lithuania destroys the pretender Svitrigaila's army – the last opportunity of reuniting the Teutonic Order's lands in Prussia and Livland is lost.

1444 First great siege of Rhodes – the Hospitallers rout the Mamelukes.

1453 Constantinople falls to the Turk.

1454 The Lizard League of Prussia rebels against Hochmeister Ludwig von Erlichshausen, offering the crown to Casimir IV of Poland.

1457 The Teutonic Knights abandon the Marienburg.

1460 King Afonso V grants the Order of Christ a levy on all merchandise from the new African lands.

1467 Peace of Thorn – the Teutonic Order surrenders West Prussia to the Poles and moves its headquarters to Koenigsberg.

1468 Frey Juan Pacheco, Master of Santiago, becomes co-adjutor of Calatrava – zenith of the military Order's political role in Castile.

1471 King Afonso V captures Tangier.

1474 Isabella becomes Queen of Castile.

1476 Isabella persuades the Trecenazgo of Santiago to leave the choice of their Master to her – the crown begins to take over the Spanish military Orders.

1479 Isabella's husband, Ferdinand, becomes King of Aragon.

1480 Second great siege of Rhodes – Pierre d'Aubusson repels the Turks.

1481 Muley Hassan of Granada storms Zahara – start of the last war of the Reconquista.

1487 Death of Garci López de Padilla of Calatrava – no new Master is appointed.

1492 Fall of Granada – end of the Reconquista.

1493 Alonso de Cárdenas of Santiago dies – no new Master is appointed.

1494 Juan de Zúñiga of Alcántara abdicates and no new Master is appointed – the three Castilian masterships are administered by the crown.

1494 The Castilian Orders are dispensed from celibacy by Pope Alexander VI and allowed to marry.

1496 The Orders of Christ and Aviz are dispensed from celibacy.

1499 The Knight of Christ, Vasco da Gama returns from India after rounding the Cape of Good Hope.

1501 First Muscovite invasion of Livland.

1503 The Grand-Duke of Moscow makes a fifty years' truce with the Landmeister of Livland.

1505 The Orders of Christ and Aviz are dispensed from poverty.

1509 The Spaniards take Oran – King Ferdinand rejects the proposal that Santiago transfer its headquarters to North Africa.

1522 The third great siege of Rhodes, which falls to the Turks.

1523 Administration of the masterships of the three great Castilian Orders is finally vested in the crown with papal permission.

1525 Hochmeister Albrecht of Hohenzollern secularises the *Ordensstaat* and becomes Duke of Prussia – the *Grosskomturei* is moved to Mergentheim.

1530 Fra. Antonio fails to reform the Order of Christ.

1530 The Knights of St John arrive in Malta.

1534 Ignatius Loyola founds the Jesuits – the Counter-Reformation abandons military Christianity.

1540 Henry VIII dissolves the English Grand Priory of St John.

1557 Ivan the Terrible invades Livland.

1561 Secularisation of the Teutonic Knights in Livland – Landmeister Gothard Kettler becomes Duke of Courland.

1561 Grand Duke Cosimo de'Medici founds the Knights of San Stefano in Tuscany – last military Order to be founded with conventual life.

1565 The Turks besiege Malta and are unsuccessful – military Christianity's most famous feat of arms.

1566 The Order of St John begins to build the convent-city of Valetta.

1568 Morisco rising in Granada – last campaign of the Reconquista.

1571 Battle of Lepanto – the Turks lose control of the Mediterranean.

1572 Foundation of the Savoyard Order of San Morizio e San Lazzaro.

1572 Frey Francisco Rades y Andrada publishes *Historia de las Tres Órdenes* – the first comprehensive history of the Spanish military Orders.

1576 The Teutonic Order refuses to move its headquarters from Mergentheim to the Turkish frontier – the last chance to fulfil a valuable military function.

1589 Death of Luys Borja of Montesa – last Master of a Spanish military Order.

1594 Fra. Giacomo Bosio publishes the first definitive history of the Order of St John of Jerusalem.

1595 Archduke Maximilian becomes the first Habsburg *Hoch-und-Deutschmeister*.

1604 Henri IV gives the French branch of St Lazarus its first Grand Master.

1606 The Teutonic Order revises its statutes.

1607 The Grand Master of St John becomes *ex officio* a Prince of the Holy Roman Empire.

1637 The Brandenburg *Ballei* of St John sends responsions to Malta – the first instance of cooperation between Catholic and Protestant branches of a religious Order.

1645 The Turks invest Candia in Crete.

1669 Candia falls – end of the last great siege undergone by military brethren.

1683 The Turks fail to take Vienna – end of the menace of Islam.

1687 Knights of St John assist in the Venetians' capture of Athens.

1694 Founding of the *Hoch-und-Deutschmeister* regiment at Vienna.

1701 The Elector of Brandenburg assumes the title 'King-in-Prussia' – protest by the *Hoch-und-Deutschmeister*.

1708 Defence of Oran – last land campaign by the Order of St John.

1716 Expedition to the Morea by the Maltese, papal and Venetian navies – the last Holy Alliance against Islam.

1726 The abbé Vertot publishes his history of the Order of St John.

1760 Turkish invasion threatens Malta for the last time.

1784 Publication of the first volume of komtur de Wal's *Histoire de l'Ordre Teutonique.*

1789 French Revolution.

1792 Louis XVI's 'Flight to Varennes' is financed by the Grand Master of St John.

1798 Napoleon Bonaparte captures Malta and evicts the Order of St John.

1801 Archduke Karl, the *Feldherr*, becomes *Hoch-und-Deutschmeister.*

1810 The Teutonic Order loses Mergentheim and all possessions outside the Austrian Empire.

1831 Foundation of the Venerable Order of St John – first Anglican revival of a religious Order.

1834 Headquarters of the Sovereign Military Order of St John (the Knights of Malta) are moved to Rome.

1834 Reorganisation and revival of the Teutonic Order.

1852 Revival of the *Johanniterorden* in Prussia.

1879 Pope Leo XIII appoints a new Grand Master for the Order of St John.

1888 The Duke of Connaught becomes Grand Prior of the Venerable Order of St John – Queen Victoria accepts the sovereignty of the English Order which becomes a national institution.

1910 Revival of the Order of St Lazarus.

1916 Alfonso XIII of Spain adopts the title 'Master of the Four Orders'.

1923 Abdication of the last military *Hoch-und-Deutschmeister,* Archduke Eugen.

1929 The Teutonic Knights become a purely clerical Order of priests.

1962 The Order of St John summons its first Chapter General since 1776 – Fra. Angelo de Mojana is elected Grand Master.

Glossary

adelantado – governor of a province
alcalde – governor of a castle
bailiff – senior officer
bailiwick – senior officer's command
balleien – bailiwicks
cadi – Moorish magistrate
cavalgada – cavalry raid
chapter-general – council attended by all brethren
chevauchée – cavalry raid
clavero – key bearer (i.e. castellan)
cofradias – confraternities
comanada – commandery (Catalan)
comanador – commander (Catalan)
comenda – commandery (Portuguese)
comendador – commander (Castilian)
comendador mayor – grand commander
confrater – honorary knight brother
Deutschritter – Teutonic Knights
domi conventuales – houses in which the rule was observed
En – Catalan 'Sir' (cf. Castilian 'Don')
encomienda – commandery (Castilian)
escudero – squire
espada – the red sword-cross emblem of Santiago
familiares – associates and employees
frares cavallers – knight brethren (Catalan)
frares clergues – priest brethren (Catalan)
freyles caballeros – knight brethren (Castilian)
freyles clerigos – priest brethren (Castilian)
ghazi – warrior for the faith (Muslim)
gomeres – negro knifemen
grosskomtur – grand commander
halbbruder – honorary knight brother

hauskomtur – house commander
hermandad – brotherhood
hermangilda – guild
hidalgo – nobleman
Hoch-und-Deutschmeister – High-and-German Master
jinetes – light horse
komturei – commandery
landkomtur – district commander
landmeister – provincial Master
langue – 'tongue' (i.e. national association)
largetto – 'lizard' – a popular name for the red sword-cross of Santiago
latifundio – great agricultural estate
maestrazgo – mastership (Castilian)
Maestre – Master (Castilian)
mestrat – mastership (Catalan or Portuguese)
Mestre – Master (Catalan or Portuguese)
mudéjar – Moor subject to Christian rule
Office – prayers and psalms to be said or sung at specified times of the day
Ordensmarschall – Marshal of the Order
Pfleger – commander
preceptor – commander
professed – having taken the monastic vows of poverty, chastity and obedience
rabito – garrison of a ribat
razzia – raid
ribat – fortified Muslim 'monasteries'
ricos-homems – noblemen (Portuguese)
Schwertbrüder – Sword Brethren
sergeant – man-at-arms
taifa – petty state
trezes – the Council of Thirteen (of the Order of Santiago)
Turcopolier – general commanding native light horse
vogt – commander (of the Sword Brethren)

Bibliography

I. BULLARIA, CARTULARIES, RULES, STATUTES, CHRONICLES, DOCUMENTS AND CONTEMPORARY HISTORIES OF THE ORDERS

General

AMMAN, J., *Cleri totius Romanae ecclesiae* (Frankfurt 1585).

BUONANNI, F., *Ordinum Religiosorum in ecclesia militanti catalogus* (Rome 1714).

GIUSTINIANI, B., *Historie Cronologiche degl'Ordini Militari e de tutte Religioni Cavalleresche*, 2 vols. (Venice 1692).

HELYOT, P., *Histoire des ordres religieux, monastiques et militaires*, 7 vols. (Paris 1714–21).

HERMANT, J., *Histoires des Religions ou Ordres Militaires* (Paris 1696).

JONGELINUS, *Originis equestrium militarium ordinis Cisterciensis* (1640).

RADES Y ANDRADA, F., *Chrónica de las tres Órdenes y Cavallerías de Sanctiago, Calatrava y Alcántara* (Toledo 1572).

Alcántara

Difiniciones [*sic*] *y Estableciementos de la Orden y Cavalleria de Alcántara* (Madrid 1609).

ORTEGA Y COTES, I. J., *Bullarium Ordinis Militiae de Alcántara, Olim Sancti Juliani de Pereiro* (Madrid 1759).

TORRES Y TAPIA, A. DE, *Crónica de la Orden de Alcántara*, 2 vols. (Madrid 1763).

Aviz

PURIFICAÕ, J. DA, 'Catalogo dos Mestres e administradores da illustre e antiquissima Ordem Militar de Aviz', *C.A.R.H.P.*, vol. 2.

Calatrava

Diffiniciones de la Orden y Cavallería de Calatrava (Valladolid 1603).

ORTEGA Y COTES, I. J., *Bullarium Ordinis Militiae de Calatrava* (Madrid 1761).

Order of Christ

Definições e estatus da ordem de Christo (Lisbon 1746).

Mercedarians

Regula et constitutiones Fratrum Sacri Ordinis Beatae Mariae de Mercede Redemptionis Captivorum (Salamanca 1588).

Montesa

RADES Y ANDRADA, F., *Diffiniciones de la sagrada Religion y Cavallería de Sancta María de Montesa y Sanct Iorge d'Alfama* (Valencia 1573).

SAMPER, H. DE, *Montesa Ilustrada*, 2 vols. (Valencia 1669).

Santiago

Bullarium Equestris Ordinis S. Iacobi de Spatha (Barcelona 1719).

Regla y Establescimientos de la orden de la Caualleria de San Sanctiago del Espada (1555).

St John

BALBI, F., *The Siege of Malta*, trans. E. Bradford (Folio Society 1965).

BOSIO, G., *Dell'istoria della Sacra religione et Illma. Militia de San Giovanni Geirosolimitano*, 3 vols. (Rome 1594).

——, *Histoire des Chevaliers de l'Ordre de S. Jean de Hierusalem*, trans. and ed. by J. Baudoin (Paris 1629).

BOURBON, J. DE, *La Grande et merueilleuse et très cruelle oppugnation de la noble cité de Rhodes prinse naguères par Sultan Séliman à present grand Turq ennemy de la très saincte foy Catholique que redige par escript par excellent et noble chevalier Frère Jacques bastard de Bourbon commandeur de Sainct Mauluiz, Doysemont e fonteynes au prieuré de France* (Paris 1525).

CAOURSIN, G., *Obsidionis Rhodiae Urbis Descriptio* (Ulm 1496), trans. John Kay, ed. H. W. Fincham (St John's Gate 1926).

'Catalogo dos Grampriores do Crato da Ordem de S. João de Malta', *C.A.R.H.P.*, vol. 4.

'Cronica Magistrorum Defunctorum' in Dugdale, vol. VI.

DELAVILLE LE ROULX, J., *Cartulaire Géneral des Hospitaliers de Saint Jean de Jérusalem 1100–1310*, 4 vols. (Paris 1894–1906).

The Knights Hospitallers in England, being the report of Prior Philip de Thame to the Grand Master Elyan de Villanova for A.D. 1338, ed. L. B. Larking, introd. J. M. Kemble (Camden Soc., London 1858).

LE GRAND, L., 'La prière qui se doit dire au Palais des Malades (à Chypre)', *La prière des malades dans les hôpitaux de l'ordre de Saint-Jean de Jérusalem*, in Bibliothèque de l'École des Chartes LVII (1896).

POZZO, B. DALL', *Historia della Sacra Religione Militare di S. Giovanni Gerosolimitano*, 2 vols. (1703, 1715).

SCICLUNA, H. P., *The Book of Deliberations of the Venerable Tongue of England 1523–1567* (Malta 1949).

VERTOT, G. AUBERT DE, *Histoire des Chevaliers Hospitaliers de S. Jean de Jérusalem*, 4 vols. (Paris 1726).

Swordbrethren

ALNPEKE, DIETLEB VON, 'Die Riterlichen Meister und Brüder zu Leiflant', *S.R.L.*, vol. 1.

LETTLAND, HEINRICH VON, 'Chronicon Livonicum Vetus', *S.R.L.*, vol. 1.

WARTBERGE, HERMANN VON, 'Chronicon Livoniae', *S.R.P.*, vol. 2.

RÜSSOW, BALTHASAR, 'Chronica der Provintz Lyfflandt', *S.R.L.*, vol. II (Bart 1584).

Templars

ALBON, MARQUIS D', *Cartulaire général de l'ordre du Temple 1119–1150. Recueil des chartes et des bulles relatives à l'ordre du Temple* (Paris 1913).

'Catalogo dos Mestres da Ordem do Templo Portugueza e em outras da Hespanha', *C.A.R.H.P.*, vol. 2.

CLAIRVAUX, BERNARD OF, 'Liber ad Milites Templi de Laude Novae Militiae', in Leclercq, J. and Rochais, H. M., *S. Bernardi Opera*, vol. III (Editiones Cistercienses, Rome 1963).

CURZON, H. DE, *La Règle du Temple* (Paris 1887).
——, *La Maison du Temple à Paris* (Paris 1888).
LECLERCQ, J., 'Un document sur les débuts des Templiers', *Révue de l'histoire ecclésiastique*, vol. LII (1957).
LIZERAND, G., *Le Dossier de l'Affaire des Templiers* (Paris 1923).
MICHELET, J., *Procés des Templiers*, 2 vols. (Paris 1841–51).

Teutonic Knights

BITSCHIN, CONRAD, 'Chronica Terrae Prussiae', *S.R.P.*, vol. III.
BLUMENAUE, L., 'Historia de Ordine Theutonicorum Cruciferorum', *S.R.P.*, vol. IV.
Chronicon Equestris Ordinis Teutonici (Netherlands 1738).
Das grosse Amterbuch des Deutschen Ordens (Danzig 1921).
DUELLIUS, E., *Debita seu statuta Equitum Theutonicorum* (1724).
'Historia Brevis Magistrorum Ordinis Theutonici Generalium ad Martinum Truchses continuata', *S.R.P.*, vol. IV.
MARTIN, K., *Minnesanger* (Baden-Baden 1953) – illuminated miniature from the Manessa Codex.
PUSILGE, JOHANN VON, 'Annalista Thorunensis', *S.R.P.*, vol. III.
PERLBACH, M., *Statuten des Deutschen Ordens* (Halle 1890).
DUSBURG, PETRUS VON, 'Cronica Terre Prussie', *S.R.P.*, vol. I.
——, *Chronicon Prussiae . . . cum incerti auctoria continuatione usque ad annum MCCCCXXXV* (Frankfurt & Leipzig 1679).
STREHLKE, E., *Tabulae Ordinis Teutonici* (Berlin 1869).
WAL, G. DE, *Histoire de l'Ordre Teutonique*, 8 vols. (Paris & Rheims 1784–90).

2. OTHER CONTEMPORARY SOURCES

AYALA, P. LOPEZ DE, *Crónicas de los reyes de Castilla*, 2 vols. (Madrid 1778–80).
BORCH, M. J., *Lettres sur la Sicile et sur l'Isle de Malte* (Turin 1782).
BRANTÔME, P. DE BOURDEILLE DE, *Les Vies des Hommes Illustrés et Grands Capitaines estrangers de son temps* (Amsterdam 1665).

——, *Les Vies des Hommes Illustrés et Grands Capitaines François de son temps*, 4 vols. (Amsterdam 1666).

BRYDONE, P., *A Tour through Sicily and Malta* (London 1773).

CELLINI, B., *The Memoirs of Benvenuto Cellini* (O.U.P. 1961).

CHARTRES, FULCHER OF, 'Historia Hierosolymitana. Gesta Francorum Iherusalem peregrinantium', *R.H.C. oc. 3.*

DICETO, RALPH DE, 'Ymagines Historiarium', *The Historical Works of Master Ralph de Diceto, Dean of London*, ed. W. Stubbs, 2 vols. (Rolls Series, London 1876).

HILL, ROSALIND (ed.), *Gesta Francorum* (Nelson 1962).

HORSEY, J., *The Travels of Sir Jerome Horsey, Kt.*, ed. A. Bond (Hakluyt Soc. 1856).

IBELIN, JEAN D', 'Le Livre du Jean d'Ibelin', *R.H.C. Lois. 1.*

JOINVILLE, J. DE, *Histoire de Saint Louis*, ed. N. de Wailly (Paris 1874); trans. M. R. B. Shaw, *Chronicles of the Crusades* (Penguin 1963).

LELEWEL, J. (ed.), *Guillebert de Lannoy et ses voyages en 1413, 1414 et 1421* (Brussels 1844).

MARIANA, J. DE, *Historiae de rebus Hispaniae* (Toledo 1592–1610), trans. John Stevens, *The General History of Spain* (London 1699).

MONTLUC, B. DE LASSERAN-MASSENCOME DE, *Commentaires de Messire de Monluc*, 2 vols. (Lyons 1593), trans. C. Cotton, *The Commentaries of Messire Blaize de Montluc* (London 1674).

PARIS, MATTHEW, *Chronica Majora*, ed. H. R. Luard, 7 vols. (Rolls Series, London 1872–83).

STUBBS, W. (ed.), 'Itinerarium peregrinorum et gesta regis Ricardi', *Memorials of the Reign of Richard I* (Rolls Series, London 1869).

VILLEHARDOUIN, G. DE, *La Conquête de Constantinople*, ed. E. Faral, 2 vols. (Paris 1938–9), trans. M. R. B. Shaw, *Chronicles of the Crusades* (Penguin 1963).

VITRY, JACQUES DE, *Historia orientalis seu Hierosolymitana*, ed. J. Bongars (Hannau 1611).

3. LATER SOURCES AND STUDIES OF THE ORDERS

Alcántara

O'CALLAGHAN, J. F., 'The Foundation of the Order of Alcántara', *Catholic Historical Review*, vol. 47 (1961–2).

S. PEDRO, M. MÚÑIZ DE, *Don Gutierre de Sotomayor, Maestre de Alcántara* (Caceres 1949).

Aviz

OLIVIERIA, M. DE, 'A Milicia de Evora e a Ordem de Calatrava', *Lusitania Sacra* I (1956).

Calatrava

GUTTON, F., *L'Ordre de Calatrava*, Commission de l'ordre de Citeaux, P. Lethellieux (Paris 1955).

O'CALLAGHAN, J. F., 'The Affiliation of the Order of Calatrava with Citeaux', *Analecta Sacri Ordinis Cisterciensis*, vols. 15 and 16 (1959–60).

——, 'Don Pedro Girón, Master of the Order of Calatrava 1445–66', *Hispania*, vol. 21 (1961–2).

General

BRASIER, L. and BRUNET, J., *Les Ordres Portugaises* (Paris 1898).

CLINCHAMPS, G. DU PUY DE, *La Chevalerie* (Paris 1961).

COCHERIL, M. M., 'Essai sur l'Origine des Ordres Militaires dans la Peninsule Iberique', *Collectanea ordinis Cisterciensium Reformatorum*, vols. 20 and 21 (1958–9).

Encyclopaedia Britannica: articles on Order of St John of Jerusalem, Teutonic Knights and Templars.

Grande Enciclopedia Portuguesa e Brasileira: articles on Alcántara, Aviz, Calatrava, Order of Christ, Santiago, etc.

LLAMAZARES, J. FERNANDEZ, *Historia Compendiada de las Cuatres Órdenes Militares* (Madrid 1862).

SALLES, F. DE, *Ordres Religieux de Chevaliers*, 2 vols. (Paris 1887–9).

Santiago

LOMAX, D. W., *La Orden de Santiago, MCLXX–MCCLXXV* (Madrid 1965).

——, 'The Order of Santiago and the Kings of León', *Hispania*, vol. 18 (1958).

MONTHERLANT, H. DE, *Le Maître de Santiago* (Paris 1947).

St John

BELABRE, F. DE, *Rhodes of the Knights* (Oxford 1908).

BOISGELIN, P. M. C. DE, *Ancient and Modern Malta and the History of the Knights of Jerusalem* (London 1805).

BOUHOURS, A., *The Life of the renowned Peter d'Aubusson* (London 1679).

BRADFORD, E., *The Great Siege* (Hodder & Stoughton 1961).

BREMOND D'ARS, A. DE, *Le Chevalier de Téméricourt* (Paris 1904).

CAVALIERO, R., *The Last of the Crusaders* (Hollis & Carter 1960).

DELAVILLE LE ROULX, J., *Les Hospitaliers en Terre Sainte et à Chypre (1100–1310)* (Paris 1904).

——, *Les Hospitaliers à Rhodes jusqu'à la mort de Phillibert de Naillac (1310–1421)* (Paris 1913).

——, *La France en Orient au XIVe siècle. Expéditions du Maréchal Boucicaut*, 2 vols. (Paris 1885–6).

——, *Mélanges sur l'ordre de St Jean de Jerusalem* (Paris 1910).

DESCHAMPS, P., *Les Châteaux des croisés en Terre Sainte. Le Crac des Chevaliers* (Paris 1934).

DUCAUD-BOURGET, F., *The Spiritual Heritage of the Sovereign Military Order of Malta* (Vatican City 1958).

EASSON, D. E., *Mediaeval Religious Houses – Scotland* (Longmans, Green 1957).

GABRIEL, A., *La Cité de Rhodes* (Paris 1921 and 1922).

HERQUET, K., *Juan Ferrandez [sic] de Heredia, Grossmeister des Johanniterordens (1337–99)* (Mulhausen i. Th. 1878).

KING, E. J., *The Knights Hospitallers in the Holy Land* (Methuen 1931).

KING, E. J. and LUKE, H., *The Knights of St John in the British Realm* (St John's Gate 1967).

KNOWLES, D. and HADCOCK, R. N., *Mediaeval Religious Houses – England and Wales* (Longmans, Green 1953).

LACROIX, A., *Déodat de Dolomieu* (Paris 1921).

LAVIGERIE, O., *L'Ordre de Malte depuis la Révolution Française* (Paris 1889).

LUTTRELL, A., 'The Aragonese Crown and the Knights Hospitallers of Rhodes 1291–1350', *English Historical Review*, vol. 76 (1961).

——, 'Jean and Simon de Hesdin – Hospitaller Theologians', *Récherches de Théologie Ancienne et Mediévale*, vol. 31 (1964).

MIFSUD, H., *Knights Hospitallers of the Venerable Tongue of England in Malta* (Malta 1914).

LA VARENDE, J., *Tourville et son Temps* (Paris 1943).

L'Ordre Souverain, militaire et hospitalier de Saint Jean de Jérusalem, de Rhodes et de Malte (Paris 1963).

PORTER, W., *History of the Knights of Malta* (London 1858).

PROKOPOWSKI, C., *L'Ordre Souverain et Militaire Jérosolymitain de Malte* (Vatican 1950).

RILEY-SMITH, J., *The Knights of St John in Jerusalem and Cyprus, 1050–1310* (Macmillan 1967).

ROSSI, E., *Storia della Marina dell'Ordene di S. Giovanni di Gerusalemme, di Rodi e di Malta* (Rome 1926).

SCHERMERHORN, E. W., *Malta of the Knights* (Heinemann 1829).

SCICLUNA, H. P., *The Church of St John in Valetta* (Rome 1955).

TAAFFE, J., *History of the Order of St John of Jerusalem* (London 1852).

St Lazarus

Regi magistrali provvedimenti relativi all'ordine dei santi Maurizio e Lazzaro (Turin 1855).

CIBRARIO, G. A. L., *Précis historique des Ordres Religieux et militaires de S. Lazare et de S. Maurice avant et après leur réunion*, trans. H. Ferrand (Lyons 1860).

GRASSIÈRE, P. BERTRAND DE LA, *Histoire des Chevaliers Hospitaliers Saint Lazare* (Paris 1932).

——, *L'Ordre Militaire et Hospitalier de Saint-Lazare de Jérusalem* (Paris 1960).

'The Hospital of Burton Lazars', *Victoria County History: 'Leicestershire'*, vol. 2 (O.U.P. 1954).

NICHOLS, J., *History of the County & Antiquities of Leicestershire*, 2 vols. (London 1795).

'The Preceptory of Locko', *Victoria County History: 'Derbyshire'*, vol. 2 (Constable 1907).

St Thomas

'St Thomas of Acon', *Victoria County History: 'London'*, vol. 1 (Constable, 1909).

STUBBS, W., *The Mediaeval Kingdoms of Cyprus and Armenia* (Oxford 1878).

WATNEY, J., *Some Account of the Hospital of St Thomas Acon in the Cheap, London, and of the Plate of the Mercers' Company* (London 1892).

Swordbrethren

BLOMBERG, C. J. VON, *An Account of Livonia with a Relation of the Rise, Progress and Decay of the Marian Teutonick Order* (London 1701).

BUNGE, F. G. VON, 'Der Orden der Schwertbrüder', *Baltische Geschichtstudien* (Leipzig 1875).

HERDER, J. G., *Der Orden Schwertbrüder* (Cologne 1965).

LEVENCLAVIUS, JOHANNES, 'De Moscovitarium bellis adversus finitimos gestis', *H.R.S.E.*, vol. 1.

SCHURZFLEISCH, H., *Historia Ensiferorum Ordinis Teutonici Livonorum* (Wittemberg 1701).

Templars

ADDISON, C. G., *The Knights Templars* (London 1842).

BORDONOVE, G., *Les Templiers* (Paris 1963).

BOUYER, L., *The Cistercian Heritage* (Mowbray 1958).

CAMPBELL, G. A., *The Knights Templars* (Duckworth 1937).

DESSUBRÉ, M., *Bibliographie de l'Ordre des Templiers* (Paris 1928).

EDWARDS, J., 'The Templars in Scotland in the thirteenth century', *Scottish Historical Review*, V, no. 17 (October 1907).

FINKE, H., *Papstumm und Untergang des Templerordens* (Munster 1907).

LIZERAND, G., *Jacques de Molay* (Paris 1928).

MARTIN, E. J. *The Trial of the Templars* (Allen & Unwin 1928).

MELVILLE, M., *La Vie des Templiers* (Paris 1951).

OURSEL, R., *Le Procés des Templiers* (Paris 1955).

PARKER, T. W., *The Knights Templars in England* (Tucson 1963).

PIQUET, J., *Les Banquiers du Moyen Age: Les Templiers* (Paris 1939).

PRUTZ, H., *Entwicklung und Untergang des Tempelherrenordens* (Berlin 1888).

SCHOTTMUELLER, K., *Der Untergang des Templer-Ordens*, 2 vols. (Berlin 1887).

SIMON, E., *The Piebald Standard* (Cassell 1959).

Teutonic Knights

BOSWELL, A. B., 'The Teutonic Order', *Cambridge Mediaeval History*, vol. VII (1932).

CARSTEN, F. J., *The Origins of Prussia* (O.U.P. 1954).

FABRICIUS, DYONISIUS, 'Livonicae Historiae Compendiosa series', *S.R.L.*, vol. II.

LAVISSE, E., 'Chevaliers Teutoniques', *Revue des Deux Mondes*, vol. 32 (1879).

MICKIEWICZ, A., *Konrad Walenrod*, (California 1925).

SALLES, F. DE, *Ordres Religieux de Chevaliers*, 2 vols. (Paris 1887–9).

SCHUMACHER, E., *Die Burgen in Preussen und Livland* (1962).

SIENKIEWICZ, H., *The Teutonic Knights* (trans. ed., London 1943).

TREITSCHKE, H. VON, *Das deutsche Ordensland Preussen* (Leipzig (1915); trans. E. and C. Paul, *Treitschke's Origins of Prussianism* (Allen & Unwin 1942).

TUMLER, P. M., *Der Deutsche Orden im Werden, Wachsen und Wirken bis um 1400* (Vienna 1955).

VOIGT, J., *Geschichte Preussens*, 9 vols. (Koenigsberg 1827–39).

——, *Geschichte des deutschen Ritterordens in seinen zwolf Balleien in Deutschland*, 2 vols. (Berlin 1857–9).

WAL, G. DE, *Récherches sur l'ancienne constitution de l'Ordre Teutonique* (Mergentheim 1807).

4. SOURCES FOR THE BACKGROUND

Latin Syria

ARCHER, T. A. and KINGSFORD, C. L., *The Crusades* (London 1894).

BARKER, SIR E., *The Crusades* (O.U.P. 1923).

BELLOC, H., *The Crusade* (London 1937).

BOASE, T. S. R., *Castles and Churches of the Crusading Kingdom* (O.U.P. 1967).

CAHEN, C., *La Syrie du Nord à l'époque des Croisades* (Paris 1940).

FEDDEN, H. R. and THOMSON, J., *Crusader Castles* (1957).

FULLER, T., *Historie of the Holy Warre* (Cambridge 1640).

GROUSSET, R., *Histoire des Croisades et du Royaume Franc de Jérusalem* (Paris 1934–6).

HAMMER-PURGSTALL, J. VON, *Histoire de l'Ordre des Assassins* (Paris 1833).

KANTOROWICZ, E., *Frederick the Second* (Constable 1957).

Koran, The, trans. J. M. Rodwell (Dent 1909).

LAWRENCE, T. E., *Crusader Castles*, 2 vols. (London 1936).

LEGGE, M. D., *Anglo-Norman Literature and its background* (O.U.P. 1963).

MASSON, G., *Frederick II of Hohenstauffen* (Secker & Warburg 1957).

OMAN, SIR CHARLES, *A History of the Art of War in the Middle Ages*, 2 vols. (Methuen 1924).

PRAWER, J. and BENVENISTI, M., 'Crusader Palestine' – Sheet 12/IX of *Atlas of Israel* (Jerusalem 1960).

REY, E. G., *Les colonies franques en Syrie au XIIe et XIIIe siècles* (Paris 1883).

——, *Etude sur les Monuments de l'Architecture militaire des Croisés en Syrie et dans l'Ile de Chypre* (Paris 1871).

RICHARD, J., *Le Royaume Latin de Jérusalem* (Paris 1953).

——, *Le Comté de Tripoli sous la dynastie toulousaine (1102–1187)* (Paris 1945).

RUNCIMAN, SIR STEVEN, *A History of the Crusades*, 3 vols. (C.U.P. 1951–4).

SMAIL, R. C., *Crusading Warfare 1097–1193* (C.U.P. 1956).

MULLER-WIENER, W., *Castles of the Crusaders* (Thames & Hudson 1966).

The Baltic

Allgemeine deutsche Biographie (Leipzig 1875–1912).

BOSWELL, A. B., 'Poland and Lithuania in the Fourteenth and Fifteenth centuries', *Cambridge Mediaeval History*, vol. VIII (1936).

FENNELL, J., *Ivan the Great of Moscow* (Macmillan 1961).

GIMBUTAS, M., *The Balts* (Thames & Hudson 1963).

GREY, I., *Ivan the Terrible* (Hodder & Stoughton 1964).

Grosser Historischer Weltatlas (II Teil, Mittelalter) (Munich 1970).

TUULSE, A., *Castles of the Western World* (Thames & Hudson 1958).

The Reconquista

BARBOUR, N., *Morocco* (Thames & Hudson, 1965)

BERTRAND, L. and PETRIE, C., *The History of Spain* (Eyre & Spottiswoode 1934).

BRAUNSCHVIG, R., *La Berberie Orientale sous les Hafsides* (Paris 1940–1).

Cambridge Mediaeval History – passim.

DOZY, R., *Spanish Islam. A history of the Moslems in Spain,* trans. F. G. Stokes (Chatto & Windus 1913).

HIGHFIELD, J. R. L., 'The Catholic Kings and the Titled Nobility of Castile', *Europe of the Later Middle Ages* (Faber & Faber 1965).

HOLE, E., *Al-Andalus – Spain under the Moslems* (Robert Hale 1958).

IRVING, WASHINGTON, 'A Chronicle of the Conquest of Granada' (from the MS. of Fray Antonio Agapida) (London 1829).

LIVERMORE, H., *A New History of Portugal* (O.U.P. 1966).

MACDONALD, I., *Don Fernando de Antequerra* (Oxford 1948).

MÉRIMÉE, P., *Histoire de Don Pedro I, roi de Castile* (Paris 1848).

MILLER, TOWNSHEND, *The Castles and the Crown* (Gollancz 1963).

MENÉNDEZ PIDAL, R., *Historia de España,* vol. XIV (Madrid 1965).

PRESCOTT, W. H., 'History of Ferdinand and Isabella', *The Works of W. H. Prescott* (Montezuma Ed., Philadelphia 1904).

——, 'History of the Conquest of Mexico', op. cit.

——, 'History of Philip II', op. cit.

SYED, AMEER ALI, *A Short History of the Saracens* (Macmillan 1889).

SORDO, ENRIQUE, *Moorish Spain* (Elek Books 1963).

VIARDOT, L., *Histoire des Arabes et des Mores d'Espagne* (Paris 1851).

WATT, W. MONTGOMERY, 'A History of Islamic Spain', *Islamic Surveys 4* (Edinburgh Press 1965).

Readjustment

ANDREWS, K., *Castles of the Morea* (Princetown, New Jersey 1953).

ATIYAH, A., *The Crusade in the Later Middle Ages* (Methuen 1938).

——, *The Crusade of Nicopolis* (Methuen 1934).

Cambridge Mediaeval History – *passim*.

GROUSSET, R., *Histoire de l'Orient Latin* (Paris 1945).

——, *L'Empire du Levant* (Paris 1946).

HILL, G., *A History of Cyprus*, 4 vols. (C.U.P. 1940–52).

KNOLLES, RICHARD, *General History of the Turks* (London 1603).

LUKE, SIR HARRY, *Cyprus – a Portrait and an Appreciation* (Harrap 1957).

LUTTRELL, A., 'The Crusade in the Fourteenth Century', *Europe in the Later Middle Ages* (Faber & Faber 1965).

MILLER, W., *The Latins in the Levant – a history of Frankish Greece* (London 1908).

RUNCIMAN, SIR STEVEN, *A History of the Crusades*, vol. 3 (C.U.P. 1954).

——, *The Fall of Constantinople 1453* (C.U.P. 1965).

The Last Crusade

BLOUET, B., *The Story of Malta* (Faber & Faber 1965).

Cambridge Modern History – *passim*.

FAURE-PIQUET, G., *Histoire de l'Afrique septentrionale sous la domination musumlane (740 à 1835)* (Paris 1905).

HAMMER-PURGSTALL, J. VON, *Geschichte des osmanischen Reiches* (Pest 1827–35); trans. J. J. Hellert, *Histoire de l'Empire Ottoman* (Paris 1841).

LANDSTRÖM, B., *The Ship* (Allen & Unwin 1961).

LUKE, SIR HARRY, *Malta – an Account and an Appreciation* (Harrap 1960).

MERRIMAN, R. B., *The Rise of the Spanish Empire in the Old World & the New* (New York 1918–25).

——, *Suleiman the Magnificent* (Cambridge, U.S.A. 1944).

OMAN, SIR CHARLES, *A History of the Art of War in the Sixteenth Century* (Methuen 1937).

PETRIE, SIR CHARLES, *Don John of Austria* (Eyre & Spottiswoode 1967).

Further Reading

The following is intended simply as an outline of the sources available.

General

Although the best-known edition of the 'De Laude Novae Militiae' is in Migne's *Patrologus Cursus Completus*, vol. CLXXXII (Paris 1854) that in *S. Bernardi Opera*, vol. III (Rome 1963) is far superior. The only comprehensive work on all orders is Helyot's *Histoire des ordres religieux, monastiques & militaires*, vols. 2, 3, & 6, which, while informative and entertaining – it contains various amusing illustrations – is unreliable and of course no use for the period after 1721; many of the books listed in its vast bibliography are of extreme rarity. Such works as Amman's *Cleri totius Romanae ecclesiae* of 1585 merit attention solely for their quaint and largely fanciful pictures of military brethren. The one modern – or comparitively modern – study of the brotherhoods as a whole is Prutz's *Die geistlichen Ritterorden* which cannot be recommended too highly; unfortunately it ends at 1300.

International Orders

The Hospitallers of St John have been called the best documented institution of the Middle Ages as they took their archives with them from Rhodes (except for those of *c.* 1300–80), which together with the entire records of 1530–1798 are in the Royal Malta Library at Valetta; in 1964 a *Catalogue of the Records of the Order of St John of Jerusalem in the Royal Malta Library* by Zammit Gabarretta and G. Mizzi began to appear at Malta. There are also many documents in the Vatican and at Venice. Between 1894 and 1906 Delaville le Roulx published his monumental *Cartulaire Géneral des Hospitaliers de Saint Jean de Jérusalem 1100–1310*, comprising 5,000 documents, but although his two great studies, *Les Hospitaliers en Terre Sainte et à Chypre jusqu'au 1310* and *Les Hospitaliers à Rhodes jusqu'au mort de Philibert de Naillac*, together with his other publications contain a mine of information they are nonetheless disappointing. Happily a splendidly definitive work on the earlier period has just appeared, as readable as it is scholarly, *The Knights of St John in Jerusalem and Cyprus, 1050–1310*, by Dr J. Riley-Smith of St Andrew's University, an author who uses Arabic sources besides having great topographical knowledge of the crusader states; Professor L. H. Butler of the same university is preparing a history of the Rhodian era. Dall' Pozzo's *Historia della Sacra Religione* of 1703 is still the only comprehensive authority for this Order in the seventeenth century, though recently the eighteenth has been well covered by Roderick Cavalliero's *The Last Crusaders*. Of general histories Bosio's history of 1594 – to which dall' Pozzo's was intended as a continuation – remains the chief source of information for the later sixteenth century, while even now Vertot is the most readable overall introduction; these three writers had access to documents since lost. In English, King's *The Knights Hospitallers in the Holy Land* and Porter's *Knights of Malta* are the main general works; both are based on Bosio and Vertot and no less inaccurate. If mannered and eccentric Taaffe's *History of the Order of St John of Jerusalem* is far better. Schermerhorn's *Malta of the Knights* contains much useful but inchoate information from good sources. The best recent account of the 1565 siege is Ernle Bradford's *The Great Siege*. Captain Brockman's *The Two Sieges of Rhodes 1480–1522* published in 1969 is an unpretentious but enjoyable account; the author has had the invaluable benefit of Professor Butler's advice. Hellwald's *Bibliographie Méthodique de l'Ordre Souverain de S. Jean de Jérusalem* published in 1885 is sadly out of date, despite Rossi's *Aggiunta alla Bibliographie Méthodique* of 1924–29. The bibliography in Riley-Smith, however, is excellent for the early period.

The Templars' archives have long since vanished, but many documents survive; d'Albon's *Cartulaire Général de l'Ordre du Temple 1119–50* (Paris 1913 and 1922) is the outstanding collection. The rule is available in de Curzon's *La Règle du*

Temple while there are various editions of papers relating to the trial – the minutes of the Papal Commission were edited by Michelet, though Lizerand's version is preferable with a French translation opposite the Latin text. Martin's study of the trial, while scholarly, is weakened by the author's strong prejudice against the Templars. The two key studies are Prutz's *Entwicklung und Untergang des Tempelherrenordens* and Finke's *Papstumm und Untergang des Temperordens*, the latter of which established the probability of their innocence. As with the Hospitallers, much useful information may be found in the Latin and Old French chronicles of the Crusades, printed in the *Receuil des Historiens des Croisades*. The standard work on their financial operations is Piquet's *Les Banquiers du Moyen Age: Les Templiers*. An excellent, if hardly definitive, modern history of the Order is Marion Melville's *La Vie des Templiers* while in English Campbell's *The Knights Templars* and Edith Simon's *The Piebald Standard* are adequate introductions. In 1928 Dessubré's *Bibliographie de l'Ordre des Templiers* appeared, and much of Riley-Smith is no less relevant to the Poor Knights than to St John.

There is no work on St Lazarus based on primary sources. Two general books, *Histoire des Chevaliers Hospitaliers de Saint Lazare* and *L'Ordre Militaire et Hospitalier de Saint-Lazare de Jérusalem*, both by Paul Bertrand de la Grassière are all that is readily available, apart from Helyot's account of the brotherhood's development in the seventeenth century. In 1860 a brief history, translated from the Italian, of the refounded Savoy branch was published at Lyon, Count Cibrario's *Précis historique des Ordres Religieux et militaires de S. Lazare et de S. Maurice avant et après leur réunion* which, as this brotherhood considered itself the Capuan priory's successor, also deals with the Palestinian period, containing several charters of great interest besides a tantalising reference to a lost seventeenth-century manuscript history. English Hospitallers of St Lazarus are dealt with in the *Victoria County History* under 'Leicestershire' and 'Derby'; there is an account of Dr Legh, last 'Master' of Burton Lazars, in the *Dictionary of National Biography*.

The Order of Montjoie falls into a special category as being both an international and a Spanish Order. Owing to its early demise many picturesque misconceptions grew up about it and these may be found in Helyot. However, Delaville le Roulx's article in the *Révue de l'Orient Latin*, vol. 1, is a definitive study of this obscure brotherhood.

German Orders

Most of the Teutonic Order's records have survived intact and various mammoth selections covering particular aspects of their activities have been published, especially since the war, such as *Regesta historico-diplomatica Ordinis S. Mariae Theutonicorum, 1198–1550, Register*, ed. Joachim and Hubatsch, 5 vols. (Gottingen 1965), and it is likely that all the Order's known documents will be available in easily accessible form in the foreseeable future. Such works as Strehlke's *Tabulae Ordinis Teutonicis* which has many Palestinian charters and *Die grosse Amterbuch des Deutschen Ordens* with its fascinating inventory of the brethren's commercial affairs in medieval Prussia are of outstanding interest. The rule is in Perlbach's *Statuten des Deutschen Ordens*. Early Prussian chronicles may be found in *Scriptores rerum Prussicarum*, those of Livland in *Rerum Livonicarum*, excellent nineteenth-century editions. Petrus von Dusburg's account of the first years in Prussia, his 'Chronica Terre Prussie' is printed in these volumes and cannot be too highly recommended – short and factual yet vivid, written in a barbarous Latin even easier to read than St Bernard's. A very general survey of the Order's history until 1400, with helpful name lists and bibliography and a sketch of the brotherhood's present state, is *Der Deutsche Orden* by the present Hochmeister, Monsignor P. Marian Tumler, but probably the most readable work is still Baron de Wal's *Historie de l'Ordre Teutonique*. The definitive outline studies, although dated, are by Voigt: *Geschichte Preussens* (first vol. published 1827), a history of the Order until 1530, and his *Geschichte des Deutschen Ritterordens in seinen zwolf Balleien in Deutschland* (Berlin 1857–9), dealing with the brethren's subsequent vicissitudes. In English the outstanding book is Carsten's *Origins of Prussia* which has chapters on the knights' colonial and administrative achievements besides some pages on Plauen's attempt to set up an estates' system while Treitschke's *Das Deutsche Ordensland Preussen*, that stimulating if wildly partisan commentary, was translated to serve for wartime propaganda! However, the sole narrative account is A. B. Boswell's single chapter in the *Cambridge Mediaeval History*; like Carsten this is provided with a valuable bibliography. Some idea of the traditional Polish view of the brethren may be obtained from Sienkiewicz's novel, *The Teutonic Knights*, of which there are several English translations.

There is nothing worthwhile in English or French on the Sword Brethren (*Porteglaives*) though a really magnificent book has recently been published in Germany – *Der Orden der Schwertbrüder* (Cologne 1965), a definitive work which makes exhaustive use of all sources.

Iberian Orders

There is a wealth of primary source material but rarely in accessible form; a vast mass of documents remains unsorted and uncatalogued. The basic work on Spanish Orders is Rades y Andrada's *Chrónica de las tres Órdenes y Cavallerías de Sanctiago, Calatrava y Alcántara* of which no new edition has been published since the original in 1572. The *bullarium* of Santiago – *Bullarium Equestris Ordinis S. Iacobi de Spatha* (Barcelona 1719) – is of value, while this Order's rule may be found in *Regla y Establescimientos de la orden de la Cavallería de San Sanctiago del Espada* printed in 1555. Montesa's rule was published in 1573, those of Calatrava and Alcántara in 1600 and 1609. The *Bullarium Ordinis Militiae de Calatrava* of 1761 is also important. *Regula et constitutiones Fratrum Sacri Ordinis Beatae Mariae de Mercede Redemptionis Captivorum* contains a largely mythical account of the founders and early Commander Generals of the Mercedarians. There are no works which examine the Order's economic and administrative roles, nor their decline. General studies, like Llamazares' *Historia Compendiada de las Cuatres Órdenes Militares* of 1862, are invariably based on Rades and add little. Gutton's *L'Ordre de Calatrava* – specially commissioned by the Cistercian Order – is not over scholarly, though pleasantly written, but covers if only sketchily the almost unknown later period up to the present day, besides containing photographs of *encomiendas* of all Spanish Orders. Recently much research has been done by American and English historians, notably D. W. Lomax, who has published a study of Santiago in the twelfth and thirteenth centuries, and by J. F. O'Callaghan, whose articles on the foundation of Alcántara and on the affiliation of Calatrava with the Cistercians are of great significance; the latter writer has also produced a most interesting article on Pedro Girón of Calatrava. Both Lomax and O'Callaghan append copious bibliographies. Nor must one overlook Múñoz de S. Pedro's study of Alcántara's Gutierre de Sotomayor. A. Luttrell's *The Aragonese Crown and the Knights Hospitallers of Rhodes, 1291–1358* though primarily concerned with the Order of St John has illuminating comments on the role of all military brotherhoods in Aragon during this period. At a different level there are various somewhat esoteric works on the brethren of the seventeenth and eighteenth centuries, e.g. *Spanish Knights of Irish Origin* by Micheline Walsh (1965), a genealogical survey of Irishmen in the Orders of Santiago and Calatrava.

It is particularly hard to find books on the Portuguese military Orders. The British Museum Library does not contain such key works as the *Constituições de S. Bento de Aviz* of 1631 though it does possess a copy of this latter Order's rule printed in 1516. The *bullarium* of Aviz was published in the early eighteenth century as well as a catalogue of the brotherhood's Masters by José de Purificao while a general work, da Costa's *Les Ordres militaires de Portugal*, appeared in 1922. There is also J. Vieira Guimaraes, *A Ordem de Christo*, published in 1936.

Other National Orders

Helyot lists two works on the Order of San Stefano – *Statuti Capituli e Institutioni dell'Ordine de Cavalieri di San Stefano* of 1562, and *Statuti e Constitutioni dell'Ordine di San Stefano* – both published at Florence – but the present writer has been unable to procure copies. However, Helyot gives an adequate if sketchy account of this Order.

For English readers the national order of St Thomas will

naturally be of some interest but the only reliable work which refers to it in any detail is Bishop Stubb's *The Mediaeval Kingdoms of Cyprus and Armenia* and in any case he is unable to spare the brethren more than a page. Their cartulary is still at the Mercers' Hall in Cheapside so one may at least hope for a definitive work in the future. Watney's *Some Account of the Hospital of St Thomas Acon in the Cheap, London, and of the Plate of the Mercers' Company* is as confused as its title because of its inaccurate source references, though it does give some interesting extracts from the cartulary. However, many useful references to sources, together with an incomplete list of Masters, are to be found in the *Victoria County History, London*, vol. I.

Index